LITTLE ROCK

COOKS

PRESENTED BY

The Junior League of Little Rock

Copies of **Little Rock Cooks** may be obtained from:

THE JUNIOR LEAGUE OF LITTLE ROCK, INC.

Post Office Box 7421

Little Rock, Arkansas 72207

$5.00 . . . . (Postage and Handling Included)

Make check payable to:

JUNIOR LEAGUE OF LITTLE ROCK — COOKBOOK

Proceeds from the sale of **Little Rock Cooks** are used for community service projects approved or sponsored by the Junior League of Little Rock.

TABLE OF CONTENTS

APPETIZERS 3

BEVERAGES 27

SOUPS 37

BREADS 51

EGGS AND CHEESE 77

FISH AND SHELLFISH 89

POULTRY 111

WILD GAME 133

MEATS 149

VEGETABLES 183

SALADS AND DRESSINGS 223

SAUCES AND ACCOMPANIMENTS 251

DESSERTS 265

COOKIES AND CANDIES 323

ABBREVIATIONS

tsp. — teaspoon(s)

Tb. — Tablespoon(s)

pt. — pint

pts. — pints

qt. — quart

qts. — quarts

gal. — gallon

gals. — gallons

oz. — ounce(s)

lb. — pound

lbs. — pounds

pkg. — package(s)

sm. — small

med. — medium

lg. — large

light cream — half and half

heavy cream — whipping cream

Trade names of products are given only when necessary.

INTRODUCTION

Arkansas tastes in foods today are a distillate of the best cooking traditions of many countries. Our forebears brought the spice of the Spanish customs, the flavor of French cuisine, the heartiness of sturdy English fare, and the piquant variety of Italian sauces.

Through five generations of history we have traditionally set a bountiful table and even now, in our servantless days we set another place for the always welcome visitor.

Just as the fish from our lakes and streams, the fruit from our flora, the game from our forests sustained the Indians and our early explorers, so are we today able to set a good table from nature's bounty and man's cultivation.

It's no wonder we have a tradition of eating well; nature has been good to us in Arkansas.

ACKNOWLEDGMENTS

Little Rock Cooks was compiled and edited by the Junior League of Little Rock from recipes submitted to us by excellent cooks in our area. We are grateful to each of those who contributed to this book. We point out to you that all recipes have been tested or evaluated before they have been included. This is not to say they must be prepared just as they are written.

Recipes are merely guides. Experimentation with them is all part of the enjoyment of cooking. We urge you to add a dash of something else—herb, spice, liqueur—make it suit your taste. Our hope is that you will use our recipes, add a little of your imagination, and let your taste buds be your guide.

Editors

Mrs. John D. Harris   Mrs. George L. Cook

Section Heads

Mrs. Elliott Bechtel   Mrs. Robert Bartlett Roach, Jr.

Mrs. William L. Cravens   Mrs. James W. Rogers

Mrs. Smith Grobmyer   Mrs. Donald F. Thompson

Mrs. Don F. Hamilton   Mrs. Leonard Thompson

Mrs. E. Jones Jacobus   Mrs. Charles H. Williamson

Sustaining Advisor
Mrs. Robert G. Carnahan

Cover Design
Mrs. George L. Cook

Introduction
Mrs. George Rose Smith

APPETIZERS

RAW VEGETABLES TO DIP

Broccoli, divided into small
  flowerets
Carrots, sliced lengthwise or
  curled
Cauliflower, divided into
  small flowerets
Celery, sliced lengthwise
Chinese Cabbage, rolled up
  leaves
Cucumber, sliced lengthwise,
  peeled
Green onions, small

Green bell pepper, lengthwise
  strips
Mushrooms, sliced or small
  whole ones
Radishes, quartered length-
  wise
Summer squash or yellow
  crookneck, sliced
Tomatoes, cherry or tiny
  pear, whole or halved
Turnips, sliced
Zucchini, sliced lengthwise

Use very fresh vegetables and serve cold and crisp. Arrange in varying colors on plate around dip. May serve with Guacamole Dip, Dill Weed Dip, Curry Dip, or Spicy Vegetable Dip.

GUACAMOLE

Yield: 3 cups

4 ripe avocados, mashed or
  pureed
½ cup diced canned green
  chilies

¼ cup minced onion
1 Tb. salt
¼ cup lemon juice

Combine all ingredients; cover and chill. Leave the avocado seeds in mixture until serving to prevent darkening. Serve with tortillas, chips, or raw vegetables.

A delicious stuffing for cherry tomatoes.

MRS. BART ROACH

DILL WEED DIP

Yield: 1⅓ cups

⅔ cup real mayonnaise
⅔ cup sour cream
1 Tb. grated onion

1 tsp. Beau Monde seasoning
1 tsp. dill weed (not seed)
1 tsp. parsley flakes

Mix ingredients and refrigerate overnight. Serve with raw vegetables.

MRS. JIM WALTON
CORVALLIS, OREGON

CURRY DIP FOR VEGETABLES

Yield: 1 cup

1 cup mayonnaise	1 tsp. grated onion
1 tsp. tarragon vinegar	1 tsp. garlic salt
1 tsp. horseradish	1 Tb. curry

Mix all ingredients thoroughly in a small mixing bowl. Refrigerate at least 2 hours before serving. Serve with raw vegetables.

MRS. TOM RAMSEY

SPICY VEGETABLE DIP

Yield: 1 cup

1 cup sour cream	½ tsp. prepared mustard
2 Tb. lemon juice	1 tsp. paprika
1 Tb. red wine vinegar	Dash cayenne
2 tsp. salt	2 Tb. horseradish
¼ tsp. dry mustard	

Combine ingredients and refrigerate at least 1 hour before serving. Serve with raw vegetables.

MRS. EDWARD D. BRISCOE

CANTALOUPE DILL DIP

Yield: 1⅓ cups

2 cantaloupes, chilled	¼ tsp. dried dill
3-oz. pkg. cream cheese	⅛ tsp. salt
1½ Tb. lime juice	1 cup sour cream
½ tsp. lime rind, grated	

Halve cantaloupes and remove seeds. Save one cantaloupe half for bowl for dip. Cut meat from remaining halves into small balls. Combine cheese, lime juice, lime rind, dill, and salt; beat until fluffy. Mix with sour cream and spoon into cantaloupe half. Serve with toothpicks for dunking cantaloupe balls into dip.

A refreshing, attractive dip. Especially nice for a brunch.

MRS. JOHN REX
OKLAHOMA CITY, OKLAHOMA

TIPSY WATERMELON

Serves: 6-8

5 cups watermelon balls	½ cup dry sherry
½ cup sugar	

Combine and refrigerate at least 2 hours.

MRS. W. MAGE HONEYCUTT

CHERRY TOMATO CANAPÉ

Small boiling onions
Cherry tomatoes
Sandwich sliced bread

Mayonnaise
Seasoning salt

Peel and slice onions very thin; soak in ice water in refrigerator all day. Cut tomatoes in half. Using a 1½-inch biscuit cutter, cut rounds of bread (you should get 4 rounds per slice). Spread mayonnaise on bread, place onion slice on mayonnaise then ½ tomato on top. Sprinkle with seasoning salt. Each onion yields about 10 slices and can be soaked up to 3 days without harm. Bread rounds may be cut and frozen until day of use.

Attractive and delicious.

MRS. WILLIAM A. SAUNDERS, JR.

ROSY RADISHES

Serves: 12

2 bunches radishes
½ tsp. salt
⅔ cup wine vinegar
½ cup olive oil

¼ cup cold water
1½ tsp. salt
½ tsp. pepper

Trim roots and stems from radishes; wash; then bring to a boil with ½ teaspoon salt in enough water to cover. Boil 1 to 2 minutes until radishes begin to lose color. Drain and cool. Make a marinade of remaining ingredients and pour over radishes. Chill at least 24 hours, turning occasionally. These keep well and improve with age.

Very unusual and tart.

MRS. JOHN BALDRIDGE

PICKLED MUSHROOMS

Yield: 3-4 doz.

1½ lbs. fresh mushrooms
1 clove garlic, crushed
¾ cup salad oil
¼ cup olive oil
½ cup lemon juice

1 cup chopped onion
1 tsp. salt
½ tsp. pepper
½ tsp. dry mustard

Clean mushrooms and mix with remaining ingredients. Refrigerate in covered container for 24 hours. Put in saucepan and bring to boil; boil 10 minutes; cool. Drain to serve. Will keep for weeks in refrigerator.

MRS. CHARLES A. SMITH

STUFFED MUSHROOMS

Yield: 36

    1 lb. fresh mushrooms   **2 Tb. butter**

Wash, dry, and stem mushrooms, reserving stems for use in some fillings. Sauté caps in butter in skillet for 2 minutes.

BACON STUFFING:

Mushroom stems, chopped	**4 Tb. parsley, chopped**
8 slices bacon, chopped	**4 Tb. butter, melted**
4 green onions and tops,	**½ tsp. salt**
chopped	**Pepper**

Cook stems with bacon, onion, and parsley. Fill caps with mixture; brush with butter, salt, and pepper. Bake at 350° for 20 minutes.

                                    Mrs. David Engelman
                                  San Francisco, California

CHEESE AND HERB STUFFING:

Mushroom stems, chopped	**¼ tsp. pepper**
3 to 4 green onions, finely	**½ tsp. garlic salt**
chopped	**⅛ tsp. mixed Italian herbs**
6 oz. sharp Cheddar, grated	**⅓ cup dry bread crumbs**
2 tsp. Worcestershire sauce	**½ cup butter**
⅛ tsp. red hot sauce	**1 tsp. Worcestershire sauce**
½ tsp. salt	**Dash hot sauce**

Mix first 10 ingredients well. Melt butter and mix with 1 teaspoon Worcestershire sauce and dash of hot sauce. Place ¼ teaspoon of this mixture in each cap; pour remaining into stuffing. Mix well and fill caps with stuffing. Bake at 350° for 15 minutes.

                                    Mrs. Paul P. Atkinson, Sr.

CRABMEAT STUFFING:

7½-oz. can crabmeat	**1 tsp. chopped capers**
1 Tb. chopped parsley	**¼ tsp. dry mustard**
1 Tb. chopped pimiento	**½ cup mayonnaise**

Combine crab, parsley, pimiento, and capers. Blend dry mustard into mayonnaise; toss with crab mixture. Fill caps and bake at 375° for 8 to 10 minutes.

                                    Mrs. Robert M. Fisher
                                  Bronxvill, New York

SHERRY CREAM STUFFING:

Mushroom stems, minced	1 Tb. sherry
1 Tb. chives, chopped	½ tsp. salt
1 Tb. butter	⅛ tsp. pepper
½ pt. heavy cream	

Sauté stems and chives in butter. Add cream, sherry, salt, and pepper. Cook until mixture thickens, about 10 minutes. Fill caps and run under broiler until bubbly.

MRS. ROBERT C. FERGUSON
BIG RAPIDS, MICHIGAN

PARMESAN STUFFING:

3 Tb. Parmesan cheese, grated	1 Tb. chopped parsley
1 clove garlic, chopped	2 Tb. melted butter
1 small onion, chopped	Salt
1 cup bread crumbs	Pepper
	6 Tb. olive oil

Mix all ingredients except olive oil and fill caps. Pour 2 tablespoons of olive oil in bottom of baking pan. Place mushrooms in pan and pour remaining 4 tablespoons of oil equally over all mushrooms. Bake at 325° for 20 minutes. For this recipe you may wish to omit initial sautéing of caps.

MRS. BEN M. HOGAN, JR.

TINY CORN FRITTERS

Serves: 6

17-oz. can cream style corn	½ tsp. grated onion
1½ cups cracker crumbs	Salt and pepper
1 large egg	

Mix all ingredients the day before cooking so crumbs will absorb moisture. Drop from a spoon into hot fat and fry until brown. Drain on paper towel. These may be kept in a warm oven for refill during a party.

MRS. DAN COTTON

NACHOS

Tortilla chips	Jalapeno peppers, chopped
Extra sharp Cheddar cheese	

Place tortilla chips on cookie sheet; top with piece of cheese, then a piece of pepper. Heat under broiler until cheese is melted. Must be served hot!

MRS. JOHN B. DYKE

PARMESAN STICKS

Serves: 10   **Oven: 400°**

1 loaf salt-rising bread   8-oz. box Parmesan cheese
1 lb. butter   Paprika

Cut the bread into strips, removing crust. Melt butter, a stick at a time, in a small saucepan. Soak bread sticks in butter, roll in Parmesan cheese and place on a cookie sheet. Sprinkle sticks with paprika. Bake about 10 minutes at 400° until toasted.

MRS. DONALD E. CHRISTIAN

CHEESE CRISPIES

Yield: 3 doz.   **Oven: 350°**

1 cup margarine   Dash salt
½ lb. sharp Cheddar cheese,   Dash red pepper
  grated   Dash Tabasco
2 cups flour   2 cups Rice Krispies

Mix margarine and cheese. Add flour, salt, red pepper and Tabasco. Stir in Rice Krispies last. Roll into a ball and then flatten. Place on ungreased cookie sheet and bake for 15 minutes. Put in cookie tin to keep.

MRS. WILLIAM L. CRAVENS

ELLA'S CHEESE STRAWS

Yields: 200   **Oven: 400°**

1 cup butter   ½ tsp. cayenne
2½ cups sifted flour   1 lb. grated sharp Cheddar
1 tsp. salt

Mix all ingredients as for pie dough. Squeeze through a pastry bag for straws or roll into small balls. Place on ungreased cookie sheets and bake until they begin to brown, 10 to 15 minutes.

MRS. JAMES R. WALT

CHEESE PUFFS

Yield: 50 medium puffs   Oven: 425°

½ cup butter
1 cup water
1 cup flour

¼ tsp. salt
1 cup grated Cheddar cheese
3 eggs

Put butter and water in a saucepan; bring to a boil. Add flour and salt; beat vigorously, cooking until mixture forms a ball and does not stick to the sides of pan. Remove from fire and add cheese; mix well; cool. Add eggs one at a time, beating after each is added. Drop from teaspoon onto buttered baking sheet one inch apart for appetizer size puffs. For larger puffs, drop from tablespoon 2 inches apart. May also force through a pastry tube. Bake 20 minutes at 425°; reduce oven to 350°; bake until light and dry. Fill puffs. May use Hot Curried Crab Meat Dip, Sherry Cream Filling in stuffed mushroom recipe, your own creamed chicken recipe, tuna fish, or grated cheese mixed with anchovy paste and soft butter. Serve hot or cold depending on filling. May bake and freeze. Thaw and stuff on day of use. May make large and use as a patty shell for a creamed main course.

This is a crisp, light patty shell for which you may invent a variety of fillings.

MISS DAISY KEATTS

EGG AND OLIVE CHEESE SPREAD

Serves: 8-10

½ lb. Old English cheese
2 Tb. chopped onion
3 Tb. chopped bell pepper
2 Tb. chopped sour pickles
   (or sweet)
2 hard-boiled eggs, chopped

8 to 9 chopped olives, with
   pimiento
½ cup cracker crumbs
¼ tsp. salt
4 Tb. mayonnaise, may need
   more

Grate cheese and mix with remaining ingredients, blending well. Form into loaf and refrigerate at least 24 hours before serving. May garnish with more sliced olives. Serve with crackers.

MRS. WILLIAM L. TEDFORD, JR.

SNAPPY CHEESE LOG

Serves: 12

½ lb. American cheese
¼ lb. blue cheese
1 small onion

½ lb. cream cheese
1½ cups chopped pecans

In a meat grinder, grind yellow cheese, blue cheese, and onion together. Knead with cream cheese. Mix with ½ cup pecans and form into 2 narrow cylinders; roll in the remaining cup of pecans. Chill for 24 hours. Serve with crackers. May be frozen.

MRS. MILFORD DAVIS, JR.

BLUE CHEESE BALL

Serves: 20-30

12 oz. blue cheese	2 Tb. Worcestershire sauce
11 oz. cream cheese	¾ cup chopped onion (opt.)
2 Tb. vinegar	Chopped pecans

Soften cheese. Mix everything except pecans, working with hands until smooth. Shape into a ball; roll in pecans. Refrigerate at least 1 hour before serving. Serve with crackers. Especially good with melba rounds. May be frozen or leftover can be mixed with sour cream to make a dip.

MRS. HOUCK REASONER, JR.

TANGY CHEESE SPREAD

Yield: 2½ cups

¾ cup beer or ale	2 dashes Worcestershire
12 oz. Cheddar cheese, grated	sauce
2 oz. blue cheese, crumbled	Dash of Tabasco
½ tsp. dry mustard	1 tsp. chopped chives or
1 Tb. soft butter	onions

Blend beer and cheese in blender; add remaining ingredients except chives and blend until smooth. Spoon into a crock or dish and chill. Garnish with chives. Serve with crackers.

This is easy to make and has a nice flavor.

MRS. B. FRANK MACKEY, JR.

SHERRY AND BLUE CHEESE DIP

Yield: 1 cup

3 oz. cream cheese	2 Tb. sherry
4 oz. blue cheese	½ clove garlic, mashed
4 Tb. milk or sour cream	Poppy seeds

Blend first 3 ingredients; add sherry and garlic. Cover with poppy seeds just before serving.

MRS. L. F. MITCHELL
LAKE LEELANAU, MICHIGAN

WINE CELLAR CHEESE

Yield: 4½ cups

1½ lbs. Cheddar cheese, grated	⅛ tsp. cayenne pepper
	¼ tsp. ground mace
1 cup sour cream	½ cup sauterne
1¼ tsp. salt	½ cup butter, melted

Mix cheese, sour cream, and seasonings. Combine wine and butter; add alternately with cheese mixture into blender. Mix a small amount then remove and continue blending until all is smooth. Chill at least 24 hours before serving with crackers or thinly sliced French bread. This is difficult to mix but worth the effort. It may be frozen.

MRS. JOHN J. TRUEMPER, JR.

CHEESE FONDUE

Serves: 12

1 clove garlic, cut	3 Tb. kirsch or 4 Tb. cognac, applejack, or slivowitz
2 cups dry white wine	
1 lb. Switzerland Swiss cheese, grated	Paprika to taste
	2 loaves Italian, French, or sourdough bread
1 tsp. cornstarch	

Rub fondue pot well with cut side of garlic. Pour in wine; set over slow heat. When wine is heated to point that tiny air bubbles rise to the surface, add cheese by handfuls, stirring constantly with wooden fork or spoon. Keep stirring until cheese is melted. Dissolve cornstarch in kirsch; add to cheese mixture. Stir again for 2 to 3 minutes, adding paprika. Serve bubbling hot with bread which has been cut into bite-size pieces, each of which must have at least one side of crust. Stale bread works well. The secret to good fondue is using good cheese and wine of a quality that you could drink, a medium price wine. This fondue will not be fluffy, instead you dip through the wine into the melted cheese. It may be a bit messy, but worth it for the flavor is marvelous.

MRS. ED D. LIGON, JR.

BELL PEPPER CHEESE DIP

Yield: 2 qts.

2 lbs. block Old English
   cheese
13-oz. can evaporated milk
2 bell peppers, finely chopped
3 large onions, finely chopped

1 cup butter or margarine
1½ Tb. chili powder
Dash cayenne pepper
2 to 3 dashes Tabasco

Melt cheese in double boiler with evaporated milk. Sauté peppers and onions in butter until wilted. Take 3 tablespoons of cheese mixture and mix with chili powder and cayenne. Add to the whole mixture. Add Tabasco just before serving. Serve hot with corn chips or tortillas. May be frozen.

This is delicious!

MRS. COOPER JACOWAY

MEXICAN CHEESE DIP

Serves: 30

16-oz. can tomatoes
10-oz. can Ro-Tel tomatoes
   and chilies
¾ cup water
½ of a 1½-oz. can chili
   powder

½ of a 1½-oz. can cumin
2 cloves garlic
2 lbs. Velveeta
½ lb. Cracker Barrel
   Cheddar

Mix first 6 ingredients, using a garlic press for the garlic. Simmer for 1 hour. Add cheeses and stir until melted. Serve hot with corn chips or tortillas.

MRS. HENRY RECTOR

HOT JALAPENOS CHEESE DIP

Serves: 30

4 Tb. butter
1 onion, chopped fine
16-oz. can tomatoes
7½-oz. can jalapenos relish

4-oz. can green chilies,
   chopped
2 lbs. Velveeta cheese
½ tsp. salt

Sauté onion in butter until clear and tender. Add tomatoes, chilies, and relish; simmer 1 hour and 15 minutes. Add cheese and salt; stir until melted. Will keep for several weeks.

MRS. LEWIS BLOCK, JR.

MEXICAN BEAN DIP

Serves: 8

15½-oz. can mashed refried   ¼ lb. Velveeta cheese, grated
  beans   1 tsp. cumin
10-oz. can Rotel tomatoes and   ¼ tsp. chili powder
  chilies

Heat beans, tomatoes, and cheese in a double boiler. Add cumin
and cook slowly about 30 minutes or until smooth. Add chili powder
only if you desire a more fiery dip. Serve in a chafing dish with
tortillas or corn chips.

MRS. DON HAMILTON

CREAM CHEESE CAVIAR MOLD

Serves: 15

16 oz. cream cheese   Cheese cloth
4 Tb. milk   4 oz. salmon caviar

Soften cream cheese with milk. Place one layer of cheese cloth in
mold; may use 4 individual jello molds. Pack the cheese in firmly
and refrigerate. Before serving drain caviar on a paper towel.
Remove cheese from mold and cover with caviar. Serve with toast
rounds.

MRS. JOHN B. DYKE

*Variation: Omit milk and add 1 tube of anchovy paste, juice of 1
lemon, 2 or 3 tablespoons Worcestershire sauce, salt, and pepper to
cheese before molding.*

MRS. FRED SCHOOLER
BATESVILLE, ARKANSAS

BRAUNSCHWEIGER BALL

½ lb. Braunschweiger   2 Tb. mayonnaise
2 Tb. mayonnaise   Worcestershire sauce to taste
1 Tb. horseradish   2 Tb. milk
1 medium onion, minced or   ¼ tsp. lemon juice
  onion juice   2 oz. caviar
Worcestershire sauce to taste   Stuffed green olives
Salt to taste   Pimiento strips
3 oz. cream cheese

Mash up Braunschweiger with mayonnaise, horseradish, onion,
Worcestershire sauce, and salt. Mold into a ball and chill until firm.
Thin cream cheese with mayonnaise, Worcestershire sauce, and
milk; ice ball with mixture. Let caviar stand with lemon juice
sprinkled on it; drain on paper towel; place on top of icing. Decorate
with olive slices and pimento strips.

MRS. WILLOUGHBY S. CHESLEY
STUART, FLORIDA

LIVERWURST MOLD

Yield: 2 molds

⅓ cup sherry
1 oz. gelatin
10½-oz. can consomme
½ lb. liverwurst

1 Tb. chives
1 Tb. Worcestershire sauce
6 oz. cream cheese

Boil together sherry, gelatin, and consomme. Pour small amount in bottom of pâté mold. Cool in refrigerator until set. In blender combine liverwurst, chives, Worcestershire, cream cheese, and remaining gelatin mixture. Pour over set gelatin mixture in mold. Refrigerate. This will freeze. May garnish with kiwi fruit slices. Serve with crackers.

MRS. WILLIAM O. BATES
WILMETTE, ILLINOIS

CHICKEN LIVER PATE

1 lb. chicken livers
¼ cup green onions, chopped
2 Tb. butter, softened
¼ cup sherry
½ oz. gelatin, softened in
  sherry
14 Tb. butter, softened

¼ tsp. garlic salt
½ tsp. nutmeg
½ tsp. salt
Dash pepper
3 Tb. brandy
Pimiento
Bell pepper strips

Sauté livers and onions in 2 tablespoons of butter. Lower heat, cover and simmer 15 minutes, stirring occasionally. Cool slightly, then pour into blender a little at a time with sherry containing gelatin. Blend until smooth. Add remaining butter, seasonings, and brandy. Rinse pâté mold with cold water and then pour mixture into mold and chill until firm. Run hot water over mold to unmold. Decorate with pimiento and green pepper strips. Sliced mushrooms and olives could also be used as a garnish. Serve with crackers.

MRS. HENRY W. RUSSELL

CHICKEN LIVER SPREAD

1 lb. chicken livers
1 medium sized onion,
  chopped
4 oz. margarine

4 hard-boiled eggs
Salt
Pepper
Pinch sugar

Boil chicken livers about 15 minutes until done. Brown ⅞ chopped onion in margarine. Put livers, browned onion, and eggs through a food grinder, not a blender. Then grind in the ⅛ raw onion, adding seasonings and sugar. If needed add more melted margarine for desired consistency. May be served on ice box bread or crackers, as appetizer, or on lettuce as a salad. May be made a day ahead but not frozen.

MRS. HERBERT BESSER

WILD DUCK COCKTAIL SPREAD

2 wild ducks
½ cup sherry
½ cup garlic wine vinegar
2 Tb. Worcestershire sauce
2 tsp. lemon pepper
2 tsp. seasoned salt
2 Tb. celery seed
Pinch thyme
Pinch marjoram
1 bay leaf
½ tsp. garlic powder

¼ cup dried sweet pepper
flakes
1 large onion, chopped
Water to nearly cover
1 hard-boiled egg, chopped
½ cup celery, chopped
½ cup mayonnaise
¼ cup Reese horseradish
sauce
½ tsp. seasoned salt

If ducks are frozen, thaw in cold water. Place thawed ducks in pan and add next 13 ingredients. Boil gently until tender, about 1 to 2 hours, depending on toughness and size. Cool in same liquid. When cool, remove, wrap, and refrigerate overnight. Next day, skin and remove meat from breasts. Cut in small cubes. Add egg, celery, mayonnaise, horseradish sauce, and seasoned salt. Mix well to a spreadable consistency. Cover and refrigerate to mellow until ready to use. Serve with crackers as a cocktail spread. Will keep several days.

MRS. RICHARD H. MCKINNEY

CHEESY CHICKEN WINGS

Serves: 8-10   Oven: 350°

2 lbs. chicken wings,
disjointed
1 cup Parmesan cheese,
grated
2 Tb. parsley

2 tsp. paprika
1 Tb. oregano
2 tsp. salt
½ tsp. pepper
½ cup melted butter

Discard tips of chicken wings, using only the largest piece. Mix together cheese and spices. Dip pieces in butter, then roll in cheese mixture. Place on a foil lined cookie sheet, forming a lip with foil, and bake for 1 hour and 15 minutes.

MRS. C. W. STEGALL, SR.

SAUSAGE PINWHEELS

Serves: 15   Oven: 375°

1 can store bought biscuits   1 lb. pork sausage

Press together biscuit dough, then roll out thinly. Spread sausage evenly over dough; roll up as a jelly roll; wrap in waxed paper; chill or freeze several hours. When ready to serve, slice thin and bake on ungreased cookie sheet 15 minutes until brown. Serve very hot.

MRS. STANLEY K. BRADSHAW

SAUSAGE CHEESE CRUMBLES

Serves: 30   Oven: 400°

1 lb. hot or mild sausage   3 cups Bisquick
½ lb. sharp cheese, grated

Have all ingredients at room temperature. Thoroughly combine cheese, Bisquick, and sausage; form into small balls. May cook immediately, refrigerate, or freeze. To freeze, place on cookie sheet and freeze individually, then put in bags and you may take out amount needed and thaw quickly. Bake for 15 minutes in a 400° oven.

Variation: Omit cheese.

MRS. WARREN A. JENNINGS
DEWITT, ARKANSAS

SAUSAGE AND CHESTNUT BALLS

Serves: 20   Oven: 350°

5-oz. can water chestnuts,   1 lb. sausage, hot
   drained and chopped   1 lb. sausage, mild

Mix and form into balls. Place on ungreased sheet and bake for 20 minutes in a 350° oven; you may want to broil for last few minutes to brown. Will freeze.

MRS. CARL FLIEGNER

BARBECUED PARTY FRANKS

2 lbs. weiners   ½ cup barbecue sauce
1 can beer   1 cup brown sugar

Cut weiners in one inch lengths. Mix remaining ingredients and pour over weiners. Marinate overnight. Cook over medium heat in a saucepan for 30 minutes. Use a large pan as they will expand. Serve in a bowl with small amount of sauce; keep warm. Serve with toothpicks.

Men love these!

MRS. EDWIN L. BAXLEY

ORIENTAL FRANKS

Serves: 6   Oven: 350°

½ cup soy sauce   ½ tsp. ground ginger
1 Tb. sugar   12-oz. jar cocktail franks
1 tsp. instant minced onion

In a shallow baking dish, mix the soy sauce, sugar, onion, and ginger. Add the franks and marinate for about 2 hours. Bake the franks in the marinade in a 350° oven for 15 to 20 minutes. Drain and serve on cocktail picks while hot.

MRS. JOHN A. RIGGS, III

CHINESE EGG ROLLS

Yield: 6-8 large rolls

FILLING:

1 cup shrimp, cooked or canned	½ cup celery
	¾ cup cabbage
1 cup pork, cooked	½ cup cold water
4 scallions	½ cup soy sauce
½ cup water chestnuts	3 Tb. oil
1 clove garlic	

Mince first seven ingredients separately, preferably in a blender. Place minced cabbage and celery in cold water; bring to a boil; drain. Heat oil in skillet. Add shrimp and pork and fry three minutes, stirring constantly. Add remaining ingredients, including celery and cabbage; fry five minutes, stirring. Set aside if to be used immediately; refrigerate if to be used the next day; freeze indefinitely. The ingredients may be gathered bit by bit as leftovers, frozen separately, and combined at time of use.

SKINS:

¾ cup sifted flour	1½ cups water
1 Tb. cornstarch	Cooking oil
1 tsp. salt	Paste: 1 Tb. flour, 2 Tb.
2 beaten eggs	water
Pinch sugar	

Sift flour, cornstarch, and salt in large bowl. Beat in eggs and sugar; add water slowly, beating constantly, until batter is smooth. Makes a very thin batter resulting in a thin pancake when fried. Heat a 6 to 8-inch enamel or non-stick skillet very hot. Drop ⅛ teaspoon of oil in skillet and distribute it along bottom and sides with a paper towel. Drop one large cooking spoon of batter into skillet and tilt skillet until batter is distributed over entire bottom. It will not be exactly the same thickness throughout. When the pancake curls at the edges, one to two minutes, turn it over. If it sticks the skillet is not hot enough. Stack pancakes; may be refrigerated if not used immediately.

To assemble, spread a layer of filling on each pancake, leaving ¼ inch unfilled around edges. Roll up pancake like a crescent roll so that filling and pancake alternate in the center. Stick the open side and ends of roll together with flour and water paste. Fry in hot oil until brown, turning once. May be refrigerated overnight and heated uncovered in a 450° oven for 15 minutes. Serve with dry mustard mixed with water as a sauce and chutney sauce. When serving, you may want to cut each large roll into pieces for hors d'oeuvres, or you may leave whole and serve as a main course. If it is too salty for you, cut down on the amount of soy sauce.

This is really not so difficult and turns out great!

MRS. WILLIAM L. PATTON, JR.

STEAK TARTARE

Serves: 10

1 lb. ground sirloin, all fat removed	1 tsp. pepper
1 bottle capers	1 tsp. Worcestershire sauce
1 yellow onion, finely chopped	1 raw egg yolk
	Coarse ground pepper
1 tsp. Louisiana hot sauce	Paprika
1 tsp. Dijon mustard	Parsley
1 tsp. salt	Dark bread
	Unsalted butter

Have the butcher grind the sirloin 3 times with all fat removed. Mix first 9 ingredients and shape into oblong mounds. Score with a knife and sprinkle coarse pepper and paprika over top. Serve on a bed of parsley with dark bread and unsalted butter. This is not meant to be cooked.

MRS. JAMES A. COYNE, JR.
ROLAND, ARKANSAS

SWEDISH MEATBALLS

Serves: 8

1 cup bread crumbs	1 egg
¾ cup water	Salt to taste
¾ cup heavy cream	¼ tsp. pepper
1½ lbs. ground chuck	Butter
1 small onion, grated	

Soak crumbs in mixture of water and cream for 30 minutes. Add gradually to meat. Add onion, egg, salt, and pepper; blend well. Shape into 1½-inch balls and cook in butter in hot skillet until done and evenly browned. Drain on paper towel. Recipe may be doubled or quadrupled. Meatballs may be frozen individually on cookie sheets, then put in bag and later heated in oven before serving.

HIBACHI STEAK

Serves: 6-8

1 lb. sirloin	1½ tsp. black pepper
¾ cup salad oil	¼ cup wine vinegar
1½ Tb. soy sauce	1 tsp. parsley
2 Tb. Worcestershire sauce	1 clove garlic, mashed
1 Tb. dry mustard	3 Tb. lemon juice
1⅛ tsp. salt	

Cut meat in bite-size pieces. Mix remaining ingredients and pour over meat. Cover and let marinate at least 4 hours or overnight. Serve with toothpicks for guests to charcoal their own on an hibachi. If you cannot use an hibachi you may broil in oven and serve in a chafing dish.

This is an elegant appetizer the men like. It is fun for guests to cook their own.

MRS. CHARLES WILLIAMSON

CHIPPED BEEF ROLL UPS

Serves: 4

3 oz. cream cheese, softened
8 green olives, chopped fine
2 to 3 tsp. horseradish

3-oz. pkg. dried, sliced beef
Melted butter

Blend cheese, olives, and horseradish. Spread on slices of beef and roll up. Cut each roll in half and fasten with toothpicks. Brush with butter and broil under medium heat until heated through. Serve immediately. If preferred, rolls may be chilled until firm and served cold. These may be prepared ahead of time. Makes 18 bite-size rolls.

MRS. ROBERT C. HICKMAN

COCKTAIL HAM BALLS

Serves: 20   Oven: 350°

3 slices bread, crust cut off
1½ cups milk
3 eggs
2½ lbs. lean pork, ground
    with 2½ lbs. cured ham

¾ cup water
1½ cups vinegar
2¼ cups brown sugar
1½ tsp. dry mustard

Soak bread in milk; add eggs; mix with meat. Shape into small balls, not too firm, and place in a single layer in a greased pan. Heat together water, vinegar, brown sugar, and dry mustard, making a syrup. Pour over ham balls. Cook for 30 minutes at 350° turning at least once. Do not let the syrup dry up. Balls may be made 1¼-inch size for a main course and cooked longer at same temperature. Also may be frozen and reheated in foil.

MRS. JOHN B. DYKE

DEVILISH HAM PUFFS

Serves: 6-8   Oven: 375°

½ lb. cream cheese
1½ tsp. baking powder
Salt
1 tsp. fresh onion juice
1 egg yolk

Cayenne pepper to taste
2 2¼-oz. cans deviled ham
3 to 4 drops Worcestershire
Dash Tabasco
24 small bread rounds

Mix cheese, baking powder, salt, onion juice, egg yolk, and cayenne. In separate dish mix ham, Worcestershire, and Tabasco. Toast bread rounds on one side. Spread untoasted side with ham mixture; cover with a mound of cheese mixture. Place on cookie sheet and bake 10 minutes at 375° or until brown. These can be prepared a few hours before baking.

MRS. FRED W. TERRY

SAUERKRAUT BALLS

Yield: 125

½ lb. lean boneless ham	1 tsp. salt
½ lb. lean boneless pork	1 tsp. dry mustard
½ lb. lean boneless corned	2 cups milk
beef	2 lbs. sauerkraut, cooked and
1 med. onion	drained
1 tsp. parsley	5 eggs, slightly beaten
3 Tb. shortening	10-oz. box corn flake crumbs
2 cups flour	

Put meats and onion through food grinder; add parsley. Blend well and sauté in shortening until pork is done. Add flour, salt, dry mustard, and milk; stir constantly until thick. Add sauerkraut, then put entire mixture through food grinder. Mix thoroughly; return to skillet and cook, stirring constantly until very thick. Cool; form into balls about the size of a walnut. Roll in flour, dip in eggs, roll in corn flake crumbs, then fry in deep fat at 370° until brown. Serve hot. May make ahead, fry, then freeze on cookie sheets one layer at a time. Thaw the day of serving and heat through in a 350° oven. Leave spaces between them for crispness and do not stack for freezing or thawing or they will flatten. Delicious served with a hot mustard sauce as a dip. This recipe makes a large amount and is very unusual.

Tasty!

MRS. ROBERT C. FERGUSON
BIG RAPIDS, MICHIGAN

PICKLED SHRIMP

Serves: 6

2 lbs. shrimp, cooked and	½ cup lemon juice
cleaned	½ cup vinegar
2 lbs. onions, sliced	1 cup French dressing
Bay leaves	1 box pickling spice

In a crock arrange in layers first shrimp, then onion, then 5 or 6 bay leaves repeating until all shrimp and onion are used. Combine lemon juice, vinegar, dressing, and pickling spice; pour over shrimp and onions; cover and refrigerate. Do not mix for 24 hours; then stir once a day for 3 or 4 days. Serve with toothpicks.

MRS. JAMES VERNON FLACK, JR.

SHRIMP POTPOURRI

Serves: 10

2 9-oz. cans artichoke hearts, drained	3 large bell peppers
2 lemons	1½ cups salad oil
3 lbs. frozen shrimp	1½ cups vinegar
2 6-oz. cans mushroom caps, drained	1 clove garlic, minced
	1½ tsp. salt
	Freshly ground pepper

Gently squeeze each artichoke heart and place it upside down on a platter. If hearts are large, cut in half, lengthwise. Sprinkle with juice of 1 lemon and let stand at least one hour. Place shrimp in boiling salted water to cover; simmer 2 to 3 minutes, or until shrimp are firm and opaque. Drain and toss with juice of the remaining lemon. Cover this and refrigerate. Wash and dry peppers; place in broiler pan, which may be foil lined, and broil 3 inches from heat for 10 minutes, turning several times until skin is blackened. Watch to prevent burning. Cool and peel off skin; cut off stem ends, cut in half, and remove seeds. Cut into large squares. Drain artichoke hearts and shrimp and place in a large container with green pepper squares and mushrooms. In a small bowl heat together oil, vinegar, garlic, salt, and pepper; pour over shrimp mixture. Cover tightly and chill at least 8 hours. Drain and serve.

MRS. JAMES W. WILSON

EASY SHRIMP DIP

Serves: 15

4½-oz. can tiny shrimp	8 oz. cream cheese
2 tsp. lemon juice	1 pk. Good Seasons Italian dressing mix
½ pt. sour cream	

Wash and drain shrimp. Mix remaining ingredients until smooth. Add shrimp. Refrigerate at least 3 hours before serving. Serve with chips or crackers.

MRS. ROBERT M. PESHEK

HOT SHRIMP AND CHEESE DIP

Serves: 12

2 10½-oz. cans cream of shrimp soup	2 6-oz. rolls garlic cheese
2 10½-oz. cans Cheddar cheese soup	1½ lbs. frozen shrimp
	Fresh ground pepper

Heat soups with cheese, which has been cut in pieces, until melted. Cook shrimp; cut in small pieces and mix well with soup mixture. Add pepper and serve with tortillas or chips. Any left over is good served over toast.

MRS. SMITH GROBMYER

SHRIMP SPREAD

Serves: 24-30

3 lbs. frozen shrimp	2-oz. carton frozen chives
1 qt. real mayonnaise	10 Tb. dried parsley flakes
4½-oz. jar horseradish	2 tsp. onion salt
mustard	Juice of 1 lemon

Boil shrimp and chop. Combine with remaining ingredients and chill for 24 hours. Serve with melba toast or chips. This sauce without the shrimp is good on hard-boiled eggs as a salad or simply as a dip for fresh shrimp.

MRS. GORDON RATHER

SPINACH CRABMEAT DIP

Serves: 15

10-oz. pkg. frozen chopped spinach	4 Tb. butter
1 bunch green onions and tops, chopped	2 7-oz. cans crabmeat
	⅓ cup Parmesan cheese

Cook spinach and drain. Sauté green onion in butter. Mix all ingredients together, heat, and serve in chafing dish with crackers or large corn chips.

MARIE SCHULTE

Variation: May omit 1 can crabmeat and add another package of spinach, another bunch of green onion, 2 tablespoons butter, Tabasco, and garlic powder.

MRS. VERNON JACKSON, III

CRAB ROLLS

Serves: 15   Oven: 350°

½ cup butter	1 loaf very thin sliced white
½ lb. Velveeta cheese	bread
7-oz. can crabmeat	Melted butter

While butter and cheese are melting, roll each slice of bread with rolling pin. Trim off crusts. Mix crabmeat with butter and cheese. Put 1 teaspoon of mixture on each slice of bread and spread evenly. Roll up bread slices and coat outside with melted butter. Cut each one into 4 pieces. Put on baking sheet and bake at 350° about 15 minutes; then run under broiler for a few minutes to brown. You may use canned lobster if preferred. This may be frozen. Serve hot.

MRS. SIDNEY BROCKMAN
ELGIN A.F.B., FLORIDA

HOT CRAB SPREAD

Serves: 10   Oven: 350°

7-oz. can crabmeat	1 Tb. chives
¼ cup lemon juice	1 Tb. onion, minced
3 oz. cream cheese	½ clove garlic, mashed
1 Tb. heavy cream	Salt
⅓ cup Hellman's mayonnaise	Dash Worcestershire sauce
(no substitute)	Dash Tabasco

Marinate crab in lemon juice for 1 hour; drain. Whip cream cheese and cream until smooth. Beat in mayonnaise; add onion, chives, garlic, and salt; blend well. Fold in crab and add Worcestershire and Tabasco. Put in ovenproof dish and bake 30 minutes at 350°. Serve with Triscuits. May use the cream cheese that comes with chives in it and omit onion.

MRS. MIKE MEHAFFY

Variation: Omit lemon juice, mayonnaise, and garlic and add an additional 5 ounces of cream cheese, ½ teaspoon horseradish, and ¼ cup slivered almonds before baking.

MRS. CASSIUS E. STREET
EAST LANSING, MICHIGAN

HOT CURRIED CRAB DIP

Serves: 20

8 oz. cream cheese	2 7½-oz. cans crabmeat,
¾ cup mayonnaise	cleaned and drained
1 Tb. lemon juice	2 Tb. melted butter
¼ tsp. Worcestershire sauce	¼ tsp. salt
1¾ oz. slivered almonds	½ tsp. curry

Mix cheese, mayonnaise, lemon juice, and Worcestershire in blender; stir in crabmeat. Brown almonds in butter until golden; add salt and stir into crab mixture. Add curry last. This can be frozen and heated later over low heat or put in casserole and baked at 350° for 40 minutes. If freezing, do not add curry until ready to serve. Serve in chafing dish as a dip.

MRS. WILLIAM A. SAUNDERS, JR.

GLAZED PECANS

Yield: 1 lb. pecans   Oven: 250°

1 lb. shelled pecans   ¼ cup light corn syrup
½ cup margarine   Salt

Spread pecans evenly in an 8½ x 13-inch aluminum pan. Scatter margarine in pats over nuts. Drizzle corn syrup over nuts. Roast in slow oven 250° to 300°, stirring occasionally until slightly browned (about one hour). Add extra margarine if spoon becomes sticky when stirring. Line counter with brown paper; spread roasted nuts on paper; salt generously, tossing nuts to insure all are covered.

MRS. FRANK BAUER, JR.

NUTTY SOYBEANS

Soybeans   Salt
Water   Paprika
Oil

Wash beans carefully; place in a covered container with four times as much water as beans. Soak 12 hours. Pour off remaining water and absorb excess moisture with paper towels. Place a few at a time in hot deep fat and fry until golden brown. It is a good idea to use a heavy pot with high sides as moisture in beans causes oil to bubble. Sprinkle lightly with salt and paprika. This can be prepared ahead of time and frozen in an airtight container. May be served in a bowl like peanuts or substituted for nuts in any recipe. Taste is similar to peanuts.

MRS. WARREN JENNINGS
DEWITT, ARKANSAS

BEVERAGES

BRIDGE DAY MINT TEA

Yield: 2 quarts

1½ cups boiling water
3 heaping tsp. tea
6 sprigs mint, leaves broken
off stems

1½ cups boiling water
1 scant cup sugar
½ cup lemon juice
1 qt. cold water

Allow tea and mint to steep in boiling water for fifteen minutes. In another 1½ cups boiling water dissolve sugar, then add lemon juice. Strain the tea and mint mixture and add to lemon juice and sugar mixture. Add one quart cold water and store in refrigerator. Will keep for days. This is a cool, refreshing drink, very light in color. The recipe doubles easily.

MRS. WILLIAM B. SIGLER

ICED RUSSIAN TEA

Serves: 20

11 cups water
2 family size tea bags
6-oz. can frozen orange juice
6-oz. can frozen lemonade

2 sticks cinnamon
6 to 8 cloves
½ cup sugar

Boil water with cinnamon, cloves, and sugar; turn off and add tea bags; let steep until tea is strong. Remove tea bags. Add juices; chill, and serve over ice. Garnish with mint. May also be served hot.

MRS. WARREN A. JENNINGS
DeWITT, ARKANSAS

INSTANT SPICED TEA

Yield: 4½ cups, dry

3-oz. pkg. instant lemonade
mix with sugar
2 cups Tang
2 cups sugar

1 cup instant tea
1 Tb. cinnamon
1 Tb. ground cloves

Mix these dry ingredients and store in an airtight jar. Mix 2 teaspoons to 1 cup of water to serve. May be iced or hot. If watching calories, you may add 1 tablespoon dried lemon peel in place of lemonade and use artificial sweetener in each cup as prepared.

MRS. WILLIAM BRUCE BISHOP

CITRUS PUNCH

2 cups sugar
2½ cups water
Juice of 6 lemons
Grated rind of 2 lemons
Juice of 2 oranges

Grated rind of 1 orange
2 handfuls fresh mint
(crushed)
Ginger ale
Vokda or gin (optional)

Boil sugar and water for 10 minutes. Pour over juice and mint; cover and let set for 1 hour. Strain and chill in refrigerator.

For Drink: Fill a glass ⅔ full of crushed ice. Add 5 tablespoons juice and equal parts of ginger ale. Vodka or gin may be added if desired.

For Punch: Fill bowl with ice; add juice and ginger ale. Garnish with orange slices or frosted grapes draped over sides of bowl.

MRS. SLOAN CUMMINS
PINE BLUFF, ARKANSAS

MULLED CIDER

Serves: 12

2 sticks cinnamon
12 whole cloves
2 tsp. allspice

½ cup brown sugar
1 gal. apple cider
Lemon slices (optional)

Tie spices in a cloth bag; place bag in cider and simmer for 15 minutes. Remove spice bag. To garnish, float thin lemon slices on top.

MRS. ROBERT D. ETTER

Variation: Add 8 tablespoons of lemon juice and 4 tablespoons of orange juice for a tart cider.

MRS. WARREN A. JENNINGS
DEWITT, ARKANSAS

HOT BUTTERED CRANBERRY PUNCH

Serves: 6

1 pt. cranberry juice
12 oz. apricot nectar

2 Tb. lemon juice
2 Tb. butter

Heat all ingredients together. Serve in mugs. May garnish with lemon slices. Addition of spirits optional.

CORDELL DOUGHERTY

BLOODY MARY

Serves: 1

4 oz. V-8 juice   1 to 1½ oz. vodka
1 oz. lemon juice   Salt
1 drop Tabasco   Pepper
1 tsp. Worcestershire sauce

Mix together and serve over ice.

J. D. HARRIS

QUANTITY BLOODY MARY MIX

Serves: 24

9 cups tomato juice   2 tsp. salt
3 cups vodka   2 tsp. pepper
⅔ cup lemon juice   2 tsp. celery salt
2 Tb. Worcestershire sauce   Dash Tabasco

Mix above ingredients. Serve over ice.

MRS. WILLIAM OVERTON

DO AHEAD DAIQUIRI

Yield: 5 cups

6 oz. frozen limeade, thawed   12 oz. rum (may use can to
18 oz. water   measure)

Combine and place in plastic container; freeze. Take out ½ hour
before serving. Spoon into champagne glasses.

MRS. W. IRA WILLIAMS
STUART, FLORIDA

*Variation: Substitute frozen lime juice for limeade and add 10
ounces frozen strawberries; mix in blender.*

MRS. ROBERT M. FISHER
BRONXVILL, NEW YORK

BANANA DAIQUIRI

Serves: 2

3 to 4 ice cubes   1 oz. simple syrup
1 medium banana, ripe   Juice of ½ lime
3 oz. rum

To make simple syrup, boil 1 part water to 2 parts sugar for 5 minutes. Keep in refrigerator as a sweetener for drinks. Mix all ingredients in blender and serve in sherbet glasses. May use more or less simple syrup depending on size and sweetness of banana. To make a lime daiquiri, eliminate banana and increase syrup and lime juice.

DR. BEN O. PRICE

YELLOW BIRDS

Serves: 4-6

4 jiggers light rum   1 jigger Tia Maria
1 jigger simple syrup (two   1 jigger banana liqueur
   parts sugar and one part   4 jiggers orange juice
   water boiled until sugar   Orange slices
   dissolves)

Blend and pour over crushed ice. Serve with half an orange slice and sip through a straw.

A Jamaican delight!

MRS. HERBERT L. THOMAS, SR.

MIMOSA

3¼ cups orange juice, fresh   1 bottle of champagne
   if possible

Mix and pour over crushed ice. Serve in deep wine goblets.

MRS. ROBERT HICKMAN

CRANBERRY SLUSH

Serves: 15

1 qt. cranberry juice   1 pt. vodka
6-oz. can frozen orange juice

Mix ingredients and freeze in plastic container for 24 hours. Serve in champagne glasses.

Very potent.

MRS. GEORGE DAVIS

GIN FIZZ

Serves: 1

1 Tb. powdered sugar	1 egg white
3 to 4 drops orange flower water	1½ oz. milk or light cream
1 squirt lime juice	1 squirt Seltzer water
1 squirt lemon juice	2 drops vanilla
1½ oz. dry gin	Cracked ice

Mix all ingredients in a blender, then strain into a glass. Do not serve over ice.

JAMES T. DYKE

WHISKEY SOUR PUNCH

Serves: 6-8

1½ cups sugar	Juice of 5 lemons
1 pt. water	Juice of 2 oranges
1 pt. good bourbon, rum, or Canadian Club	Rinds of 2½ lemons
	Rinds of 2 oranges

Dissolve sugar in water. Add remaining ingredients. Let rinds sit in mixture in refrigerator overnight. Next day squeeze juice from rinds. Strain if desired. Refrigerate 24 hours. Serve very cold. May be kept for a long time as a ready cocktail.

MRS. EUGENE MASON

GLÖGG

Serves: 18-20

5 sticks cinnamon	1 fifth brandy
1 Tb. whole cloves	1 cup blanched almonds
½ lb. dried peaches	1 or 2 fifths wine (sherry,
1 cup raisins	burgundy, port, madeira,
1 qt. water	may be mixed)

Tie spices in a cheesecloth bag and place in water with peaches and raisins. Cook until tender and leave until ready to complete preparations for serving. This part can be done ahead. Remove bag and heat fruit and juices. Add brandy, almonds, and wine. Add sugar if needed. Continue to heat but do not boil. Pour into glass, enamel, or silver container. Ladle into punch cups or glasses and accompany with a small coffee spoon. Include some of the fruits and almonds. This is delightful for a Christmas punch.

MRS. ROBERT G. CARNAHAN

MAGNOLIA MANOR JULEP

Serves: 1

6 or 7 sprigs fresh mint	Crushed ice
Sugar to cover	2 to 3 oz. bourbon
Water	Fresh mint

Place mint in bowl, cover with sugar and add enough water to moisten thoroughly. Crush leaves, stems, and sugar with a wood pestle to make mint essence. Fill beaker half full of crushed ice and add half the mint infusion. Fill to brim with ice and add balance of mint infusion. Pour in bourbon until beaker brims and refrigerate for 1 hour. Before serving add a sprig of fresh mint.

A. HALL ALLEN

MRS. WITT'S EGGNOG

Serves: 8

6 eggs, separated	6 Tb. sugar
¾ cup whiskey, or to taste	1 pt. cream, heavy

Beat egg yolks well. Beat in whiskey a little at a time. Beat egg whites, adding sugar. Fold whites into yolk mixture, then fold in cream.

MRS. ROBERT G. CARNAHAN

GRASSHOPPER

Serves: 2

2⅔ cups vanilla ice cream or	2 oz. green creme de menthe
ice milk	1 oz. white creme de cocoa

Blend ingredients in blender; thin with light cream if necessary. Should be the consistency of a milk shake.

J. D. HARRIS

MOCHA PUNCH

Serves: 35

1 oz. instant coffee	½ gal. chocolate ice milk
1 cup sugar	½ gal. vanilla ice milk
2 cups hot water	Whipped cream (optional)
1 gal. milk	Liquor (optional)

Dissolve the sugar and coffee in hot water. Add milk and chill overnight. Just before serving, add the ice milk, breaking into chunks. May garnish with whipped cream. May add creme de cocoa or light rum if desired. If making for 50, leave amount of sugar, water, and chocolate ice milk the same and use 2 ounces coffee, 1½ gallons milk, and 1 gallon vanilla ice milk.

MRS. DON F. HAMILTON

RUM RUNNER'S PUNCH

Yield: 1 gal.

3 pts. tea	1 cup sugar
1 pt. lemon juice	1 pt. rum
1 pt. orange juice	2 pts. whiskey

Mix and chill. Serve over ice. Can be made ahead of time.

Bourbon flavored and potent.

MRS. E. R. NEFF
MRS. CHARLES WITSELL

HOT BUTTERED RUM

Serves: 30

1 cup butter	2 tsp. each of nutmeg,
1⅓ cups light brown sugar	cinnamon, and vanilla
6 Tb. honey	Water or apple cider
6 oz. rum	Rum

Cream butter; mix in sugar and then add vanilla, spices, honey, and rum. Mixture will refrigerate indefinitely. When ready to use add one heaping tablespoon of mixture and one jigger of rum to each cup of boiling water or hot apple cider.

MRS. WARREN A. JENNINGS
DeWITT, ARKANSAS

COFFEE BRANDY

Yield: 9 cups

1 whole vanilla bean	2 cups boiling water
2 oz. powdered instant coffee	1½ pts. brandy
4 cups sugar	

Split vanilla bean half way down middle. Mix other ingredients, add bean and let brew in closed jar in dark place for one month. Remove bean.

MRS. JOHN E. ARNOLD

SOUPS

BEAN SOUP

Serves: 6

1 lb. dried Navy or Great Northern beans	3 to 4 ribs celery, chopped
	6 to 8 sprigs parsley
End of ham	3 Tb. butter
2 qts. water	Salt and pepper to taste
1 large onion, chopped	1 tsp. sugar
3 to 4 carrots, chopped	¼ cup flour

Soak beans in enough water to cover well overnight; drain. Slowly cook beans with end of ham in 2 quarts water, covered, for about 2 hours, or until beans are tender. Chop onion, carrots, celery, and parsley and cook covered slowly in butter until tender. Season to taste; add sugar. Remove end of ham from beans. Cut ham into chunks; return to beans. Add vegetable mixture; season to taste. Cook together for about 30 minutes. To thicken make a paste with flour and water; add to soup; cook slowly for about 30 minutes.

BROCCOLI SOUP

Serves: 8

2 10-oz. pkgs. frozen chopped broccoli	10½-oz. can condensed cream of chicken soup
2 chicken bouillon cubes	½ tsp. oregano
1½ cups milk (about)	Salt and pepper
2 cups cream or half and half	Croutons

Cook broccoli as label directs, but add bouillon cubes instead of salt. Drain well, reserving liquid. Add milk to reserved liquid to make 2 cups. Place liquid, broccoli, cream, undiluted soup, and oregano in blender. Cover and blend until smooth, about 30 seconds. Pour mixture into pan and heat; do not boil. Add salt and pepper to taste. Garnish with croutons.

MRS. STANLEY K. BRADSHAW, JR.

FRESH CREAM OF CORN SOUP

Serves: 6

5 ears sweet corn	Salt and pepper to taste
2 small onions, chopped	2 cups milk
1 medium bell pepper, seeded and chopped	2 egg yolks
	1 cup cream, heavy
3 Tb. butter	Slivered almonds

Scrape corn kernels from cob with sharp knife. Sauté onions and green pepper in butter; add salt and pepper. Add corn and milk; simmer for 10 minutes. Put soup through food mill or puree in blender. Beat egg yolks. Bring cream just to boiling point; pour over egg yolks, stirring briskly; add to hot soup. Garnish with slivered almonds that have been slightly browned in butter. This soup may be made ahead if you wait until the last minute to add egg yolks and cream.

MRS. DON THOMPSON

COLD CUCUMBER SOUP

Serves: 6

3 medium cucumbers, peeled
  and quartered
3 Tb. butter
1 Tb. flour

3 cups chicken broth
2 Tb. sour cream
Salt and pepper to taste

Remove seeds from cucumbers, mince fine. Cook ⅔'s of minced cucumbers in butter, do not brown, stirring constantly for about 5 minutes. Add flour, stirring thoroughly; cook an additional 3 to 4 minutes; stir in chicken broth. Simmer about 10 minutes. Add salt and pepper. Remove from heat; force through fine sieve. Add remaining ⅓ of uncooked cucumbers; chill. When ready to serve, add sour cream. May garnish with chives, nutmeg, or slivered toasted almonds. Pass croutons if you wish.

THE CAPITOL CLUB

COLD CURRY-CRAB SOUP

Serves: 8

1 Tb. chopped chives
2 Tb. butter
2 tsp. curry
2 Tb. flour
3 cups milk

2 cups crab meat, cleaned
  and drained
¼ cup sherry
2 cups heavy cream

Sauté chives in butter for 1 minute. Add curry and flour; cook until well blended. Add milk; cook until thick. Heat crab meat in sherry; add cream; add to curry mixture. Serve very cold. This may be made a day ahead.

MRS. DAVID SNOWDEN

GAZPACHO

Serves: 8

3 medium bell peppers,
  chopped and seeded
3 medium cucumbers, peeled
  and chopped
5 medium ripe tomatoes,
  peeled and chopped
2 medium red onions,
  chopped
2 cloves garlic, chopped
2 10-oz. cans Snap-E-Tom

3 tsp. salt
½ tsp. oregano leaves
½ tsp. basil leaves
½ tsp. Tabasco
1 Tb. Worcestershire sauce
½ cup salad oil
½ cup red wine vinegar
2 Tb. lemon juice
Garlic croutons

Mix all ingredients together except croutons; put in refrigerator for 2 hours. Take about 2 cups of mixture; put in blender for about 15 seconds; stir all together. Chill. Serve topped with garlic croutons.

MRS. JOSEPH P. WARD

MULLIGATAWNY SOUP

Serves: 10

4-lb. chicken	1 cup diced carrots
3 qts. water	1 to 2 tsp. curry powder
2 tsp. monosodium glutamate	½ tsp. saffron
3 tsp. salt	¼ tsp. pepper
3 Tb. butter	Salt to taste
1 clove garlic, minced	¼ cup cornstarch
⅔ cup rice	½ cup milk
1 cup chopped onion	1 cup light cream

Put chicken, water, monosodium glutamate, and salt in 5-quart pan. Cover and simmer until tender. Remove meat; reserve broth and skim fat off. Melt butter in large skillet; sauté garlic and rice until straw colored. Add onion and carrots; sauté 1 to 2 minutes. Bring 10 cups chicken broth to boil; add to vegetables. Season with curry powder, saffron, salt, and pepper. Simmer until rice is cooked. Add chicken (cut into pieces). Blend cornstarch with milk; add to soup. Cook and stir until thick. Add cream just before serving and heat.

GUMBO

Serves: 12

4 Tb. olive oil	20-oz. can tomatoes
4 Tb. butter	1 Tb. Worcestershire sauce
4 Tb. flour	1 chicken, cooked in water
1 large onion	(save 2 qts. stock)
¼ cup garlic, chopped	2 or 3 lbs. shrimp, cleaned
2 Tb. parsley, chopped	Oysters
1 bell pepper, chopped	Crab
3 cups center cut ham, diced	Rice, cooked
2 10-oz. pkgs. okra, chopped	

Make a roux from olive oil, butter and flour; cook over moderate heat, stirring constantly until very black. Add onion, garlic, parsley, green pepper, and ham; cook until tender. Add okra, tomatoes, and Worcestershire sauce. Debone chicken; put in large kettle; add first mixture and 2 quarts stock; simmer, covered, for 2 hours. About 45 minutes before serving add shrimp, oysters, and crab as desired. Serve either over rice or with mound of rice in each serving.

MRS. ALLEN ALWORTH

LEEK SOUP

Serves: 4

2 large leeks or yellow onions	1 Tb. butter
1 potato, pared and diced	⅛ tsp. paprika
1 cup chicken broth (canned	⅛ tsp. pepper
may be used)	1 tsp. salt
2 Tb. minced chives	1 cup milk or cream

Cut leeks and about 4 inches of their green tops into pieces; boil with the potato in about 2 cups boiling water until soft. Drain off water. Run through blender, return to saucepan; add rest of ingredients. Stir to mix well; reheat. Serve very hot.

MRS. GEORGE ROSE SMITH

ONION SOUP GRATINEÉD WITH CHEESE

Serves: 6-8   **Oven: 325°**

5 cups yellow onions, thinly	Salt and pepper to taste
sliced	3 Tb. cognac (optional)
3 Tb. butter	12 to 16 slices French bread
1 Tb. oil	cut ¾-inch thick
1 tsp. salt	Olive oil
¼ tsp. sugar	Garlic clove, cut
3 Tb. flour	2 oz. Swiss cheese, slivered
5 cups canned beef broth	1 Tb. onion, grated
3 cups water	1½ cups Swiss cheese, grated
½ cup dry white wine	1 Tb. butter melted

Cook sliced onions slowly in butter and oil in covered, heavy 4 quart saucepan for 15 minutes. Uncover, raise heat, stir in salt and sugar. Cook slowly 30 to 40 minutes, stirring frequently. Onions should be an even deep golden brown. Sprinkle in flour and stir for 3 minutes. In another pan bring liquids to boil; stir into onion mixture. Simmer, partly covered, for 30 to 40 minutes. Salt and pepper to taste. Just before serving stir in cognac.

To make the bread topping place sliced bread in one layer in roasting pan; bake in 325° oven for 30 minutes or until thoroughly dried and lightly browned. Half way through baking, baste each side with olive oil. After baking rub with cut garlic.

To gratineé bring soup to boil; stir in 2 ounces Swiss cheese; pour into casserole or individual onion soup pots. Float toast rounds on top of soup; sprinkle with grated cheese, sprinkle with melted butter. Bake in 325° oven for 20 minutes. Serve immediately.
This soup may be served without the cheese topping. If so, pass grated cheese.

MRS. MIKE MEHAFFY

POTAGE CRÈME DE CHAMPIGNONS
CREAM OF MUSHROOM SOUP

Serves: 4-6

1½ lbs. fresh mushrooms	2 egg yolks
9 Tb. butter	¾ cup heavy cream
2 finely chopped shallots	Salt
6 Tb. flour	White pepper
6 cups chicken stock	

Separate mushroom caps and stems; slice half of the caps about ⅛-inch thick and coarsely chop the remaining caps and stems. In skillet, melt 2 tablespoons of butter; add the sliced mushrooms to the butter and sauté for 2 minutes or until lightly colored. Transfer to another bowl and set aside. In the same skillet, add additional 2 tablespoons of butter and cook the remaining stems and caps with the shallots. Set aside in the skillet.

In a heavy 4 to 6 quart saucepan, melt the remaining 5 tablespoons of butter over moderate heat. Remove pan from heat and stir in flour; then cook over low heat, stirring constantly, for 1 to 2 minutes. Do not let this roux brown. Remove pan from heat and allow to cool for a few seconds, then pour in chicken stock, beating constantly with a wire whisk. Return to heat and stir until cream soup base comes to a boil, thickens, and is perfectly smooth. Then add the chopped mushrooms and shallots; simmer, stirring occasionally, for 15 minutes.

Puree the soup through food mill into a mixing bowl, then back through a fine sieve to the saucepan. With wire whisk, blend the egg yolks and cream together in a bowl. Whisk some of the hot soup into the egg-cream mixture, 2 tablespoons at a time, until ½ cup has been added. Then reverse the process and slowly whisk the now warm egg-cream mixture into the soup.

Bring to a boil; boil for 30 seconds, stirring constantly. Remove the pan from the heat. Taste and season with salt and white pepper. Add reserved sliced mushrooms and serve in a tureen.

Sherry may be added to taste if desired.

MRS. DONALD E. CHRISTIAN

CREAMED ONION SOUP

Serves: 6

2 medium onions, chopped fine	10-oz. can beef consommé
2 Tb. butter	1 cup light cream
3 Tb. flour	Salt and pepper
	Paprika or parsley

Brown onions in butter; remove from heat; stir in flour until smooth. Add consommé; stir until smooth. Add cream; cook until soup thickens. A little milk may be added if too thick. Season with salt and pepper to taste. Garnish with paprika or parsley.

MRS. MARTHA DEAN

OYSTER BISQUE

Serves: 2-3

½ pt. fresh oysters	2 Tb. butter, softened
¼ cup water	1½ Tb. flour
Salt	½ cup milk
Cayenne pepper	½ cup cream or half and half
2 Tb. chopped parsley	1 beaten egg yolk

Drain liquid from oysters; save liquid. Add water to liquid and bring to a boil. Season with salt, cayenne pepper, and parsley. Cream butter and flour until smooth; add to liquid. Stir until smooth; add a few chopped oysters, milk, and cream. Cook for 5 minutes. Stir in well beaten egg yolk. To serve, add rest of oysters. Bring to a boil. When edges of oysters begin to curl, serve immediately.

MRS. CHARLES M. TAYLOR, II

SPLIT PEA SOUP

Serves: 6

1½ cups split peas	2 bay leaves
1 ham bone	8 cups boiling water
½ cup carrots, diced	½ cup light cream
2 ribs celery, diced	Salt and pepper to taste
2 medium onions, sliced	¾ tsp. sugar
8 peppercorns	

Wash peas and drain. Put peas with ham bone, vegetables, seasonings, and water in kettle. Cover and simmer over low heat until peas are soft, about 3 hours, stirring occasionally to prevent burning. Remove bone. Force soup through sieve or blend in blender. Add cream, salt and pepper to taste, and sugar. Reheat and serve.

MRS. FRANK PADBERG

POT-AU-FEU

Pot-au-Feu is a modest French dish, and is an example that French cooking is not always expensive but can be economical and good. Pot-au-Feu is served as a soup or a one-dish meal of meat and vegetables. This dish is easy to make but requires long, slow cooking.

Serves: 6

2 lbs. beef brisket	2 ribs celery
Salt and pepper to taste	1 onion stuck with 3 cloves
3 leeks	1 tsp. thyme
5 carrots	3 sprigs parsley
1 parsnip	1 bay leaf
1 turnip	Croutons

Place brisket in large stew pot. Cover with cold water; add salt and pepper; bring to boiling point; skim off all foam. Add remaining ingredients; bring to boil; cover and allow to simmer 4 hours. When ready to serve, remove grease, strain soup, and serve over croutons. Serve meat on platter with mustard or horseradish; garnish with the vegetables.

MISS ELIZABETH TAYLOR

IRISH POTATO SOUP

Yield: 3 quarts

1 cup butter	Water
4 medium onions, thinly sliced	2 cloves garlic, crushed or 1 Tb. dried minced garlic
8 baking potatoes, peeled and sliced thin	1 Tb. dried parsley
2 qts. milk (less for thicker soup)	2 pinches each thyme and crushed red pepper
	Salt and pepper

Melt butter; add onions and potatoes. Cook until thoroughly done (about 30 minutes), adding just enough water to keep from browning. Add milk and seasonings; heat thoroughly before serving. Do not boil.

This is much better if made the day before.

MRS. GUY W. BEARD

NANCY'S DEEP SEA CHOWDER

Serves: 8

2 16-oz. pkgs. fish (sole, flounder, etc.)	2 potatoes, sliced
	¼ cup flour
6 cups boiling water	2 cups light cream
4 tsp. salt	⅛ tsp. pepper
2 carrots, sliced	1 Tb. lemon juice
2 leeks (if available) or 1 onion, chopped	Salt to taste

Cook fish in water and salt. When flakey, take out and separate. Cook vegetables in broth, covered, for 15 minutes or until tender. Add fish. Blend flour with a little cream until smooth. Add to soup with the pepper, lemon juice, and rest of cream. Salt.

MRS. BART ROACH

LOUISIANA SEA FOOD SOUP

Serves: 8

4 cups okra, cut up	Salt and pepper
2 onions, chopped	A good size pinch each of marjoram, thyme, and basil
½ cup butter	
2 Tb. flour	3 lbs. raw shrimp
2 16-oz. cans stewed tomatoes	7-oz. can crab meat
2 13¾-oz. cans chicken broth	½ pt. oysters (optional)
1 chicken bouillon cube	Rice

Using a large kettle or Dutch oven, sauté cut okra and onions in butter for about 15 minutes over low heat. Stir in flour. Add stewed tomatoes, chicken broth, bouillon cube, salt, pepper, and herbs to taste. Simmer over low heat for 1½ to 2 hours. While this mixture cooks, clean shrimp (shell and devein). After the above mixture has cooked, add cleaned shrimp, crab meat, and oysters. Continue cooking for 15 minutes.

Serve in large soup bowls, topped with a mound of rice.

MRS. GRIFFIN SMITH

SHRIMP CHOWDER

Serves: 8

4 large onions, sliced
¼ cup butter
2 cups boiling water
6 medium raw potatoes,
  cubed
1 Tb. salt
½ tsp. seasoned pepper

1½ qts. milk
2 cups (½ lb.) grated process
  Cheddar cheese
2 lbs. cooked shrimp (about
  3 10-oz. pkgs. frozen)
3 Tb. snipped parsley

Sauté onion slices in butter until tender. Add water, potatoes, salt, and pepper. Simmer covered until potatoes are done (about 30 minutes). Do not drain. Heat milk with cheese until melted, do not boil. Add shrimp and milk and heat. Serve with parsley sprinkled on top.
Variation: For Clam Chowder use 1½ lbs. of clams. Process American cheese may be substituted for process Cheddar.

MRS. JOHN J. TRUEMPER, JR.

COLD SPINACH SOUP

Serves: 8

2 10-oz. pkgs. frozen chopped
  spinach
3 green onions
4 sprigs parsley
4 sprigs dill

3 cups chicken broth
Salt and pepper to taste
Dash of sugar
2 slices smoked salmon
  (optional)

Defrost spinach completely. Put into blender container; cover; puree. Add the onion, parsley, dill, and broth; puree. (May have to half mixture for this process.) Season with salt, pepper, and sugar. Chill. Serve cold. Garnish with salmon cut into strips, if you wish.
May be prepared a day ahead.

MRS. B. FRANK MACKEY, JR.

SPRING SOUP

Serves: 8

2 Tb. butter
1 cup leeks or yellow onion,
  chopped
1 green onion, chopped
1½ qts. hot water
2 potatoes, peeled, quartered,
  and thinly sliced
2 carrots, peeled and sliced

Salt to taste
¼ cup raw rice
8 stalks fresh or frozen
  asparagus, cut in ½-inch
  pieces
½ lb. spinach, washed and
  chopped
1 cup light cream

Melt butter in 3 quart kettle; add leeks and onions; cook covered over low heat about 5 minutes. Add water, potatoes, carrots, and salt; bring to boil; reduce heat; simmer covered 15 minutes. Add rice and asparagus; simmer covered 25 minutes. Add spinach; simmer 10 minutes longer. Stir in cream. Bring just to boiling. The flavor is enhanced by preparing soup the day before. Refrigerate overnight; reheat at serving time.

MRS. ROBERT D. DICKINS

TOMATO SOUP

Serves: 8

¾ cup butter
2 Tb. olive oil
1 large onion, thinly sliced
  (about 2 cups)
½ tsp. dried thyme
Salt and freshly ground
  pepper
½ tsp. dried basil
3 Tb. tomato paste

2½ lbs. fresh ripe tomatoes,
  peeled and cored, or a 2 lb.
  3-oz. can Italian style
  tomatoes
¼ cup flour
3¾ cups fresh or canned
  chicken broth
1 tsp. sugar
1 cup heavy cream

Heat ½ cup butter in kettle; add olive oil. Add onion, thyme, salt, pepper, and basil. Cook, stirring occasionally, until onion is wilted. Add tomatoes and tomato paste; stir to blend. Simmer 10 minutes. Place the flour in a small mixing bowl; add about 5 tablespoons of broth, stirring to blend. Stir this into tomato mixture. Add remaining chicken broth and simmer 30 minutes, stirring frequently all over the bottom of kettle to make certain soup does not stick or burn. Put soup through the finest sieve or food mill possible. Return to heat; add sugar and cream. Simmer, stirring occasionally, for 5 minutes. Add remaining butter, swirling it around in the soup.

MRS. JAMES T. DYKE

VEGETABLE SOUP

Serves: 10

1 large knuckle bone
2 lbs. stew meat
2 tsp. seasoned salt
2 tsp. lemon-pepper marinade
2 10½-oz. cans tomato puree
2 onions, diced
1 cup celery, diced
½ cup cabbage
½ cup rice

½ cup barley
½ 10-oz. box frozen okra
1 bell pepper, diced
16-oz. can lima beans
16-oz. can peas and carrots
16-oz. can green beans
Seasoned salt
Lemon-pepper marinade
3 10-oz. cans beef broth

In large kettle put bone, meat, seasoned salt, and lemon-pepper marinade. Cover with water; cook covered until meat is tender. When tender, leave in liquid until nearly cool. Remove meat and bone from liquid; refrigerate separately overnight. Next day skim fat off broth. Broth may have jelled; if so, add 2 cups water and heat. To broth add tomato puree, onions, celery, and cabbage. Cover and simmer about 2 hours. Add rice, barley, okra, green pepper, lima beans, peas and carrots, green beans, and meat cut in bite-size pieces. Add seasoned salt and lemon-pepper marinade to taste. Add canned beef broth. Simmer about 1½ hours, stirring occasionally. This may be thinned if desired by adding water or more beef broth.

MRS. RICHARD H. McKINNEY, SR.

VICHYSSOISE

Serves: 6-8

3 cups sliced potatoes   1½ qts. canned chicken broth
3 cups sliced white onions   1 cup heavy cream
Salt to taste   3 Tb. minced chives

Simmer potatoes, onions and salt in chicken broth, partially covered, about 45 minutes, or until vegetables are tender. Do not overcook. Puree the soup in a blender. Stir in cream. Taste for seasoning. Chill. Serve in chilled soup cups with minced chives.

MRS. MIKE MEHAFFY

WATERCRESS SOUP

Serves: 8

2 lbs. potatoes, peeled and   1 cup watercress, packed
  sliced   1 cup heavy cream
2 lbs. leeks or yellow onions,   Salt and pepper to taste
  sliced   Minced chives
2 qts. chicken stock

Simmer, covered, potatoes and leeks in stock for 45 minutes. Add watercress; cook 5 minutes. Puree in blender. Add cream, salt, and pepper. Chill. Serve cold and decorate with minced chives.

Variation: Substitute 1 cup spinach or 2 cups asparagus cooked until tender and cut in pieces. Serve hot or cold.

MRS. BART ROACH

QUICKIE SOUPS

POTAGE CRÈME D'ARTICHOKE

Serves: 8

2 9-oz. pkgs. frozen artichoke   1 cup heavy cream
  hearts   ¼ cup chicken stock
16 oz. condensed mushroom   ¼ cup dry white wine
  soup, undiluted

Cook artichokes according to package directions. Combine with remaining ingredients and puree in electric blender. Chill thoroughly; garnish with parsley sprig.

MRS. BEN PRICE

QUICK CONSOMME

Serves: 3-4

10 oz. beef consomme	3 cloves
12 oz. V-8 juice	1 Tb. lemon juice
1 Tb. sugar	3 to 4 lemon slices

Mix all ingredients except lemon slices. Simmer 15 to 20 minutes. Strain and serve. Garnish with thin lemon slices.

MRS. JAMES T. BECKER

EASY CUCUMBER SOUP

Serves: 2

1½ medium cucumbers, peeled and chopped	Dash hot sauce
13-oz. can vichyssoise	Salt to taste
	Sour cream

In blender blend all but sour cream. Chill well; serve with dollop of sour cream.

MRS. LAWRENCE BURROW

JELLIED MADRILENE WITH CAVIAR

Serves: 8

½ cup sour cream	4 13-oz. cans jellied madrilene
½ cup red caviar	Parsley

Put 1 tablespoon of sour cream in 8 small bowls; add 1 tablespoon of caviar to each one. Cover with one-half can of congealed madrilene for each. Refrigerate. Garnish top with parsley.

MRS. WILLIAM BOND

COLD TOMATO SOUP

Serves: 6

2 10-oz. cans tomato soup	Dash Worcestershire sauce
2 pts. heavy cream	½ cup sour cream
1 cucumber, grated	2 tsp. chives
1 small onion, grated	

Add cream to undiluted soup; add cucumber, onion and Worcestershire sauce. Mix well. Chill overnight. To serve top with teaspoon of sour cream; sprinkle with chives.

MRS. ALLAN EDWARD MEADORS

48 SOUPS

SENEGALESE SOUP

Serves: 3

13-oz. can senegalese soup
½ cup chicken stock
Dash sherry

Curry powder to taste
¼ cup cream, whipped

Strain canned soup; heat and add chicken stock. When bubbly, add sherry; add curry powder to taste. Serve with float of whipped cream.

MRS. ROBERT D. LOWRY

DO YOUR OWN THING SOUP

Serves: 6

2 10-oz. cans potato soup
1 Tb. onion, minced
13 ¼ -oz. can chicken stock

½ cup sour cream
Salt to taste

In blender, mix potato soup and onion; add stock and blend. Stir in sour cream. Chill. In 6 separate serving dishes or wooden bowls put these items:

Chopped tomatoes
Cut up cucumbers
Thin slices of onion and eggplant marinated for 3 days
  in olive oil with garlic and
  oregano

Broken pretzel sticks and
  almonds
Sliced bell pepper and thin
  strips of Jack cheese
Chutney

Serve each guest a bowl of basic soup; pass mixtures to add to soup. Guests use own imagination and embellish soup several times in own way.

MRS. HENRY W. RUSSELL

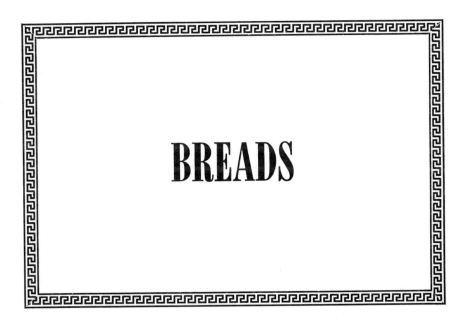

BREADS

BREADS

Warning: This section may be habit forming! Making your own bread is indeed a gratifying experience. Once you begin to treat your family to delicious homemade breads, they will probably become addicted and will no longer be happy with the "store-bought" kind. Absolutely nothing equals the aroma of bread baking in the oven and the joy of cutting a fresh warm slice. As if these rewards were not enough, it is truly a pleasure to create a loaf of bread. The kneading, punching, and shaping allow you to put a lot of yourself into it. This may explain why many breadmakers are an uninhibited, happy lot.

The Breads are divided into three sections: Yeast Breads, Quick Breads, and Sourdough Breads.

YEAST BREADS

Breads made with yeast are not difficult to make, but require some time at home. YEAST grows and produces carbon dioxide which causes the dough to expand or rise. The liquid used must be warm enough to allow the yeast to grow, but not too warm, because excessive heat can kill the yeast. Have all ingredients at room temperature. More yeast may be added if it is a very cold day, or if you wish to hasten the process. SUGAR aids in fermentation and is food for the yeast. SALT helps control the fermentation. MILK makes a finer textured bread and adds nutrients. WATER makes a coarser bread and a crisp crust. FAT or BUTTER add flavor to the bread and makes it stay fresh longer. Bread made with unbleached flour tastes better and is more nutritious. Tell your grocer you want unbleached flour and he will have it on hand for you. When using any flour or wheat germ, keep it in the refrigerator to keep fresh.

ELIZABETH YOUNG'S HOMEMADE BREAD

Yield: 2 loaves   Oven: 375°

2½ cups lukewarm water   1½ tsp. salt
2 Tb. sugar   2½ Tb. bacon fat, melted
1 pkg. dry yeast (2 may be   (or any other drippings)
  used on a cold day)   6 cups unsifted flour
½ cup sugar   Butter or margarine

Stir into 2½ cups lukewarm water 2 tablespoons sugar and yeast.
Let mixture set 5 to 15 minutes. Add ½ cup sugar, salt, and bacon
fat. Stir in flour, cup by cup until too thick to stir, then work in by
hand. Turn onto floured board or counter; add more flour if necessary and knead at least 10 minutes. Place in large greased bowl and
brush top with melted butter or margarine (or bacon drippings).
Cover and let rise in warm place (76° to 85°) to twice its bulk
(about 1½ hours).

Divide into 2 equal portions gently. (DO NOT KNEAD.) Mold
into 2 individual loaves. Place each into a greased loaf pan
(9¼ x 5¼ x 2¾-inch). Be sure sides and bottoms of pans are well
greased. Brush entire top surface of each loaf with melted margarine. Cover pans with light cloth and let rise, rounding to top of
each pan (approximately 1½ hours). Preheat oven to 375°. Place
pans on center rack of oven, allowing air space between each pan.
Bake at 375° for 15 minutes, then lower temperature to 275° and
bake 15 to 20 minutes. Test loaf for doneness by trying to slip out
of pan easily. If it doesn't, return it to oven for 5 to 10 minutes.

Remove from oven. Brush each loaf on top with margarine or butter while still in pan. Lift loaves gently out of pan. Let cool on
wire rack. For a softer crust, brush sides of loaves with butter or
margarine while hot. Leave loaves uncovered while cooling.

TIME TO MAKE BREAD:

Yeast-sugar mixture to set _____5 to 15 minutes

Mix batter and knead _____10 to 15 minutes

First rise in bulk _____1½ hours

Folding into loaves _____5 minutes

Second rise (loaf pans) _____1½ hours

Baking time _____30 to 40 minutes

Cooling on racks _____30 minutes

    Total _____4⅓ to 4¾ hours

MRS. GORDON YOUNG

FRENCH BREAD

Yield: 2 loaves   **Oven: 400°**

- 1 ¾ cups warm water
- 1 pkg. active yeast
- 3 Tb. melted shortening
- 1 Tb. salt
- 4 cups flour
- Corn meal
- 1 egg white
- 2 Tb. water

Pour 1¾ cups water into bowl. Sprinkle yeast in, stirring. Add shortening, salt, 4 cups flour gradually. Beat until smooth. Mix with hands only if necessary. Turn out onto floured board. Knead only until dough is smooth. Put dough in greased bowl, turning once to grease top. Cover with damp cloth and let rise 1½ hours or until doubled.

Punch down. Turn onto board and knead to remove bubbles. Shape into long oval. Slice lengthwise to make 2 loaves. Place on greased cookie sheet which has been sprinkled with corn meal. Make gashes with sharp knife across tops of loaves ½ inch deep. Do not cover. Let rise until double, about 1 hour.

Preheat oven (400°). Place shallow pan of water on bottom of oven to insure a crisp crust. Beat egg white with water. Brush loaves. Bake 20 minutes. Brush with egg white again. Bake 20 minutes longer or until glaze is brown. Cool on racks.

This recipe may also be made into smaller individual loaves.

BROWN BREAD

Yield: 4 loaves   **Oven: 350°**

- 2 yeast cakes
- ½ cup lukewarm water
- 2 cups rye flour
- ¾ cup dark molasses
- ⅓ cup shortening, melted
- 2 tsp. salt
- 2 cups boiling water
- 6 cups sifted white flour
- Egg, slightly beaten

In a small bowl soften yeast in water. In a large bowl combine rye flour, molasses, shortening, and salt. Add boiling water and stir well. Cool this mixture to lukewarm. Add softened yeast. Stir in 2 cups white flour, using electric mixer. Then add remainder of flour and stir by hand. Remove dough from bowl and place on well floured surface. Cover with towel and let rest 10 minutes. Knead until smooth, about 10 minutes. Place in well-greased large bowl, turning dough to grease both sides. Cover and let rise in warm place until double (about 2 hours).

Punch dough down. Cover and let rise again until double, about 30 minutes. Turn out on lightly floured surface. Divide into 4 parts. Form into mounds. Cover and let rise 15 minutes. Shape into 4 loaves. Place into greased baking pans. Cover and let rise until doubled (1 to 1½ hours). Brush loaves with slightly beaten egg and bake at 350° for 30 minutes. Remove from pans and let cool on rack.

May be wrapped in foil and frozen. When ready to use, thaw and heat in foil.

MRS. CLAUDE DURRETT, JR.

MONKEY BREAD

Serves: 12   **Oven: 350°**

½ cup warm water	½ cup sugar
2 pkgs. dry yeast	1 tsp. salt
½ cup milk	2 eggs, beaten
1 cup margarine, used separately	5 cups flour

Stir yeast in warm water until dissolved. Heat milk and ½ cup margarine in saucepan until melted. Measure sugar and salt in large mixing bowl; pour in milk mixture; stir until dissolved. When lukewarm, add eggs and yeast mixture. Add 2½ cups flour; stir; add remaining flour and mix well. Turn out on a lightly floured board and knead until smooth and elastic (about 5 minutes). Place in greased bowl; cover with a damp cloth; let rise until double in bulk (about 2 hours). Punch down and let dough rest for 30 minutes. Roll dough very thin on lightly floured board. Cut dough in squares; dip pieces in ½ cup melted margarine and place in ring mold with edges overlapping; fill half full. Let rise until double (about 2 hours). Bake 20 to 30 minutes at 350°.

CINNAMON RING:

Mix 1 cup sugar with 2½ teaspoons cinnamon. Dip dough squares in melted margarine and then in cinnamon-sugar mixture and place in ring mold. Proceed as for plain monkey bread. Let rise until double and bake 20 to 30 minutes at 350°. Turn out on serving plate and drizzle a glaze of 1 cup powdered sugar, moistened with enough milk or light cream to spread.

Do not cut; this is a pull-apart bread.

A special treat for holiday buffets!

MRS. ALLAN DISHONGH

DILL BREAD

Yield: 2 loaves   **Oven: 350°**

1 pkg. dry yeast	1 tsp. salt
¼ cup warm water	¼ tsp. soda
1 cup creamed cottage cheese	1 Tb. onion, minced
2 Tb. sugar	1 Tb. butter
1 egg	2¼ to 2½ cups flour (after
2 tsp. dill seed or weed	sifting)

Mix yeast in water; set aside until yeast starts bubbling. In blender jar put yeast mixture, cottage cheese, sugar, egg, dill, salt, soda, onion, and butter; blend well. Put mixture in bowl. Sift flour; add gradually to mixture; mix well; cover and let rise in warm place until doubled, about 1 hour. Stir dough down; turn into 2 well-greased loaf pans. Cover; let rise in warm place about ½ hour. Bake at 350° for 30 to 40 minutes. Brush top with butter after done. Salt top if desired. May be frozen.

DR. UNA ROBINSON
BLOOMINGTON, INDIANA

CHEESE BREAD

Yield: 2 large loaves   Oven: 375°

About 7 cups sifted flour   1 lb. extra sharp Cheddar
2 Tb. sugar   cheese, grated
1 Tb. salt   2 eggs
2 pkgs. dry yeast   1 Tb. caraway seeds
2 ¼ cups milk   (optional)
3 Tb. margarine

In large bowl combine 2½ cups flour, sugar, salt, and yeast. Combine milk and margarine in saucepan. Bring to a boil. Cool to lukewarm.

Add to dry ingredients; beat until blended (may be done in mixer). Add 1 cup flour, beat; add cheese and eggs. Gradually add remaining flour; knead until smooth and elastic.

Put in greased bowl, turning to grease top. Cover. Let rise in warm place until double in bulk.

Punch dough down, divide into loaves. Place in well-greased pans (2 large, 3 medium, or 4 small). Cover. Let rise in warm place until double in bulk.

Bake at 375° for 35 to 45 minutes, depending on size of pans. Remove from pans at once. Cool on wire rack.

MRS. BOOKER WORTHEN

PATIO HERB BREAD

Yield: 2 loaves   Oven: 375°

2 cups warm water   2 Tb. soft butter or
2 pkgs. dry yeast   margarine
2 Tb. sugar   1 Tb. dried rosemary leaves
2 tsp. salt   4½ cups all-purpose flour

Sprinkle yeast over water in large bowl of electric mixer. Let stand 1 minute. Stir to dissolve. Add sugar, salt, butter, rosemary, and 3 cups flour. Beat at low speed until blended. Beat at medium speed until smooth, about 2 minutes. Scrape down sides of bowl and beaters with spatula.

With a wooden spoon beat in rest of flour by hand. Cover bowl with waxed paper, then a towel. Let rise in warm, draft-free place about 45 minutes or until doubled in bulk.

Preheat oven to 375°. Grease a 1½ or 2 quart casserole or 2 loaf pans. With a wooden spoon, stir down batter and beat 25 strokes. Turn into casserole or pans and bake 55 to 60 minutes (casserole) or 35 to 40 minutes (loaf pans) until nicely browned.

Remove from pan, let cool on a wire rack. Serve cold or slightly warm cut into wedges.

Variation: Instead of rosemary try 1 tsp. thyme and 2 tsp. marjoram.

MRS. B. FRANK MACKEY, JR.

OATMEAL BREAD

Yield: 2 loaves   Oven: 350°

2 cups rolled oats (oatmeal)	¼ cup boiling water
2 cups boiling water	2 tsp. salt
1 cake yeast	1 Tb. sugar
½ cup warm water	5 cups flour
¼ cup molasses	

Pour 2 cups boiling water over oats; cool. Mix yeast and ½ cup warm water; add to oats. Mix molasses, ¼ cup boiling water, salt, and sugar; add to oats. Gradually stir in flour; knead until well blended. Put in bowl; cover; let rise in warm place until doubled, about 1 hour. Put into 2 greased loaf pans; let rise until doubled. Bake at 350° for 50 to 60 minutes. This freezes well.

MRS. ISAAC SCOTT, JR.

BRAIDED POPPY SEED BREAD

Yield: 1 loaf   Oven: 350°

4 Tb. melted butter, cooled	½ cup warm water
¼ cup sugar	3½ cups sifted flour
1 tsp. salt	1 beaten egg
½ cup scalded milk	Poppy seeds
1 pkg. yeast	1 beaten egg

Melt butter and set aside. Dissolve sugar and salt in milk. Cool. Add yeast which has been dissolved in warm water. Blend. Add 1 cup flour, blend, add 1 beaten egg and another cup flour. Mix thoroughly and add melted butter. Blend, adding 1½ cups (more or less, as needed) to make smooth dough. Knead well for 5 minutes or more. Cover and let rise in warm place until double. Punch down and knead again for another 5 minutes. Cover and let rise again until double. Punch down, knead and let rest 5 minutes. Divide dough into 3 parts and, with palms of hands, make strands about 12 inches long. Braid and seal each end. Place on large greased cookie sheet. Brush with beaten egg and sprinkle heavily with poppy seeds. Let rise until almost double. Bake at 350° for 30 to 35 minutes, until deep golden brown. This recipe makes 1 large, very impressive, loaf of bread. Time consuming, but not hard. The trick is to have the dough as smooth as a "baby's bottom."

MRS. DON THOMPSON, JR.

RAISIN BREAD

Yield: 2 loaves   Oven: 375°

3½ to 3¾ cups pre-sifted   ½ cup water
  flour   4 Tb. butter
¼ cup sugar   2 eggs
1½ tsp. salt   1 tsp. vanilla extract
2 pkgs. active dry yeast   3 cups seedless raisins
½ cup milk   2 Tb. soft butter

Mix 1¼ cups flour with sugar, salt, and undissolved yeast in large electric mixer bowl. Heat milk, water, and butter until warm and butter melts. Slowly stir into dry mixture; beat with electric mixer for 2 minutes at medium speed. Beat in eggs one at time; add vanilla and ¾ cup flour; beat for 2 minutes at high speed. Stir in raisins and remaining flour. Turn out on lightly floured board and knead for 5 minutes. Put dough in greased bowl; turn to coat all sides; cover; let rise in warm place for about 1 hour or until doubled. Punch down dough; form a ball; place on lightly floured board; cover and let rest for 15 minutes. Divide dough in half; place each half in greased loaf pan. Cover and let rise about 25 minutes. Bake 25 to 30 minutes at 375°. Remove from pans; brush with butter; slice when cool.

RYE BREAD

Yield: 2 loaves   Oven: 450°

3 pkgs. dry yeast   ½ cup hot water
1 cup warm water   2 Tb. shortening
3 tsp. salt   3 cups sifted flour
2 Tb. caraway seeds   2½ cups sifted rye flour
¼ cup molasses   Corn meal

Dissolve yeast in warm water. In large bowl mix salt, seeds, molasses, hot water, and shortening; add yeast. Blend white and rye flour; gradually stir into yeast mixture. On floured board, knead dough until smooth. This is a stiff dough. Place dough in greased bowl; turn to bring greased side to top. Cover and let rise until doubled, about 2 hours. Punch down dough; cover and let rest 10 minutes. Shape into 2 loaves. Sprinkle corn meal in bottom of two loaf pans; place loaves in pans. Cover and let rise until doubled, about 1 hour. Brush lightly with cold water. Bake at 450° for 10 minutes; reduce heat to 350°; bake for 25 to 30 minutes.

STUFFED SOUR CREAM BREAD

Yield: 1 loaf   Oven: 375°

BREAD:

1 pkg. dry yeast
1¼ cups warm water
4 tsp. dried onion flakes
1¼ tsp. salt
½ tsp. monosodium
  glutamate

2 tsp. salad oil
1 pkg. (1½ oz.) sour cream
  mix
2½ to 3 cups flour
1 egg white, beaten
1 Tb. cold water

FILLING:

3 Tb. sour cream
3 Tb. butter, soft
¼ tsp. garlic powder
¼ tsp. dried onion flakes

¼ tsp. monosodium
  glutamate
2 tsp. dried parsley flakes

In large bowl soften yeast in water. Stir in onion, salt, monosodium glutamate, oil, and sour cream mix. Blend well. Gradually add flour to make stiff dough. Knead on floured surface until smooth (2 to 3 minutes). Place in greased bowl, turning to grease all over. Cover and let rise 45 minutes or until light.

Roll out dough on floured surface to 14 x 10-inch rectangle. Spread with filling. Starting with 14-inch side roll up jelly roll style, pinching edges to seal. Taper ends. Place seam side down on greased cookie sheet. Let rise 45 minutes. Make six diagonal slashes with sharp knife across top of loaf (½ inch deep). Bake at 375° for 35 to 40 minutes. Brush with egg white mixed with water. Bake 5 minutes more. Cool on wire rack.

MRS. DON THOMPSON, JR.

WHOLE WHEAT BREAD

Yield: 2 loaves   Oven: 375°

1 pkg. active dry yeast
2 cups warm water
2 Tb. sugar
2 tsp. salt
4 cups sifted flour

½ cup hot water
½ cup brown sugar
3 Tb. shortening
4 cups whole wheat flour

Soften yeast in warm water. Add sugar, salt and flour. Beat until smooth. Set mixture in warm place for about 1 hour until it is light and bubbly. Combine hot water, brown sugar and shortening, stir and cool to lukewarm. Add to yeast-flour mixture. Add whole wheat flour and mix until smooth. Turn onto floured board. Knead until smooth, about 10 minutes. Place in greased bowl and turn over to grease all sides. Cover and let rise in warm place until double in bulk. Knead down dough and divide into 2 parts. Shape each into a ball. Cover and let rise 10 minutes. Roll to 10 x 14-inch rectangle. Roll up, sealing ends as you go. Place loaves, seam side down, in 2 lightly greased loaf pans. Cover and let rise until doubled. Bake in 375° oven for 45 to 50 minutes.

WHEAT GERM BREAD

Yield: 2 loaves   Oven: 400°

2 pkgs. active dry yeast
½ cup warm water
1¾ cups milk, scalded and
  cooled to lukewarm
⅓ cup honey
1 Tb. salt
¼ cup margarine, soft

5 to 6 cups flour, unsifted
1 cup wheat germ
1 Tb. grated lemon rind
  (orange rind may be
  substituted)
Salad oil

In large warm bowl, dissolve yeast in warm water. Add warm milk, honey, salt, margarine, and 2 cups flour. Beat in electric mixer at low speed until smooth. Add 1 cup flour. Beat 2 or 3 minutes until thick and elastic. Scrape sides of bowl occasionally.

With wooden spoon stir in wheat germ and lemon rind. Gradually work in remaining flour to make a soft dough that leaves sides of bowl, adding more if necessary. Turn out onto floured board; knead 5 to 10 minutes until dough is smooth, elastic, and no longer sticky. Cover with a towel; let rest 20 minutes.

Punch down. Divide into 2 equal portions. Roll each portion into an 8 x 12-inch rectangle. Roll up tightly into loaves beginning with 8-inch sides. Seal final seam and edges well. Place in 2 greased loaf pans. Brush surface of dough with salad oil. Cover pans loosely with waxed paper. Refrigerate 2 to 24 hours.

When ready to bake, remove from refrigerator, uncover and let stand while pre-heating oven. Just before baking puncture any surface bubbles with an oiled toothpick.

Bake in a 400° oven for 35 to 40 minutes. May be frozen.

Unbleached flour makes healthier and tastier bread. Use it if you can.

MRS. ROBERT NEUBAUER
EASTON, CONNECTICUT

SALLY LUNN

Yield: 1 loaf   Oven: 350°

¼ cup warm water
1 pkg. dry yeast
1 cup milk
½ cup butter

1 tsp. salt
¼ cup sugar
3 eggs, beaten
3 cups flour

Dissolve yeast in ¼ cup warm water. Scald milk; add butter, salt, and sugar; stir until well mixed. After mixture has cooled slightly, add yeast and eggs. Add flour and beat until well blended. Put bowl in warm place, cover, let rise 1 hour. Pour into greased and floured bundt pan. Allow bread to rise another hour in pan. Bake at 350° 25 to 30 minutes.

Note: Batter is runny; not bread dough consistency.

MRS. ALBERT GORNATTI

PARTY ROLLS

Yield: 4 dozen   Oven: 400°

1¼ cups milk   2 tsp. salt
2 yeast cakes   ⅓ cup melted butter
3 eggs   4½ cups sifted flour
½ cup sugar   Melted butter

Heat milk until lukewarm. Stir in 2 yeast cakes. Let stand or stir until dissolved. Beat eggs in a very large greased bowl. Add sugar, stir in salt and yeast mixture and beat until smooth. Add melted butter. Blend in flour by hand, 1 cup at a time. Cover and let stand in warm place until double in size. Dough will be sticky, so sift a little flour on top of dough until you are able to pick it up and roll out on board. Roll out one-half of dough at a time, about ½ inch thick. Cut with 1½ to 2 inch cutter. Dip each round in melted butter, fold over and place in greased pan. Let rise. Bake in 400° oven for about 15 minutes or until brown.

These rolls may be frozen if wrapped tightly. Allow about 6 hours to thaw and rise. Makes 5 or 6 pans of rolls.

MRS. CLAUDE DURRETT, JR.

REFRIGERATOR DINNER ROLLS

Yield: 8 dozen   Oven: 375°

1 cup warm water   2 egg yolks
2 pkgs. yeast   6 cups flour
¾ cup margarine or butter   1 tsp. salt
¾ cup sugar   2 beaten egg whites
1 cup boiling water

Dissolve yeast in cup of warm water. Cream margarine and sugar; add cup of boiling water and cool to lukewarm. Add egg yolks and yeast mixture and stir thoroughly. Stir in flour and salt (may be done in electric mixer). Fold in stiffly beaten egg whites. Dough will be very soft looking. Leave in mixing bowl, cover, and place in refrigerator overnight or until needed. (It must be in refrigerator at least 2 hours and will keep 4 days.) Two hours before baking, roll out dough and cut as you would biscuits and place on well-greased pan to rise. Bake 15 to 20 minutes at 375°.

These may be partially baked, then covered with plastic wrap to be frozen. Brown and serve when desired.

MRS. JAMES ROGERS

BAGELS

Yield: 32 bagels   Oven: 425°

2 pkgs. dry yeast	8 cups flour
2 cups warm potato water	Sugar
4 medium eggs	Boiling water
1 Tb. salt	2 Tb. sugar
1 Tb. sugar	2 egg yolks beaten with 2 Tb.
¼ cup salad oil	water

Stir yeast into ½ cup warm potato water. (This is water in which peeled potatoes have been cooked. Save it when you next cook potatoes.) Beat eggs in large bowl; add yeast mixture and rest of potato water, salt, sugar, oil and 2 cups flour. Stir in remaining flour. Knead on floured surface for 10 minutes, adding more flour if necessary. Place in greased bowl, cover and let rise in a warm place until double in bulk.

Punch down, knead lightly until smooth. Roll out dough into rectangle and divide into 32 pieces. Make each piece into a 6-inch "rope" which is ¾ inch in diameter. Moisten ends and seal together (doughnut shapes). Let rise for 15 minutes.

Boil 2 quarts of water in a deep pot; add 2 tablespoons sugar. Drop bagels into water, one at a time. As they rise to the top, turn them over. Boil 3 minutes on second side. Remove with slotted spoon and place on greased baking sheets. Brush with egg yolk glaze (egg yolks and water). Bake at 425° for 20 to 25 minutes, until golden brown and crispy.

To serve bagels, slice in half and toast. Spread with butter or cream cheese. Serve hot. Can also be used for sandwiches but are best when toasted. Use the same day you make them or freeze and use later. They get stale easily.

STICKY BUNS

Yield: 2 dozen   Oven: 400°

2 pkgs. dry yeast	3¼ cups flour
¼ cup sugar	2 Tb. melted butter
1 tsp. salt	1 cup brown sugar
1 egg, slightly beaten	½ cup chopped pecans
1 cup warm milk	1 cup butter

In large bowl place yeast, sugar, salt, egg, and milk. Add flour and 2 tablespoons butter; mix and let rise in warm place until doubled. Prepare a muffin pan by placing in each cup 1 teaspoon butter, 1 teaspoon brown sugar, 1 teaspoon pecans. For extra rich rolls, add more butter, sugar, and pecans.

Roll dough into a rectangle about 8 x 16 inches and ¼ inch thick. Spread with butter and sprinkle with sugar. Roll up starting with long side. Cut into 24 pieces; place one piece in each cup. Let rise until doubled. Bake at 400° for 15 to 20 minutes. Invert immediately onto rack and let topping drip down. Serve warm. If served later, cover with foil and reheat.

MRS. ELLIOTT BECHTEL

ONION BUNS

Yield: 2 dozen   Oven: 375°

1 pkg. dry yeast
1 cup lukewarm milk
2 Tb. sugar
1 tsp. salt
3 cups flour
3 egg yolks, beaten slightly

2 tsp. onion juice
12 Tb. butter, softened
1 onion, sliced thin
1 egg yolk
1 Tb. heavy cream

Sprinkle yeast into ½ cup warm milk; add sugar and salt; stir until
dissolved. Place mixture in warm place until it bubbles and has
almost doubled, 5 to 8 minutes. Pour flour into large mixing bowl.
Make well in center; add yeast mixture, 3 egg yolks, remaining ½
cup milk, 8 tablespoons butter, and onion juice; stir slowly until
mixed. Cover bowl; put in warm place; let rise until doubled, about
45 minutes. Punch down dough with your fist; cover loosely; let
rise again until doubled.
Meanwhile, cook onions in 2 tablespoons butter; drain. Preheat oven
to 375°; grease 2 cookie sheets with remaining butter. Work onions
in dough; divide dough in half; roll each half in circle about ⅛ inch
thick. Cut with 3 to 4 inch cutter; place on cookie sheet; let rise
until double, about 15 minutes. Bake for 10 minutes. Mix egg yolk
and cream, brush mixture on buns; bake another 10 minutes.

HOT CROSS BUNS

Yield: 24 buns   Oven: 350°

1 cup milk, scalded
¼ cup butter
¼ cup sugar
1 yeast cake
3½ cups flour
1 egg, beaten

1¾ tsp. salt
⅛ tsp. nutmeg
1 tsp. lemon rind
2 Tb. chopped citron
½ cup seedless raisins

Mix together milk, butter, and sugar; cool until lukewarm; add
yeast cake crumbled into small pieces. Add 1½ cups flour; beat
vigorously. Cover in a warm place until light and fluffy and bubbles
appear. Add egg, salt, nutmeg, lemon rind, and one more cup of
flour. Beat until smooth; add remaining flour, citron, and raisins.
Knead lightly; place in greased bowl; let rise until doubled in bulk
(about 1 hour). Punch down in bowl. Pinch off pieces about the
size of eggs; form into balls and place in 8-inch square pan, three to
a row. Bake 20 minutes at 375°.

ICING:

3 egg whites
1½ cups powdered sugar

1 Tb. lemon juice

Put unbeaten egg whites in bowl; add sugar and lemon juice. Add
more sugar if too thin. Make a cross on each bun.

MRS. BART ROACH

QUICK BREADS

Quick breads are those which may be made up in one to two hours. The rising and expanding in these breads comes from baking powder, soda, or both, rather than from yeast.

BAKING POWDER BISCUITS

Yield: 18 Oven: 400°

2 cups sifted flour
4 tsp. baking powder
½ tsp. salt

5 Tb. shortening
⅔ cup milk
Butter

Mix flour, baking powder, and salt. Cut in shortening with two knives or fingertips. Slowly add milk until a soft dough has formed. Pat out on floured board until ⅓ inch thick. Cut with biscuit cutter and place in greased pans. Brush tops with melted butter or milk. Bake for 12 minutes at 400°, or cover tightly and place in refrigerator for last minute baking.

Cheese Biscuits: Add ¼ to ½ cup sharp Cheddar cheese after cutting in shortening.

MRS. JAMES KALMBACH
DALLAS, TEXAS

LOU'S BUTTERMILK BISCUITS

Yield: 38 small Oven: 450°

2 cups Bisquick
⅔ cup buttermilk
4 Tb. softened butter

¼ tsp. soda
8 to 12 Tb. melted butter

Cut butter into Bisquick until the size of peas. Add soda to buttermilk; stir well; add to first mixture; stir with a fork until batter follows the fork. Put melted butter on hands to keep batter from sticking; knead batter gently 10 to 15 strokes on a floured pastry cloth. Pat dough to ¼ inch; cut with small cutter which has been put in flour. Dip biscuits in melted butter and place in pans; pour remaining butter over biscuits. May be frozen immediately or kept in refrigerator for 2 or 3 days. Bake 10 to 15 minutes at 450°.

Scant ⅔ cup milk plus 1 Tb. vinegar may be substituted for buttermilk.

MRS. BILL ANDERSON
TULSA, OKLAHOMA

YORKSHIRE PUDDING

Serves: 6-8 Oven: 425°

1 cup flour
½ tsp. salt
1 cup milk

2 eggs
½ cup hot roast beef drippings

Beat all ingredients except drippings with rotary beater just until smooth. Heat 9 x 9 x 2-inch pan in oven; add drippings; pour batter on top of drippings. Bake 35 minutes at 425°. Cut in squares.

MRS. DON THOMPSON

BRAN MUFFINS

Yield: 8 muffins   **Oven: 425°**

¾ cup sifted flour	1 egg, beaten
2½ tsp. baking powder	¾ cup milk
¼ tsp. salt	3 Tb. melted shortening
⅓ cup sugar	1½ cups bran flakes

Sift together flour, baking powder, salt, and sugar. Combine egg and milk. Add to flour mixture; add shortening; mix only enough to dampen flour (it will be lumpy). Fold in cereal. Grease muffin tins; fill ⅔ full. Bake 15 to 20 minutes at 425°. The batter may be prepared the evening before, put in muffin tin, covered with damp cloth, refrigerated, and baked the following morning.

MRS. WILLIAM BISHOP

6-WEEKS BRAN MUFFINS

Yield: 5-6 dozen   **Oven: 350°**

2 cups boiling water	1 cup shortening
2 cups 100% Bran	3 cups sugar
5 cups flour	4 eggs
5 tsp. soda	4 cups All Bran
1 tsp. salt	1 qt. buttermilk

Mix water and Bran. Let stand. Sift together flour, soda, and salt. Cream shortening and sugar; to this add eggs one at a time beating after each addition; add All Bran and buttermilk. Combine and mix all three mixes only until moistened. Put in greased muffin tins. Bake 15 to 20 minutes at 350°.

The batter may be covered, refrigerated, and baked as needed. It will keep for 6 weeks.

MRS. ED LESTER

DATE MUFFINS

Yield: 12 muffins   **Oven: 425°**

1 cup flour	½ cup margarine, softened
1 cup wheat germ	1 cup milk
⅔ cup sugar	2 eggs, beaten
3 tsp. baking powder	½ cup dates, cut up

Grease muffin tins very well or use paper cup cake liners as dates tend to stick. Combine dry ingredients; add margarine, milk and eggs; stir, but do not beat. Fold in dates. Pour into muffin tins; bake at 425° for 20 minutes.

MRS. ELLIOTT BECHTEL

GINGER CHEESE MUFFINS

Yield: 12   Oven: 350°

2 cups flour
1 Tb. baking powder
¼ tsp. soda
½ tsp. ginger
½ tsp. salt
½ cup molasses

⅔ cup grated cheese
1 egg
½ cup milk
¼ cup salad oil
Ginger and sugar

Combine all ingredients except ginger and sugar; fill greased muffin tins ⅔ full; sprinkle tops with ginger and sugar. Bake for 20 minutes at 350°.

DAISY KEATS

PEABODY HOTEL MUFFINS

Yield: 12   Oven: 450°

2 cups flour
1 Tb. baking powder
½ tsp. salt
4 Tb. sugar

1 egg
4 Tb. melted butter
1 cup milk
1 tsp. vanilla

Sift together flour, baking powder, salt, and sugar. Beat egg; add butter to egg and beat again; add milk and vanilla and beat again. Combine liquid and dry ingredients; stir quickly until dry ingredients are just moist. Put quickly into greased muffin tin. Bake 20 minutes at 450°

Hints: Do not grease sides of muffin tins. Do not mix batter very well; definitely not with mixer. Do not drop batter; slide off spoon with spatula.

MRS. EUGENE MASON

APRICOT BREAD

Yield: 1 loaf   Oven: 325°

1 cup dried apricots
1 cup warm water
1 cup sugar
2 Tb. butter, melted
¼ cup reserved juice or
    apricot nectar

½ cup orange juice
    concentrate
2 cups flour
2 tsp. baking powder
¼ tsp. soda
1 cup chopped nuts

Chop apricots; soak 30 minutes in water; drain excess water and reserve (if there is none, use apricot nectar). Stir in sugar, butter, ¼ cup reserved juice, and orange juice concentrate. Sift flour, baking powder, and soda together; add nuts and coat with flour mixture. Combine all ingredients; stir only enough to mix well; let stand 20 minutes before cooking. Grease and flour a loaf pan; bake for 1 hour and 15 minutes at 325°.

Good with cream cheese.

MRS. JOHNNY BRANNAN

BANANA NUT BREAD

Yield: 1 loaf   Oven: 325°

1 cup sugar
½ cup softened butter
2 eggs
2 cups flour
1 tsp. baking soda

½ tsp. cinnamon
½ tsp. ground cloves
3 crushed bananas
½ cup chopped nuts

Cream sugar and butter; add eggs; beat well. Sift in flour, soda, cinnamon, and cloves; beat well. Mix in bananas and nuts. Pour into greased loaf pan; bake 1 hour at 325°.

MRS. BILL COOPER

CRANBERRY BREAD

Yield: 1 loaf   Oven: 325°

2 cups flour
1 cup sugar
2 tsp. baking powder
½ tsp. salt
½ tsp. soda
1 egg, beaten

1 orange: juice and grated
   rind to ¾ cup
2 Tb. salad oil
½ cup chopped nuts
2 cups cranberries, cut in
   half

Sift dry ingredients. Add juice, rind, egg, and oil. Mix until dampened. Add nuts and cranberries; mix. Bake in greased loaf pan at 325° for 50 to 60 minutes. Cool before slicing.

MRS. BART ROACH

LEMON BREAD

Yield: 1 loaf   Oven: 350°

½ cup shortening
1 cup sugar
2 eggs, well beaten
1½ cups flour
½ tsp. salt

1 tsp. baking powder
½ cup milk
1 lemon, juice and rind
½ cup sugar, for glaze

Cream shortening and sugar; add eggs; mix well. Sift together flour, salt, and baking powder. Add dry mixture to first mixture, alternating with milk. Grate rind of lemon; add; mix well. Bake in greased loaf pan for 45 minutes at 350°. Mix juice of lemon and sugar. Immediately after removing bread from oven, pour lemon mixture over it. Don't remove from pan until cool.

Can be doubled and frozen.

MRS. GEORGE DANGERFIELD

ORANGE BREAD

Yield: 2 small loaves   Oven: 350°

3 cups flour
4 tsp. baking powder
1 Tb. grated orange rind
½ cup sugar

1 egg
¼ cup orange juice
1¼ cups milk
2 Tb. melted butter

Have all ingredients at room temperature. Sift, then measure 3 cups flour; resift into large bowl with baking powder. Add orange rind and sugar. Combine and beat egg, juice, milk, and butter; add to dry ingredients; stir until barely blended. Bake in two greased 8 x 3½-inch loaf pans at 350° for 50 minutes. This freezes well. Serve warm with butter.

MRS. WILLIAM A. SAUNDERS, JR.

PRUNE LOAF

Yield: 1 loaf   Oven: 350°

1 cup salad oil
2 cups sugar
3 eggs
2 cups flour
Dash of salt

1 tsp. vanilla
1 cup chopped nuts
1 cup chopped prunes
1 tsp. soda
1 cup buttermilk

Mix in order all but last two ingredients. Mix soda in buttermilk; add to mixture. Bake in extra large greased loaf pan for 1 hour at 350°.

MRS. STANLEY K. BRADSHAW, JR.

PUMPKIN BREAD

Yield: 3 loaves   Oven: 350°

3½ cups sifted flour
2 tsp. soda
1½ tsp. salt
2 tsp. cinnamon
2 tsp. nutmeg
3 cups sugar

4 eggs, beaten
⅔ cup water
1 cup salad oil
16-oz. can pumpkin (2 cups)
1 cup chopped pecans

Combine flour, soda, salt, cinnamon, nutmeg, and sugar in large mixing bowl. Add eggs, water, oil, and pumpkin; stir until blended. Add nuts; mix well. Pour mixture into 3 greased and floured one-pound coffee cans. Bake 1 hour at 350°. Cool slightly in cans; turn out on rack to finish cooling. Flavor is best if baked day before using.

Keeps for weeks in refrigerator or freezes beautifully. Delicious with spiced tea.

CORN BREAD

Serves: 6-8   Oven: 450°

1 egg
1 cup buttermilk
1 cup yellow corn meal
1 tsp. sugar
½ tsp. salt

1 Tb. melted bacon drippings
½ tsp. soda
1 tsp. baking powder
1 Tb. warm water

Break egg in buttermilk; beat well. Add meal, sugar, and salt; add bacon drippings. Mix soda and baking powder in water; add to above mixture. Just before baking, stir mixture well. Pour in hot, greased iron skillet; bake for 20 minutes at 450°. Corn bread is done when it begins to pull away from pan.

MRS. CARL SCOTT HUNTER

MEXICAN CORN BREAD

Serves: 6-8   Oven: 375°

1 cup white corn meal
1 tsp. salt
2 tsp. baking powder
½ tsp. soda
2 eggs, beaten
¾ cup milk
17-oz. can creamed style corn

½ cup melted bacon
  drippings
1 heaping cup grated
  American cheese
3 finely chopped jalapeno
  peppers

Combine corn meal, salt, baking powder, and soda. Stir in eggs, milk, and bacon drippings until blended thoroughly. Add corn. Pour half mixture into iron skillet or heavy baking dish. Spread cheese and peppers evenly over mixture. Spread remaining batter on top. Bake for 45 minutes at 375°. Done when brown on top and firm to touch.

MRS. WILLIAM L. PATTON, JR.

CORN CAKES

Serves: 4

⅔ cup corn meal
¼ cup flour
2 Tb. sugar
1 tsp. salt
2 tsp. baking powder

½ cup milk
2 Tb. melted shortening
1 egg
1 Tb. shortening

Sift all dry ingredients together; add milk, 2 tablespoons shortening and egg. Melt 1 tablespoon shortening in skillet; heat to medium hot. Drop tablespoonful of batter in skillet; cook until golden; turn and cook other side. Do not mash them. Stack cakes with butter between; good with syrup, too.

Great with fried catfish!

MRS. GENEVA WARREN

CORN STICKS

Yield: 14   Oven: 500°

1½ cups white corn meal   1 Tb. flour
1 tsp. salt   1 tsp. baking powder
¼ tsp. sugar   ⅔ cup cool water
1⅓ cups boiling water   1 Tb. bacon grease

Use cast iron corn stick pans. Place in oven to heat while making batter. In a bowl mix corn meal, salt, sugar, and boiling water. Then add flour, baking powder, and cool water. Remove hot pans from oven and grease with bacon grease, pouring any excess into batter. Stir batter and pour into pans. Bake 35 minutes at 500°. These are old fashioned corn sticks and will be crunchy.

MRS. ETHEL STEVENSON
EARLE, ARKANSAS

HUSH PUPPIES

Yield: 2 dozen

2 cups yellow corn meal   2 Tb. sugar
1 finely minced onion   2 eggs, beaten slightly
¼ cup shortening   Salt and pepper to taste
2 tsp. baking powder   1 cup boiling water

Mix all ingredients except water. Add water; stir quickly to mix. Shape into balls and fry in deep fat.

SPOON BREAD

Serves: 8   Oven: 325°

3 Tb. melted butter   2 tsp. salt
1 cup white corn meal   4 egg yolks, beaten
1 cup cold milk   4 egg whites, beaten
3 cups scalded milk

Heat 7 to 8-inch souffle dish with 3 tablespoons butter in it. Mix corn meal with cold milk; slowly stir into scalded milk. Cook 10 minutes, stirring well. Add the melted butter, salt, and egg yolks; cool slightly. Fold in stiffly beaten egg whites; bake in souffle dish at 325° for 1 hour. Serve immediately.

MRS. CHRISTOPH KELLER, JR.

CHEESE SPOONED BREAD

Serves: 4   Oven: 350°

2 cups milk   Dash cayenne pepper
½ cup Cream of Wheat   1 cup Cheddar cheese, grated
1 tsp. salt   1 egg, beaten slightly
4 Tb. butter, cut up

Cook milk and Cream of Wheat together until thick; add salt, butter, cayenne, and cheese. Remove from fire; stir until cheese is melted. Put beaten egg in medium size bowl; add hot mixture by spoonfuls mixing after each addition for 5 or 6 spoonfuls; then add remaining mixture; mix well. Pour into greased 1½ quart baking dish. Bake for 45 minutes at 350°.

MRS. CHARLES H. WILLIAMSON

CREPES

Yield: 20 crepes

4 eggs	1 Tb. butter, melted
1 ¾ cups milk	½ tsp. salt
1 ½ cups flour	¼ tsp. baking powder

Beat eggs slightly; add milk and flour; beat until smooth. Add butter, salt, and baking powder; beat until smooth. This may be done in blender. Let stand 5 minutes. To cook, brush 6-inch skillet lightly with butter or margarine. Over moderately high heat, add ¾ tablespoon of batter to skillet; tip skillet quickly so batter will run around skillet thinly and completely cover bottom. Turn heat down; let cook through; they need not be turned, but bottom should be golden. If crepes are too thick, use less batter. Stack crepes; cover with towel; keep warm in a slow oven. If they are made in advance, place waxed paper between each crepe; they may be reheated.

MRS. CLIFF WOOD

GERMAN PANCAKE

Serves: 2   Oven: 425°

3 eggs	3 Tb. sugar
3 Tb. flour	¼ tsp. cinnamon
1 Tb. sugar	¼ cup melted butter
6 Tb. milk	Powdered sugar
Juice of ½ lemon	

Beat eggs until thick; add flour, sugar, and milk. Pour into large, buttered skillet. Bake uncovered for 8 minutes at 425°; reduce heat to 375°; bake for 8 more minutes. Put pancake on platter; sprinkle with lemon juice, sugar, cinnamon, and butter. Roll it up; sprinkle with powdered sugar. Serve with homemade applesauce if possible.

MRS. B. FRANK MACKEY, JR.

BAVARIAN BREAKFAST ROLLS

Yield: 24   Oven: 350°

2 cups flour	½ pt. sour cream
1 cup butter	1 cup coconut
16-oz. jar apricot-pineapple jam	1 cup finely chopped nuts (optional)

Blend flour, butter, and sour cream as you would pie dough. Wrap in wax paper; refrigerate overnight. Divide dough in half. Roll each half in a 12 x 18-inch rectangle. Spread each half with jam; sprinkle with coconut and nuts. Starting with shorter end, roll up each piece; pinch ends together and seal seam. Bake on greased cookie sheet for 40 to 45 minutes at 350°. Slice and serve. This may be wrapped in foil and reheated, or may be frozen.
Great for morning meetings.

MRS. HARRY McDERMOTT, JR.

CHEESE ROLL

Serves: 8   Oven: 350°

½ lb. American or mild   1 cup apple jelly
  Cheddar cheese, grated   ½ cup chopped nuts
½ cup butter, softened   Cinnamon
2 cups flour   Sugar

Mix together and knead cheese, butter, and flour. Roll into rectangle 24 x 4-inch on waxed paper. Spread with jelly and sprinkle with nuts, cinnamon, and sugar. Roll as jelly roll, starting with long side. Refrigerate for 24 hours. Slice thin and bake on greased cookie sheet at 350° for 10 to 15 minutes.

MRS. ED I. MCKINLEY, JR.

SOUR CREAM COFFEE CAKE

Yield: 1 large coffee cake   Oven: 350°

1 cup softened butter   1 tsp. vanilla
2 cups sugar   2 cups sifted cake flour
2 eggs   1 tsp. salt
1 cup sour cream   1 tsp. baking powder

TOPPING:

½ cup chopped pecans   4 Tb. brown sugar
2 tsp. cinnamon

In large bowl, cream butter and sugar; add eggs one at a time, beating well after each addition. Fold in sour cream and vanilla. Sift dry ingredients; add to mixture. Put half the batter in greased and floured 10-inch tube pan; sprinkle half the topping over batter; add rest of batter; sprinkle remaining topping on top. Bake 55 to 60 minutes at 350°. Cool thoroughly before removing from pan; sprinkle with powdered sugar.

MRS. DONALD TATMAN
PINE BLUFF, ARKANSAS

WAFFLES OR PANCAKES

Serves: 4

2 cups sifted flour   1 cup milk
1 tsp. soda   1 cup buttermilk
1 tsp. baking powder   1 egg
1 tsp. salt   4 Tb. melted oleo or oil

Mix all ingredients and beat well. May be mixed in blender. If batter used for pancakes, pour from pitcher into very hot skillet. If used for waffles, pour into hot waffle iron.

Variations for pancakes:

Blueberry—Add ½ pint fresh blueberries.

Apple—Quarter apples; slice thinly. Pour batter on hot griddle; place a few apples on each pancake. Turn when batter begins to bubble. Sprinkle with cinnamon and sugar.

MRS. THOMAS G. GREAVES, III
GREENVILLE, SOUTH CAROLINA

SOURDOUGH

"If at first you don't succeed . . ." When about to embark on a sour-dough baking adventure you need patience, perseverance, and room in your refrigerator. There is no flavor like that of sourdough and if you are especially fond of it, be prepared to gain a few pounds.

Here are two ways to get a starter going. Use whichever one you prefer, or both. You must use the starter at least once a week.

No. 1—Pour 1 cup milk into a crock (don't use metal) and let stand at room temperature 24 hours. Add 1 cup flour and stir. Leave uncovered in a warm place for 2 to 5 days. After it becomes bubbly and is sour smelling it can be used in recipes. Maintain about 1½ cups at all times. When you use some, replace it with 1 cup milk and 1 cup flour. Let set overnight and then refrigerate.

No. 2—Mix together 1 cup milk, 1 cup flour and ¼ cup sugar. Let stand for 1 or 2 days at room temperature until it bubbles. It may then be refrigerated. Use often and replenish or "feed" it once a week with 1 cup milk, 1 cup flour and ¼ cup sugar.

The leavening action in the sourdough recipes comes from reaction of acid (sourness) and soda, which you can increase or decrease according to the sourness you prefer and from the bacterial action in the starter.

If it is a cool day allow more time for the dough to rise.

Sourdough breads and biscuits don't stay "fresh" for very long, so do try to use them on the day they are baked. They dry out easily.

Do not cover; it will explode.

SOURDOUGH BREAD

Yield: 2 loaves   **Oven: 400°**

1 cup starter	2 tsp. salt
1½ cups warm water	2 cups flour
4 cups flour	½ tsp. soda
2 tsp. sugar	

Mix together starter, water, 4 cups flour, sugar, and salt. Place in pottery crock or bowl and leave at room temperature about 18 hours or until double. Stir in 1 cup flour mixed with ½ tsp. soda. Turn out onto floured board and knead 9 minutes, working in remaining 1 cup flour.

Shape into 2 long loaves and place on lightly greased cookie sheet. Cover and let set in warm place for 3 to 4 hours, until almost double. Brush tops with water (for a crispy crust) and make 3 diagonal slashes across tops with sharpest knife. Place shallow pan of water in bottom of oven. Bake at 400° about 45 minutes. Can be reheated briefly to restore crisp crust.

SOURDOUGH BLUEBERRY PANCAKES

1 cup starter
2 cups warm water
2½ cups flour
2 eggs, beaten
2 Tb. sugar

2 Tb. salad oil
½ cup milk
1 tsp. soda
1 cup blueberries, fresh or
frozen

Mix starter, warm water and flour. I et stand in covered bowl (pottery preferred) overnight. Do not refrigerate.

In the morning add eggs, sugar, oil, milk, soda and blueberries. Let batter stand 10 to 15 minutes. Cook on hot griddle and serve with hot maple syrup or blueberry syrup.

SOURDOUGH ENGLISH MUFFINS

Yield: 12 muffins   Griddle: 275°

½ cup starter
1 cup milk
2¾ cups flour
2 Tb. sugar

¾ tsp. salt
½ tsp. soda
2 or 3 Tb. corn meal

Combine starter, milk and 2 cups flour in a large pottery bowl. Don't use metal. Mix and cover with tea towel for 8 hours or overnight at room temperature. Mix ½ cup flour, sugar, salt, and soda and add to dough. Turn out onto board floured with remaining ¼ cup flour. Knead 3 to 5 minutes until smooth, adding more flour if necessary.

Roll out dough to ¾ inch thickness. Cut 12 3-inch square muffins. Place on waxed paper which has been sprinkled with ½ of the corn meal. Sprinkle remainder on tops. Cover and let rise in a warm place for 45 minutes. Cook on lightly greased griddle at 275° for 9 or 10 minutes per side. Serve split and toasted with butter, cream cheese or jelly. Can also be used for open face sandwiches.

SOURDOUGH BISCUITS

Yield: 2 dozen   Oven: 400°

¼ cup shortening
1 cup flour
1 tsp. baking powder

¼ tsp. baking soda
½ tsp. salt
1 cup starter

Cut shortening into flour with pastry blender or fork. Add remaining ingredients and knead until smooth. Roll and cut out. Bake at 400° for 10 to 15 minutes.

EGGS AND CHEESE

EGGS AND EGG DISHES

Eggs may be cooked in many ways: Poached, fried, scrambled, soft- or hard-cooked in the shell, omelettes, etc., and in any of these ways may be served alone or in combination with other foods. One fundamental rule applies to all forms of egg cookery: Cook with low to moderate heat, never high heat, and for exactly the length of time specified in the recipe. A properly cooked egg has a tender white and a smooth yolk.

TO POACH AN EGG:

Pour into a skillet enough water to cover eggs and add ¼ teaspoon vinegar for each cup water. Heat water to just below boiling point. Break one egg at a time into a saucer and slip into the water. When all eggs are in, reheat water to simmering. Cover, remove from heat, and let stand 3 to 5 minutes, until eggs are of desired firmness. Eggs may be poached ahead of time and reheated before serving. Remove eggs when done and place them in a bowl of cold water. This stops the cooking and removes the vinegar. Set the uncovered eggs in the refrigerator. They will keep perfectly for 2 or 3 days. When ready to serve, drain the eggs and place in very hot salted water for about one minute. Remove with a slotted spoon, trim edges and drain over a folded towel.

TO SOFT-COOK EGGS IN THE SHELL:

Place eggs in a saucepan with enough water to cover to a depth of one inch. Cover, bring to boiling point, remove from heat, and let stand 3 to 5 minutes, allowing the longer time for more eggs or firmer consistency.

TO HARD-COOK EGGS IN THE SHELL:

Place eggs in a saucepan with enough water to cover one inch. Cover, bring to boiling point, remove from heat, let stand 25 minutes. Cool eggs immediately in cold water.

TO SCRAMBLE EGGS:

Break eggs into a bowl. For creamy scrambled eggs add one tablespoon milk or light cream for each egg; for dry scrambled eggs, add ½ tablespoon milk or light cream for each egg. Beat mixture until yolks and whites are blended. Season with salt and pepper. Pour mixture into a heated skillet containing one tablespoon melted butter. Stir and cook slowly until eggs are set.

TO MAKE AN OMELETTE:

Beat eggs with a pinch of salt and pepper in a mixing bowl until yolks and whites are blended. Place a lump of butter in a no-stick skillet and set over high heat. As butter melts, tilt skillet in all directions to coat bottom and sides. Pour eggs in when butter has ceased to foam. Let eggs settle 3 or 4 seconds then move pan rapidly back and forth over heat. When eggs have set into a soft custard (about 10 seconds) tilt the skillet away from you. Flip the near end of the omelette toward the far lip of the pan using a fork. Shake pan to slide omelette to edge. Have warm serving plate ready and quickly turn omelette pan upside down over plate. A filling may be placed in the omelette either while it is in the pan and before you have folded over to one side, or after it is on the serving plate it may be scored and filling placed on top.

CHEESE SOUFFLE

Serves: 6   Oven: 350°

4 Tb. butter	4 eggs, separated
4 Tb. flour	2 tsp. dry mustard
1½ cups milk	2 tsp. catsup
½ lb. sharp cheese, grated	Salt to taste

Melt butter; stir in flour. Add milk and cheese, stirring until smooth; add beaten egg yolks, mustard, catsup and salt; cool. Fold in stiffly beaten egg whites. Pour into greased 2 quart casserole or 8 individual casseroles. Place in pan of water and bake for 1 hour at 350°.

Tip: If an extra egg white is added, the souffle will hold its shape when cutting into it.

MRS. BART ROACH

CUP BAKED EGGS

Serves: 4   Oven: 350°

4 tsp. butter	4 tsp. butter
4 tsp. parsley, minced	4 tsp. light cream
4 eggs	4 muffins or slices toast
Salt and pepper to taste	

Grease 4 small custard cups with 1 teaspoon butter each; sprinkle with 1 teaspoon minced parsley each. Break an egg into each cup, season with salt and pepper, add 1 teaspoon cream and 1 teaspoon butter. Arrange cups in a pan of hot water; cover with waxed paper and bake in 350° oven for 15-20 minutes or until eggs are set. Unmold on hot buttered muffins or toast.

CRAB MEAT EGGS AU GRATIN

Serves: 4

6 eggs	4 oz. American cheese,
6½-oz. can crab meat,	crumbled
drained	Salt and pepper to taste
3 Tb. milk	2 Tb. butter

Beat eggs until lemon colored; add crab meat, milk, cheese, butter, salt and pepper. Put in top of double boiler over barely boiling water. Cook and stir until eggs are done.

MRS. WARREN JENNINGS
DEWITT, ARKANSAS

BAKED EGGS IN CHEESE SAUCE

Serves: 6   Oven: 325°

1 tsp. prepared mustard   1½ cups medium white sauce
½ lb. American Cheddar   6 eggs
   cheese   Salt and pepper to taste

Add mustard and cheese to white sauce and stir until cheese has melted. Put half of sauce in buttered casserole, break in eggs and cover with remaining white sauce. Bake 20 to 25 minutes in 325° oven.

This is nice for breakfast served with sausage and hot biscuits.

MRS. STANLEY K. BRADSHAW, JR.

BASIC QUICHE

Serves: 8   Oven: 450°

10-inch unbaked pie shell,   Pinch of nutmeg
   chilled   6 eggs
1 Tb. butter, softened   1 pt. light cream
1 cup grated Swiss cheese   ¼ cup Parmesan cheese,
1 Tb. flour   grated
¼ tsp. salt   2 Tb. butter, melted and
Pepper to taste   browned

Spread butter on bottom of pie shell. Sprinkle Swiss cheese in bottom of pie shell. Sift dry ingredients. Add eggs and cream to dry ingredients and beat until mixed but not frothy. Pour custard over cheese. Bake at 450° for 10 minutes. Reduce heat to 325° and bake 25 minutes longer. Remove from oven and sprinkle with Parmesan cheese and butter. Return to oven for 10 minutes or until a knife inserted in custard comes out clean. Let set 10 minutes before cutting into wedges to serve.

Variations of Basic Quiche:

Quiche Lorraine: 8 slices of crisp bacon, crumbled and added to Basic Quiche.

Shrimp Quiche: 1 to 1½ cups cooked shrimp added to Basic Quiche.

Crab Quiche: 1 to 1½ cups picked and drained crab meat added to Basic Quiche.

Lobster Quiche: 1 to 1½ cups shredded boiled lobster added to Basic Quiche.

Mushroom Quiche: 1½ cups mushrooms sliced and sautéed in 3 Tb. melted butter lightly seasoned added to Basic Quiche.

Asparagus Quiche: Arrange cooked asparagus (1 box frozen asparagus or ½ lb. fresh asparagus) in a pinwheel design in bottom of pie shell. Proceed with Basic Quiche recipe.

BRUNCH EGGS

Serves: 8-10

8-oz. can sliced mushrooms,
   drained
½ cup butter
12 hard-cooked eggs, chopped
   fine
1 can mushroom soup,
   undiluted

½ cup milk
2 Tb. Worcestershire sauce
⅓ cup lemon juice
2 pkgs. dried beef, chopped
   fine
Salt and pepper to taste
Tabasco to taste

Sauté mushrooms in butter. Add remaining ingredients; blend well and heat. If mixture is too thin, thicken with a paste of 2 tablespoons flour, and ¼ cup milk. This recipe is best served over toast points or English muffins.

MRS. GILBERT BUCHANAN

DEVILED EGGS AND ASPARAGUS

Serves: 8-10   Oven: 350°

2 pkgs. frozen asparagus
10 hard-cooked eggs
1 large can deviled ham
1 tsp. grated onion
½ tsp. Worcestershire sauce
¾ tsp. dry mustard
1 tsp. cream, heavy
6 Tb. butter

6 Tb. flour
3 cups milk
2 cups grated Cheddar cheese
¼ tsp. dry mustard
1 tsp. salt
Dash of pepper
2 cups cornflakes, crushed
2 Tb. melted butter

Cook asparagus according to directions on package; drain and cut up. Place on the bottom of a buttered casserole. Slice eggs in half. Mix yolks with ham, onion, Worcestershire, ¾ teaspoon dry mustard, and cream. Stuff egg whites and place on top of asparagus. Make a cheese sauce by melting butter in a saucepan and adding flour. Gradually add milk; stir until thick. Add cheese and seasonings; pour over casserole. Top with cornflake crumbs mixed with melted butter. Bake at 350° for 20 minutes.

MRS. BART ROACH

EGGS OBSTACULOS

Serves: 6

2 Tb. butter or oil
¾ cup hot tomato sauce

8 eggs
1 cup beer

Heat oil and sauce in a shallow dish, rolling it well around the edges. When bubbling, break eggs into it. Heat slowly until the eggs are done, pour the beer over, and serve at once with hot toast.

EGGS AND CHEESE CONTINENTAL

Serves: 6   Oven: 350°

1 cup thinly sliced onion
1 Tb. butter
9 hard-cooked eggs, sliced
2 cups shredded Swiss cheese
10½-oz. can cream of mushroom soup
¾ cup milk

1 tsp. prepared mustard
½ tsp. seasoned salt
¼ tsp. dill weed
¼ tsp. pepper
6 slices caraway rye bread,
   buttered

Sauté onion in butter till tender. Spread in bottom of 11½ x 7½ x 1½-inch baking dish. Top with slices of egg; sprinkle with cheese. Beat remaining ingredients except bread in bowl with electric mixer. Pour soup mixture over. Cut each slice of bread into 4 triangles. Place slices on top of casserole with points up. Bake 30 to 35 minutes or until heated through at 350°. Set oven on broil or 550°. Place casserole 6 inches from heat—broil one minute or until bread is toasted.

MRS. DON THOMPSON

EGG CROQUETTES

Serves: 8

9 hard-cooked eggs
3 Tb. butter
3 Tb. flour
1 cup hot milk
1 Tb. parsley, chopped
½ Tb. onion juice

½ tsp. lemon juice
Dash cayenne
1½ tsp. salt
White pepper
2 eggs, slightly beaten
2½ cups dry bread crumbs

Rice the eggs. Make a white sauce of the butter, flour, and milk. When thick, add riced eggs and seasonings. Refrigerate until stiff. Form into croquettes; roll in bread crumbs, dip in egg, then roll in crumbs again. Fry in hot deep fat and drain on paper towels. May be kept warm in oven for a time. Makes 12 medium size croquettes.

MRS. A. HOWARD STEBBINS, III

GREEN EGGS AND HAM

Serves: 8

1 doz. eggs
¼ cup milk
1½ oz. bourbon (optional)
½ cup cubed avocado

½ cup grated Swiss cheese
½ cup boiled ham, chopped
¼ cup chopped green onions
3 Tb. butter

Beat eggs. Add rest of ingredients and scramble gently in hot butter.

EGGS HUSSARDE

Serves: 8

16 thin slices grilled ham   16 poached eggs
16 Holland Rusks   2 cups hollandaise sauce
3 cups marchand de vin sauce   Paprika
16 slices grilled tomato

Lay a slice of ham across each Holland Rusk and cover with
marchand de vin sauce. Lay slices of tomato on the sauce and place
poached eggs on tomato slices. Top with hollandaise sauce and
garnish with a sprinkling of paprika.

MARCHAND DE VIN SAUCE:

Yield: 4 cups

1 ½ cups butter   4 Tb. flour
⅔ cup mushrooms, chopped   1 tsp. salt
1 cup minced ham   ¼ tsp. pepper
⅔ cup green onions, chopped   Cayenne pepper to taste
1 cup onion, chopped   1 ½ cups beef stock
4 Tb. minced garlic   1 cup red wine

Melt butter and lightly sauté mushrooms, ham, green onion, onion,
and garlic. When onion is golden brown, add flour, salt, pepper, and
cayenne. Brown well, about 7 to 10 minutes, blend in the stock and
wine and simmer over low heat 35 to 45 minutes.

                                    MRS. BRONSON COOPER JACOWAY

FLORENTINE EGGS EN COCOTTE

Serves: 6   Oven: 325°

10-oz. pkg. frozen spinach   6 Tb. heavy cream, warm
2 Tb. butter   6 Tb. grated cheese, Cheddar
6 eggs   or Parmesan
Salt and pepper

Cook and season spinach according to package directions. Drain
well and sauté in butter 2 to 3 minutes. Spread over bottoms and
sides of 6 buttered cocotte dishes or ramekins. Break one egg into
each. Sprinkle with salt and pepper. Place dishes in a shallow pan
of hot water. Cook over surface heat 3 minutes, never allowing the
water to boil. Pour one tablespoon cream over each egg, then
sprinkle each with one tablespoon grated cheese. Cover and cook
5 minutes in a preheated slow oven (325°).

FLUFFY OMELET

Serves: 2   Oven: 350°

3 Tb. shortening   4 eggs, separated
½ tsp. salt   4 Tb. milk
¼ tsp. cream of tartar   Pepper to taste

Heat shortening in large skillet on low heat. Add salt and cream of tartar to egg whites and beat to form stiff, pointed peaks. Beat egg yolks until thick. Add milk and pepper to egg yolks, stirring until blended. Fold egg whites gently into yolks. Pour egg mixture into skillet. Cook for 5 minutes on top of stove, moving skillet gently several times. Bake at 350° for 10 to 12 minutes, or until gloss disappears and omelet is light brown. Crease omelet through center when set; fold over with a spatula, and roll from the skillet to a heated platter. Serve immediately.

PARTY EGGS

Serves: 18   Oven: 140°-200°

3 doz. eggs   ¼ cup butter
1⅓ cups light cream   2 cups medium white sauce
3 tsp. salt   Chopped parsley
Pepper to taste

Beat eggs with cream, salt, and pepper. Melt butter in large frying pan. Pour in egg mixture, stirring occasionally until almost set. Fold in hot white sauce while eggs are still creamy. Keep hot in a very slow oven (140°-200°) or place over hot water on top of range. Sprinkle with parsley.

These eggs are great for late night breakfast. They stay very moist in a chafing dish.

Variation: This can be served over hot toast with deviled ham.

MRS. GENE MASON

SCRAMBLED EGGS CHASSEUR

Serves: 6

½ lb. chicken livers   Salt and pepper
2 Tb. butter   8 eggs, scrambled with ⅓
½ cup sautéed, sliced mush-   cup milk or light cream
    rooms   Chopped parsley
¾ cup white sauce

Cook livers in butter until they are no longer pink. Remove from heat and dice the livers. Add mushrooms, white sauce, salt, and pepper. Put the mixture in the center of a warmed serving dish and spoon scrambled eggs around it. Garnish with parsley.

Good for breakfast, lunch, or supper!

RAMEKIN FORESTIER

Serves: 6   Oven: 400°

FILLING:

1 cup mushrooms, minced	1 Tb. flour
1 Tb. butter	4 Tb. cream, heavy
1 Tb. salad oil	¼ tsp. salt
1 Tb. onions, minced	Pepper

Sauté mushrooms and onions in butter and oil for 5 minutes, stirring often. Lower heat, sprinkle with flour and cook a minute. Remove from heat, add cream, stir over heat until thick; add salt and pepper. Set aside.

MIXTURE:

½ cup flour	⅛ tsp. pepper
2 cups milk, cold	Nutmeg, dash
3½ Tb. butter, melted	4 eggs, large
½ tsp. salt	1⅓ cups cheese, grated

Put flour in a saucepan; gradually beat in milk, using a wire whip or a fork. Stir over moderate heat until it boils and thickens. Remove from heat, beat in butter, seasonings, and eggs one at a time. Then beat in 1 cup of cheese.

Turn one-half the mixture into a greased baking dish (9 x 1½-inch or individual ramekins). Spread mushroom filling on top; cover with remaining mixture. Sprinkle with ⅓ cup cheese and dot with butter (1 tablespoon).

Bake at 400° for 25 to 35 minutes or until set in middle. When done it will have doubled in size and browned. Serve immediately.

This may be prepared a day ahead and refrigerated before baking. Baking time may be increased if casserole is cold.

MRS. FRANK MACKEY, JR.

STUFFED FRENCH LOAF

Serves: 4-6   Oven: 375°

6 hard-cooked eggs	1 tsp. grated onion
2¼-oz. can ripe olives, drained and sliced	1 tsp. prepared mustard
1 cup grated Cheddar cheese	¼ tsp. seasoned pepper
8-oz. can tomato sauce	1 loaf French bread

Peel and chop eggs. Combine with remaining ingredients except bread. Slice French loaf in half lengthwise. Scoop out part of soft center. Spoon egg mixture into bread shell. Put loaf back together, return to foil wrapper, and bake in 375° oven 45 minutes, or until cheese melts.

MRS. ROBERT CARNAHAN

WELSH RAREBIT

Serves: 4

1 tsp. butter
2 cups Cheddar cheese,
  grated
⅜ tsp. salt
¼ tsp. pepper

1 tsp. dry mustard
⅛ tsp. cayenne pepper
1 Tb. Lea and Perrin
1 cup beer or milk
2 eggs, slightly beaten

Melt butter in the top of a double boiler. Add cheese, salt, peppers, mustard, Lea and Perrin, and beer; stir until smooth. Add eggs and cook, stirring until thick. (This will take about 20 minutes.) Serve over toast.

MRS. DREW LANDER

FISH AND SHELLFISH

BEER BATTER FOR FRIED SHRIMP

Serves: 6-8

2 eggs, separated
12 oz. beer
1 Tb. melted butter
1 tsp. dry mustard
Salt and pepper to taste

1½ cups flour and flour for
dredging
Shrimp for 6 to 8
Hot oil

Beat yolks with beer and butter. Add dry mustard, salt and pepper.
Pour into flour and mix until smooth. Whip whites until stiff and
fold into batter mixture. Dredge shrimp first through flour, then
through batter. Fry in hot oil until golden.
Serve with tartar or red sauce.

MRS. RICHARD S. WOODS
DALLAS, TEXAS

GARLIC SCAMPI

Serves: 6   Oven: 400°

½ cup butter
1 tsp. salt
3 cloves garlic, crushed
¼ cup chopped parsley

2 lbs. large raw shrimp
2 tsp. grated lemon peel
2 Tb. lemon juice
6 lemon wedges

Preheat oven to 400°; melt butter in 13 x 9 x 2-inch baking dish in
oven. Add salt, garlic and one tablespoon parsley; mix well. Arrange cleaned shrimp in single layer in baking dish; bake, uncovered, for 5 minutes. Turn shrimp and sprinkle with lemon peel,
lemon juice and remaining parsley and bake 8 to 10 minutes, until
tender. Arrange shrimp on heated serving platter (or individual
plates if used as first course), pour garlic butter over all, and
garnish with lemon wedges.

MRS. WILLIAM MCLEAN

FINGER LICKIN' SHRIMP

Serves: 8

8 lbs. large unpeeled shrimp
¼ cup salt
1½ to 2 tsp. black pepper
1 tsp. red pepper
¾ cup salad oil
3 cups chopped white onions

3 cups chopped celery
3 cups chopped bell pepper
½ cup chopped green onions,
include tops
½ cup chopped parsley

Fry shrimp combined with salt and black and red pepper in salad
oil over medium heat until red. Add white onions, celery and bell
peppers. Turn to high heat. Cover and bring to boil. Reduce heat
and cook 15 to 20 minutes. Then add green onions and parsley.
Serve, peel 'em and eat 'em style, in the sauce. Dip French bread
in sauce or serve with rice.

MRS. J. W. GUTHRIE
OKLAHOMA CITY, OKLAHOMA

SHRIMP REMOULADE

2 lbs. cooked shrimp
2 cloves garlic
⅓ cup Zatarain's horseradish
  mustard
2 Tb. catsup
2½ Tb. paprika
¾ tsp. cayenne pepper

1 tsp. salt
⅓ cup tarragon vinegar
½ cup olive or corn oil
½ cup chopped green onions
  with tops
Chives

Combine all ingredients except shrimp in blender, blend 2 to 3 minutes, until thoroughly and finely blended. If no blender, crush garlic, and chop onions finely.

Serve over cooked shrimp on a bed of shredded lettuce. This amount of sauce is sufficient for two pounds of shrimp, the smaller the better, and the flavor will be improved if the sauce is made ahead and the shrimp allowed to marinate in it in the refrigerator.

BILL LEWIS

IMMEDIATE SHRIMP

Serves: 4

1 lb. frozen shrimp, cleaned
  and shelled
1 large onion, sliced
1 large bell pepper, sliced

Olive oil
1 to 2 tsp. oregano
Salt
Pepper

Cover bottom of skillet with olive oil; when hot, add shrimp, onion, and bell pepper. Stir constantly, add more oil if needed to keep glossy. Cook about 15 minutes or until shrimp are done. Add oregano, salt, and pepper. Serve.

MRS. HENRY RUSSELL

SHRIMP DE JONGHE

Serves: 4   Oven: 400°

1 lb. cooked small shrimp
1 cup butter
1 cup bread crumbs
¼ cup sour cream
¼ cup chopped parsley
2 cloves minced garlic

1 tsp. salt
1 tsp. Worcestershire sauce
1 tsp. A-1 sauce
Coarsely ground black pepper
Juice of ½ lemon

Cream the butter, blend in crumbs, and sour cream. Add the parsley, garlic, salt and pepper, sauces, and lemon juice. Arrange shrimp in one layer in bottom of oven-proof serving dishes, or fish shaped shells. Apply a coating of the mixture, smoothing it over the shrimp. Bake in 400° oven til tops are lightly browned. You may flute the edges of the dishes with Duchess potatoes (mashed potatoes with butter and an egg mixed in), and garnish with a slice of green stuffed olive for a fish eye, and a sprig of parsley added after removal from the oven, for the tail.

BILL LEWIS

LEMON WILD RICE WITH SHRIMP

Serves: 6   Oven: 375°

2 tsp. chopped bell pepper
2 tsp. chopped onion
3 tsp. butter
2 cups (packed) cooked wild rice
1 can cream of mushroom soup

3 Tb. lemon juice
½ tsp. Worcestershire sauce
½ tsp. mustard
1 cup cheese, cubed
1 lb. cleaned raw shrimp
Paprika
Parsley

Sauté green pepper and onion in butter until soft. Stir into cooked wild rice. Mix soup, lemon juice, Worcestershire sauce, and mustard with wild rice. Add cheese and shrimp. Place in buttered casserole. Bake in 375° oven for 30 minutes. Garnish with paprika and parsley.

MRS. SAM KUYKENDALL

SHRIMP CURRY

Serves: 8   Oven: 300°

4 Tb. butter
1 large onion, finely chopped
½ cup apple, finely chopped
½ cup celery, finely chopped
1½ cups water
2 Tb. curry powder

Salt and pepper to taste
1 pt. heavy cream
3 lbs. cooked shrimp
5 cups cooked rice
4 whole fresh pineapples

Melt butter, add onion, apple, and celery. Simmer for a few minutes, then add water. Let all simmer gently until tender and most of liquid has cooked away. Stir curry, salt, and pepper into mixture; add cream and cooked, cleaned shrimp. Cook gently until cream is reduced to sauce consistency. Serve over rice with condiments, such as roasted peanuts, chutney, coconut, etc. For a special dinner, cut fresh pineapples in half down the middle of the green tops. Scoop out core of pineapple, fill with hot rice and curried shrimp. Bake pineapple with stem unremoved in 300° oven for 5 minutes. Serve immediately. Tuck a fresh flower in the green stem.

MRS. GEORGE COOK

SHRIMP HARPIN

Serves: 6-8   Oven: 350°

2½ lbs. shrimp, peeled
1 Tb. lemon juice
3 Tb. salad oil
¾ cup raw rice
¼ cup chopped onion
2 Tb. butter

½ tsp. pepper
1 cup heavy cream
1 tsp. salt
1 can tomato soup, undiluted
½ cup sherry
½ cup toasted almonds

Cook shrimp according to directions on package; drain; sprinkle with lemon juice and oil and place in a 10-inch buttered casserole. Cook rice; drain and add to shrimp. Sauté onion in butter; add remaining ingredients to onions and mix well. Pour over shrimp; garnish with almonds and bake in a 350° oven for 35 minutes. May be prepared ahead and reheated.

MRS. BART ROACH

SHRIMP ROCKEFELLER

Serves: 6   Oven: 400°

2 lbs. shrimp, cooked and
   cleaned
½ cup butter
1½ tsp. Worcestershire
   sauce
1 tsp. salt
½ tsp. Accent
¼ tsp. Tabasco
1 tsp. celery salt
½ cup chopped green onions
½ cup chopped parsley

2 cloves garlic, minced
2 pkgs. frozen chopped
   spinach, thawed and
   drained
3 slices white bread, without
   crusts
¾ cup water
2 tsp. melted butter
½ cup dry bread crumbs
¼ cup grated Parmesan
   cheese

Melt ½ cup butter and blend in seasonings. Add onions, parsley, garlic, and spinach and sauté 10 minutes. Pour water over bread and break up. Add to vegetable mixture and stir. Arrange shrimp either in bottom of casserole or in individual dishes and cover with vegetable-bread mixture. Combine melted butter, crumbs, and cheese. Sprinkle mixture over top and bake at 400° for 15 minutes. May be refrigerated overnight before baking. If used as an appetizer it will serve 10 to 12.

MRS. ALBERT OTTEN

SHRIMP AND ARTICHOKE HEART CASSEROLE

Serves: 8-10   Oven: 350°

3 Tb. butter
3 Tb. flour
1 cup milk
1 cup heavy cream
½ tsp. paprika
¼ tsp. cayenne pepper
1 Tb. catsup
1 Tb. fresh lemon juice

1 cup grated cheese (sharp)
1 Tb. Worcestershire sauce
3 Tb. medium dry sherry
2 lbs. large shrimp, deveined,
   shelled and boiled about 3
   minutes or until pink
4 small cans artichoke hearts

Melt butter in heavy saucepan, add flour, stir in milk, then cream. As the mixture thickens, stir in paprika and cayenne pepper. Add catsup, lemon juice, grated cheese, Worcestershire sauce, and sherry. Remove from heat. Place shrimp on the bottom of a flat, oblong casserole or baking dish. Cut drained artichoke hearts in quarters (halves if they are small) and lay on top of the shrimp. Pour sauce over all and heat in 350° oven until bubbly hot. Sliced water chestnuts are a pleasant addition to this dish, for texture contrast, but add little to the flavor.

MRS. ROLLO RILLING

SHRIMP CREOLE

Serves: 12

5 lbs. raw shrimp, fresh or
    frozen
Onion
Salt
Garlic
Mustard seed
Dill seed
Black and red pepper
Celery
Lemon
¾ cup salad oil (¼ cup may
    be olive oil)
3 Tb. flour

1 large onion, sliced thin
2 cloves garlic, minced
½ lb. mushrooms, raw and
    sliced
1 bay leaf
2 tsp. oregano
2 tsp. chili powder
2 tsp. salt
1 to 2 tsp. black pepper
1 can tomato paste
2 bell peppers, sliced
1 small jar sliced pimientos

Drop shrimp into large kettle of boiling water that is well seasoned
with onion, salt, garlic, mustard seed, dill seed, black and red pepper,
celery and lemon. Bring to a second boil and cook for 5 minutes.
Clean shrimp and reserve stock. Using a heavy pot, make a roux by
heating oil and mixing in flour, stirring constantly until brown.
Add onion, garlic, and mushrooms. Continue cooking, stirring constantly, until mixture is slightly browned. Add shrimp and spices
and continue stirring until the shrimp is coated with roux. Add
tomato paste, green peppers and pimientos. Cook for 15 minutes
over moderate heat. Pour in 3 cups hot shrimp stock. Cook for 1
hour over low heat, adding more shrimp stock if desired. Best
served over hot rice.

MRS. A. JOSEPH JOHNSON, JR.

SHRIMP BAKE IN AVOCADO

Serves: 2   Oven: 300°

1 avocado
10-oz. pkg. of frozen shrimp
1 Tb. lemon juice
Celery leaves
4 Tb. butter
2 Tb. flour

½ cup heavy cream
Small can sliced mushrooms
2 Tb. sweet wine
½ cup Pepperidge Farm
    stuffing mix

Peel, split and slightly salt avocado. Boil shrimp for 1 minute in
salted water with lemon juice and celery leaves (don't overcook).
Drain. Melt butter, then add flour and cream to make a white sauce.
Cook a minute, then remove from heat. Add mushrooms, wine and
shrimp to the sauce. Pour over each avocado half and top each half
with Pepperidge Farm mix and heat thoroughly in 300° oven.

MRS. WILLIAM H. MCLEAN

SHRIMP JAMBALAYA

Serves: 6

½ cup butter	1 tsp. oregano
3 Tb. flour	2 tsp. salt
2 large onions, chopped	½ tsp. cayenne pepper
1 large bell pepper, chopped	2 tsp. black pepper
3 cloves garlic, chopped	½ tsp. coriander
5 ribs celery, chopped	2 bay leaves
1 lb. 12-oz. can whole	2 tsp. thyme
tomatoes, chopped	2 tsp. celery salt
16-oz. can whole tomatoes	1 tsp. ground cloves
½ cup chopped fresh parsley	¼ tsp. cardamon
¾ cup chopped ham	½ tsp. ground ginger
2 tsp. rosemary	2½ to 3 lbs. shrimp

Melt butter in heavy Dutch oven or roaster. Stir in flour; stir and cook until light brown and bubbly. Add onions, bell pepper, garlic and celery to flour roux and cook for about 20 minutes. Add tomatoes and juice, parsley, ham and all the seasonings. Stir occasionally, cover and simmer 2 to 3 hours. Just before serving, stir in shrimp and cook until shrimp are done. Serve over hot fluffy rice.

MRS. CHARLES M. NOLAN

DEVILED CRAB

Serves: 6   Oven: 375°

2 cups crab meat	½ tsp. salt
¼ cup sherry	1 tsp. dry mustard
1 tsp. Worcestershire sauce	2 cups light cream
3 egg yolks, beaten	½ cup buttered bread
3 Tb. butter	crumbs
2 Tb. flour	

Mix crab meat with sherry, Worcestershire sauce and egg yolks. Melt butter, stir in flour mixed with seasonings. Add cream and stir until thick. Gently add flaked crab and blend well. Fill shells, sprinkle with buttered crumbs and bake at 375° for 10 minutes.

Some recipes call for minced hard-boiled egg, minced parsley, lemon juice, horseradish. Their use depends on whether you like highly seasoned dishes. For the above recipe, use ½ teaspoon of horseradish, 2 tablespoons of lemon juice, 2 tablespoons of parsley or 2 hard-boiled eggs.

CRAB MEAT IMPERIAL

Serves: 6   Oven: 375°

3 6-oz. pkgs. frozen crab
  meat or 3 7½-oz. cans crab
  meat
2 Tb. butter
2 Tb. bell pepper, minced
2 Tb. flour
½ tsp. dry mustard

½ tsp. salt
⅛ tsp. paprika
½ cup light cream
½ cup mayonnaise
1 Tb. sherry
2 Tb. pimiento, minced

Melt butter in saucepan and lightly cook the green pepper. Blend in flour, mustard, salt and paprika. Cook for a minute and stir in cream. Remove from heat and add mayonnaise. Gently add crab meat, sherry and pimiento. Place in shells or casserole and bake in 375° oven for 15 to 20 minutes or until bubbly.

CRAB MEAT MORNAY

Serves: 6-8

8 Tb. butter
½ small bunch green onions,
  chopped
2 Tb. flour
10½-oz. can cream of mushroom soup
¾ cup milk

½ lb. Swiss cheese, grated
1 Tb. sherry
½ cup parsley, chopped fine
Salt and pepper
1 lb. crab meat
Toast points or shells

Melt butter in heavy pot. Sauté onions. Blend in flour. Add soup, milk, and cheese. Cook until cheese melts and sauce is smooth. Add other ingredients, gently fold in crab meat. Serve in chafing dish on toast points or in patty shells.

MRS. FRED W. TERRY

CRAB MEAT SYCAMORE

Serves: 8   Oven: 325°

2 lbs. white lump crab meat
  (4 cups)
¾ lb. Swiss cheese, diced
2 pkgs. frozen artichoke
  hearts, cooked and drained
3 Tb. butter
2 Tb. flour

1¼ cups milk
2 Tb. dry sherry
Hot sauce
Worcestershire sauce
Salt and pepper to taste
Bread crumbs

Alternate layers of crab, cheese, and artichokes in a greased 1½ quart casserole. Make a cream sauce by melting butter and adding the flour, stirring until smooth. Add milk a little at a time, cooking until thickened. Remove from heat and add sherry, hot sauce, Worcestershire, salt, and pepper to taste. Spoon cream sauce over top of casserole and sprinkle with bread crumbs. Bake uncovered at 325° 30 to 40 minutes or until bubbly.

MRS. DON F. HAMILTON

CRAB OR SHRIMP GAYLORD

Serves: 4   Oven: 350°

1 garlic clove, cut
2 lbs. lump crab meat or
  2 lbs. shrimp, cooked and
  cleaned
1½ cups small curd cottage
  cheese
2 Tb. dry sherry
1 Tb. grated Parmesan cheese

1 tsp. Worcestershire sauce
Monosodium glutamate
1 tsp. lemon juice
½ tsp. salt
¼ tsp. pepper
½ cup fine dry bread crumbs
1 Tb. thinly sliced almonds
Melted butter

Rub 4 sizable shells or ramkins with the cut garlic clove. Divide crab meat or shrimp among the four dishes. Combine thoroughly cottage cheese, sherry, Parmesan, Worcestershire, monosodium glutamate, lemon juice, salt, and pepper. Spread the mixture over the sea food. Sprinkle bread crumbs over the mixture to cover it completely and sprinkle the crumbs with melted butter. Bake in 350° oven until the cheese mixture is hot and begins to soften. Remove the dishes from oven and sprinkle the top of each with almonds. Return to oven and bake until almonds are lightly browned.

MRS. J. BRIAN FRAZIER

SEASHELL CRAB CASSEROLE

Serves: 4-6   Oven: 350°

7½-oz. can crab meat
1 cup uncooked shell
  macaroni
4 oz. Cheddar cheese, grated
2 hard-boiled eggs, chopped

10½-oz. can cream of mushroom soup
1 cup milk
1 Tb. chopped chives

Drain crab and combine all ingredients in 1 quart casserole. Cover and refrigerate at least 8 hours. Bake, covered, in 350° oven for one hour.

MRS. ROWE HILL

CRAB MEAT AND RICE CASSEROLE

Serves: 4-6   Oven: 325°

10½-oz. can cream of celery
  soup
¼ cup milk
½ tsp. salt
Worcestershire sauce
½ cup mayonnaise

7½-oz. can crab meat
1 cup cooked rice
1 whole chicken breast,
  cooked and cut up
Cracker crumbs

In saucepan, heat soup with milk. Blend in salt, Worcestershire and mayonnaise. Fold in drained crab meat, rice and diced chicken. Put in greased casserole. Bake at 325° for 20 minutes. Sprinkle on cracker crumbs and brown.

MRS. WILLIAM A. SAUNDERS, SR.

CRAB MEAT SALAD CASSEROLE

Serves: 6   Oven: 350°

2 7½-oz. cans crab meat   1 cup mayonnaise
¾ cup milk   1 tsp. salt
½ cup chopped onion   Pepper
6 hard-boiled eggs, chopped   1 cup croutons
1 cup croutons   6 Tb. butter

Mix together all ingredients except 2nd cup of croutons and butter.
Place in greased casserole or in 6 individual shells. Soak remaining
1 cup croutons in melted butter and place on top of mixture. Bake
at 350° until bubbly, about 20 minutes.

MRS. JACK EAST, JR.

DEVILED CORN AND CRAB MEAT

Serves: 6   Oven: 350°

4 Tb. butter   7½-oz. can crab meat
2 Tb. flour   2 hard-boiled eggs, chopped
1 tsp. prepared mustard   1 lb. can whole kernel corn
½ tsp. Worcestershire sauce   1 lb. can cream style corn
1 Tb. lemon juice   ½ cup grated Parmesan
½ tsp. monosodium gluta-   cheese
  mate   ½ cup cracker crumbs (14)
½ tsp. salt   1 Tb. butter, melted
Pepper   Hard-boiled eggs
½ cup milk   Olive slices

Melt 4 tablespoons butter in saucepan. Stir in flour, mustard,
Worcestershire, lemon juice, M.S.G., salt, and pepper. Add milk all
at once. Cook and stir until mixture is thickened and boiling. Carefully stir in crab meat (be sure all cartilage is removed), chopped
eggs, whole and cream corn. Spoon into a 1½ quart casserole.
Sprinkle cheese over top. Combine cracker crumbs and the tablespoon melted butter. Sprinkle over cheese. Bake in 350° oven for
45 minutes. Garnish with hard-boiled eggs and olive slices. Also
makes nice individual casseroles.

MRS. EUGENE J. WALTER

WINKUM

Serves: 6

½ cup melted butter   1 small jar pimientos
1 cup grated sharp cheese   ½ onion, chopped
1 can tomato soup   ½ cup heavy cream
7½-oz. can crab meat   1 egg, beaten
10½-oz. pkg. shrimp

Cook in double boiler, adding ingredients in order given above,
except for egg. Cook 20 minutes. When almost ready to remove
from fire, add beaten egg. Serve in patty shells.

MRS. GEORGE RYLAND
PINE BLUFF, ARKANSAS

BAKED CRAB MEAT SANDWICH

Serves: 10   Oven: 400°

20 slices sandwich bread
2 7½-oz. cans crab meat
1 small can mushrooms,
  sliced
⅔ cup mayonnaise

2 5-oz. jars Old English
  cheese
1 cup butter
2 raw eggs

Trim crusts from bread and fill with mixture of crab meat, drained mushrooms, and mayonnaise. Cream together cheese, butter, and eggs in mixer until fluffy. Frost sides and tops of sandwiches generously. Place, not too close together, on cookie sheet and refrigerate for 12 hours. Bake at 400° for 12 to 15 minutes. May be frozen; let thaw 2 hours before baking.

MRS. CRAIG WOOD

CRAB-SHRIMP PIE WITH BECHAMEL SAUCE

Serves: 6   Oven: 325°

BECHAMEL SAUCE:

⅓ cup butter
⅓ cup flour
3 cups hot milk
1 tsp. salt
¼ tsp. pepper

¼ tsp. nutmeg
1 cup grated Gruyere cheese
  (Swiss, or Mozzarella may
  be used)

Melt butter in saucepan. Stir flour in smoothly; cook a few more minutes. Gradually add milk and seasonings and stir well. Cook slowly for 25 minutes stirring gently but steadily until sauce is thick and smooth. Add cheese and allow to melt.

PIE FILLING:

1½ cups frozen lump crab
  meat
1½ cups shrimp (fresh are
  best), cooked
¾ cup fresh sliced mush-
  rooms
3 Tb. butter
1 Tb. parsley

1 Tb. grated onion
1 tsp. nutmeg
2 Tb. dry vermouth
3 cups Bechamel sauce
9-inch unbaked pie shell
1 Tb. cracked black pepper
Paprika

Line a greased 9-inch pie pan with your favorite pastry. Bake 5 minutes in 325° oven. In a large bowl mix crab meat, shrimp, and mushrooms browned in 3 tablespoons butter. Add parsley, onion, nutmeg, vermouth and one tablespoon cracked black pepper. Mix with Bechamel sauce and fill pastry. Sprinkle with paprika for color. Bake covered for 20 minutes in a 350° oven.

MRS. DAVID SNOWDEN

CRAB SUPPER PIE

Serves: 6   Oven: 325°

1 cup natural Swiss cheese,   3 eggs, beaten
  shredded   1 cup light cream
9-inch unbaked pie shell   ½ tsp. salt
7½-oz. can crab meat,   ½ tsp. lemon peel, grated
  drained and flaked   ¼ tsp. dry mustard
2 green onions and tops,   Dash of mace
  sliced   ¼ cup sliced almonds

Sprinkle cheese evenly over bottom of pastry shell. Top with crab
meat; sprinkle with onions. Combine eggs, cream, salt, lemon peel,
dry mustard, and mace. Pour over crab meat. Top with almonds.
Bake at 325° for 45 minutes or until set. Remove from oven and let
stand 10 minutes before serving.

MRS. HESTER MEYER

CRAB PIE

Serves: 6   Oven: 375°

Pastry shell, baked 4 to 5   1 Tb. cracked black pepper
  minutes   2 Tb. grated onion
4 cups frozen or canned crab   Salt
  meat   1 Tb. butter
2 cans cream of shrimp soup   Gruyere cheese
¼ cup heavy cream   Slivered almonds
1 tsp. parsley   4 Tb. butter
2 Tb. dry vermouth   Paprika

Thaw crab meat if frozen. Drain. Mix shrimp soup with cream.
Add parsley, vermouth, pepper, salt and onion, that has been sautéed
in butter. Mix with crab meat. Add more cream if mixture seems
too dry. Place in pastry shell that has been baked 4 to 5 minutes
in a 375° oven. Sprinkle cheese, almonds, butter, paprika on top.
Bake at 350°, covered with foil, for 10 minutes. Remove foil and
bake until crust is brown. (Does not set.)

MRS. DAVID SNOWDEN

SCALLOPS NEWBURG

Serves: 4

1 pt. scallops   2 slightly beaten egg yolks
2 Tb. butter   ½ tsp. salt
1½ tsp. flour   Few grains cayenne
½ cup heavy cream   Patty shells
2 Tb. sherry

Cook scallops in their own juice for 3 minutes. Add butter and
cook 5 minutes more. Shake flour and cream together in a small
jar until well blended; add slowly to scallops, stirring constantly,
until sauce boils. Stir in sherry and egg yolks. Cook 1 minute.
Remove from heat and serve in patty shells or over toast.

MRS. DON HAMILTON

CREPES OF CRAB MEAT MARYLAND

Serves: 8

2 Tb. butter
2 Tb. minced green onions
1 small garlic clove, minced
2 Tb. flour
½ cup canned tomato sauce
2 13-oz. cans lobster bisque
½ tsp. leaf tarragon

3 7½-oz. cans lump crab
   meat
16 crepes
3 Tb. grated Parmesan
   cheese
Parsley sprigs

Melt butter in 10-inch skillet over low heat; add green onion and garlic; cook one minute. Stir in flour; add tomato sauce, lobster bisque and tarragon; bring to boil, stirring occasionally. Simmer 5 to 8 minutes. Correct seasoning. Remove and reserve one cup of sauce for glazing. Add crab meat to sauce remaining in skillet, stirring gently so as not to break crab meat lumps; simmer 10 minutes. Remove from heat. Place about 3 tablespoons of mixture on each crepe; roll into cylinder shape. Arrange crepes on an oven proof platter. Spoon reserved sauce over crepes. Sprinkle with Parmesan. Broil until golden brown. Garnish with parsley.

MRS. MONROE FRANK

STUFFED LOBSTER TAILS THERMIDOR

Serves: 6   Oven: 350°

6 lobsters tails (8-10 oz.)
4 Tb. butter
1 small onion, minced
1 cup mushrooms, sliced
4 Tb. flour
1½ cups milk
1 cup heavy cream
1 tsp. dry mustard
1 tsp. celery salt

1½ tsp. salt
Dash of cayenne
2 egg yolks, beaten
1½ cups mild Cheddar
   cheese, grated
4 Tb. sherry
1 Tb. lemon juice
½ cup buttered bread crumbs

Clean lobster tails and boil as directed on package. Let stand in water 10 minutes after finished. Remove meat from shells and cut in bite-size pieces. Set shells aside. Sauté onions and mushrooms in butter. Blend in flour and add milk slowly. Cook until thick. Add cream and seasonings. Add a little sauce to eggs and then eggs to sauce. Add 1 cup cheese, sherry, lemon juice, and lobster. Fill shells. Sprinkle top with buttered crumbs and remaining ½ cup of cheese. Place on cookie tray and bake at 350° for 15 minutes or until heated through.

MRS. JAMES K. HAMILTON

ASPARAGUS WITH LOBSTER SAUCE

Serves: 4-6

1 frozen rock lobster tail
  (about 8-oz.)
Boiling salted water
20 to 30 medium sized fresh
  asparagus spears

4 Tb. melted butter
2 Tb. brandy
½ cup heavy cream
Salt to taste

Cook lobster tail in boiling salted water according to the package directions. Remove meat from shell and cut in crosswise slices. Lay asparagus spears flat in a wide shallow pan or skillet in just enough boiling salted water to cover. Cook until spears are tender when pierced with the tip of a sharp knife; drain. Add butter and shake pan gently to rotate and coat the spears. Take from pan and group in sets of five, tips pointing in the same direction. Heat lobster slices in the same butter. Warm brandy and pour over lobster; flame. Remove lobster slices and arrange over spears. Add cream to the pan and boil very rapidly, until thickened (3 to 4 minutes). Pour over asparagus and lobster. Serve immediately.

COQUILLES SAINT JACQUES

Serves: 8   Oven: Broiler

1 tsp. lemon juice
½ tsp. salt
2 lbs. scallops
4 Tb. butter
¼ cup finely chopped onions
¼ lb. or 3-oz. can mush-
  rooms, sliced
⅓ cup flour
Salt and pepper

1 cup light cream
½ cup milk
1 cup Swiss or Gruyere
  cheese, grated
½ cup dry white wine
1 Tb. lemon juice
1 Tb. parsley
½ cup buttered bread crumbs

Cook scallops in 1 cup water, lemon juice and salt. Simmer 6 minutes. Drain. In butter, sauté onions and mushrooms until tender (5 minutes). Remove from heat. Stir in flour, salt and pepper until blended. Add cream and milk. Bring to boil, reduce heat and simmer until quite thick. Add cheese; stir until melted. Add wine, lemon juice, parsley and scallops. Turn into 8 scallop shells or 1½ quart casserole. Sprinkle bread crumbs over top. Broil 4 inches from heat until golden brown—2 or 3 minutes.

MRS. BART ROACH

OYSTERS ON THE HALF SHELL—HOW TO OPEN

Raw oysters that have been opened just before serving are judged to be at their best. Shucking should be done by a strong hand with a sturdy instrument. But, there is a trick . . . and it works. Scrub your oysters well under running water with a stiff vegetable brush. Then put your oysters on a cookie sheet in a moderately hot oven, 400°, for 5 or 6 minutes depending upon their size. Remove from oven and drop into ice water. The heat relaxes the muscle and they can be opened very easily with a table knife. The shell is so heavy, the heat does not affect the oyster at all. Oysters to be eaten raw are left loose in the deeper half of the shell, arranged on a chilled plate and served with a cut lemon and freshly ground pepper.

MRS. CHARLES M. NOLAN

CREOLE OYSTERS

Serves: 12

½ slice bacon, minced
1½ tsp. onion, chopped
1 Tb. parsley
1 Tb. butter
2 tsp. flour
½ tsp. salt

½ tsp. pepper
1 cup light cream
Oyster liquor
4 doz. oysters, cut in 4 parts
Cracker crumbs

Fry bacon. Add onion and parsley. Cook until soft. Melt butter. Add flour, salt and pepper. Add cream and oyster liquor, bacon, onion and parsley. Thicken slightly. Add oysters. Put in shells and cover with cracker crumbs. Serve very hot.

MRS. ROBERT EUBANKS

SCALLOPED OYSTERS

Serves: 8   Oven: 350°

2 pts. fresh oysters
1 cup cracker crumbs
Salt
Pepper

4 Tb. butter
1 cup light cream
½ cup liquid from oysters

Drain oysters, save ½ cup liquid. Grease a 1 quart casserole dish. Layer the ingredients, putting ⅓ of the crumbs on the bottom, then ½ of the oysters, sprinkling them with salt and pepper. Dot with butter. Repeat, ending with cracker crumbs. Dot with rest of butter. Pour over light cream and oyster liquid. Bake uncooked in a 350° oven for 40 to 45 minutes, until golden and bubbly.

MRS. WILLIAM P. BOND, JR.

LULLA'S OYSTERS

Serves: 4   Oven: 350°

1 pt. oysters
1 cup celery, chopped
1 onion, chopped
4 Tb. butter
Thyme
Bay leaf

Salt
1 can cream of mushroom
  soup
4 hard-boiled eggs
Bread crumbs

Cook oysters in own liquid until sides curl. Sauté celery and onion in butter. Add other ingredients adding oysters and liquid last. Put in casserole, top with crumbs. Bake uncovered about 12 minutes in a 350° oven.

MRS. HENRY MENTZ
HAMMOND, LOUISIANA

OYSTERS DUNBAR

Serves: 6   Oven: 450°

3 artichokes (whole)
1½ Tb. flour
3 Tb. butter
¾ tsp. salt
¾ tsp. pepper
¼ tsp. hot sauce
½ tsp. thyme

2 doz. oysters and oyster
  liquor
1 oz. sherry
¾ cup cracker crumbs
Butter
Paprika

Boil artichokes until very tender—1½ hours. Scrape leaves and mash hearts. Brown flour in butter, add seasonings, oyster liquor and artichoke mixture. Broil oysters in butter until they curl. Mix with other ingredients. Add sherry. Place in ramekins or shells, top with crumbs, dot with butter, sprinkle with paprika. Heat in 450° oven for 10 minutes or until mixture is bubbling and crumbs brown.

MRS. BART ROACH

STUFFED OYSTERS

Serves: 3   Oven: 425°

1 doz. oysters
7-oz. can crab meat
1 Tb. minced green onion
¼ cup mayonnaise

½ tsp. salt
¼ tsp. dry mustard
¼ tsp. Tabasco
½ cup bread crumbs

Place 4 oysters, well drained, on bottom of ramekin or shell. Combine other ingredients except crumbs. Place a heaping tablespoon over each oyster. Sprinkle crumbs on top. Heat in 425° oven about 12 minutes or until moisture around edge of shells is bubbly. Do not overcook. Serve with lemon wedges.

This is a good luncheon or first course dish.

MRS. DAN COTTON

WHITE CLAM SAUCE FOR SPAGHETTI

Serves: 6-8

1 large onion, finely chopped
½ cup olive oil
3 garlic cloves, crushed
1 can whole baby clams

¼ cup chopped parsley
½ tsp. cracked pepper
½ tsp. crushed red pepper
Pinch dried basil

In saucepan, sauté onion in hot oil until soft; add garlic and cook one minute. Add clams with juice and other ingredients. Salt to taste, simmer 30 minutes on very low heat, toss with one pound cooked spaghetti.

MRS. CHARLES McKENZIE

SALMON CROQUETTES

Serves: 6-8

4 Tb. margarine
5 Tb. flour
½ tsp. salt
1 cup milk
2 cups salmon, flaked
1 tsp. lemon juice

½ tsp. onion juice
Dash pepper
½ cup fine bread crumbs
2 eggs, slightly beaten
2 Tb. water
Cooking oil

Melt margarine in top of double boiler or heavy saucepan. Add flour and salt and blend. Add milk and cook until smooth and thick, stirring constantly. Remove from fire. Add salmon, lemon juice, onion juice, and pepper. Blend well. Spread mixture in shallow pan and chill until stiff. Cut into cutlets with 2½-inch biscuit cutter or shape into patties with hands. Roll in crumbs, then in eggs beaten with water, then in crumbs. Fry in hot shortening (375°) 1-inch deep in heavy frying pan until brown. Drain on paper towels.

MRS. G. BURNS NEWBILL
BENTON, ARKANSAS

SALMON SOUFFLE

Serves: 4   Oven: 350°

2 tsp. chopped onion
2 tsp. butter
2 tsp. flour
⅛ tsp. salt
Dash pepper
Dash nutmeg

½ cup milk
2 beaten egg yolks
1-lb. can salmon, drained and
     flaked
2 beaten egg whites

Sauté onion in butter. Stir in flour and seasonings. Add milk gradually, stirring until it boils. After 1 minute remove from fire. Stir in egg yolks and salmon. Fold salmon mixture into stiffly beaten egg whites. Put in 1 quart casserole. Bake at 350° for 25 minutes. Serve immediately.

MRS. NELS STAVENAS
MINNEAPOLIS, MINNESOTA

SALMON LOAF

Serves: 4-6   Oven: 350°

1-lb. can salmon, drained
2 eggs, slightly beaten
1 tsp. salt
1 tsp. prepared mustard
2 cups whole wheat bread
   crumbs

Pepper to taste
½ cup shredded Cheddar
   cheese
1 Tb. melted butter
1 cup milk

Combine all ingredients and mix thoroughly. Turn into well greased loaf pan and bake 30 minutes in 350° oven. Serve with white sauce or catsup.

MRS. STANLEY BRADSHAW

CHOPSTICK TUNA

Serves: 4   Oven: 375°

1 can cream of mushroom
   soup, undiluted
¼ cup water
3-oz. can Chow Mein noodles
6½-oz. can tuna fish
1 cup chopped celery

¼ cup chopped onion
8-oz. pkg. cashew nuts
Mandarin oranges for
   garnish
Parsley

Combine soup and ¼ cup water. Add 1 cup chow mein noodles, tuna, celery, onions and nuts. Place in ungreased 10 x 6 x 1½-inch baking dish; sprinkle remaining noodles (1 cup) over top. Bake in preheated 375° oven until bubbly. Garnish with a ring of mandarin orange sections and a cluster of parsley.

Variation: Add 6-oz. can water chestnuts, sliced and drained, and a 16-oz. can Chinese vegetables, drained.

MRS. A. HOWARD STEBBINS, III

BAKED SOLE

Serves: 4   Oven: 350°

4 small Sole
2 Tb. butter
1 Tb. onion, chopped
3 Tb. parsley, chopped
Salt

Freshly ground pepper
½ cup dry white wine
¼ lb. small mushroom caps
Bread crumbs
Lemon slices

Prepare the Sole by removing the black skin only. Put butter in large shallow oven-proof platter. Place the Sole on platter and spread with onions and parsley. Sprinkle with salt and pepper. Moisten Sole with wine and mushroom caps (which have been thoroughly washed). Cover with bread crumbs, dot with butter and bake in 350° oven for 30 minutes. Serve with lemon slices. (Frozen fillet of Flounder, Haddock or Cod may be substituted for the Sole.)

MRS. SAM KUYKENDALL

FISH FILLETS PROVENCIAL

Serves: 4   Oven: 350°

2 Tb. butter	1 Tb. basil
6 mushrooms, sliced	1 small clove garlic
1 onion, sliced	Salt and freshly ground
1 carrot, chopped	pepper
4 ripe tomatoes, cut up	4 fish fillets
2 Tb. chopped chives	

In skillet, melt butter and sauté mushrooms for a few minutes. Add onion, carrot, tomatoes, herbs, garlic, salt and pepper to taste. Simmer for 10 minutes. Remove garlic. Place fillets in buttered baking dish 8 x 10-inch ; pour sauce over them. Bake in 350° oven for 20 to 30 minutes, or until the fish flakes.

MRS. DONALD THOMPSON

SHRIMP SAUCE FOR FLOUNDER

Serves: 8

2 Tb. butter	2 cups milk
2 Tb. chopped onion	2 egg yolks
2 Tb. chopped celery	Salt and pepper to taste
2 Tb. grated raw carrot	1 Tb. lemon juice
3 Tb. flour	2 cups cooked shrimp

Melt butter in top of double boiler over heat. Put in vegetables and stir. Add flour, blend; add milk; stir constantly until thick. Add beaten egg yolk, stirring vigorously. Salt and pepper to taste, and stir in lemon juice. Add cleaned, cooked whole shrimp. Keep warm until ready to serve. Pour over broiled flounder on large platter. Garnish with parsley.

MRS. BUFORD BRACY

CHARCOAL BROILED FISH

The proportions for this recipe vary with number of fish, size, and your particular taste. A very general guide would be to melt about ¼ cup of butter in a saucepan ; add 2 tablespoons of lemon juice and seasonings such as lemon-pepper marinade, seasoned salt, and pepper. Several hours before grilling, coat the chilled fish with the seasoned melted butter. Butter will congeal on fish. Refrigerate fish. Place heavy foil on grill and punch holes in it so that charcoal flavor can penetrate fish. Place fish on foil and baste as it cooks with remaining seasoned butter. Fish cooks quickly so do not overcook! Watch for flesh to turn white and flake.

SOUTHERN FRIED CATFISH

Serves: 6-8

3 lbs. catfish fillets
2 cups yellow corn meal
Salt and pepper

3 inches cooking oil in a deep
fat fryer

Wash and drain fillets. Salt and pepper. Place corn meal and fish in a large plastic bag and shake until fish is well coated. Preheat oil and cook fish at 350° until fish is brown on both sides, turning only once.

YOUNG'S FISH AND SEA FOOD

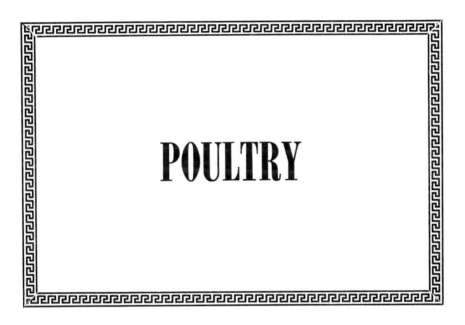

POULTRY

MARIE'S KENTUCKY FRIED CHICKEN

Serves: 4

1 fryer, cut up, 2½ or 3 lbs.	¼ tsp. pepper
3 cups water	1 cup flour
1 Tb. salt	Salad oil for frying
2 tsp. fines herbs*	Chicken broth (recipe
2 tsp. onion powder	follows)
2 envelopes instant chicken	Chicken gravy (recipe
broth	follows)
2 tsp. seasoned salt	

Cover cut up chicken in salt water in medium size bowl and chill for 1 hour. Make a fine powder of fines herbs, onion powder, seasoned salt, instant chicken broth, and pepper with electric blender or mortar and pestle. Combine herbs with flour in a plastic bag. Remove chicken from water one piece at a time and shake in flour mixture while still wet (save salt water for later use). Coat thickly with flour. Pour enough salad oil in skillet to make 1 inch deep and heat to 375°. Fry chicken pieces 5 minutes on each side. Turn with slotted spoon. Drain on paper towel. Remove oil from skillet (don't wash) and add 1 cup chicken broth to skillet (recipe below). Return chicken to skillet. Cover and cook 20 minutes. Keep warm in oven while making gravy.

CHICKEN BROTH:
Place salted water, in which chicken soaked, in a pan. Add chicken giblets, 2 onion slices, several celery tops. Cover and simmer 30 minutes. Makes about 3 cups.

CHICKEN GRAVY:
Strain remaining 2 cups of chicken broth and add to skillet in which chicken was cooked. Heat to boiling while stirring and scraping baked-on juices from side and bottom of pan. Make paste of 4 tablespoons flour and ½ cup cold water in a small cup. Stir into boiling liquid. Continue stirring for 1 minute. Salt and pepper to taste. Add chopped giblets if desired and simmer 2 minutes longer.

*This is a premixed blend available in the spice section.

MRS. CHARLES A. VINES, JR.

POLLO EN JUGO DE NARANJA

Serves: 3-4   Oven: 325°

1 frying chicken, disjointed	½ cup blanched ground
Seasoned flour	almonds
Oil for frying	½ cup crushed pineapple
1 cup orange juice	2 Tb. sugar
1 cup white wine	¼ tsp. cinnamon
½ cup raisins	⅛ tsp. cloves

Dredge chicken with seasoned flour. Brown in oil. Place chicken in shallow glass baking dish. Combine all other ingredients and pour over chicken. Bake at 325°, basting often, for 30 minutes. Raise temperature to 350° and bake 15 minutes longer.

MRS. HAMILTON WEBRE

SESAME CHICKEN FONDUE

Serves: 6-8

1 egg
½ cup water
¾ tsp. salt
2 tsp. sesame seeds
½ cup flour

4 whole chicken breasts,
boned and cut in bite-size
pieces
1 quart oil

Mix egg, water, salt, seeds and flour. Dip chicken pieces in batter and drain. Fill skillet ⅓ full of oil, heat to 375° and cook one layer at a time. Fry 3 to 5 minutes until golden. Serve with sauces.

DILL SAUCE:

1 cup sour cream
½ cup mayonnaise

1 tsp. dill weed
2 Tb. dill pickle relish

PINEAPPLE SAUCE:

½ cup pineapple preserves
2 Tb. mustard

2 Tb. horseradish

ROYALTY SAUCE:

1 cup catsup
½ tsp. mustard
1 Tb. brown sugar

2 Tb. vinegar
½ cup oil

Cook 5 minutes.

CHICKEN INDIENNE

Serves: 8   Oven: 350°

1 Tb. butter
1 3-lb. frying chicken or
  3 lbs. chicken parts
1 onion coarsely chopped
1 bell pepper, seeded and
  chopped
2 cups chicken stock or
  canned chicken broth

2 Tb. lemon juice
1⅓ cups ready to use
  mincemeat
1 tsp. salt
Dash pepper
1 cup uncooked long grain
  rice
1 Tb. curry powder

Melt butter and brown chicken for 15 minutes on all sides. Remove chicken and in same skillet sauté onion and green pepper until shiny. Add lemon juice, chicken stock, mincemeat, salt, pepper, rice, and curry powder. Mix well, then turn mixture into buttered 2½ quart baking dish. Arrange browned chicken pieces over rice mixture and cover. Bake at 350° for an hour.

For fancy occasion, small lotus bowls can be added filled individually with chutney, chopped peanuts, sieved egg yolks, golden raisins, and bacon bits.

CAMPING CHICKEN

Serves: 1   Oven: 350°

½ fryer chicken per person   Salt
1 small white onion per   Pepper
  person   Aluminum foil
4 Tb. butter

For each person, wrap ½ chicken, 1 onion, butter, salt, and pepper
in a generous sheet of aluminum foil. Fasten ends and center fold
tightly. Handle carefully and do not puncture foil. Place in 350°
oven or on campfire and bake for 45 minutes or more. For a complete dinner, a potato, zucchini, carrots, etc., may be added to
packet.

DR. J. B. GOFF, JR.
TEXARKANA, ARKANSAS

CHICKEN CHABLIS

Serves: 4   Oven: 350°

5 Tb. butter   2 chicken breasts, halved
3-oz. can mushrooms   ⅔ cup dry white wine
Flour   (Chablis, Vermouth)
Salt and pepper to taste   Sliced Swiss cheese

Melt 2 tablespoons butter in a skillet, stir in drained mushrooms
and cook for 5 minutes over low heat. Remove mushrooms from
skillet; lightly flour, salt and pepper chicken breasts. Add 3 more
tablespoons butter to skillet and brown chicken breasts. Remove
chicken from skillet and add wine to skillet and bring to boil while
scraping bottom and sides of pan. Stir mushrooms in and remove
from heat. Place chicken breasts skin side down in a casserole dish.
Pour wine and mushrooms over and bake uncovered for 35 minutes
in 350° oven. Turn chicken up, spoon mushrooms over and top with
thin slices of Swiss cheese. Bake 15 minutes longer, basting
frequently.

MRS. HENRY RECTOR

SAUTÉED CHICKEN SUPREME

Serves: 8

8 chicken breasts   1 cup chicken stock
½ cup butter   1 pt. sour cream
2 Tb. brandy   2 Tb. Parmesan cheese
1 tsp. tomato paste   1 Tb. lemon rind
2 Tb. flour

Sauté chicken in butter in skillet until brown. Pour brandy over
chicken. Remove breasts, add tomato paste and flour to the butter.
Gradually add stock and cook until thickened. Add sour cream,
Parmesan cheese and lemon rind. Do not boil. Place chicken back
in skillet with sauce and simmer, covered, for 45 minutes. Serve
with rice.

MRS. ROBERT G. CRESS

CHICKEN KIEV

Serves: 4-6

4 chicken breasts, whole	Flour
Salt	2 eggs, beaten
8 Tb. green onion, chopped	1 cup dry bread crumbs
8 Tb. fresh parsley, chopped	Deep, hot fat—340°
¼ lb. chilled butter	Lemon wedges

Cut chicken breasts lengthwise in half. Remove skin and bone (try not to tear meat) and place each piece between two pieces of waxed paper. With wooden mallet, pound until ¼-inch thick. Peel off wrap and sprinkle with salt and 1 tablespoon each of green onion and parsley. Cut butter into 8 pieces. Place at end of each cutlet and roll like jellyroll, tucking in sides. Press to seal well. Dust with flour and dip in beaten egg, then roll in dry bread crumbs. Chill at least one hour. Fry in deep, hot fat (340°) for about 5 minutes or until golden brown. Serve with lemon wedges.

MRS. DONALD F. THOMPSON, JR.

STUFFED CHICKEN BREASTS

Serves: 4   Oven: 300°

4 whole chicken breasts, boned	Olive oil
	1 small can mushrooms
Salt and pepper to taste	4 slices bacon
1 tsp. tarragon	½ to 1 cup vermouth
¼ cup finely chopped onion	Marinated artichoke hearts
½ cup chopped celery	

Flatten chicken breasts with mallet. Sprinkle each with salt and pepper and ¼ teaspoon tarragon on each. Sauté onion and celery in olive oil, which just covers bottom of skillet, until onion is just transparent. Add mushrooms and toss lightly; remove from heat. Divide the onion mixture equally among breasts, spread on half of flattened breast and fold other side over. Wrap a slice of bacon around the breast and secure with toothpick. Place chicken in a baking dish and pour vermouth over. Place in oven and cook at 300° for one hour or until chicken is done. Cover chicken with aluminum foil while baking. Baste frequently. When chicken is done, remove foil and allow chicken to brown. Serve on warm platter with marinated artichoke hearts.

MRS. ROBERT C. LOWRY

GIPSEY'S STUFFED CHICKEN

Serves: 6   Oven: 325°

3 broilers   2 Tb. butter
1 cup heavy cream   ½ cup blanched almonds,
Salt and pepper to taste   ground
½ to ¾ cup dry white wine   Finely chopped parsley
½ lb. mushrooms

Split broilers in half. Take about ¼ cup of cream and rub it into
the chicken thoroughly, sides and cavity as well as the outside.
Sprinkle with salt and pepper. Cover the bottom of a baking pan or
large casserole with wine to a depth of about ¼ inch. Arrange
chicken pieces in pan, breast side down, using two pans if necessary. Place in 325° oven and bake, basting several times, about 50
to 60 minutes or until done. Chop mushrooms fine and sauté lightly
in butter. Add remaining cream and ground almonds. Give the
almond meat a minute or two to puff up and drop spoonfuls of the
mixture into chicken cavities. Sprinkle with parsley. Turn oven
down to very low (250°) and let chicken hold until ready to serve.

MRS. PAUL P. ATKINSON, SR.

SESAME CHICKEN

Serves: 6-8   Oven: 350°

8 chicken breasts or   ½ cup soy sauce
  2 broilers, quartered   2 tsp. powdered ginger
Lemon juice   1 tsp. monosodium glutamate
4 cloves garlic, chopped   (Accent)
1 cup salad oil   ¾ cup sesame seeds

Place chicken in large bowl and sprinkle with lemon juice. Mix
chopped garlic with salad oil, soy sauce, ginger and monosodium
glutamate. Pour mixture over chicken and marinate for 30 minutes.
Remove from oil mixture; brown in heavy skillet; then coat each
piece with seeds; add marinade and bake in 350° oven 1½ hours or
until tender. Baste from time to time with marinade.

FOR OUTDOOR BARBEQUE:

Cut 8 large squares of foil. Top each chicken with 1 tablespoon
marinade. Wrap tightly; arrange on grill and cook 45 to 60 minutes
or until tender. Unwrap, coat pieces with seeds and put on grill
until seeds are golden brown.

MRS. ROBERT CARNAHAN

CHICKEN RICHELIEU

Serves: 4

4 boned whole chicken   ½ lb. chicken livers
    breasts   ¼ cup flour
¼ cup butter   1 pt. brown sauce
2 cloves garlic, crushed   1 Tb. parsley, chopped
4 green onions, chopped   ½ cup claret
¼ lb. mushrooms   Salt and pepper

Brown chicken breasts in butter. Remove from pan. Brown garlic, onions, mushrooms and livers. Add flour and stir. Add brown sauce, parsley, claret and salt and pepper to taste. Return chicken and simmer until tender.

BROWN SAUCE:

1½ Tb. clarified butter   2 cups consomme,
1½ Tb. flour   undiluted

Melt butter, add flour. Cook slowly over low heat until blended and slightly browned. Add consomme gradually. Bring to a boil and cook 3 to 5 minutes, stirring constantly. Simmer gently for 30 minutes. Makes 2 cups.

MRS. COOPER RILEY

BROILED CHICKEN TEMPLE BELLS

Serves: 8   Oven: Broil

1 cup salad oil   4 small broilers, split
6 Tb. vinegar   Softened butter
1 tsp. salt   Sliced bananas
2 small cloves garlic, peeled   Radish flowers
1 cup mango chutney   Link sausages

Mix first five ingredients in blender to make basting sauce. Place chicken halves, skin side down, on broiler pan 7 inches from broiler. Baste alternately with butter and chutney basting sauce until brown; turn and repeat. When chicken is brown, remove from broiler and bake at 350° until tender (20 minutes or so). Baste frequently and, if desired, cover with foil and keep in low oven (250°) until ready to serve. (They will stay moist if tightly covered.) Serve over curried rice and garnish with sliced bananas, radish flowers and link sausages.

MRS. F. WILLIAM TERRY, JR.

CHICKEN WITH CHIPPED BEEF

Serves: 6 Oven: 300°

1 small jar of chipped beef
6 slices bacon
6 chicken breasts, boned
Pepper to taste
1 can cream of mushroom
  soup

1 pt. sour cream
3-oz. pkg. cream cheese
1 medium can sliced button
  mushrooms
¼ cup dry sauterne

Place chipped beef (no salt), crumbled, in bottom of buttered casserole; wrap bacon around the chicken breasts and sprinkle with pepper. Lay chicken breasts in casserole. Combine soup, sour cream and cream cheese in a blender or electric mixer. Stir in mushrooms and pour mixture over chicken breasts in casserole. Cover with foil and cook in 300° oven for two hours. Remove foil and add sauterne and cook for one more hour.

MRS. M. J. KILBURY, JR.

CHICKEN BREASTS WITH SHRIMP SAUCE

Serves: 6-8 Oven: 350°

4 chicken breasts, split
¼ cup milk

4 Tb. butter.

Place 4 chicken breasts (8 pieces) in roasting pan and pour ¼ cup milk over them. Place ½ tablespoon butter on each piece. Cover and bake in 350° oven for 1 hour and 15 minutes.

SHRIMP SAUCE:

3 Tb. butter
⅓ cup flour
1 cup milk
¼ tsp. salt
⅛ tsp. pepper
1 tsp. paprika

1 cup cooked shrimp, cut in
  small pieces
1 can (2½-oz.) mushrooms
¼ cup dry white wine or
  sherry
1 Tb. Worcestershire sauce

About 15 minutes before chicken is done, make cream sauce by melting 3 tablespoons butter over low heat. Gradually stir in flour, then slowly stir in 1 cup milk. Blend together until smooth and cook until thickened. Add salt and pepper, then add cooked shrimp, mushrooms (drained), paprika, wine and Worcestershire sauce. Cook and stir over low heat about 10 minutes. Place 2 pieces of chicken breast on plate and spoon sauce over top.

MRS. MONROE FRANK, II

CHICKEN PARISIENNE

Serves: 12   Oven: 450°-375°

12 small chicken breasts,   ¼ cup lemon juice
  boned   2 Tb. Worcestershire sauce
2 8-oz. jars currant jelly   2 tsp. allspice
1 Tb. cornstarch   3 tsp. salt
1 cup water   1 tsp. pepper

Put chicken in uncovered roaster. Mix remaining ingredients in
saucepan and bring to a boil, then simmer 5 minutes. Remove from
fire and pour over chicken. Bake in 450° oven for 15 minutes, then
reduce to 375° and bake for 1 hour, basting frequently. Serve the
sauce separately.

MRS. JOHN J. TRUEMPER, JR.

CHICKEN WITH PECANS

Serves: 6   Oven: 350°

1 frying chicken (cut up)   1 cup chopped pecans
½ cup butter   ¼ cup sesame seeds
1 cup buttermilk   ¾ tsp. salt
1 egg, slightly beaten   1 Tb. paprika
1 cup flour   ½ tsp. pepper

In large shallow baking dish melt butter. In flat bowl combine
buttermilk and egg, slightly beaten. In another bowl mix flour,
pecans, sesame seeds and seasonings. Dip chicken pieces first in
milk mixture then in flour mixture. Put skin side down in butter
and turn so that chicken is coated with butter. Arrange skin side
up and bake 1½ hours, uncovered, at 350°. Baste 2 or 3 times.

MRS. ROBERT GLISSON
MEMPHIS, TENNESSEE

CHICKEN KOREAN

Serves: 4-6   Broiler

½ cup olive oil   ½ tsp. pepper
½ cup soy sauce   ½ tsp. dry mustard
½ cup dry white table wine   2 tsp. gingerroot
½ cup sliced green onions   6 chicken breasts, boned and
2 cloves garlic, mashed   cut in half

Combine all ingredients and pour over chicken breasts. Marinate
several hours, covered in the refrigerator. Turn several times.
Place in glass casserole with the marinade. Broil 3 inches from
heat, 15 minutes on each side, until tender. Serve with rice that has
pineapple chunks cooked in butter mixed with it.

MRS. DAVID KANE

BREAST OF CHICKEN HONDURAS

Serves: 6   Oven: 400°

6 chicken breasts, boned,   3 cups fine, fresh white
   skinned and halved   bread crumbs
3 bananas   Salt and pepper
1 cup flour   1 cup butter
3 eggs

Put chicken breasts between 2 sheets of waxed paper and pound them with flat side of a cleaver. Place 2 tablespoons of mashed bananas on each breast and fold chicken breasts over the filling to form six cutlets of even shape. Dip the cutlets in flour, then in beaten eggs and roll them in fine fresh white bread crumbs. Salt and pepper them to taste. Melt butter in skillet and sauté each side until golden, then bake in hot oven, 400°, for 15 minutes or until tender.

MRS. DONALD F. THOMPSON, JR.

CHICKEN PAPRIKA

Serves: 8

2 chickens, 3 or 3½ lbs. each,   ½ large bell pepper
   disjointed   1 tsp. salt
½ cup butter   1 cup sour cream
2 large onions, chopped   2 Tb. flour
3 Tb. Hungarian or sweet
   paprika

Put disjointed chicken in ice water and let soak about ½ hour. (Remove pieces of chicken from water when ready to put in skillet.) Melt butter in heavy skillet and sauté onions until golden brown. Remove skillet from fire and add paprika (paprika burns easily and can taste bitter if burned). Mix well. Add drained chicken pieces, stir with paprika and onions, getting each chicken piece well coated with paprika. Add green pepper and salt. Cover and simmer over low heat until chicken is done or tender, about one hour. (Don't let chicken get too done or it will fall apart.) Remove pieces of chicken to a platter and keep warm. Discard green pepper. Blend flour into sour cream, add to gravy stirring with whisk until smooth. Cook over low heat stirring constantly until hot. Taste; add salt if necessary. Do not let it boil or the sour cream might curdle. If you are not ready to serve the chicken, put the chicken in the gravy, ladle gravy over the chicken and cover. Keep flame low.

Serve with drop dumplings, egg barley, rice or noodles.

MRS. R. B. ELWOOD

GRILLED ORIENTAL CHICKEN

Serves: 8

8 chicken legs	4 Tb. brown sugar
8 chicken thighs	2 tsp. dry mustard
1 cup salad oil	1 Tb. oregano
½ cup vinegar	1 Tb. thyme
1½ bottles soy sauce	1½ tsp. Accent

Combine all the ingredients except the chicken to make marinade. Use an enamel, glass or crockery container for marinade. Cook chicken legs and thighs in water for 20 minutes, covered. Remove from water, place in marinade and refrigerate not less than 4 hours. Broil over charcoal fire until done.

MRS. CURTIS TATHAM, JR.
NORTHBROOK, ILLINOIS

CHICKEN DANA

Serves: 4-6　　　　　　　　　　　　　Oven: 350°

2 Tb. butter	8-oz. carton sour cream
1 cup uncooked rice	½ cup white wine
6 to 8 chicken pieces	3-oz. can mushrooms
Salt and pepper to taste	Parmesan cheese
10-oz. can asparagus soup	2 14-oz. cans asparagus

Melt butter in bottom of pan; put in uncooked rice; lay chicken pieces on top; salt and pepper to taste. Mix soup, sour cream, wine and mushrooms; pour half of mixture over chicken and sprinkle Parmesan cheese over all. Place drained asparagus on top and cover with remaining soup mixture. Bake 55 minutes at 350°.

MRS. VICTOR MENEFEE

CHICKEN ADOLPHUS

Serves: 10-12

1 medium hen, cooked and cut up into bite size pieces (can use canned chicken)	½ lb. toasted almonds
	1 large can mushrooms, drained
½ cup butter	1 large can ripe olives, pitted and drained
6 Tb. flour	Paprika
2 cups milk	Red pepper
2 cups chicken stock	Sherry
Salt and pepper to taste	
½ cup chopped pimiento	

Make a cream sauce by combining the butter, flour, milk, chicken stock and salt and pepper. Add the remaining ingredients to the cream sauce and heat through. Stir in chicken. Serve over rice or Chinese noodles.

MRS. J. LOUIS CHERRY
BLYTHEVILLE, ARKANSAS

COQ AU VIN

Serves: 6

2 (2½-3 lb.) chickens, cut up
1 tsp. salt
½ tsp. pepper
¼ cup butter
2 Tb. salad oil
2 cups fresh mushrooms,
   sliced, or 2 6-oz. cans sliced
   mushrooms, drained

2 cups dry red wine
   (or white)
¼ cup flour
1 clove garlic, crushed
4 or 5 strips bacon, cooked
   and crumbled
2 1-lb. cans small whole
   white onions, drained

Sprinkle chicken with salt and pepper. Brown in large kettle or skillet, in butter mixed with salad oil. Remove. Keep warm. In same pan, sauté mushrooms (fresh or canned). Remove with slotted spoon. Mix together dry red wine and flour. Slowly pour into pan, stirring constantly. Bring to a boil and cook 2 or 3 minutes, until thick. Add 1 clove garlic, crushed, and then the chicken. Cover and cook over low heat 35 to 40 minutes until chickens are fork-tender. Meanwhile, cook and crumble 4 or 5 strips bacon. About 5 minutes before end of cooking time for chicken, add 2 cans whole white onions that have been drained. When ready to serve Coq au Vin, place chicken on platter and spoon the onions around and sprinkle with cooked bacon.

MRS. B. FRANK MACKEY, JR.

CHICKEN SURPRISE

Serves: 6   Oven: 350°

WHITE SAUCE:

4 Tb. butter
4 Tb. flour

2 cups milk
3 beef bouillon cubes

Make the white sauce, using butter, flour, 2 cups milk and bouillon cubes and stir it until it thickens, then cool slightly.

FILLING:

2 beaten eggs
½ cup mayonnaise
1 small can chow mein
   noodles

½ cup chopped almonds
2 cups chopped chicken
Lemon juice

To sauce add the beaten eggs, mayonnaise, chow mein noodles, and almonds. Then add the cooked chopped chicken sprinkled with a little lemon juice for flavor. Put in a covered casserole and bake in 350° oven for 25 to 30 minutes.

TOP SAUCE:

1 can mushroom sauce
¾ cup milk

½ cup grated cheese
1 tsp. herb seasoning

Heat ingredients together until cheese melts. Serve hot.

MRS. VERNON L. JACKSON

HOT CHICKEN SALAD

Serves: 8　　　　　　　　　　Oven: 350°

2 cups cooked chicken
(full cup)
2 cups finely cut celery
½ cup toasted slivered
almonds
½ tsp. salt
2 Tb. finely chopped onion

½ cup mayonnaise
1 Tb. chopped bell pepper
2 Tb. chopped pimiento
½ cup cream of chicken soup
2 Tb. lemon juice
3 cups crushed potato chips
½ cup grated cheese

Toss all ingredients well together except potato chips and cheese. Spoon into 2 quart casserole and sprinkle chips and cheese on top. Bake at 350° for 20 minutes. This may be baked in individual baking dishes at the same temperature for 10 minutes.

MRS. WILLIAM RALPH COOK
WYNNE, ARKANSAS

KING RANCH CASSEROLE

Serves: 8　　　　　　　　　　Oven: 350°

2 cups cooked diced chicken
1 can Ro-tel tomatoes and
green chilies
1 can cream mushroom soup
1 can cream chicken soup
½ can chicken broth

1 pkg. soft tortillas, cut in
small pieces
1 large onion, chopped
1 cup grated sharp Cheddar
cheese

Layer the chicken, tomatoes, soups, broth and tortillas in a greased 2 quart casserole. Add chopped onions. Repeat layers and onions. Sprinkle grated cheese over top and bake at 350° for one hour.

MRS. MARK BELEW
VERNON, TEXAS

CHICKEN AND WILD RICE CASSEROLE

Serves: 6-8　　　　　　　　　Oven: 350°

1 cup wild rice
½ lb. sliced mushrooms
4 Tb. butter
3 cups cooked, cut up chicken
1½ cups cream, light

2 Tb. chives or onions
2½ cups chicken stock
1 tsp. salt
½ tsp. cracked pepper
½ cup Parmesan cheese

Rinse wild rice in lukewarm water several times, then soak for two hours. Slice and sauté mushrooms in 2 tablespoons butter until brown. Drain rice, blend with chicken, cream, mushrooms, chives and 1¼ cups stock, salt and pepper.

Butter 3 quart casserole with 1 tablespoon butter, add ingredients, cover and bake one hour at 350°. Add 1½ cups stock. Return to oven 30 more minutes. Just before serving, remove cover, sprinkle with cheese, dot with 1 tablespoon butter and brown 10 minutes.

MRS. LEWIE A. WATKINS, JR.

CHICKEN CACCIATORE

Serves: 6

2½ lbs. chicken pieces	1 or 2 cloves garlic, minced
½ cup flour with salt and	1 tsp. oregano
pepper	1 tsp. celery salt
¼ cup butter	1 cup diced celery
2 onions, diced	1 tsp. salt
1 can tomato sauce	¼ tsp. pepper
1 can water	

Skin chicken. Coat with seasoned flour, brown in butter then remove chicken from pan. Cook onions until soft, add remaining ingredients and chicken. Cover and simmer 40 minutes or until tender, turning chicken occasionally. Add water if needed.

MRS. W. MAGE HONEYCUTT

MARGARELLA

Serves: 8

1 Tb. butter	½ lb. mushrooms
4 medium onions, chopped	½ pt. light cream
2 bell peppers, chopped	4 cans tuna or chicken
2 sweet red peppers, chopped	½ cup chutney
2 10½-oz. cans tomato soup	Salt and pepper

Melt butter in skillet. Add onions, peppers and mushrooms. Cook until onions are transparent. Add tomato soup and cream and bring to a boil. Drain meat. Break into bite-size pieces. Add seasoning and chutney and serve over wild rice or fried noodles.

This is a good Lenten recipe!

CHICKEN SPAGHETTI

Serves: 20   Oven: 250°

4½ lb. hen (or 2 small)	20-oz. can tomatoes
1 bell pepper, chopped	1½ lb. chili brick (remove
1 button garlic, chopped	any fat)
3 medium onions, chopped	2 8-oz. cans mushroom pieces
Salad oil	2 boxes (8-oz.) vermicelli
1 qt. chicken broth	1 lb. Cheddar cheese, grated

Cook hen until tender in small amount of water; remove from bone and cut into bite-size pieces. Sauté green pepper, garlic and onion in a little salad oil. Add chicken broth and to this add tomatoes, chili and mushroom liquid. Simmer all slowly until chili is dissolved, about 30 minutes. Cook vermicelli in salted, boiling water (directions on box). In large casserole put layers of vermicelli, cheese, chicken, chili mixture. On top layer, place mushrooms and more cheese and bake 1½ hours at 250°.

CHICKEN SPAGHETTI

Serves: 15-20   Oven: 350°

3 cups chopped celery
1 cup chopped onion
1 bell pepper, chopped
1 cup margarine
1 can mushroom soup,
  undiluted
1 can tomato soup, undiluted
1 pt. chicken broth
1 Tb. chili powder

1 tsp. Tabasco sauce
Salt to taste
1 hen or 2 large fryers, boiled
  until tender; remove meat
  from bones and cut into
  bite-size pieces
1 lb. elbow spaghetti
1 lb. grated Cheddar cheese

Cook celery, onion and bell pepper in margarine until tender. Add
mushroom and tomato soup, chicken broth, chili powder, Tabasco
and salt to taste. Mix with cooked deboned chicken and spaghetti,
cooked and drained. Put into a 15 x 11-inch pan, sprinkle with
grated cheese and cook at 350° until bubbly—about 30 minutes.

MRS. G. BURNS NEWBILL
BENTON, ARKANSAS

CHICKEN TETRAZZINI

Serves: 10   Oven: 375°

½ cup butter
½ cup flour
1 pt. milk
¼ lb. American cheese
¼ lb. Old English cheese
1 can mushroom soup

1 onion, chopped
3 to 4 stalks celery, chopped
5 lb. hen, boiled
4 oz. spaghetti
Cracker crumbs

Make white sauce with butter, flour and milk. Add cheese, cut in
small pieces, and soup, without diluting. Stir well. In another pan,
sauté chopped onion and celery until tender. Boil hen until tender.
Cool and cut into bite-size pieces. Cook spaghetti in broth. Drain
spaghetti. Combine everything in a buttered casserole dish and top
with cracker crumbs. Bake, uncovered, at 375° for 30 minutes.

MRS. RICHARD S. WOODS
DALLAS, TEXAS

MUSHROOMS AND CHICKEN LIVERS

Serves: 8

1 lb. chicken livers
4 Tb. butter
2 6-oz. cans broiled, sliced
  mushrooms or 1 pt. fresh
  mushrooms, sliced

½ cup chopped green onions
1 cup sour cream
3 tsp. soy sauce
3 tsp. chili sauce
Pepper to taste

Cook livers, covered, in butter until almost tender. (About ten
minutes.) Add mushrooms and green onions, and cook until onions
and livers are tender. Combine remaining ingredients and add to
livers. Heat and stir just until sauce is hot. Serve over rice or hot
buttered toast.

MRS. ROBERT CARNAHAN

OPEN-FACED BREAST OF CHICKEN SANDWICH
WITH REMOULADE SAUCE

Serves: 2

Butter	2 Tb. remoulade sauce
2 slices dark rye bread	2 thin slices Swiss cheese
Escarole lettuce leaves	2 slices cold chicken breast
4 Tb. shredded lettuce	4 slices crisp bacon

Butter large slices of rye bread and cover with escarole and shredded lettuce. Add Swiss cheese and cold chicken. Top with remoulade sauce and bacon. Garnish with chopped hard-cooked eggs and green olives.

REMOULADE SAUCE:

1 cup mayonnaise	½ tsp. anchovy paste
¼ cup olive oil	½ tsp. chopped parsley
2½ Tb. chopped dill pickle	½ tsp. dried tarragon
1 Tb. capers	½ tsp. dried basil
1½ tsp. Dijon-style mustard	

Beat all ingredients together until well blended. Refrigerate.

CHICKEN LIVERS WITH MADEIRA SAUCE

Serves: 4

1 lb. chicken livers	Flour
Milk	½ lb. mushrooms
Salt and pepper to taste	3 Tb. butter

Soak livers in milk for ½ hour, then dry and sprinkle with salt, pepper and dredge in flour. Sauté chicken livers and mushrooms 3 to 4 minutes in butter.

MADEIRA SAUCE:

2 Tb. butter	⅓ cup Madeira
2 Tb. flour	Salt and pepper
1 cup chicken broth	Parsley, minced

To make Madeira sauce, brown flour in butter; add broth, wine and seasonings. Reheat livers in sauce and serve on toast.

ROASTED ROCK CORNISH HENS

Serves: 1 per person   Oven: 425°

Rock Cornish Hens	Parsley
Lemon juice	Rosemary
Salt	Butter
Pepper	Bacon slices

Thaw hens overnight in refrigerator. Wash and pat dry. Sprinkle cavities with lemon juice, salt and pepper. Put 1 or 2 sprigs of parsley, a pinch of crushed rosemary and 1 tablespoon butter in each bird. Place breast side up in roasting pan. Cover breasts with bacon slices. Roast in hot oven, 425°, 45 to 50 minutes, or until fork-tender.

MRS. JAMES HATHAWAY

CHICKEN LIVERS IN ONION CREPES

Serves: 8   Oven: 375°

CREPES:

1 cup flour	1 cup milk
½ onion, finely grated	2 Tb. melted butter
2 beaten eggs	

CHICKEN LIVERS:

16 chicken livers, cut in half	¼ tsp. paprika
4 Tb. butter	

SAUCE:

¼ onion, chopped	1 cup Bearnaise sauce
½ apple, peeled and chopped	1 cup cream, whipped
1 tsp. chives	Salt and pepper
2 Tb. brandy	

Make crepes according to directions listed in the Bread section. In a separate pan, sauté chicken livers 3 to 4 minutes in butter and paprika. In another pan, simmer for 2 minutes, onion, apple, chives, with drippings from livers and brandy. Add livers and season to taste. Remove from fire and add ½ cup of bearnaise sauce. Spread on crepes and roll. Arrange on fireproof platter. Mix other ½ cup of bearnaise sauce with whipped cream. Cover each crepe lightly. Bake in 375° oven until brown.

MRS. BART ROACH

ROCK CORNISH HENS WITH ORANGE-RAISIN SAUCE

Serves: 4   Oven: 350°

4 Cornish hens	1 cup orange juice
Salt	¼ cup butter
Melted butter	¼ cup flour
1 box Uncle Ben's Wild and Long Grain Rice	1 tsp. salt
14-oz. can chicken broth	¼ tsp. paprika
½ tsp. salt	⅛ tsp. pepper
1 cup raisins	2 cups milk

Thaw hens. Wash and pat dry. Sprinkle insides with salt and brush with butter. Place hens on shallow rack and bake for 1 hour in a 350° oven. In a large saucepan, measure broth and water to make 3 cups. Bring to a boil and add rice and mixture from box. Reduce heat and simmer for 45 minutes. While rice is cooking, combine raisins and orange juice, bring to a boil and simmer 5 minutes. Set aside. Melt butter, add flour and seasonings. Take off heat and add milk. Stir until smooth. Add orange juice and raisin mixture. Serve hens on a bed of rice with sauce over top. Serve remaining sauce separately.

STUFFED ROCK CORNISH HENS

Serves: 6   Oven: 400°

1 box wild rice   6 Cornish hens

WINE GLAZE:

¼ cup red wine   ¾ tsp. salt
⅛ tsp. pepper   3 Tb. melted butter
½ tsp. sugar   1½ tsp. lemon juice

Cook rice according to package directions. Salt and pepper hens. Stuff cavity of hens lightly with rice. Place hens in shallow roasting pan and cover loosely with foil. Roast in hot oven, 400°, for 30 minutes. Uncover; baste with Wine Glaze; bake 1 hour more, basting occasionally with the glaze.

MRS. JACK FROST, JR.

TURKEY WITH HONEY AND GINGER GLAZE

Oven: 350°

12-lb. turkey   ⅓ cup honey
½ cup Chablis   Salt
1-inch piece gingerroot,   Pepper
  grated

Dissolve honey and wine together. Add gingerroot; sprinkle with salt and pepper; pour honey-wine mixture over bird. Cover turkey loosely with foil to prevent burning the skin. Cook at 350° for 25 minutes to the pound. Baste every 30 minutes. When done, you will have a delightful, dark brown glaze. Serve with chestnut dressing.

RICE DRESSING (for CHICKEN, TURKEY or DUCK)

Serves: 4-6   Oven: 350°

1½ cups of raw rice   ¼ cup fresh parsley, chopped
1 tsp. salt   3 Tb. oil
2 large onions, chopped   ½ tsp. thyme
1 large bell pepper, chopped   Pepper
6 ribs celery, chopped   3 bay leaves
1 can mushrooms   Chicken broth

Cook rice in salted, boiling water according to package directions. In skillet, sauté onions, pepper, celery until soft. Add dry, cooked rice and all other ingredients and seasonings, except bay leaves and broth. Fill the cavity of the bird and place the remainder of the dressing under the bird in the roasting pan. Place breast side down and put bay leaves at various places on the top of the loose rice. Moisten the dressing with chicken broth and roast at 350° until breast is tender; turn fowl over and brown breast before serving.

FRANCES M. GARING

CHESTNUT DRESSING

Oven: 350°

1 can chestnut puree
1 cup melted butter
1 cup cream, light
2 cups dry bread crumbs

4 Tb. chopped parsley
½ cup chives
½ cup white raisins
Salt and pepper

Add chestnut puree to rest of ingredients. Bake at 350° for 45 minutes in pre-oiled or buttered casserole.

BASIC BREAD DRESSING

Serves: (1 cup per 1 lb. of dressed bird)   Oven: 325°
       Makes 4 cups

¼ cup butter
Chopped giblets, cooked
4 Tb. chopped onion
4 cups crustless, diced white
   or corn bread crumbs, one
   day old
4 Tb. chopped parsley

1 cup chopped celery
1 tsp. dried tarragon or basil
¾ tsp. salt
½ tsp. paprika
⅛ tsp. nutmeg
Stock to moisten the dressing
   very lightly

Sauté the chopped giblets and onion in butter. Combine with other ingredients. Stuff bird lightly or bake in greased ring mold, loaf pan or casserole at 325° until thoroughly heated.

Variations:

MUSHROOM: Add ½ pound mushrooms, chopped, and sautéed in 1 tablespoon butter.

OYSTER: Add 1 pint oysters, chopped and sautéed in 2 tablespoons butter. Use part oyster liquor to moisten dressing.

WALNUT or PECAN: Add 1½ cups of nut meats.

SAUSAGE: Add ¾ pound sausage. Dressing should be dry as liquid from sausage will moisten it as it cooks.

MARY ANN'S ORANGE SAUCE FOR DUCKLING

Serves: 4

¾ cup orange marmalade
1 tsp. orange rind, grated
½ cup orange juice
¼ cup vinegar
1 tsp. prepared mustard

2 tsp. cornstarch
¼ tsp. rosemary
¼ tsp. leaf tarragon
¼ tsp. salt

Combine ingredients in saucepan; mix well. Bring to boil stirring constantly and cook until thickened. Brush duckling several times during last 30 minutes of roasting. Serve remaining sauce with duckling. You may add Grand Marnier or Cointreau to this if you like.

MRS. WARREN JENNINGS
DEWITT, ARKANSAS

DUCK BIGARADE

Serves: 8-10   Oven: 350°

3 Long Island ducklings   1 carrot
Salt and pepper   1 rib celery
½ cup butter   1 pt. water
1 onion

Remove necks, wings, gizzards and livers. Season ducklings with
salt and pepper; roast for 1½ hours at 350°. Prick skin often to
achieve crispness. Brown necks, wings, gizzards and livers in butter
with onion, carrot and celery. Add salt and pepper; simmer in water
for 1½ hours. While stock is cooking make sauce.

SAUCE BIGARADE:

3 oranges   4 Tb. cider vinegar
1 grapefruit   ½ cup cornstarch
½ cup sugar   4 Tb. Grand Marnier

Peel the oranges and grapefruit as thin as possible in slender strips,
julienne. Boil 2 minutes in enough water to cover; then strain.
Brown sugar and vinegar to make caramel; add peel. Squeeze
orange and grapefruit juice into caramel. Add strained stock, cornstarch and simmer 1 hour. Add Grand Marnier at the last minute
before serving. Carve ducks and serve with sauce.

BARBEQUE SAUCE FOR CHICKEN

Yield: 2 cups

1 5-oz. bottle of A-1 sauce   1 small onion, chopped
½ 5-oz. bottle Worcester-   1 button garlic
   shire sauce   3 round slices of lemon
½ cup butter   Juice of ½ lemon

Combine all ingredients in a saucepan. Simmer, and do not let boil,
for 15 to 30 minutes.

MRS. ROBERT H. WICKARD

BARBEQUE SAUCE FOR CHICKEN

Yield: 2 cups

1 small bottle catsup   Tabasco
1 cup dark corn syrup   Juice of 1 lemon
2 Tb. Worcestershire sauce   Salt and pepper
1 Tb. mustard   1 tsp. garlic salt or powder

Mix all ingredients and baste chicken while cooking over charcoal
grill.

MRS. VERNON JACKSON, III

DRESSING FOR TURKEY

Serves: 10-12 or 15-lb. turkey

8-oz. pkg. Pepperidge Farm
  Herb Seasoned Stuffing
8-oz. pkg. Pepperidge Farm
  Corn Bread Stuffing
1 12-oz. pkg. frozen onions
1 bunch celery, chopped
1 cup butter
¼ to ½ lb. lean sausage,
  uncooked
2 large apples, chopped

4 eggs, well beaten
½ cup raisins (optional)
Salt
Pepper
¾ tsp. nutmeg
¾ tsp. garlic salt
1½ Tb. parsley
Sage or poultry seasoning to
  taste
½ tsp. cayenne pepper
1 qt. chicken broth

Sauté chopped onions and celery in butter until tender. In large bowl, mix packages of stuffing. Crumble sausage and add to bread mix. Add onions and celery, apples, raisins (if used). Stir in beaten eggs. Add all seasonings. Mix with 2 cups of chicken broth. Place dressing in 9-inch baking dish. May be frozen or refrigerated overnight. Dressing may be stuffed inside bird or baked separately. If baked separately add enough chicken broth to float. Bake 1 hour in 350° oven.

I like to bake dressing covered for 30 minutes and uncovered for 30 minutes to barely brown.

MRS. JAMES MADIGAN

WILD GAME

BASIC RECIPE FOR WILD DUCKS

Serves: 8   Oven: 300°

4 ducks   Salt
2 onions   2 cans consomme, undiluted
2 apples   2 cups orange juice

Rinse ducks. Salt cavity. Stuff ½ apple and ½ onion in each duck.
Place in roasting pan. Cover with consomme and orange juice.
Cover pan with foil. Roast in 300° oven for 3 hours. Carve ducks.
Place meat in juices and cook for 1 hour, uncovered. Serve with
wild rice and curried fruit.

MRS. BART ROACH

CREOLE DUCK

Serves: 4   Oven: 300°

2 ducks   Salt and pepper
½ apple   Salad oil
1 onion   Bacon
Celery

Cover duck with water and parboil 5 to 8 minutes. Take out. Salt
cavity and stuff with apple, onion, and celery. Rub outside of duck
with salt, pepper, and salad oil. Turn breast down in roaster. Strip
back with bacon and cover with creole sauce.

CREOLE SAUCE:

½ cup butter   1 can tomatoes, chopped
1 onion, chopped   Salt and pepper
2 bay leaves

In saucepan, combine butter, onion, bay leaf, tomatoes, salt and
pepper and boil 30 minutes. Pour over duck. Cover and bake in
300° oven for 2 hours or until tender. Remove duck and thicken
liquid with flour. Serve sauce over duck. Serve with sausage
dressing.

MRS. ROBERT CRESS

SAUSAGE DRESSING FOR DUCK

Serves: 4

3 pats country sausage   ¾ cup liquid in which duck is
1 large onion, diced   parboiled
1 stalk celery, diced   2 eggs, slightly beaten
1 cup cooked rice, hot

Brown crumbled sausage with onion and celery. Cook until brown.
Add liquid in which duck was parboiled. Add hot cooked rice. Fold
in eggs and serve immediately. Add salt and pepper to taste.

MRS. ROBERT CRESS

SPORTSMAN'S DELIGHT

Serves: 4   Oven: 300°

2 ducks   1 bell pepper, chopped
1 pkg. sauerkraut   4 Tb. butter or olive oil
1 onion, chopped   Salt and pepper

Mix sauerkraut, onion, and pepper. Salt and pepper duck and stuff
with mixture. Cover breast with remaining sauerkraut, dot with
butter or oil and wrap tightly in foil. Cook at 300° for 3 hours.

Men love this!

PHIL FOSTER
SHREVEPORT, LOUISIANA

BARBARA'S POTTED DUCK

Serves: 4   Oven: 300°

2 ducks   ½ bay leaf
4 Tb. butter   2 sprigs parsley
½ onion, chopped   1 can cream of chicken soup
1 clove garlic, minced   1 cup dry red Burgundy
1 pinch thyme   Salt and pepper

Split ducks in two. Brown pieces in butter, remove and place in
casserole. Sauté onion and garlic, add to casserole with other seasonings, undiluted soup and wine. Add salt and pepper to taste.
Cover tightly and roast in 300° for 3 hours or until tender. If liquid
gets low during cooking, add water or more wine. Serve duck with
liquid from pan as gravy.

MRS. GORDON WITTENBERG

WILD DUCK IN BARBECUE SAUCE

Serves: 4-6

3 ducks   ½ cup Worcestershire sauce
3 Tb. shortening   ½ cup catsup
1 pt. vinegar   ½ cup chili sauce
½ lb. margarine   2 Tb. lemon juice
1 tsp. dry mustard   1 clove garlic, crushed
2 Tb. minced onion   1 Tb. liquid smoke
2 Tb. brown sugar   Hot sauce to taste

Brown ducks in shortening in Dutch oven. Combine all other ingredients and pour over ducks. Cover and simmer for 2 to 2½
hours until meat falls from bone. Duck may be served as whole
breast or chopped and served on buns.

People will eat this who don't like duck. It is very spicy and moist.

MRS. CHARLES A. SMITH

TOP OF THE STOVE DUCK

Serves: 4

2 ducks
½ cup butter
4-oz. can mushrooms and
   liquid
1 pod garlic

1 onion, chopped
1 bell pepper, chopped
1 pkg. Pepperidge Farm
   Dressing
Salt and pepper

Place ducks in Dutch oven with butter, garlic, mushrooms, onion, and bell pepper. Salt and pepper generously. Cover and cook on low heat for 2½ to 3½ hours. Remove duck and carve. Add dressing to juices and mix well. Serve together.

TAP HORNER

WILD DUCK IN APPLE JUICE AND BRANDY

Serves: 6-8   **Oven: 375°**

4 ducks
Salt and pepper
4 small onions
4 small apples
Celery
Rosemary

Garlic salt
Celery salt
½ cup sherry
½ cup apple juice
¼ cup peach brandy

Thoroughly wash each duck inside and out. Rub inside of cavity with salt and pepper. Place onion, apple and celery inside each duck. Sprinkle with rosemary, garlic salt and celery salt. Arrange in deep roasting pan. Add sherry, juice and brandy. Roast covered for 2 hours at 375°. Baste every 15 minutes. Top may be removed last 30 minutes to insure browning.

MRS. JAMES FLACK, JR.

WILD DUCK BUTTON WILLOW

Serves: 2   **Oven: 275°**

1 duck, well cleaned
1 small onion
1 small orange

4 Tb. barbecue sauce
4 Tb. sherry
Salt and pepper

Stuff duck with onion and orange. Rub well with salt and pepper. Place duck, breast down, in aluminum foil large enough to completely seal the duck. Pour barbecue sauce and sherry over duck and seal. Bake in 275° oven for 3 hours.

Very little duck taste left!

BUTTON WILLOW CLUB
MRS. VERNON JACKSON

WILD DUCK DELUXE

Serves: 6-8   Oven: 450°

¼ cup margarine
2 Tb. flour
1 or 2 cloves garlic, mashed
3 or 4 duck breasts
2 onions, finely chopped
2 carrots, finely chopped

¼ cup parsley, chopped
2 cups tomato juice
1 cup orange juice
1 can consomme
½ cup sherry

Make a paste of the first three ingredients and spread on the duck breasts that have been blotted dry, salted and peppered. Place breast side up in a 450° oven for 15 minutes, uncovered. Meanwhile, combine onions, carrots, parsley, juices and consomme. Bring to a boil and simmer 20 minutes. Pour over ducks, then turn them breast side down in the liquid. Cover, reduce heat to 350° and continue cooking for 2 hours. Uncover during last 20 minutes and add sherry. Serve with long grain or wild rice.

The gravy is glorious. You will never believe that wild duck can be so moist.

WILD DUCK IN SHERRY

Serves: 2   Oven: 300°

1 wild duck
1 Tb. butter
1 tsp. salt
1 tsp. Worcestershire sauce
3 dashes Tabasco

1 onion, chopped
1 garlic button
1 cup Roma Sherry
1 small can sliced mushrooms

Melt butter in pot. Brown duck. Add other ingredients, except mushrooms. Cover and bake at 300° for 3 hours. Carve duck and add mushrooms. Return to oven, uncovered, for final 30 minutes.

HENRY ANTHONY
LAKE VILLAGE, ARKANSAS

MARINATED DUCK BREASTS

Serves: 2-4

2 ducks (4 boneless breasts)
½ cup Wishbone Italian
   Dressing
1 Tb. Worcestershire sauce

Juice of one lemon
¼ tsp. each garlic powder,
   ground cloves
Bacon slices

Soak ducks in salt water for 3 hours. Remove the breast, dry pieces with paper toweling and place in shallow pan. Combine the rest of the ingredients, pour over duck, and marinate at least 30 to 40 minutes. Wrap each breast in bacon and secure with toothpick. Cook on grill over a slow fire, 7 minutes per side, or until bacon is done. May be sliced thin and served with barbecue sauce as an hors d'oeuvre.

MRS. GEORGE DAVIS

DUCK CASSEROLE

Serves: 6-8

2 ducks	1½ cups light cream
1 onion	1 Tb. chopped parsley
2 ribs celery	1½ tsp. salt
½ cup butter	¼ tsp. pepper
½ cup chopped onion	1 pkg. Uncle Ben's Wild Rice
¼ cup flour	and Long Grain Rice
6-oz. can mushrooms	1 pkg. slivered almonds

Boil ducks for 2 hours with sliced onion and celery. Cook rice according to directions on package. In a deep skillet, melt butter. Sauté onion. Stir in flour. Add mushrooms and their liquid. Add cream, parsley, salt, pepper, and cooked rice. Debone ducks and add chunks of meat to other ingredients. Put into 2 quart casserole and sprinkle with almonds. Bake at 350° for 25 minutes.

MRS. TOMMY STOBAUGH
PINE BLUFF, ARKANSAS

MARIE SCHULTE'S DUCK CASSEROLE

Serves: 6　　　　　　　　　　　　　　　　　　Oven: 350°

2 ducks	4 Tb. butter
Onion	1 tsp. Worcestershire sauce
Celery	Salt and pepper
16-oz. can tomato wedges	2 cups cooked rice
¼ cup onions, chopped	Buttered bread crumbs
½ cup celery, chopped	and/or Parmesan cheese

Boil ducks in water with onion and celery until done (2 to 3 hours). Take meat off bone and cut up in bite-size pieces. Combine tomatoes, onions, celery, and sauté in butter. Season with salt, pepper and Worcestershire sauce. Thicken with flour as needed. Line a 2 quart casserole with 2 cups of cooked rice. Place meat over rice and pour sauce over all. Top with buttered crumbs and/or Parmesan cheese. Bake at 350° until bubbly and thoroughly heated.

This can be made ahead and frozen.

MARIE SCHULTE

CURRANT JELLY SAUCE

Serves: 8

½ to 1 small jar currant jelly	½ cup butter
⅓ cup Worcestershire sauce	

Simmer in double boiler for 15 minutes. Serve with duck.

MRS. WILLIAM SIGLER
MRS. JAMES STUCKEY

WILD DUCK STUCKEY

Serves: 4   **Oven: 500°-350°**

2 ducks   3-oz. can mushrooms
Butter or bacon drippings   4 cups cooked wild rice
Salt and pepper   1 cup raw minute rice
1 can consomme, undiluted

Clean and dry ducks. Rub with butter or drippings; salt and pepper
inside and out. Brown in 500° oven for 30 minutes. Remove from
oven and smother them with consomme, mushrooms, wild rice and
minute rice. Cover tightly and return to 350° oven for 2 hours.
Remove from oven. Carve ducks and serve with rice and currant
jelly sauce. This may be doubled as needed. Ducks will be well done
and very moist.

MRS. JAMES STUCKEY

KINGDOM-COME DUCK

Serves: 6-8   **Oven: 350°**

4 ducks   2 cans consomme, undiluted
2 apples   1 can water
Celery   Cooked, crumbled bacon

Stuff ducks with apple and celery. Place breast down in consomme
and water. Cover tightly and cook for 3 hours at 350°. Duck should
be very tender. Slice breast away. Place duck breast in greased,
shallow casserole. Pour sauce over duck, cover and bake at 350°
just until hot. Place breast on mound of rice, sprinkle with bacon
and pass sauce as gravy. This is a must!

SAUCE:

1½ cups butter   5-oz jar currant jelly
⅔ cup sherry   4 Tb. Worcestershire sauce
½ cup bourbon

In a saucepan, slowly heat butter, sherry, bourbon, jelly, and
Worcestershire sauce. If too thin, thicken with a little flour.

MRS. DAVID SNOWDEN

CHAMPAGNE SAUERKRAUT FOR DUCK

Serves: 8

1 large onion, diced   1 medium potato, grated
4 Tb. margarine   1 can spiced grapes and juice
1 large can sauerkraut   1 cup Champagne or white
½ 8-oz. can applesauce   wine

Mix all but wine and cook until potato and onion are soft. When
ready to serve, add wine and heat until piping hot. Serve immediately with duck.

LETHA CHEATHAM

ORANGE SAUCE FOR WILD DUCK

Serves: 4

2 medium oranges
½ cup sugar
1 Tb. red wine vinegar

¼ cup orange liqueur
Juices from roast duck

Grate peel from one orange (2 teaspoons). With vegetable parer, cut peel from other orange in long thin strips. Squeeze juice from both oranges. In heavy skillet, cook and stir sugar and vinegar until sugar caramelizes to a rich brown. Remove from heat; add peel, juice and liqueur. Return to heat and simmer, stirring constantly, until caramelized sugar dissolves. Skim off fat from juices in roasting pan. Add orange juice mixture. Stir in strips of peel.

MRS. ROBERT L. DORTCH, JR.
SCOTT, ARKANSAS

SMOTHERED DOVE BREASTS

Serves: 4-6

16 dove breasts, cleaned
Salt
Pepper
Garlic powder
1 cup flour

3 Tb. bacon drippings
½ cup chopped onion
2 5¾-oz. cans Dawn Fresh
    Mushroom Sauce
⅛ cup water

Rinse dove breasts thoroughly in cold water. Sprinkle sparingly with salt, pepper, and garlic powder. Put flour in bag and shake dove in it, to coat well. Brown dove in a skillet, uncovered, over medium heat, using the bacon drippings. Turn frequently. Add onions, mushroom sauce and water. Stir well. Reduce heat to simmer and cook, covered, for 45 minutes or until tender when pierced with a fork.

MRS. JERRY LIGHT

DOVE A LA COMO

Serves: 4

12 doves
Flour
1 cup butter
2 cans consomme
½ can water

1 Tb. cracked black pepper
Salt to taste
4 cups fried, crisp bacon
½ cup sherry
Buttered whole wheat toast

Rinse dove. Lightly salt. Roll in flour. Brown in skillet in butter. Add consomme, water, pepper and salt to taste. Cover and simmer, breast down, for 1½ hours. When done, may be served on buttered toast. Be sure to completely cover dove with bacon and serve with gravy, to which you have added the sherry. The bacon is the secret!

MRS. DAVID SNOWDEN

DOVE IN WINE

Serves: 6

24 doves	1 cup butter
Salt	2 cups dry red wine
Pepper	¼ cup vinegar
Flour	¼ cup Worcestershire sauce

Salt, pepper and lightly flour doves. Brown in skillet in butter. Add other ingredients. Cook, covered, very slowly for 1 hour. Thicken pan juices with flour and serve with dove.

MRS. A. HOWARD STEBBINS

ROASTED QUAIL

Serves: 1 bird per person   Oven: 350°

FOR EACH BIRD:

¼ cup dry bread crumbs	Flour
1 Tb. butter	½ cup butter
1 Tb. broken pecans	¼ cup sherry
Salt and pepper	

Prepare stuffing by sautéing bread crumbs in 1 tablespoon of butter. Add pecans. Roll birds in salt, pepper and flour and brown in melted butter. Spoon stuffing into cavity. Place breast down in roaster. Add 2 cups of water to skillet. Add ¼ cup of sherry for each bird. Pour over quail. Cover tightly and cook in 350° oven for 1½ hours. Use juices in pan as gravy.

MRS. GEORGE WITTENBERG

FRIED QUAIL

Serves: 1-2 birds per person

Clean each quail and split it down the back, leaving halves attached. Season both sides with salt and pepper. Put birds in paper bag with flour and shake to cover all parts. Remove from bag and flatten them, breast down, in hot cooking oil. Use enough oil so birds are at least half immersed. Turn until well browned on both sides. Add small amount of water to steam. Cover and cook an additional ½ hour at a lower heat. Make a gravy by using pan liquids, thickened with flour and milk. Serve with hot biscuits.

MRS. MALLORY CRANK

CHARCOAL-BROILED QUAIL

Serves: 4

8 fresh quail	Bacon
Lemon-pepper marinade	

Wash and dry quail; sprinkle with lemon-pepper marinade. Wrap each bird with a piece of bacon, covering as much of the meat as possible; secure with a toothpick. Cook for about 15 minutes over a slow charcoal fire.

FINLEY VINSON

SMOTHERED QUAIL

Serves: 6   Oven: 350°

6 quail   ½ cup sherry
6 Tb. butter   Salt and pepper
3 Tb. flour   Cooked rice
2 cups chicken broth

Clean quail. Brown in heavy skillet or Dutch oven in butter. Remove quail to baking dish. Add flour to butter in skillet and stir well. Slowly add chicken broth, sherry, salt and pepper. Blend well and pour over quail. Cover baking dish and bake at 350° for 1 hour. Serve with cooked rice.

MRS. DREW LANDER

HUNTER'S QUAIL

Serves: 8

8 quail   ¼ cup Worcestershire sauce
Vinegar   ¼ cup A-1 sauce
Salt and pepper   2 cups water
½ cup butter   Buttered toast

Rub quail with vinegar, salt and pepper. Sear quickly in butter in iron skillet or Dutch oven. Mix Worcestershire, A-1 and water; pour over quail. Cover and cook 1 hour. Remove quail and cook liquid down to 1 cup. Serve quail on buttered toast using liquid for gravy.

MRS. ROBERT CRESS

SAVORY GOOSE

Serves: 2-4   Oven: 300°

1 wild goose   ¾ cup currant jelly
2 apples, quartered   1 tsp. cinnamon
16-oz. can applesauce   ½ cup corn syrup

Rinse goose. Place quartered apples in cavity. Make a sauce by heating other ingredients. Pour over and cook, covered, for 3½ hours or until very tender.

WILD GOOSE

Serves: 2-4   Oven: 475°

1 wild goose   1 cup red wine
4 strips bacon   1½ cups chicken stock
1 tsp. rosemary   1 cup dry white wine
1 tsp. tarragon   1 cup orange juice
1 tsp. salt   1 cup heavy cream

Place bacon over breast of goose and place in roasting pan. Sprinkle with rosemary, tarragon and salt. Add red wine and stock. Place uncovered in 475° oven for 10 minutes. Reduce heat to 350° and cook, covered, for 2 to 3 hours. Add white wine, orange juice and baste often for 1 more hour. To make gravy, add cream to liquids and drippings. This makes the most divine gravy!

MRS. VERNON JACKSON, III

GOURMET DELIGHT PHEASANT

Serves: 6-8   Oven: 350°

4 pheasants, breasts only   Salt
1 cup brandy   Pepper
2 cups chicken stock   2 pt. heavy cream
1 onion, chopped   1 jar horseradish
1 clove garlic, crushed   ½ lb. mushrooms

Brown pheasant breasts in butter. Place in baking dish. Pour over brandy. Light and let burn out. Add stock, onions, garlic, salt and pepper. Bake at 350° for 1 hour, basting occasionally. Remove from oven. Pour over cream and horseradish and bake another 1½ hours. Just before serving, add mushrooms sautéed in butter. Good with wild rice.

PHEASANT WITH GRAVY

Serves: 4

2 pheasants, quartered   1 can beef gravy
Salt and pepper to taste   4-oz. can mushrooms
Seasoning salt to taste   ¼ cup chopped parsley
Flour to dredge   4 green onions, chopped
4 Tb. butter   1½ tsp. monosodium
½ cup sherry   glutamate
10½-oz. can consomme

Clean pheasant and season with salt, pepper, seasoning salt, and dredge with flour. Brown in butter until golden on each side in large heavy skillet with tight fitting lid. Add sherry, consomme, gravy, onions, and mushrooms. Cook covered at 300° F. 45 minutes. Add parsley and monosodium glutamate and heat another 10 minutes.

RABBIT STEW

Serves: 6

1 rabbit, cut into serving   2 qt. water
   pieces   2 cups potatoes, diced
6 small white onions   2 cups carrots, sliced
1½ cups chopped celery   ½ lb. mushrooms
1 bay leaf   ½ cup flour
5 tsp. salt   ½ cup water
½ tsp. pepper

Place first seven ingredients in kettle. Simmer, covered, for 2 hours. Add potatoes, carrots and mushrooms and simmer, covered, another 45 minutes until all is tender. Blend flour and cold water and add to stew. Cook until thickened. Decorate with parsley and serve.

WILD TURKEY STEAKS

Take a sharp knife, run the blade down alongside the keel bone, removing the flesh from one end to the other. By this process, each half breast can be taken off whole. Lay the slab of white meat, skin side down and cut off ½ inch thick steaks until all the meat is gone. Sprinkle with salt and pepper and pile the steaks up together—thus the salt will quickly penetrate. **Do not salt anymore than you want for one meal.** As soon as salt dissolves and juices begin to flow, spread out steaks, and sprinkle dry flour lightly on both sides. Take care to do this right or you will get the flour too thick. The flour mixes with the juices, forming a crust around the steak, like batter. Have the frying pan on the stove with plenty of grease and sizzling hot so that the steak will fry the moment it touches the grease. Brown on both sides. By this method you retain all the juice from the meat and the flour prevents any grease from penetrating the meat. Will melt in mouth.

GRAVY IF DESIRED:

To pan drippings and about a teaspoon of the leftover grease, add ½ pint cold water to hot frying pan. Let boil about 5 minutes, season and have a rich, brown gravy.

This is a 60-year-old recipe taken from a rare book about wild turkey hunting. The book says, "Having eaten turkey this way, you would not care for baked or roast turkey again."

MRS. WILLIAM TEDFORD

VENISON SWISS STEAK

Serves: 4

1½ lbs. venison steak	2 Tb. Worcestershire sauce
(1½-in. thick)	Salt
3 large onions, sliced	Pepper
6 ribs celery, cut in thirds	1 to 2 Tb. flour dissolved in
2 cups canned tomatoes	¼ cup water

Dust venison steak with flour, salt and pepper. Brown in hot fat. Mix other ingredients, except flour, and spread over meat. Cook, covered, over low heat, 1¼ to 1½ hours. Remove meat and thicken juice by adding flour mixed with water.

This is for people who don't like the strong "gamey" flavor of venison.

MRS. CHARLES WITSELL

ROAST VENISON WITH POIVRADE SAUCE

Serves: 8-10   Oven: 450°

4½ lb. boneless venison   ½ cup cognac
   roast   Salt
4 Tb. butter   Pepper

Sprinkle the meat with salt and pepper to taste. Melt butter in open
skillet and turn roast in the butter until coated without browning.
Place roast, uncovered, in 450° oven and bake, basting and turning
the meat frequently, for 30 minutes. Reduce heat to 400°. Continue
basting and roasting 15 minutes for medium rare or longer for well
done. Remove meat and keep warm. Add cognac to skillet and
ignite it. Stir. This liquid will be added to poivrade sauce. Serve
the meat sliced with sauce.

POIVRADE SAUCE:

3 Tb. olive oil   2½ cups canned beef gravy
⅓ cup carrots, chopped   1½ Tb. cracked black pepper
⅓ cup onion, chopped   Cognac and juices from roast
4 Tb. parsley, minced   roast
1 cup dry red wine

Sauté vegetables in oil for 5 minutes. Add wine and simmer until
reduced by one-half. Add gravy and cook over low heat for 30
minutes. Strain. Add pan juices and pepper and serve with roast
venison.

MRS. PHILIP S. ANDERSON, JR.

VENISON STEW OR POT ROAST

Oven: 300°

MARINADE:

Equal parts red wine and   1 bay leaf
   water   10 to 12 cloves
6 to 8 peppercorns   1 sliced onion

ADD LATER:

1 tsp. grated lemon rind   ⅓ cup port
3 Tb. lemon juice   1½ Tb. butter

Cover venison with marinade and leave from 2 to 6 days. Turn
occasionally. Dry meat, dredge in flour and brown in fat. Pour
marinade over and bake, covered, for 3 to 4 hours. Skim fat from
drippings and add rind, juice, port and butter. Serve with seasoned
drippings.

For less tender cuts.

MRS. BART ROACH

VENISON AND ALE

Serves: 6

Flour
2 lbs. venison, cubed
$\frac{1}{4}$ cup salad oil
1 cup onion, chopped
2 or 3 cloves garlic, chopped
2 ribs celery, chopped
6 sprigs parsley
$\frac{1}{2}$ tsp. peppercorns

$\frac{1}{2}$ tsp. leaf thyme, crumbled
1 bay leaf
4 to 5 carrots, sliced
2 parsnips, sliced
12 to 14 onions, small
1 lb. mushroom, sliced
2 12-oz. bottles ale
2 cans consomme, undiluted

Dredge meat cubes in flour and brown on all sides in oil in a large Dutch oven; remove meat and reserve. Add onion, garlic and celery to fat remaining in pot and cook until lightly browned. Make a bouquet garni of parsley, peppercorns, thyme, and bay leaf in a double thickness of cheesecloth; add to pot. Return meat to pan and add vegetables, ale and enough consomme to cover meat and vegetables. Cover; bring to a boil; reduce heat and simmer 1½ to 2 hours or until meat is tender. Correct seasoning. Thicken with flour, if desired.

JIM WILSON

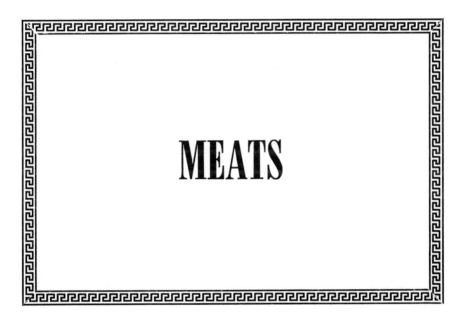

MEATS

BEEF TENDERLOIN

Serves: 6-8   Oven: 450°

Whole tenderloin   **Seasoned salt**
Olive oil   **Freshly ground pepper**

Rub tenderloin with olive oil, and sprinkle liberally with seasoned salt and pepper. Let meat stand at least 1 hour before roasting. Put meat in roasting pan. Place in 450° oven, and reduce heat to 350°. Roast to 140° on meat thermometer for rare (about 30 minutes). Slice tenderloin ½-inch thick.

Delicious topped with warm artichoke hearts and Bernaise sauce.

MRS. L. F. MITCHELL
LAKE LEELANAU, MICHIGAN

STANDING RIB ROAST BEEF

1 standing rib roast   **Garlic powder**
Salt and pepper

Rub the roast well with seasonings and let stand at room temperature. Place in roasting pan with rib side down. In the morning put in cold oven. Roast for 1 hour at 375°. Turn off oven until ½ hour before serving. Again turn oven to 375° for 30 minutes.

IMPORTANT:

Do not open oven door from time you put roast in until you are ready to eat.

Roast will be beautifully brown on the outside and rare on the inside, regardless of size. If a less rare roast is desired, the temperature should remain the same, but the final reheating time may be increased by 10 minutes.

MRS. SMITH DAVIS

ROAST BEEF WITH COFFEE

3 to 5 lb. roast beef, any cut   **2 cups black coffee**
Garlic or onion slivers   **2 cups water**
1 cup vinegar   **Salt and pepper**
2 Tb. salad oil

Use a large knife to cut slits completely through the meat. Insert slivers of garlic (or onion) down into the slits. Pour vinegar over meat, making sure it runs down into the slits. Marinate in refrigerator 24 to 48 hours. When ready to cook, place in a big heavy pot and brown well on all sides in oil. Cover with coffee and water. Simmer covered on top of stove 2 to 4 hours. Season with salt and pepper 20 minutes before serving.

MRS. BRONSON COOPER JACOWAY

ROAST BEEF TERIYAKI

Serves: 10-12   Oven: 325°

6-lb. rolled roast of beef
2 cups beef broth
2/3 cup soy sauce
1/2 cup red wine
3 Tb. brown sugar

1/4 cup finely chopped green
  onions
2 Tb. lemon juice
2 tsp. powdered ginger
2 cloves garlic, crushed

Place meat in a deep bowl. Mix together broth, soy sauce, wine, green onions, sugar, lemon juice, ginger, and garlic. Stir marinade until sugar dissolves. Pour over meat, cover, and let marinate in the refrigerator overnight or for at least 10 hours. Turn meat occasionally. Preheat oven to 325°. Remove meat from marinade and place on a rack in a foil-lined roasting pan. (The foil is important as the sugary marinade tends to burn on the bottom of the pan.) Pour marinade into a saucepan and set aside. It will be used for basting, then heated later and served as a sauce. Insert a meat thermometer into the center of the roast. Allow approximately 32 minutes per pound for rare, 38 minutes per pound for medium. Brush beef 3 or 4 times with marinade during roasting. Allow meat to rest about 20 minutes after removing from oven. Heat remaining sauce and serve with the meat.

MRS. WAYNE UPTON

POT ROAST DUBONNET

Serves: 6-8

3 to 5 lb. rump roast
  (shoulder or chuck)
2 large onions, sliced
1 lemon, sliced
2 Tb. sugar
1 tsp. salt

12 peppercorns
1 Tb. ginger
1 1/2 cups Dubonnet
2 Tb. bacon drippings
2 Tb. melted butter
2 Tb. flour

Marinate roast in next 7 ingredients, covered in refrigerator for 18 to 24 hours. Turn meat occasionally.

When ready to cook, drain meat well, saving marinade liquid. Brown meat in bacon drippings in Dutch oven or deep skillet. Strain marinade; add liquid to meat and simmer approximately 3 hours, or until meat is tender. Remove meat and strain remaining liquid into a bowl. Blend flour and butter in pan and add strained liquid. Stir until smooth and slightly thickened. Add salt to taste. Place meat in gravy; heat for 5 minutes. Serve sliced meat on a hot platter, pouring gravy over the roast.

MRS. L. F. MITCHELL
LAKE LEELANAU, MICHIGAN

SAUERBRATEN

Serves: 6-8

4 lbs. boneless rump or round
   roast
½ cup dry red wine
½ cup red wine vinegar
2 cups cold water
5 peppercorns and 4 whole
   juniper berries coarsely
   crushed with a mortar and
   pestle

1 onion, sliced
2 small bay leaves
3 Tb. salad oil
½ cup chopped onion
½ cup chopped carrots
½ cup chopped celery
2 Tb. flour
½ cup water
10 gingersnaps, crushed

In a 2 to 3 quart saucepan combine wine, vinegar, water, sliced onion, crushed peppercorns and juniper berries, and bay leaves. Bring marinade to a boil over high heat. Cool to room temperature. Place beef in a deep crock or a deep stainless steel or enameled pot just large enough to hold it comfortably. Pour marinade over meat. Marinade should come at least halfway up the sides of the meat; if necessary, add more wine. Turn meat to moisten all sides. Cover pan tightly with foil or plastic wrap. Refrigerate 2 to 3 days, turning meat over at least twice a day.

Remove meat from marinade and pat completely dry with paper towels. Strain marinade through a fine sieve over a bowl, reserving liquid. Discard spices and onions.

Heat oil in heavy 5 quart container. Add meat and brown on all sides, turning frequently and regulating heat so that it browns deeply and evenly without burning. This should take about 15 minutes. Transfer meat to a platter. Pour off all but 2 tablespoons of oil. Add chopped onions, carrots, and celery and cook over moderate heat 5 to 8 minutes, stirring frequently. Sprinkle flour over vegetables and cook, stirring constantly, 2 to 3 minutes longer. Pour in 2 cups of the reserved marinade and ½ cup water. Bring to a boil over high heat. Add meat, cover tightly and simmer over low heat for 2 hours, or until meat shows no resistance when pierced with the tip of a sharp knife. Remove meat to serving platter and keep warm. Stir in cookie crumbs and heat to boiling. Spoon gravy over sliced meat and serve.

HANS BACH

BARBECUED BRISKET

Serves: 12-16   Oven: 275°

4 lbs. brisket of beef	½ cup sugar
Salt and pepper	1 tsp. celery salt
¼ cup Worcestershire sauce	½ tsp. Tabasco
½ tsp. sage	1½ cups catsup

Liberally salt and pepper brisket. Combine remaining ingredients in small saucepan. Heat just until sugar melts. Pour ⅓ of sauce in bottom of roasting pan. Place brisket on sauce. Pour ⅓ of sauce on top of brisket. Cover and cook in 275° oven 4½ hours. Slice thinly and serve with remainder of sauce on buns.

Variation: Marinate meat overnight in liquid smoke (1 small bottle). Pour off. Salt and pepper meat and cover with small bottle of Worcestershire sauce and barbecue sauce. Wrap in foil. Cook 6 hours at 300°. Chop and serve on buns.

MRS. STEPHEN W. CREEKMORE, JR.
FORT SMITH, ARKANSAS

BRISKET ROAST WITH BEER

Serves: 6 to 8 (hot), 12 to 20 (cold)   Oven: 225°

4 to 5 lb. brisket roast	Freshly ground pepper
2 medium onions, sliced	12-oz. can beer
12-oz. bottle chili sauce	Worcestershire sauce
Seasoned salt	

Place brisket in roaster, fat side up. Cover with sliced onions, then add chili sauce. Rinse out bottle with water and pour over roast. Add salt and pepper. Cook uncovered in 225° oven for 3 hours. Baste every 30 minutes, adding small amounts of water if needed. Pour beer over meat and cook covered 1½ hours more. For sauce or gravy, skim grease off liquid in pan and add a dash of Worcestershire sauce. Slice roast and serve hot with parsleyed new potatoes and a tossed salad.

To serve cold, cook the day before, chill overnight, then have butcher slice roast thin as bacon. Cut long slices in half to serve as cocktail food, and serve with slices of thinly sliced rye or French bread. Serve with sauce, cold or hot, mayonnaise and mustard.

MRS. NORMAN FAUST

LONDON BROIL

Serves: 4

Flank steak, 1½ to 2 lbs.	½ tsp. powdered rosemary
1½ tsp. monosodium	¼ tsp. ground ginger
glutamate	1 tsp. whole peppercorns
1½ tsp. salt	¼ cup lemon juice
1 tsp. sugar	½ cup salad oil
1 Tb. instant minced onion	1 clove garlic, split
½ tsp. dry mustard	

Mix seasonings together with lemon juice, salad oil and garlic to make marinade. Place steak in glass or enamel container, cover with marinade and place in refrigerator 3 to 4 hours, turning steak occasionally. Remove steak from marinade and broil about 4 to 5 inches from heat for 5 minutes on each side. Meat should be rare. Cut steak across the grain in thin diagonal slices.

MRS. JAMES M. MCGAUGHY

BEEFSTEAK AU ROQUEFORT

Serves: 2

1 Porterhouse steak, 2-inches	¼ cup butter
thick	2 to 4 Tb. Roquefort cheese
2 Tb. melted butter	Juice of ½ lemon
1 beef bouillon cube	2 to 4 Tb. fresh parsley,
Salt and freshly ground	chives or chervil
pepper	

Trim excess fat off steak. Brush with mixture of bouillon cube melted in butter, salt and pepper. Broil on grill until cooked to your liking. While steak is cooking, cream Roquefort cheese and butter with lemon juice, chopped herbs and a little salt and pepper. Serve steak immediately, topped with Roquefort butter.

MRS. EUGENE MASON

STEAK DIANE

This steak is quickly and easily made at the table in a chafing dish, if there aren't too many people. It definitely requires best cut of meat.

FOR EACH SERVING:

Rib eye steak, ½ inch thick	1 Tb. minced shallots
2½ Tb. butter	1 Tb. cognac
1 Tb. minced chives	2 Tb. sherry
1 Tb. minced parsley	1 tsp. Worcestershire sauce
Salt and pepper to taste	(optional)

Pound meat as flat as possible with flat mallet. Cream together 1½ tablespoons butter, chives, parsley, salt and pepper. Melt remaining butter over medium heat with shallot, which should soften but not brown. Increase heat and sauté steak quickly, about ½ minute per side (until just seared). Remove and keep warm. Flame pan with cognac; reduce heat. Add seasoned butter, sherry and Worcestershire (if desired). When blended, replace steak for an instant, turning once, then serve with sauce.

MRS. DONALD F. THOMPSON, JR.

BAKED STEAK WITH MUSHROOMS

Serves: 6-8   Oven: 375°

3½ lb. sirloin steak
  (2 inches thick)
1 Tb. salad or olive oil
2 Tb. butter
½ tsp. salt
¾ tsp. thyme

2 garlic cloves, peeled
¼ lb. fresh mushrooms or
  can drained sliced mushrooms
½ cup Burgundy
2 Tb. chopped parsley

Preheat oven to 375°. Wipe steak with damp paper towels. Heat oil in large heavy skillet until very hot. Brown steak well, about 5 minutes, on each side. Remove steak and pour off all fat. Replace steak and spread with 1 tablespoon butter; sprinkle with salt and thyme. Place garlic beside steak. Insert meat thermometer into side of steak, being sure point is near center of meat. Bake uncovered, 25 to 30 minutes, or until thermometer registers 140° F. for rare or 150° F. for medium rare. Remove steak to serving platter. Discard garlic. Keep steak warm. Sauté mushrooms in skillet until browned. Add wine and heat to boiling over high heat. Stir to dissolve browned bits in pan. Boil, uncovered a few minutes, to reduce liquid slightly. Remove from heat. Stir in 1 tablespoon butter. Pour over meat. Sprinkle with parsley. To serve, carve steak thinly on diagonal. Spoon sauce over slices.

MRS. H. WILLIAM GOODMAN

SAVORY STUFFED FILET OF BEEF

Serves: 16   Oven: 300°

1 filet, about 6 to 7 lbs.
  (or 2 filets, 3½ lbs. each)
3 large onions, sliced thinly
6 Tb. olive oil
4 Tb. butter
2 cloves garlic, minced
18 ripe olives, chopped

½ cup ham, diced
1 tsp. salt
1 tsp. freshly ground pepper
1 tsp. thyme
2 egg yolks, beaten
2 Tb. chopped fresh parsley

Sauté onion in oil and butter until limp. Add garlic, olives, ham, salt, pepper, and thyme. Cook until well blended. Stir in beaten egg yolks and parsley. Cook 2 to 3 minutes. Cut filets in thick slices not quite all the way through lengthwise. Spoon stuffing into slices. Run needle and thread in lacing manner to close it. Place on a rack. Brush with butter and roast in 300° oven for 30 minutes for rare, 45 minutes for medium, 1 hour for well done. Let meat rest 10 minutes before serving. May be served with Bordelaise sauce.

MRS. DONALD F. THOMPSON, JR.

GERMAN ROULADEN

Serves: 4-6

2 lbs. top round beef, sliced	3 Tb. horseradish
¼-inch thick	2 to 3 Tb. cornstarch
4 slices thick bacon, diced	3 cups beef bouillon
2 to 3 dill pickles	1 Tb. salad oil
3 Tb. prepared mustard	2 Tb. butter

Cut meat into 6 to 8 slices; trim off fat. Slice pickles lengthwise. Spread each piece of meat with mustard and horseradish; sprinkle with diced bacon. Place dill pickle slice in center of meat, roll up and fasten with small skewers or toothpicks. Heat butter and oil in skillet and brown roulades; then remove. Stir in bouillon, bring to boil and thicken with cornstarch dissolved in small amount of water. Add roulades to gravy and simmer, covered, about 1 hour. Serve with potato dumplings.

POTATO DUMPLINGS:

4 to 6 medium potatoes	1 tsp. salt
1 cup flour	Dash nutmeg
2 eggs, beaten	6 cups beef bouillon

Cook potatoes and peel off skins while warm. Grate with fine grater. Add flour, eggs, salt, and nutmeg. Knead with fingers and shape into balls 1 to 2 inches in diameter. Bring bouillon to boil and drop dumplings in. Lower heat and simmer about 10 minutes, until dumplings rise to top. (Try one dumpling in the bouillon, if it falls apart, add more flour to mixture.)

MRS. DAN DANIELS
FAIRFIELD BAY, ARKANSAS

BEEF AND HAM BIRDS IN WHITE WINE

Serves: 4

4 ¼-inch slices sirloin tip	¼ cup raisins
(about 3 by 5 inches)	6 Tb. Parmesan cheese,
¼ lb. ham, sliced paper thin	grated
(Virginia ham preferred)	1 cup sharp cheese, grated
½ cup parsley, finely	4 to 6 Tb. margarine
chopped	¾ cup white wine
¼ cup almonds, chopped	

Place beef slices between two sheets of waxed paper and pound very thin. Lay a slice of ham on each slice of beef. Make a filling of parsley, almonds, raisins, and cheeses. Spread filling on each of the meat slices. Roll up slices and tie with string. Brown birds on all sides in margarine. Add wine and simmer covered, for about 30 minutes, or until meat is tender. Carefully remove strings to serve.

MRS. JOHN BALDRIDGE

PAPRIKA BEEF ROLL

Serves: 6   Oven: 350°

2 round steaks, 1½ lbs. each
1 tsp. salt
½ tsp. pepper
1 Tb. paprika (Hungarian)
2 4-oz. cans sliced mush-
  rooms
1 onion, thinly sliced
2-oz. jar pimiento
¾ cup bread crumbs
½ cup melted butter

1 Tb. boiling water
1 egg, beaten
½ cup stuffed green olives,
  sliced
Flour
¼ cup salad oil
8 oz. whole mushrooms
3 small onions
2 cups dry red wine

Pound steaks thin. Rub with salt, pepper, and paprika. Overlap steaks on meat board, making one large steak. Spread with mushrooms, onion, pimiento, and cover with finely rolled bread crumbs. Dribble mixture of butter, water, and egg over bread crumbs. Add layer of sliced olives. Roll meat up and tie firmly with twine in 3 or 4 places. Sprinkle with flour and brown in oil in roasting pan. Place onions and whole mushrooms around meat and sprinkle lightly with salt and pepper. Add wine. Cook covered in 350° oven for 2 hours.

MRS. EUGENE MASON

WINE MARINADE FOR SHISH KABOBS

1 cup red wine
2 tsp. Worcestershire sauce
2 cloves garlic
1 cup salad oil
4 Tb. catsup
2 Tb. vinegar

1 tsp. salt
1 tsp. black pepper
2 tsp. sugar
1 tsp. marjoram
1 tsp. rosemary
½ tsp. basil leaves

Mix all ingredients together and use as marinade for sirloin steak cubes and small vegetables such as onions, tomatoes, green pepper pieces, and mushrooms. Marinate all together at least 10 hours. Alternate meat and vegetables on skewers. Cook on grill on foil punched with holes.

MRS. ALLAN DISHONGH

SPAGHETTI SAUCE DI COCCO

1½ lbs. round steak, cut in individual portions, trimmed, pounded, sprinkled with chopped garlic, parsley, salt and pepper, and rolled and secured with toothpicks
1 lb. pork chops, cut in bite-size pieces

Meatballs, mixed with parsley and garlic
2 qts. canned tomatoes, preferably pear-shaped Italian style
3 6-oz. cans tomato paste
1 to 2 tsp. sweet basil
1 to 2 garlic cloves
Salt and pepper to taste

Brown the roulades in bacon fat, then the pork and meatballs. Put all ingredients in a large heavy kettle and cook for about 3 hours at a gentle simmer, covered, stirring occasionally. This is best served on homemade spaghetti. The machines are available in Italian specialty groceries. Otherwise, vermicelli is preferred. Remove all of the meat and serve it as a side dish to the spaghetti. This freezes well, and improves with limited age.

BILL LEWIS

OLD-FASHIONED BEEF RAGOUT

Serves: 8

¼ cup salad oil
6 lbs. chuck, cut for stew
2 cups finely chopped onion
1 cup finely chopped celery
1 clove garlic, crushed
⅓ cup flour
16-oz. can undrained tomatoes
1 cup sauterne wine
2 10½-oz. cans beef bouillon
2 Tb. chopped parsley

1 tsp. dried rosemary
2 bay leaves
½ tsp. dried tarragon
2¼ tsp. salt
½ tsp. pepper
2 cups sliced carrots
2 lbs. new potatoes, bite-size
10-oz. pkg. frozen peas
10-oz. pkg. frozen mushrooms

Brown beef in hot oil in 6 quart Dutch oven. Remove beef and add onion, celery, and garlic; sauté. Remove from heat, stir in flour. Brown flour lightly over low heat, stirring for 2 minutes. Add tomatoes, wine, undiluted bouillon, parsley, herbs, salt, and pepper. Bring to boil; add beef. Reduce heat; simmer, covered, 2½ hours or until meat is tender. Skim off any fat. Add carrots and potatoes; cook 1 hour. Cook peas and mushrooms by label directions; drain. Sprinkle over stew.

MRS. CHARLES A. SMITH

CARBONADE OF BEEF FLAMANDE

Serves: 4-6   Oven: 325°

3 lbs. chuck, cut in 2-inch   1 pint beer
   pieces   1 tsp. sugar
Salt and pepper   1 tsp. vinegar
3 Tb. salad oil   1 clove minced garlic
5 onions, sliced   1 tsp. thyme
4 Tb. butter   1 bay leaf
3 Tb. flour   2 tsp. chopped parsley
1 cup bouillon

Season chuck with salt and pepper. Brown meat in oil in Dutch oven. Melt butter in another skillet and brown onions slowly, about 20 to 30 minutes. When meat is brown, remove from Dutch oven. Add flour to remaining oil. Brown until dark. Add beer and bouillon and cook until thick, stirring constantly. Add seasonings, then meat and onions. Cook covered about 2½ hours at 325°. Good with boiled potatoes and beer.

MRS. MIKE MEHAFFY

HUNGARIAN GOULASH

Serves: 4-6   Oven: 350°

2 lbs. lean beef or veal, cut   1½ Tb. flour
   into 1-inch cubes   1½ cups beer
Salt and freshly ground   ½ cup fresh or canned
   pepper to taste   chicken broth
2 Tb. peanut oil (or salad oil)   1 tsp. Dijon or Duseldorf
2 tsp. butter   mustard
2 cups onions, thinly sliced   1 tsp. caraway seeds
1½ Tb. paprika   1 cup sour cream

Season meat with salt and pepper. Heat oil and butter in skillet and brown meat on all sides. Transfer meat to heavy casserole. Add onions to skillet and cook, stirring, until wilted, adding more butter if necessary. Stir in paprika and flour. Add beer and chicken broth, then mustard and caraway seeds, and bring to a boil. Add salt to taste and pour mixture over meat. Cover and bake at 350° 1 to 1½ hours. Just before serving, stir in sour cream. Serve with noodles or dumplings.

MRS. JOHN M. HARRISON

BEEF BURGUNDY FLAMBE

Serves: 6

2 slices bacon
2 Tb. flour
1 tsp. seasoned salt
2 lbs. sirloin tip steak, cut in
short strips
1 pkg. beef stew seasoning
mix
1 cup Burgundy

1 cup water
1 Tb. tomato paste
12 small boiling onions
4 oz. fresh mushrooms
16 cherry tomatoes, stems
removed
¼ cup brandy

Fry bacon in a Dutch oven, then remove. Coat meat strips with flour and seasoned salt. Brown in bacon fat. Add beef stew seasoning mix, Burgundy, water, and tomato paste. Cover and simmer gently 45 minutes. Peel onions and pierce each end with a fork so they will retain their shape when cooked. Add onions to beef mixture and simmer about 40 minutes, until meat and onions are tender. (Recipe may be prepared ahead of time to this point. If prepared ahead, reheat and proceed.) Add mushrooms and cherry tomatoes; simmer 5 minutes. Pour into a shallow dish or chafing dish. Heat brandy quickly and gently over hot water. Pour over beef mixture. Set aflame at the table. Stir gently and serve immediately.

MRS. B. R. JUDKINS

BEOUF BOURGUIGNON

Serves: 6

½ lb. mushrooms
2 Tb. butter
2 cups red wine
3 Tb. salad oil
4 oz. salt pork, cut into small
pieces (or 4 strips bacon
cut up)
12 small boiling onions
3 lbs. shoulder roast, cut into
2-inch cubes

3 Tb. flour (or more if
necessary)
2 cloves garlic
1 Tb. chopped parsley
2-inch piece orange peel
1 bay leaf
¼ tsp. thyme
¼ tsp. nutmeg
1 tsp. salt

Sauté mushrooms in butter, set aside. Heat wine in a separate pan. Heat oil in Dutch oven; add salt pork. Brown and remove. Next, brown onions and remove. Dredge meat in flour. Add to pan and brown on all sides. Return salt pork to pan; add warm wine, garlic, parsley, orange peel, and seasonings. Cover tightly and cook over low heat about 3½ hours. Remove cover, add onions, and cook 15 minutes. Remove orange peel, garlic, and bay leaf. Mushrooms may be added to the mixture or reheated and served as a garnish around the side of the serving dish. Serve over parslied rice.

This is a very easy, very good dish, and will hold through the most prolonged cocktail hour.

MRS. C. W. BLACKWOOD, JR.

BEER BEEF STROGANOFF

Serves: 4-6

2 lbs. sirloin steak, cut in   ⅛ tsp. paprika
  1-inch cubes   2 Tb. flour
2 Tb. salad oil   1 tsp. Worcestershire sauce
1½ tsp. salt   12-oz. can beer
2 onions, sliced   1 cup sour cream
3-oz. can sliced mushrooms

Brown meat in oil in large skillet. Add salt. Remove meat. In same
skillet cook onion and undrained mushrooms, covered, for 3 to 4
minutes. Push to side. Blend flour and paprika in drippings. Add
beer and Worcestershire. Stir and cook until thickened and bubbly.
Return meat; stir in sour cream. Cook slowly about 10 minutes.
Serve over noodles or rice.

MRS. DAVID CLINTON

LEBANESE STEW

Serves: 8

1½ lbs. round steak, cut in   ⅛ tsp. oregano
  1-inch cubes   2 cups okra
2 Tb. butter   2 Tb. butter
2 16-oz. cans green beans,   2 cups long grain rice, soaked
  drained and rinsed   before cooking
3 8-oz. cans tomato sauce   4½ cups water
2 cups beef broth   1 tsp. salt
2½ tsp. salt   ⅛ tsp. pepper
1¼ tsp. black pepper   ¼ cup butter
2 cloves garlic

Brown meat in butter in large heavy skillet. Add beans, tomato
sauce, beef broth, salt, pepper, oregano, and garlic. Fast-brown
okra in 2 tablespoons butter to prevent stringing. Add to mixture.
Simmer 1½ hours. Cook rice in water, salt, pepper, and butter.
Pour meat mixture over buttered rice and serve.

MRS. MARK BELEW
VERNON, TEXAS

OUR TOWN STEW

Serves: 8

This is a stew for the purist. It is not confused with the usual "stew" vegetables. When it is well made the result should be beautifully brown gravy containing tender pieces of meat, whole small onions and mushrooms.

3 lbs. good beef stew meat cut in chunks or cubes	12 oz. beer
Flour	30 to 35 small pearl onions, peeled
Shortening (or half olive oil and half butter)	30 to 35 fresh mushroom caps
Salt and pepper	Cayenne
2 cloves garlic, sliced	

Salt and pepper meat well. Dredge in flour making sure that all sides are well coated.

Brown meat well in the shortening in a heavy pot, along with one sliced clove of garlic. When the meat is richly brown, pour over it the 12 ounces of beer. Then add water to cover the meat. (More beer may be used if desired, but too much will give the stew a slightly bitter taste. This can be remedied by the judicious addition of a small amount of sugar.)

Add the second clove of garlic—or more if you desire—and a small amount of cayenne. (Careful.) Bring to a boil, reduce heat and simmer 1½ to 2 hours.

Correct seasoning and add pearl onions, cooking until the onions are tender but still whole. During the last 10 minutes stir in the mushroom caps from which the stems have been removed. (The removal of stems is purely for visual effect. Leave them on if you want.)

A little water may be added at this point or during cooking to increase the liquid volume slightly. The rich brown gravy is imperative.

The stew should be served with potatoes, preferably mashed with a hand masher and enriched with milk, butter, salt and pepper. It can also be served with noodles. Serve beer with it, or wine. This stew, incidentally, can be made with red wine instead of beer as a variation.

It freezes well and its flavor improves if made one day and served the next.

RICHARD ALLIN

TIM'S CHEESE 'N BUTTER BURGERS

Serves: 8

2 ½ lbs. ground beef
   (not round or chuck)
Worcestershire sauce
Tabasco
Garlic powder
½ tsp. Accent
1 tsp. salt
¼ tsp. pepper

8 pats butter (1 ½ tsp. each)
5 oz. sharp Cheddar cheese,
   grated
8 strips bacon (optional)
8 hamburger buns, buttered
   and lightly toasted
Unseasoned meat tenderizer
Barbecue sauce

Season meat with generous shakes of Worcestershire, Tabasco, and garlic powder according to individual preference. Add Accent, salt, and pepper. Mix well. Divide meat into 16 portions. Shape each into flat pattie; turn up sides slightly on 8 of these. In center of each turned up pattie place grated cheese and top with pat of butter. Top with second pattie. Shape hamburgers until round and edges are sealed. If using bacon, wrap around seam and fasten with toothpick. Sprinkle with meat tenderizer on both sides and grill over hot coals, basting frequently with barbecue sauce. Serve on toasted buns with assortment of relishes.

TIM DE NOBLE

STUFFED PEPPERS

Serves: 6

6 to 8 large bell peppers
½ cup rice
1 large onion, chopped
1 ½ lbs. ground beef, ground
   with ½ lb. ground pork
1 tsp. salt

¼ tsp. pepper
16-oz. can tomatoes
1 cup water
1 cup sour cream
2 Tb. cornstarch

Trim the stem ends from the peppers and carefully remove the seeds and pith. Cook rice in salted boiling water for 10 minutes. Sauté onion in bacon fat until tender. Mix ground meat, onion, rice, salt and pepper. Stuff peppers with the mixture. Arrange peppers in a Dutch oven, cover with tomatoes and water. Cook covered on top of stove over low heat for approximately two hours. Remove peppers to warm platter. Strain liquid. Mix sour cream and cornstarch and add slowly to the liquid. Heat to boiling point. Serve as gravy for peppers.

MRS. R. B. ELWOOD

CHILI

Serves: 6-8

4 lbs. ground chuck	6-oz. can tomato paste
4 Tb. salad oil	5¼ cups (or 4 10½-oz. cans)
2 cups chopped onion	beef stock
1 to 2 Tb. chopped garlic	1 Tb. salt
6 to 8 Tb. chili powder	Pepper to taste
1½ tsp. oregano	1½ cups kidney beans
1½ tsp. ground cumin	

Brown meat in oil; remove to 5 quart pan. Cook onions and garlic in same oil until onions are clear; remove to pan. To meat and onions, add chili powder, oregano, cumin, tomato paste, stock, salt and pepper. Blend well. Bring to boil, reduce heat and simmer, covered, for 1½ to 2 hours. Add beans last 30 minutes.

MRS. LEONARD THOMPSON

MEAT BALLS

Serves: 6

1½ lbs. ground meat	2 garlic cloves, pressed
2 slices bread soaked in	1 Tb. Parmesan cheese
water then squeezed well	Salt
2 eggs	Pepper
1 tsp. parsley	

Mix well. Roll into medium size balls and brown.

SAUCE:

3 to 4 Tb. salad oil	2 cans water
1 medium onion, chopped	½ tsp. parsley
2 6-oz. cans tomato sauce	½ tsp. salt
1 small carrot, chopped very	¼ tsp. basil
fine	½ tsp. oregano

Heat oil in large saucepan or skillet; add onions and brown. Add remainder of ingredients. Bring to a slow boil; cook at least one hour. Add meat balls at beginning of boil. Serve over noodles or macaroni.

MRS. GEORGE STEWART

HAMBURGER STROGANOFF

Serves: 6

1½ lbs. ground beef
2 Tb. butter
2 Tb. salad oil
1 cup chopped onion
6-oz. can mushrooms
1 can beef bouillon soup
1½ Tb. flour
½ tsp. caraway seed
Dash of nutmeg
Dash Worcestershire sauce
Salt and pepper to taste
2 cups sour cream

Brown meat. Remove from skillet and pour off fat. Melt butter and oil in skillet and sauté onions and mushrooms until onions are clear. Remove from skillet. Add flour to skillet and brown. Add bouillon and blend. Stir in salt, pepper, caraway, nutmeg, and Worcestershire. Return meat, onions, and mushrooms to skillet. Simmer all together for 15 minutes. Before serving stir in sour cream. Serve over noodles.

ANNE EASLEY STEBBINS

TALLERINI

Serves: 10-12   Oven: 350°

2 lbs. ground beef
1 onion, chopped
2 8-oz. cans enchilada sauce
6-oz. can tomato paste
1 can cream style corn
Salt and pepper
6-oz. can ripe pitted olives, drained
Dash chili powder
1 lb. Cheddar cheese, grated
5-oz. pkg. noodles, cooked

Brown meat in Dutch oven. Add onion and let wilt. Cut olives in half. Add remaining ingredients. Cook 30 minutes in 350° oven.

MRS. VERNON JACKSON, III

HERB MEAT LOAF

Serves: 4-6   Oven: 350°

1 lb. ground beef
¼ lb. lean sausage
½ onion, grated
¼ tsp. garlic salt
1 rib celery, chopped
1 egg, beaten
1 tsp. Accent
6 oz. chili sauce
¼ cup milk
1 cup herb seasoned stuffing (Pepperidge Farm)
1 tsp. salt
½ tsp. pepper
8-oz. can tomato sauce

Mix all ingredients except tomato sauce. (The best method for mixing this is with your hands.) Press into a greased loaf pan. Bake in 350° oven for 1 hour. Remove from oven and pour off grease. Cover with tomato sauce. Return to oven for 5 minutes.
For a spicier sauce, mix 16-oz. can tomatoes, 6-oz. can tomato paste, 2 tablespoons chopped onion, sautéed in 1 tablespoon butter, and 2 teaspoons oregano.

MRS. RICHARD FREELING

BILLIE'S CABBAGE ROLL

Serves: 18   Oven: 250°

6 lbs. lean ground beef
2 cups cooked rice
Milk to moisten
4 Tb. chopped parsley
1 Tb. onion salt
1 Tb. garlic salt

2 tsp. pepper
½ tsp. nutmeg
2 large heads cabbage
4 8-oz. cans tomato sauce
2 Tb. brown sugar

Mix together ground beef, rice, and enough milk to make mixture very moist (approximately 2 cups). Add parsley, salts, pepper, and ¼ tsp. nutmeg. Form into small individual loaves about the size of your fist, well patted. Separate cabbage leaves and boil a few at a time until pliable, approximately 1 minute. Wrap loaves in cabbage leaves, securing with toothpicks and pack tightly into a 10 x 13-inch pan. Pour tomato sauce over and sprinkle with the remainder of the nutmeg and the brown sugar. Cover tightly with aluminum foil and bake 2½ hours in 250° oven. This may be made several days ahead and refrigerated. In fact, the flavors blend better if this is done. It freezes well too.

MRS. JAMES B. SPEED
FORT SMITH, ARKANSAS

ITALIAN BEEF PATTIES

Serves: 4

1½ lbs. lean ground beef
2 eggs
⅔ cup Italian style bread or
  2 slices bread soaked in
  milk
1 medium onion, chopped
½ cup grated Parmesan
  cheese

3 cloves garlic, chopped
2 tsp. oregano leaves
1 tsp. basil
Salt and pepper
4 slices onion
4 slices bell pepper
4 Tb. sliced mushrooms
8-oz. can tomato sauce

Mix first 9 ingredients together as for meat loaf. Make 4 large hamburger shaped patties. On each patty put 1 slice onion, 1 slice green pepper, and 1 tablespoon mushrooms. Pour tomato sauce over each patty. Simmer 45 minutes in electric skillet, covered, or in Dutch oven in 350° oven for 1 hour.

MRS. EUGENE MASON

SPAGHETTI SAUCE

Serves: 6-8

1 lb. ground beef	¼ tsp. pepper
½ cup chopped onion	1 bay leaf
2½-oz. can mushrooms	Dash basil
¼ cup chopped parsley or	6-oz. can tomato paste
2 tsp. dried parsley	8-oz. can tomato sauce
1 tsp. garlic salt	16-oz. can tomatoes
1 tsp. salt	8-oz. pkg. spaghetti
1 tsp. oregano	

Brown ground beef and onion in Dutch oven or large skillet. Add all other ingredients except spaghetti. Simmer covered 1 hour, then uncovered one-half hour. Serve over cooked spaghetti.

MRS. VERNON JACKSON, III

LASAGNE

Serves: 6-8   Oven: 375°

1 Tb. salt	½ tsp. pepper
1 Tb. olive oil	2 Tb. parsley flakes
3 qts. boiling water	½ cup grated Parmesan
8 oz. lasagne noodles	cheese
1 lb. ricotta or cottage cheese	1 recipe meat sauce
2 eggs, beaten	1 lb. Mozzarella cheese, sliced
2 tsp. salt	thin

Add olive oil and 1 tablespoon salt to rapidly boiling water. Gradually add lasagne noodles so that water continues to boil. Cook uncovered, stirring occasionally, until tender. Drain. Mix ricotta, eggs, salt, pepper, parsley, and Parmesan together. Cover bottom of 13 x 9 x 2-inch baking dish with ⅓ meat sauce. Place ⅓ Mozzarella cheese over sauce and top with ricotta cheese mixture. Add a layer of ½ the lasagne. Repeat layers. Cover with remaining meat sauce and cheeses. Bake in 375° oven for 30 minutes.

MEAT SAUCE:

¼ cup olive oil	½ cup tomato puree
½ cup butter	2 Tb. tomato paste
1 medium onion, finely	2 ribs celery, finely
chopped	chopped
1 lb. ground beef	1 carrot, finely chopped
4 minced garlic cloves	Salt
3 Tb. finely chopped parsley	Pepper
2 Tb. Chianti wine	2 tsp. oregano
1 cup canned tomatoes	

Heat olive oil and butter together. Add onion and ground beef, sauté until brown, stirring occasionally. Add garlic and parsley. Cook over low heat for 10 minutes. Stir in wine; cover and steam for 2 minutes. Add tomatoes, tomato puree, and tomato paste. Bring to boiling point and add celery, carrot, and seasonings. Cover and cook over low heat, stirring occasionally, until flavors have penetrated.

MRS. A. JOSEPH JOHNSON, JR.

STUFFED MUSHROOM CASSEROLE

Serves: 4   **Oven: 350°**

2 pkgs. frozen spinach
  (or 2 bunches fresh)
1 cup sour cream
1 cup Cheddar cheese
1 cup Monterey Jack cheese
½ cup Parmesan cheese
¼ cup green onions, sliced

¼ cup green onion tops,
  chopped
1½ tsp. salt
1 tsp. Italian herb seasoning
12 giant mushrooms
1 lb. ground chuck
Nutmeg

Cook spinach briefly in hot water; drain and chop. Mix with sour cream, ½ cup each shredded Cheddar, Monterey Jack, and Parmesan cheeses, chopped green onion tops, ½ tsp. salt, and herb seasoning. Place 12 stemmed fresh mushrooms, cup side up, in center of large baking dish. Spoon spinach around edges. Sauté ground beef lightly with sliced green onions and 1 tsp salt. Spoon over mushrooms. Top with ½ cup each shredded Cheddar and Monterey Jack. Sprinkle lightly with nutmeg. Bake covered in 350° oven for 25 minutes.

MRS. BEN WITSELL
LAS VEGAS, NEVADA

SPICY MEATBALL CASSEROLE

Serves: 8-10   **Oven: 350°**

1½ lbs. ground beef
¾ cup soft bread crumbs
3 Tb. milk
1 egg
¼ cup minced onion
1½ tsp. salt
Pepper
¼ tsp. thyme
¼ tsp. oregano
1 clove garlic, crushed
¼ cup margarine
¾ cup onion, chopped
16-oz. can tomatoes

6-oz. can tomato paste
1 clove garlic, crushed
1 Tb. parsley flakes
1 tsp. oregano
Pinch of basil
Pinch of thyme
¼ cup cooked crumbled
  bacon
½ lb. spaghetti
1 cup small curd cottage
  cheese
½ cup sour cream
Parmesan cheese

Combine beef, bread crumbs, milk, egg, minced onion, salt, pepper, thyme, oregano, and 1 clove garlic. Shape into balls and cook in margarine. Drain. In same skillet sauté onion. Stir in tomatoes, tomato paste, 1 clove garlic, parsley flakes, oregano, basil, and thyme. Add bacon and meatballs. Simmer covered for 45 minutes. Meanwhile, cook and drain spaghetti. Grease 3 quart casserole. Place one-half of cooked spaghetti in bottom. Spread with cottage cheese, sour cream, and one-half of meatball mixture. Add remainder of spaghetti and top with rest of meatball mixture. Top with Parmesan cheese if desired. Bake in 350° oven for 30 minutes.

This is a good and spicy company spaghetti dish.

MRS. ALLEN BULLARD

MOUSSAKA

Serves: 8   Oven: 375°

1½ lbs. ground lamb or
    chuck
1 large onion, chopped fine
¼ cup butter
28-oz. can tomatoes, drained
2 Tb. chopped parsley
½ cup red wine
Salt and pepper to taste
2 eggs, well-beaten
½ cup grated Parmesan
    cheese

3 Tb. bread crumbs
2 medium eggplants
¼ cup melted butter
⅓ cup bread crumbs
3 Tb. butter
3 Tb. flour
1½ cups milk
2 eggs, well-beaten
¼ cup grated Parmesan
    cheese

Brown meat and onion in ¼ cup butter; add tomatoes, parsley, wine, salt, and pepper. Cook slowly until liquid is absorbed; set aside to cool. Then add eggs, cheese, and 3 Tb. bread crumbs. Mix well and season to taste. (For variety try nutmeg or garlic.) Meanwhile, peel and slice eggplants lengthwise into ½-inch slices; brush with melted butter and broil until brown on each side. (May be fried if desired, using additional butter.) Sprinkle the bottom of a 9 x 13-inch pan with bread crumbs; place a layer of eggplant over this; cover with meat mixture; repeat eggplant and meat layers. In a saucepan, prepare a cream sauce by melting butter, adding flour, and stirring until blended; add milk gradually. Cook until thick, stirring constantly. Remove from heat and slowly add heated sauce to eggs; add cheese and mix. Pour over casserole and bake uncovered for 1 hour at 375°, or until top is golden. Cool at least 30 minutes before serving.

The flavor of moussaka improves if it is baked the day before serving and is reheated. This Greek dish is good served with a green salad, Greek olives, and Feta cheese.

MRS. J. LARRY LAWSON
PARAGOULD, ARKANSAS

LEG OF LAMB

Serves: 6-8   Oven: 325°

1 leg of lamb
Salt
Pepper
¼ cup vinegar

¼ cup Worcestershire sauce
Brown sugar
2 garlic buds

Wipe lamb with damp cloth. Rub lamb with salt and pepper. Put in an open pan with no water. Mix vinegar and Worcestershire sauce and pour over lamb. Cover roast with brown sugar. Slice garlic buds very thin and put on top. Place in cold oven. Heat to 325°. Cook 30 minutes per pound.

MRS. F. PRESTON HALL

DOLMADES (GREEK STUFFED GRAPE LEAVES)

Serves: 6

1 lb. ground lamb or chuck	½ cup chopped celery
⅓ cup raw rice	¼ cup butter
1 egg	½ cup chicken broth
2 Tb. chopped parsley	Salt and pepper to taste
2 Tb. chopped mint leaves	10-oz. jar grape leaves
1 large onion, finely chopped	Additional chicken broth

Mix first 5 ingredients in a large bowl. Sauté onion and celery in butter until golden brown; add to meat mixture. Add ½ cup chicken broth and season to taste with salt and pepper. Carefully unroll grape leaves, rinse, and boil in water for 5 minutes; drain well. Place 1 Tb. meat mixture on the longest point of each grape leaf; fold over once; fold edges toward center and roll again to complete each little package. Place in layers in a large pan; cover with additional chicken broth (about 2½ cups), cover if desired, and simmer for 1 hour. Makes about 40.

AVGOLEMONO SAUCE:

3 eggs	2 tsp. flour
Juice of 1 lemon	Additional chicken broth

This sauce should be prepared just before serving.

Beat eggs well, adding lemon juice gradually. Remove dolmades from pan; add enough chicken broth to make 2 cups. (You may not need to add any.) Stir flour into broth and then gradually add hot broth to eggs, stirring constantly. Return to heat and cook until thickened, stirring constantly. Pour over dolmades and serve immediately.

Fresh grape leaves may be used instead of canned and should be parboiled also. Fresh leaves may be frozen for future use.

MRS. THEODORE POLYCHRON

BACHELOR'S BARBECUE LAMB

Serves: 4-6

Leg of lamb	½ cup dehydrated onions
8-oz. bottle Italian dressing	½ cup bourbon
12-oz. bottle chili sauce	

Have butcher "butterfly" leg of lamb by cutting out bone and stretching meat out flat. Mix remaining ingredients and marinate lamb overnight, turning occasionally. Cook over low charcoal fire for 1 hour, turning and basting every 15 minutes.

This is good served hot but also makes delicious sandwiches served cold.

MRS. BILL MATTHEWS

LAMB STEW

Serves: 6-8

3 lbs. boneless lamb, cut in
chunks
2 Tb. flour
1½ tsp. salt
¼ tsp. pepper
2 Tb. salad oil
1 garlic clove, minced
1 cup celery, thinly sliced
1 onion, chopped
1 tsp. tarragon

1 pt. cranberry juice cocktail
1½ tsp. sugar
8 carrots, cut in 1-inch
chunks
8 small onions, peeled
2 potatoes, pared and
quartered
10-oz. pkg. frozen green peas
(or 16-oz. can Lesueur
peas, drained)

Roll lamb in mixture of flour, salt, and pepper. Brown in oil in a Dutch oven. Add garlic, onion, and celery; brown slightly. Add tarragon, cranberry juice, and sugar. Simmer, covered, 1 to 1½ hours, or until lamb is tender. Add all vegetables except peas and simmer, covered, about 30 minutes more. Add peas; cook 15 minutes longer. Thicken gravy with more flour if desired.

MRS. GIL BUCHANAN

ARTICHOKES STUFFED WITH LAMB

Serves: 4   **Oven: 375°**

4 whole fresh artichokes
1 lb. ground lamb
¾ cup chopped onion
2 Tb. salad oil
½ cup fine dry bread crumbs

¼ cup snipped parsley
2 eggs, beaten
½ tsp. salt
¼ tsp. pepper
¼ tsp. nutmeg

Wash artichokes and cut off stem close to base. Cook in boiling salted water 25 to 30 minutes, or until stalk can be pierced easily with a fork. Drain upside down. Cut off top third of leaves. Remove center leaves and chokes. Lightly brown lamb and onion in oil. Drain well. Add remaining ingredients. Mix well. Fill centers of artichokes with mixture. Place in a 9 x 9 x 2-inch baking dish. Pour hot water around artichokes to depth of 1 inch. Bake, uncovered, in 375° oven for 35 minutes. Serve with Sauterne Sauce.

SAUTERNE SAUCE:

¼ cup sauterne
1 Tb. minced onion
¾ cup mayonnaise

2 Tb. parsley
1 Tb. lemon juice

Combine sauterne and onion in small sauce pan. Let stand 10 minutes. Add and mix remaining ingredients. Cook and stir until mixture is heated through. **Do not boil.** Pour over artichokes.

MRS. MONROE FRANK

ARMENIAN MARINADE

Serves: 6

2 lbs. lamb cut in 2-inch
  cubes
½ cup salad oil
½ cup fresh lemon juice
1 tsp. marjoram

1 tsp. thyme
1 tsp. pepper
1 clove garlic, crushed
½ cup chopped onion

Mix all ingredients except lamb in large glass bowl. Add meat and marinate covered at least 2½ days. Turn meat occasionally during the day and refrigerate at night. Alternate pieces of meat on skewers with tomatoes, mushrooms, peppers, and onions. Broil over low charcoal fire until vegetables are done.

MRS. BILL GRACE

VEAL PARMIGIANA

Serves: 8   Oven: 350°

1 cup chopped onion
2 minced garlic cloves
¾ cup olive oil
2 1-lb. cans tomatoes
6-oz. can tomato paste
1 tsp. sugar
2 tsp. ground oregano
2 eggs

1 tsp. salt
1 cup cracker crumbs, finely
  crushed
8 veal cutlets (2 lbs.)
2 8-oz. pkgs. Mozzarella
  cheese, sliced thin
½ cup grated Parmesan
  cheese

Sauté onion and garlic in 2 tablespoons of olive oil until soft; stir in tomatoes, tomato paste and sugar. Simmer 45 minutes, stirring often; stir in oregano and simmer 15 minutes longer. Meanwhile beat eggs and salt slightly. Dip veal cutlets into egg mixture and then into cracker crumbs to coat well. Brown cutlets, a few at a time, in part of remaining olive oil, adding oil as needed; drain. Pour about one cup of the tomato sauce into a 13 x 9 x 2-inch baking dish. Top with one-half of the cutlets; spread with one cup of sauce; sprinkle with one-half portion each of the Mozzarella and Parmesan cheeses. Repeat to make another layer. Bake for 30 minutes in 350° oven. Serve with cooked spaghetti.

MRS. HOWARD JONES, JR.

VEAL SCALLOPPINE

Serves: 6

½ cup grated Parmesan
   cheese
¼ cup flour
1 tsp. salt
¼ tsp. pepper
1½ lbs. veal, sliced and
   pounded very thin

2 Tb. olive oil
1 garlic clove, chopped
¾ cup Marsala wine
¼ cup consomme
1 Tb. lemon juice
Parsley, chopped

Mix cheese, flour, salt, and pepper together. Dry meat with paper towels, cut into 3-inch slices, sprinkle with flour mixture and pound it into the veal. Veal should be very thin. Heat olive oil, add chopped garlic and then brown meat lightly on both sides. Add wine, consomme, and lemon juice. Cover and simmer slowly for 30 minutes. Sprinkle with parsley before serving.

MRS. CHARLES M. NOLAN

CROWN PORK ROAST

Serves: 14   Oven: 350°

12 to 14 lbs. rib loin, back-
   bone removed, bones
   frenched
⅔ cup raw rice
¼ cup butter
1½ cups chicken stock

14-oz. can pineapple chunks
1 cup celery, chopped
4 cups bread crumbs
2 tsp. leaf sage, crumbled
Black pepper
2 onions, chopped

Have butcher prepare roast and tie to form ring. Rub all over with salt and pepper. Place in shallow roasting dish. To make rice stuffing, sauté raw rice in butter until grains are golden. Add chicken stock; simmer until liquid is absorbed. Drain pineapple, reserving liquid. Combine rice with remaining ingredients, reserving a few pineapple chunks for decoration. Fill center of roast with rice stuffing.

Cover the stuffing and wrap the rib ends with foil. Skewer bacon or foil to lower part of roast. Cook 35 minutes per pound in 350° oven. Remove roast to platter and make pan gravy, using pineapple juice as part of liquid. Garnish with pineapple chunks.

MRS. C. RAY WILLIAMS

CHERRY SAUCE FOR PORK ROAST

12-oz. jar cherry preserves
2 Tb. light corn syrup
¼ cup red wine vinegar
¼ tsp. salt

¼ tsp. cinnamon
¼ tsp. nutmeg
¼ tsp. cloves
¼ cup blanched almonds

Combine all ingredients except almonds in saucepan, bring to a boil stirring frequently. Reduce heat, simmer 2 minutes. Add almonds. Baste pork roast last 30 minutes of cooking, spoon more over and let cool 30 minutes before serving.
Serve remainder of sauce in a sauce boat.

MRS. ROBERT SHULTS

STUFFED PORK CHOPS

1½-inch thick pork chops
Raisins
Apple, chopped fine
Orange peel, grated
Ginger

Cloves
Peppercorns
Salt
Butter

Have butcher slice a pocket in pork chops. Into each pocket put a mixture of ⅛ teaspoon ginger, and 1 teaspoon each raisins, apple, and orange peel. Take equal parts of cloves and peppercorns and grind until fine with a mortar and pestle. Rub into each side of chops. Salt to taste. Simmer slowly in butter over low heat until done, turning often.

SWEET AND SOUR PORK

Serves: 4

6 pork chops
2 Tb. margarine
2 bell peppers
2 onions
13½-oz. can pineapple
  chunks

1 Tb. vinegar
2 Tb. brown sugar
1 tsp. salt
Pepper to taste
2 tsp. cornstarch
⅓ cup water

Cut pork from bones and trim fat. Cut in 1-inch pieces. Melt margarine in Dutch oven or deep skillet. Brown pork well. Chop onion and bell pepper in 1-inch pieces and add to pork. Sauté until onions are clear. Add liquid from pineapple and cook on low heat for about 10 minutes. Add pineapple chunks, salt, pepper, brown sugar, vinegar, and small amount of water if necessary. Cook 10 minutes longer, then add cornstarch dissolved in ⅓ cup water. Stir carefully as mixture thickens. **Do not allow to boil.** Serve over boiled rice with almonds sprinkled on top and soy sauce available.

MRS. JAMES B. KALMBACH
DALLAS, TEXAS

PORK CHOPS WITH ARTICHOKES

Serves: 6

6 pork chops	1 can artichokes
3 Tb. butter	3 green onions
1 Tb. salad oil	Thyme
4 carrots	Basil
4 boiling potatoes	1 clove garlic
Salt and pepper	

Pat pork chops dry with paper towel. Brown in butter and oil. Peel and slice carrots, cube potatoes, and parboil both 3 to 4 minutes in boiling, salted water and drain. Remove pork chops from skillet; put vegetables in and stir. Salt and pepper to taste. Drain artichokes and add to skillet. Place pork chops on top of vegetables and sprinkle with salt, pepper, thyme, and basil. Add garlic and chopped green onions. Cover and simmer for about 30 minutes, basting occasionally with bulb baster.

MRS. LEONARD THOMPSON

PORK CHOPS IN WINE

Serves: 6

6 pork chops	¼ tsp. dried dill
2 tsp. prepared mustard	¼ cup brown sugar
Salt	6 thin lemon slices
Pepper	1 cup dry white wine

Trim fat from chops and grease skillet with it. Brown chops well. Drain fat. Spread one side of chop with mustard, seasonings, and brown sugar. Put slice of lemon on each chop. Add wine. Cover and cook 50 to 60 minutes or longer.

MRS. JOHN J. TRUEMPER, JR.

RUTH'S PORK CHOPS WITH SAUERKRAUT

Serves: 6   **Oven: 300°**

6 thick pork chops	Black pepper
2 tsp. garlic salt	2 16-oz. cans sauerkraut

Sprinkle chops generously with garlic salt and pepper. Grease skillet with pork fat or bacon drippings. Brown chops well on both sides. Rinse kraut well in collander. Drain. Brown kraut in same drippings. Salt and pepper kraut and place in baking dish. Place chops on top. Pour any remaining drippings over all. Cover tightly with foil. Bake in 300° oven for 2 hours, until well done.

RUTH ANDERSON

GLAZED PORK CHOPS

Serves: 6

6 thick pork chops   1 can consomme
Lemon-pepper marinade

Marinate pork chops according to directions on lemon-pepper jar at least 6 hours or overnight. Trim fat from chops and use small piece of fat to grease hot heavy skillet. Blot chops with paper towel and brown. Turn heat very low, cover, and cook slowly 25 to 30 minutes, turning once. (Pork is done when juice runs clear yellow with no trace of rose where pricked deep with fork.) Remove chops to serving dish and keep warm. Turn heat very high under skillet and pour can of consomme in with juices. Boil down rapidly and stir up all pan scrapings until volume is reduced and thickens into a glaze. Pour over chops and serve. Glaze is also good over accompanying potatoes, carrots, etc.

MRS. SAM BOELLNER

SWEET AND SOUR RIBS

Serves: 6   Oven: 425°

3 lbs. country style pork ribs   ⅔ cup brown sugar
2 Tb. cornstarch   2 tsp. dry mustard
⅔ cup vinegar   1 cup crushed pineapple
½ cup catsup   ½ cup water
¼ cup diced onion   2 Tb. soy sauce

Brown ribs meaty side up in Dutch oven or heavy casserole 20 to 30 minutes at 425°. Pour off fat. Combine remaining ingredients and pour over ribs. Bake uncovered at 350° for 1½ hours, basting approximately every 15 minutes.

MRS. PURCELL SMITH, JR.

COUNTRY CURED HAM
(Cooking Instructions)

If ham is aged and hard, soak overnight in cold water. Scrub mold, etc., off thoroughly with stiff brush and soda if necessary. Place ham in covered roaster. Pour 4 cups liquid over ham. Coke, wine, peach, pineapple or orange juice are suggested. Place roaster in cold oven. Heat to 500° and cook ham for 1 minute per pound. Turn oven off promptly and let ham set in unopened oven for 3 hours. Turn oven on again and when it reaches 500°, allow ham to cook for 1 minute per pound. Turn oven off and leave ham in oven for 10 hours or overnight. Skin (and bone if desired), score and glaze as preferred.

ELIZABETH YINGLING
ALEXANDRIA, VIRGINIA

BARBECUE SAUCE FOR HAM

Yield: 2 cups

¾ cup chopped onion	⅛ tsp. thyme
⅓ cup chopped celery	¼ tsp. allspice
1 clove garlic	3 Tb. Worcestershire sauce
½ cup butter	1 Tb. vinegar
3 Tb. chopped parsley	1 small bottle catsup
1 bay leaf	1 cup water

Sauté onion, celery, garlic in butter until soft. Add all other ingredients, bring to a boil. Reduce heat, simmer a few minutes. Add thinly sliced ham, cooking until heated. Serve on small buns.

MRS. JAMES E. HATHAWAY

PECAN STUFFED HAM

Serves: 8-10   Oven: 325°

6 to 7 lb. boned, rolled ham (casing removed)	1½ cups pecans, coarsely chopped
¼ cup butter	1 egg, beaten
1 cup chopped onion	2 Tb. prepared mustard
2 cups packaged cornbread stuffing mix	½ cup honey
½ cup chopped parsley	2 Tb. frozen orange juice concentrate, thawed

Have butcher remove a cylinder of meat lengthwise from center of ham, leaving a 2-inch shell. (Meat removed may be ground and used for ham salad.) Sauté onion in butter 2 or 3 minutes. Combine with cornbread mix, pecans, parsley, egg, and mustard to make dressing. Fill ham cavity lightly with dressing. Reserve remaining dressing for stuffed onions. Place ham on rack in shallow roasting pan and bake 1 hour in 325° oven. Mix orange juice and honey and baste ham. Continue baking for 30 minutes, basting occasionally. Let ham rest 30 minutes before slicing. Serve with baked stuffed onions.

BAKED STUFFED ONIONS:

Serves: 8   Oven: 325°

8 medium yellow onions	2 Tb. butter
Stuffing from ham	½ cup water

Cut ends off onions; peel. Remove centers, leaving a shell ¼ to ½ inch thick. Place onion shells in saucepan. Cover with salted cold water. Bring to boil; simmer 10 minutes. Drain onions well. Spoon stuffing into shells. Top with pat of butter. Place in baking pan and add water. Cover loosely with foil and bake in 325° oven 1 hour.

MRS. R. J. CROWDER

HOT HAM SALAD

Serves: 4-6   Oven: 400°

2 cups ham, chopped or
  ground
1 cup celery
½ cup pecans
1 Tb. onion, chopped

¼ cup sweet pickle, chopped
1 tsp. salt
1 cup mayonnaise
½ cup grated cheese
1 cup potato chips, crushed

Mix first 7 ingredients together in a casserole or baking dish. Sprinkle with grated cheese and top with potato chips. Bake in 400° oven for 20 minutes.

MRS. JOHN A. WILLIAMS

HAM FRIED RICE

Serves: 4

4 cups firm cooked rice
1½ cups (½ lb.) cooked ham,
  cut in strips
1 medium onion, chopped
½ cup celery, cut diagonally
  into small pieces

½ cup diced bell pepper
2 Tb. salad oil
Salt and pepper to taste
1 tsp. Accent
2 Tb. (or more) soy sauce
2 eggs

Cook rice according to package directions for firm texture; cool. Place ham, onion, green pepper and celery in a large skillet; sauté in oil until onions are soft. Add salt, pepper, and Accent, mixing well. Add rice and soy sauce, stirring after the addition of each. Break eggs into the mixture and cook over medium heat, stirring constantly, until eggs are set. Serve immediately.

This is a delicious way to use the last of a ham and is a hearty one-dish dinner.

MRS. PAUL B. GEAN
FORT SMITH, ARKANSAS

OPEN FACED HAM SANDWICH

Serves: 4   Oven: 400°

½ cup mayonnaise
1 tsp. horseradish
4 slices bread

4 slices Swiss cheese
4 slices ham
Asparagus spears

In a saucepan mix mayonnaise and horseradish; heat. Layer bread, cheese, ham, and asparagus. Heat in oven for about 10 minutes, or until cheese is melted. Top with mayonnaise sauce and serve hot.

MRS. JOHN P. COBB

HOT HAM SANDWICHES

Serves: 4   Oven: 325°

8 slices bread   3 eggs, beaten
Butter   2 cups milk
2 cups cooked ham, ground   ¼ tsp. salt
2 Tb. mustard   Dash pepper
2 cups grated cheese

Cut crust from bread and butter both sides. Put 4 slices bread on bottom of a 9-inch square pan. Mix ham and mustard and spread on bread. Sprinkle with cheese and cover with remaining 4 slices bread. Combine eggs, milk, and seasonings and pour over bread. Chill at least 1 hour, although it is better if chilled overnight. Bake at 325° for 45 minutes. (It may take a little longer for edges to brown.)

MRS. WILLIAM B. SIGLER

SCRAPPLE VON KOLNITZ

2 lbs. lean ground pork   1 tsp. red chili pequins
3 pts. bouillon   1 tsp. poultry seasoning
½ tsp. freshly ground pepper   1 Tb. Worcestershire sauce
½ tsp. sage   1½ tsp. salt
½ tsp. dried thyme   1½ cups yellow corn meal

Simmer ground pork in bouillon for about 1½ hours, or until tender. After meat is tender, draw off 1 quart of the stock, place in a saucepan, and add the pepper, sage, thyme, red chili pequins, crushed (these are bottled by Spice Islands Company), poultry seasoning, Worcestershire sauce, and salt. Bring the whole to a boil.

When mixture is boiling rapidly, beat in over a low flame yellow corn meal and cook until mixture thickens (the best way to beat in corn meal is with an electric beater to keep mixture from lumping). Add the meat mixture, and cook for another 5 minutes. Stir mixture into two 9 x 5 x 3-inch loaf pans, and refrigerate overnight so mixture will solidify.

When ready to cook the scrapple, slice with a sharp ham slicer into ⅛-inch thick slices, being careful not to break the slices. Rub a heavy frying pan with a thin coating of fat, but make certain that there is no excess fat in the pan. Place the first batch in a cold pan, and cook over a medium-low flame. When it has browned on one side, use a pancake turner, inverted, and carefully cut the strip of scrapple from the pan, turn, and brown on the other side. The second batch will be easier to turn.

This is really a breakfast delicacy, and should be served with fried eggs. But the cooked scrapple, as finger pieces or hot hors d'oeuvres, goes excellently with beer.

MRS. A. HOWARD STEBBINS, III

SAUSAGE AND RICE SUPREME

Serves: 6-8   Oven: 350°

1 lb. lean sausage
½ cup onion, chopped
1 cup celery, chopped
3-oz. can mushrooms
½ cup almonds, toasted

1 can water chestnuts
1½ pkgs. chicken noodle soup
  (dehydrated)
2½ cups water
3 cups cooked rice

Cook rice according to package directions. Reserve. Slice and fry sausage in skillet. Coarsely crumble sausage. Remove sausage from drippings. In drippings add onion and celery. Sauté. Add mushrooms, almonds, water chestnuts, soup, water, cooked rice and sausage. Mix and bake covered in ungreased 1½ quart casserole 45 minutes to 1 hour at 350°.

MRS. LAWRENCE FAUBER
FORT WORTH, TEXAS

POLISH SAUSAGE AND LENTILS

Serves: 4-5   Oven: 350°

1 cup lentils
2 Tb. salad oil
1 onion, chopped
1 clove garlic, chopped
2 cloves garlic
16-oz. can tomatoes

3 medium size Polish
  sausages, peeled
1 tsp. sugar
1½ tsp. pepper
1 bay leaf
Salt to taste

Put lentils in a large saucepan and cover with salted water. Bring to boil. Cover and cook 20 minutes or until they are tender but hold shape. Drain and reserve juice. Heat vegetable oil in skillet. Add onion and garlic. Cook until onion is tender. Drain and chop tomatoes. Add to skillet and cook until free of liquid. Peel sausage and cut in ½-inch thick slices. Mix sausage, lentils, and tomato mixture together and put in 2 quart casserole. Add sugar, pepper, bay leaf and salt. Cover and bake in 350° oven for 30 minutes. Add lentil liquid for moisture, if necessary.

This is a very highly seasoned dish.

MRS. DAVID KANE

SWEETBREADS NEW YORKER

Serves: 6

3 sets or pairs sweetbreads   1 qt. water
6 slices broiled cured ham   1 Tb. vinegar

Like all organ meats sweetbreads are highly perishable and should
be prepared for use as soon as purchased. First soak them at least
1 hour in large quantity cold water to release any blood. Parboil in
water and vinegar. Simmer uncovered from 2 to 5 minutes depending on size. Drain. Firm sweetbreads by plunging at once into cold
water. Drain. Remove some of the membranes, but leave enough
to hold sweetbreads together. Chill overnight. Sauté sweetbreads
in butter until golden brown. Place on a piece of broiled ham and
top with sherry sauce.

SHERRY SAUCE:

6 large onions, chopped   1 qt. cream
3 Tb. butter   ¼ tsp. cayenne
1 Tb. concentrated chicken   1 cup sherry
  base

Sauté onions in butter until transparent. Add cream, chicken base,
and cayenne. Bring to boil, thicken lightly, strain, return to heat
and add sherry. Stir well.

BEN MITCHELL
WINROCK FARMS

VEGETABLES

BASIC RULES FOR COOKING FRESH VEGETABLES

It has been said that the principal weakness in American cooking is the improper preparation of vegetables. Because the South is favored with an extended growing season which provides an abundant supply of beautiful vegetables, perhaps we may rightfully claim to have used our ingenuity to master the fine art of preparing delectable vegetables.

To attain the best flavor and nutritional value, always choose fresh vegetables before frozen, but frozen before canned. Fresh vegetables that are to be cooked should be washed, dried, and chilled in a dark place as quickly as possible. For if they are left at room temperature and in the light or if they are soaked or allowed to remain wet, both nutrients and flavor are lost. Remember that most vitamins are stored near the skin, so deep paring should be avoided. It is preferable to peel vegetables just before cooking, not allowing them to reach room temperature.

If the best flavor and most nutrients are to be retained, cook chilled vegetables very quickly, using very little water, and for the shortest length of time necessary to make them tender. Try not to lift the lid while cooking, for contact with oxygen destroys vitamin C. Because salt attracts moisture, avoid salting a vegetable during the cooking process, for the juices, which carry the vitamins, minerals, sugars, and flavors, will be drawn out. Except when they are cooked in a sauce or casserole, vegetables should be salted just before serving.

If vegetables are properly stored and cooked, their natural colors are also preserved. Color should never be maintained by adding baking soda, for this method not only destroys nutrients, but also results in a mushy texture. However, the addition of vinegar or lemon juice to the cooking water will help to stabilize the color of green vegetables. Another method of preserving both color and nutrients is cooking vegetables in milk. If simmered, the milk will not curdle and will often result in a sweeter, milder vegetable.

ARTICHOKES ALSATION

Serves: 6   Oven: 350°

2 8½-oz. cans artichoke	½ cup milk
hearts	½ cup cream, light
2 slices lemon	1 cup grated Cheddar cheese
1 button garlic	Salt to taste
2 Tb. butter	Paprika
2 Tb. flour	Riced egg yolks

Cook artichoke hearts, lemon, and garlic slowly for 20 minutes. Drain, remove garlic and lemon. Put in baking dish and cover with cheese sauce. (To make cheese sauce, melt butter in pan; add flour and blend until smooth. Slowly add milk and cream, stirring constantly until it thickens. Add cheese and stir until it melts. Add seasonings.) Cover with riced egg yolks. Bake 20 minutes, covered, in 350° oven.

Variation: Use ½ cup Swiss cheese instead of 1 cup Cheddar cheese.

MRS. BOOTH SMITH

ARTICHOKE AND SPINACH CASSEROLE

Serves: 6   Oven: 350°

2 pkgs. frozen chopped	1 tsp. salt
spinach	½ cup Parmesan cheese
8½-oz. can artichoke hearts	1 can mushroom or celery
Tabasco to taste	soup, undiluted
1 tsp. Worcestershire sauce	2 Tb. butter

Cook spinach according to package directions; drain well. Meanwhile rinse artichoke hearts in cold water and cut each into 4 to 6 pieces. Combine hot spinach, artichoke hearts, seasonings, ¼ cup Parmesan cheese, and soup by folding together. Pour into a buttered 2½ quart casserole and top with remaining cheese. Dot with butter. Bake uncovered at 350° until well heated.

MRS. JAMES B. KALMBACH
DALLAS, TEXAS

FRESH ARTICHOKES

Serves: 18

6 artichokes	8 qts. water
Lemon juice	Cheesecloth
4 Tb. salt	

Wash artichokes thoroughly. Break off the small, tough leaves around the base of each artichoke, then cut off the stem even with the base. With a sharp, heavy knife, cut about an inch off the top portion of leaves. Trim the sharp points of the remaining leaves with scissors. Rub the cut leaves and base with lemon juice immediately.

Bring water and salt to a boil in a large kettle. Drop in the artichokes, and cover them with a double fold of cheesecloth, or single layer of some other thin material. Boil slowly without a lid for 35 to 45 minutes, checking occasionally to see that the exposed tops of the artichokes remain covered by the cloth. When the leaves pull out easily and the bottoms are tender, remove the artichoke carefully from the water and turn upside down to drain.

When cool enough to handle, turn right side up and gently force a small opening in the center of the artichoke. Remove enough of the yellowish center leaves to expose the choke. With a spoon, carefully scrape this fuzzy prickly portion from the bottom of the artichoke. Serve cold with a mayonnaise, hollandaise, drawn butter, or vinaigrette sauce for dipping leaves.

MRS. PHILIP ANDERSON, JR.

ASPARAGUS CASSEROLE

Serves: 6   Oven: 375°

1 lb. fresh asparagus or	¾ tsp. seasoned salt
1 pkg. frozen	3 tsp. chopped chives
4 to 5 hard boiled eggs	½ cup grated Cheddar cheese
¼ cup butter	1 large tomato
¼ cup flour	¼ cup dry bread crumbs
1½ cups milk	1 tsp. melted butter
½ cup sauterne wine	

Cook asparagus until tender; drain and cut into bite size pieces. Place in a 1½ quart casserole; put sliced cooked eggs over asparagus. Make a white sauce by melting butter in a saucepan; stir in flour and gradually add milk and sauterne; add salt, chives, and cheese; stir constantly until thick. Pour sauce over eggs and asparagus. Arrange sliced tomato over sauce. Combine bread crumbs and melted butter and sprinkle over top of casserole. Bake uncovered at 375° for 25 minutes.

This is delicious!

MRS. B. R. JUDKINS

CHINESE ASPARAGUS

Serves: 6-8

2 lbs. fresh asparagus
1 can chicken or beef broth,
   undiluted
2 tsp. soy sauce
2 tsp. Accent

2 tsp. cornstarch
6 pieces bacon, fried crisp
1 Tb. hot bacon grease
¼ cup toasted almonds

Prepare asparagus by cutting in 2 inch diagonal slices. (Even the fairly tough stalks can be used if the tough outer layer is removed.) Mix broth, soy sauce, Accent, and cornstarch. (This can be done ahead.) Place crumbled bacon in a skillet with hot bacon grease. Add asparagus and cook over medium high heat for about 5 minutes, stirring and turning often. Add soup mixture, cover, and cook over low heat for 5 to 10 minutes, or until asparagus has a clear look but is NOT soft. Garnish with almonds and serve immediately.

This is an unusual way to serve fresh asparagus; the secret is not to overcook!

MRS. JOSEPH MULLEN

SPRING GARDEN MEDLEY

Serves: 4

2 bunches fresh asparagus
1 small can tiny green peas
1 cup shredded lettuce
1 green onion, sliced thin

2 tsp. salt
⅛ tsp. pepper
4 Tb. butter

Cut ends off asparagus, wash, and slice on the diagonal. Combine all ingredients except butter in large bowl. Toss. Cut 6-inch squares of aluminum foil and place equal servings in each. Top with a tablespoon of butter each and fold securely. Place in steamer with one inch of boiling water in bottom and cover. Steam for 30 minutes, turn off heat, let stand 10 minutes, open and serve.

BAKED BARLEY WITH MUSHROOMS AND ALMONDS

Serves: 6   Oven: 350°

½ cup finely chopped onion
½ cup barley
3 tsp. butter
Salt and pepper to taste
3 cups chicken broth

½ lb. fresh mushrooms or
4-oz. can mushrooms
pieces and stems, drained
2 Tb. butter
½ cup slivered almonds

Sauté onions and barley in butter; brown lightly; season to taste. Pour into 1½ quart casserole; add 1½ cups broth. Bake 30 minutes at 350°. Add other 1½ cups broth and mushrooms which have been sautéed in butter. Top with almonds. Bake at 350° until liquid is gone, about 1½ hours.

MRS. WILLIAM P. BOND

CARAWAY GREEN BEANS

Serves: 8-10   Oven: 350°

4 slices bacon, diced
2 medium onions, diced
4 16-oz. cans whole green
 beans
1 Tb. caraway seeds
1 cup grated Cheddar cheese

1 can cream of mushroom
 soup, undiluted
1 can water chestnuts, sliced
1 tsp. lemon pepper marinade
Ritz cracker crumbs
Butter

Sauté bacon and onions; add green beans and caraway seeds; simmer 1 hour on top of stove. Pour off all juice except ¼ cup. Add mushroom soup, cheese, water chestnuts, and pepper; place in a 1½ quart casserole. Cover with cracker crumbs; dot with butter. Bake uncovered at 350° for about 30 to 40 minutes. This can be prepared the day before. It can also be frozen.

MRS. JAMES K. HAMILTON

DILL BEANS

Serves: 6-8   Oven: 350°

2 16-oz. cans French style
 green beans
1¼ tsp. dill seed
6 Tb. flour
6 Tb. margarine
1½ cups milk
3 Tb. grated onion

2½ tsp. Accent
1 cup bean juice
Dash of Tabasco
Salt and pepper to taste
Cracker crumbs
Paprika

Cook beans (including liquid) with dill seed, boiling for 45 minutes. Let cool; drain and save liquid. Make white sauce of flour, margarine, milk, onion, Accent, bean juice, Tabasco, salt, and pepper. Put beans in a greased 2 quart casserole; pour white sauce over. Cover with cracker crumbs and sprinkling of paprika. Bake uncovered for 30 minutes at 350°.

This is a good recipe for company and is easy to prepare ahead.

MRS. GRIFFIN SMITH

GREEN BEANS AMANDINE

Serves: 6

2 cans French style green
 beans
8 to 10 slices bacon
½ cup chopped onion

5 Tb. vinegar
Salt and pepper to taste
3 Tb. browned, slivered
 almonds

Drain beans early in day and set aside. Fry bacon, dice, and save. Brown onions in bacon fat; add beans, vinegar, salt, and pepper. Heat ingredients, then refrigerate all day. Just before serving add bacon and almonds and heat.

MRS. EDWIN CROMWELL

GREEN BEANS AU GRATIN

Serves: 4   **Oven: 350°**

2 Tb. butter
2 Tb. flour
½ tsp. salt
⅛ tsp. dry mustard
¾ cup milk
¼ cup grated Longhorn
   cheese

1 pkg. frozen French style
   green beans or 16-oz. can
   French style green beans
Paprika
Slivered almonds
Parmesan cheese
⅓ can fried onion rings

Make a white sauce with first five ingredients; when thick, add cheese and melt. Stir in drained beans and pour into buttered 1 quart casserole. Sprinkle with Parmesan cheese, almonds and paprika. Bake uncovered for 30 minutes at 350°. Put onion rings on top during last 5 to 10 minutes.

MRS. CHARLES H. WILLIAMSON

GREEN BEANS SUPREME

Serves: 8

2 pkgs. frozen French cut
   green beans
6 slices bacon, cooked and
   drained

2 Tb. bacon drippings
⅔ cup sour cream

Cook beans according to directions on package; drain. Stir bacon drippings into sour cream; add to beans. Add crumbled bacon and stir over low heat until hot.

Variation: Shredded cabbage may be substituted for green beans.

DAISY KEATTS

GREEN BEANS WITH SWISS CHEESE

Serves: 6   **Oven: 400°**

2 Tb. flour
2 Tb. butter
1 cup sour cream
½ tsp. grated onion
1 tsp. salt
¼ tsp. sugar

2 16-oz. cans green beans,
   drained
½ lb. Swiss cheese, grated
Corn flake crumbs, sautéed
   in butter

Make a white sauce with flour, butter, and sour cream. Add onion, salt, and sugar. Place layers of beans and cheese in a 2 quart casserole. Pour sauce over; top with crumbs. Bake for 20 minutes, uncovered, at 400°.

Variation: Substitute bacon or almonds for corn flake crumbs.

MRS. DREW LANDER

LIMA BEANS

Serves: 8

1½ pkgs. frozen lima beans
1 cup sour cream
2 Tb. salad oil
1 Tb. vinegar
1 tsp. salt

1 tsp. sugar
2 tsp. chopped parsley
1 button garlic, pulverized
Dash of paprika

Cook and drain lima beans. Mix all other ingredients; add beans. Refrigerate overnight. Serve hot or cold.

MRS. RALPH DOWNS

BROCCOLI CASSEROLE

Serves: 6   Oven: 350°

2 10-oz. pkgs. frozen chopped
  broccoli
Salt to taste
1 Tb. lemon juice
2 Tb. butter

2 Tb. flour
¾ cup milk
¾ cup mayonnaise
¾ cup buttered bread
  crumbs

Cook broccoli according to directions on package; drain. Add salt and lemon juice. Make white sauce, using butter, flour, and milk. Add mayonnaise; mix. Place in buttered 2 quart casserole; cover with bread crumbs. Bake uncovered at 350° for 30 minutes or until crumbs are brown and mixture bubbly.

MRS. BART ROACH

BROCCOLI CASSEROLE

Serves: 10   Oven: 350°

3 pkgs. frozen chopped
  broccoli
2 cans cream of mushroom
  soup

6 oz. grated Cheddar cheese
½ cup grape nuts
½ can onion rings, crumbled

Cook broccoli according to package directions. Drain, place in a 2 quart buttered baking dish. Add soup and cheese. Place grape nuts and onion rings on top. Bake covered for 30 minutes at 350°. Take cover off and bake 15 minutes more. This can be frozen before it is baked.

MRS. DON MURPHY

BROCCOLI MUSHROOM CASSEROLE

Serves: 18   Oven: 350°

2 large onions, chopped
½ cup butter
6 pkgs. chopped broccoli,
   frozen
3 cans cream of mushroom
   soup, undiluted
3 rolls garlic cheese

2 tsp. Accent
8-oz. can mushrooms,
   drained
1 cup blanched almonds or
   pecans
1 cup bread crumbs

Sauté onions in butter; add frozen broccoli and cook until tender, about 30 minutes. Add soup, cheese, Accent, mushrooms, and ¾ cup nuts. Pour in one large deep or two smaller casseroles. Sprinkle remaining nuts and bread crumbs on top. Bake uncovered at 350° until bubbly.

This is good used as a dip, too.

MRS. RAYMOND C. COOK

BROCCOLI WADDILE

Serves: 6   Oven: 375°

2 pkgs. frozen chopped
   broccoli
1 Tb. melted butter
½ cup mayonnaise

1 Tb. flour
3 eggs, beaten
1 cup light cream
½ tsp. salt

Cook broccoli according to directions on package; drain. Add butter, mayonnaise, and flour; fold in eggs and cream. Pour into a greased, medium size ring mold; place in a pan of water. Bake uncovered at 375° for 55 minutes, or until a knife comes out clean when inserted near the center. Unmold and serve hot.

MRS. VERNON JACKSON, III

SOUR CREAM-BACON SAUCE FOR BRUSSELS SPROUTS

Serves: 3-4

¾ Tb. chopped chives
½ tsp. lemon-pepper
   marinade
¼ tsp. chopped dill weed
6 slices bacon, fried and
   crumbled

Salt to taste
½ cup sour cream
1 pkg. frozen brussels
   sprouts

Cook brussels sprouts according to package directions. Drain and keep warm. Combine first 5 ingredients with sour cream. Heat through but do not boil. Pour over brussels sprouts. Sprinkle with paprika for color.

CREPES THEODORA

Serves: 8   Oven: 350°

20 crepes
2 10-oz. pkgs. frozen chopped
  broccoli
2 Tb. margarine
2 Tb. chopped onions
6-oz. can chopped
  mushrooms, drained
2 Tb. flour

½ cup light cream
¼ cup chicken broth
2 Tb. grated Parmesan
  cheese
4-oz. can water chestnuts,
  chopped
1 tsp. salt
⅛ tsp. pepper

For crepe recipe see index.

Cook broccoli according to package directions. Drain. Melt butter and sauté onion and mushrooms until lightly browned. Stir in flour. Add cream and chicken broth slowly and cook, stirring until thickened. Add remaining filling ingredients including broccoli. Mixture will be thick. Correct seasonings.

SAUCE:

¼ cup butter
¼ cup flour
1¾ cups light cream
2 cups milk

1½ cups grated Parmesan
  cheese
2 tsp. prepared mustard
1 tsp. salt

Melt butter and stir in flour. Add cream and milk. Cook and stir until smooth and thickened. Add remaining sauce ingredients and cook gently until smooth and cheese has melted completely.

To assemble, spread each crepe with filling, roll up and place seam side down in 2 greased shallow casseroles. Pour sauce over all and bake at 350° for 25 to 30 minutes.

MRS. CLIFF WOOD

COMPANY BRUSSELS SPROUTS

Serves: 6

2 10-oz. pkgs. frozen brussels
  sprouts
2 Tb. butter
5-oz. can water chestnuts,
  drained and sliced

¼ tsp. crushed dried
  rosemary
1 can cream of chicken soup,
  undiluted
2 to 3 Tb. sherry

Cook brussels sprouts according to package directions; drain. Heat butter in a saucepan; add water chestnuts and rosemary; cook until lightly browned. Stir in soup and sherry; heat, stirring occasionally. Add brussels sprouts to sauce; heat; serve hot.

MRS. FINLEY VINSON

CABBAGE POTPOURRI

Serves: 6-8

5 slices bacon
1 medium head cabbage, chopped
1 cup celery, chopped
1 medium bell pepper, chopped

1 medium onion, chopped
2 or 3 tomatoes or 16-oz. can tomatoes, drained
1 Tb. sugar, scant
Seasoned salt to taste
Pepper to taste

Fry bacon in a large skillet until crisp; remove bacon and add remaining ingredients to the bacon grease. Cook covered about 20 minutes, or just until tender, stirring frequently. Arrange on a large platter and sprinkle crumbled bacon on top.

This would be good served with chicken or pork.

MRS. GEORGE PURYEAR
JONESBORO, ARKANSAS

CABBAGE STROGANOFF

Serves: 6   Oven: 350°

1 head green cabbage, finely shredded
1 tsp. salt
1-inch water in large pan
2 Tb. butter

1 Tb. white vinegar
1 Tb. sugar
1 cup sour cream
Salt to taste
Paprika

Boil cabbage in salted water, tightly covered, for 5 to 10 minutes; drain well. Add butter to cabbage and toss. Add vinegar, sugar, sour cream, and salt to taste; toss again. Place in a 1½ quart buttered casserole; garnish with paprika. Bake uncovered at 350° for about 20 minutes, or until hot.

Good served with pork roast, sauerbraten, or ham; has an unusually delicate flavor and a crisp texture.

MRS. HALL BUCHNER

SWEET AND SOUR CABBAGE

Serves: 4-6

Head of cabbage, sliced
2 Tb. water
4 Tb. butter
1 tsp. salt
½ cup chopped onion

Dash cayenne pepper
Dash nutmeg
4 Tb. vinegar
1 Tb. sugar

Soak the sliced cabbage in water to cover for 20 minutes. Drain. Combine cabbage, 2 tablespoons water, butter, salt, onion, cayenne, and nutmeg in saucepan and cook covered for 15 to 20 minutes. Add vinegar and sugar and cook 5 minutes more.

MRS. LEONARD THOMPSON

CARROTS, ARTICHOKE HEARTS, AND MUSHROOMS

Serves: 8

2 cups fresh mushrooms
2 Tb. butter
1 Tb. salad oil
2 Tb. green onions, chopped
10-oz. pkg. frozen artichoke
  hearts, quartered

2 lbs. carrots, quartered and
  cooked
½ cup beef broth
Salt and pepper to taste
Parsley

Sauté mushrooms in butter and oil; add onions and cook until tender. Add artichokes, carrots, beef broth, salt, and pepper. Cover and simmer for about 5 minutes. Sprinkle with parsley.

MRS. LEONARD THOMPSON

CARROT CASSEROLE SUPREME

Serves: 4   Oven: 350°

2 cups diced, cooked carrots
½ cup mayonnaise
¼ cup onion, grated

¼ cup horseradish
Crushed Ritz crackers

Combine all ingredients; place in buttered 1 quart casserole and cover with crumbs. Bake at 350° for 30 minutes.

Variation: Serve in a nest of English peas.

MRS. ROBERT G. CARNAHAN

CARROTS-IN-HONEY AU GRATIN

Serves: 4   Oven: 450°

8 to 10 young fresh carrots
2 Tb. honey
1 tsp. marjoram, or oregano,
  or chopped mint

Salt to taste
1 cup grated Swiss cheese

Scrub and trim carrots; cook in lightly salted water until tender, but not too soft. Split carrots from end to end; add honey mixed with seasonings. Arrange in a 1 quart casserole; cover with cheese. Brown under broiler, or bake in 450° oven for 10 minutes.

Try these with pork or chicken.

MRS. E. JONES JACOBUS

CARROTS DI PROSSEDI

Serves: 6

12 large carrots	Salt and pepper to taste
½ cup butter	Basil

Rinse and peel carrots thoroughly. With a potato peeler, reduce carrots to a pile of shavings, trying to keep the shavings as long and wide as possible. This step can be done several hours ahead of dinner if kept moist and covered. Twenty minutes before dinner is served, heat butter in large skillet. Place carrots in skillet and cook slowly, turning often; carrots will cook down to a fraction of original bulk. They are done when limp. Add salt and pepper; toss with basil. Serve immediately.

ARCHIE TAYLOR
SAN FRANCISCO, CALIFORNIA

CARROT RING

Serves: 8   Oven: 350°

2 lbs. fresh carrots (2 cups, mashed)	½ cup cream, light
2 tsp. sugar	¼ tsp. ground ginger (optional)
2 well-beaten eggs	1 tsp. ground orange peel (optional)
Salt to taste	
¼ tsp. pepper	

Boil carrots in sweetened water until tender; drain and mash well. Add all other ingredients and mix well. Pour into a small greased ring mold and place mold in a pan of water. Bake uncovered in a 350° oven for 30 minutes; serve hot. May be prepared ahead of time and refrigerated, but allow 45 to 60 minutes to bake if cold.

MRS. ROBERT H. WICKARD

MARINATED CARROTS

Serves: 8-10

2 lbs. carrots	½ cup vinegar
½ medium onion, thinly sliced	½ cup salad oil
¼ bell pepper, thinly sliced	½ cup sugar
1 can tomato soup, undiluted	Tabasco to taste

Scrub carrots and slice in thin rounds; boil in salted water for 10 minutes, or until crisp; do not overcook. Drain well; add onion and bell pepper; mix gently. Put tomato soup, vinegar, oil, and sugar in saucepan and bring to a boil; add Tabasco. Pour over the carrots, in a container of your choice; cover and refrigerate overnight. Keeps indefinitely.

MRS. JOHN WILLIAMS

SAUCY CARROTS

Serves: 4

8 to 10 carrots	1 Tb. light corn syrup
2 Tb. prepared mustard	2 Tb. butter
¼ cup brown sugar	¼ tsp. salt

Pare carrots and cut into one inch chunks. Cover with salt water and cook until tender; drain. Meanwhile, put remaining ingredients in a saucepan in the order listed. Heat, stirring constantly until blended. Pour sauce over carrots and toss gently. Serve hot.

This sauce is sweet and sour and is very delicious.

MRS. DON F. HAMILTON

CAULIFLOWER AU GRATIN

Serves: 8   Oven: 350°

2 medium heads of cauliflower or 3 pkgs. frozen cauliflower	3 Tb. butter
	3 to 4 Tb. cornstarch
	1 cup milk
½ lb. grated Cheddar cheese	Butter

Soak cauliflower heads in salted water for 20 minutes; break into sprigs and put them into boiling salted water. Cook until tender, then drain; remove sprigs into a greased 2 quart oblong baking dish. Add most of the grated cheese on top of the cauliflower. In a saucepan melt butter; gradually add cornstarch, stirring constantly until it is thick. Gradually thin this mixture with milk. Pour this mixture over the cauliflower; sprinkle the remaining cheese over this. Dot with butter. Bake uncovered at 350° about 20 minutes or until the top begins to brown. This may be prepared ahead and refrigerated or frozen.

MRS. J. B. GOFF, JR.
TEXARKANA, ARKANSAS

ITALIAN CAULIFLOWER

Serves: 4

1 head cauliflower or 2 pkgs. frozen cauliflower	½ tsp. salt
	1 cup chopped, peeled tomatoes
Boiling water	
4 Tb. olive oil	¼ cup Parmesan cheese
¼ clove garlic, minced	Chopped parsley

Cook cauliflower in small amount of boiling water, covered, for 10 minutes. Heat oil in skillet; sauté garlic, add tomatoes, salt and well drained cauliflower. Sprinkle with Parmesan cheese. Garnish with chopped parsley when served.

TANGY CAULIFLOWER

Serves: 6-8

3 pkgs. frozen cauliflower
10-oz. can tomatoes with
green chilies

1 pkg. taco seasoning
6 oz. grated American cheese

Cook cauliflower according to package directions. Drain well, add tomatoes with chilies undrained. Sprinkle taco seasoning over top, mix well. Add cheese—reheat until cheese melts.

MRS. POLLY STYERS

CELERY AMANDINE

Serves: 6

4 cups celery, diagonally
sliced
½ cup slivered almonds
4 Tb. butter
1 Tb. minced onion

1 Tb. Spice Island chicken
seasoned stock base
2 Tb. dry white wine
1 tsp. parsley

Use large outer green stalks of celery; slice ¼-inch thick. Sauté almonds in one tablespoon butter; remove from pan; melt rest of butter. Add celery, sprinkle with chicken stock base and add onions. Cover and cook over low heat, turning celery several times, for about 10 minutes. Add wine and almonds; cook 2 or 3 minutes. Sprinkle with parsley and serve. (The texture of the celery is the important thing in this and is best tested by taste. It can be done ahead, up to the point of adding the wine and almonds and reheating, if you don't cook the celery too much.)

This is a nice change for a "green" vegetable.

MRS. R. NORMAN FARRIS

CELERY WITH ALMONDS

Serves: 6

4 cups celery, cut diagonally
½-inch long
¼ cup butter
½ cup consomme, beef or
chicken

1 Tb. flour
Salt
Pepper
Toasted slivered almonds

Sauté celery in butter for 3 to 4 minutes. Stir flour into consomme and add to celery. Season to taste. Garnish with almonds.

MRS. CLIFF WOOD

CELERY AU GRATIN

Serves: 6-8   Oven: 350°

5 cups chopped celery
2 cans mushroom soup,
  undiluted

2 cups grated Cheddar cheese
Buttered bread crumbs
Blanched slivered almonds

Cook celery in salted water until tender; drain; pour into a shallow 2 quart greased casserole. Pour soup over celery; top with grated cheese, bread crumbs, and almonds. Bake uncovered for 20 minutes, or until cheese is melted and bread crumbs are brown.

MRS. LEWIS BLOCK, JR.

CELERY, MUSHROOM & WATER CHESTNUT CASSEROLE

Serves: 6

4 cups sliced celery
3 cups water
1 tsp. salt
4 Tb. butter
¼ cup flour
1 can water chestnuts,
  drained and sliced

1 cup light cream
6-oz. can mushrooms,
  drained, or 8-oz. fresh
  mushrooms sautéed in
  butter
Salt and pepper to taste

Cook celery in salted water, covered, until tender but still crisp. Drain and reserve 1 cup liquid. Melt the butter and stir in flour; gradually add celery liquid and cream. Stir constantly while cooking over low heat until mixture bubbles and thickens. Simmer over low heat for five minutes, still stirring. Add celery, mushrooms, and water chestnuts. Season to taste with salt and pepper. Pour into casserole and serve hot.

MRS. ROBERT G. CARNAHAN

CRUNCHY CELERY

Serves: 6   Oven: 350°

1 bunch celery
1 pt. chicken broth
1 tsp. salt
½ tsp. lemon-pepper
  marinade
4 Tb. cornstarch

4 Tb. cold water
7-oz. can water chestnuts,
  sliced
¼ cup blanched almonds
Buttered bread crumbs
Paprika

Cook celery and broth with seasonings just until crisp. Mix cornstarch with cold water; add to broth. Add water chestnuts and almonds. Pour into a buttered 1 quart casserole and cover top with buttered crumbs and paprika. Dot top with extra butter and bake uncovered at 350° for 40 minutes.

MRS. EUGENE MASON

CHILIES RELLENOS

Serves: 6-8   Oven: 300°

1 lb. Monterey Jack cheese   4 eggs, separated
2 3½-oz. cans El Paso large   3 Tb. flour
  green chilies, chopped

Cover bottom of lightly greased 2 quart baking dish with sliced
cheese; add a layer of chilies. Alternate layers. Beat egg whites
stiff; add flour and fold in beaten yolks. Pour over cheese and
chilies. Bake at 300° for 40 minutes.

MRS. VERNON JACKSON, III

CORN PUDDING

Serves: 6-8   Oven: 350°

¼ cup butter   ¼ cup finely chopped onion
¼ cup flour   1¾ cups milk
2 tsp. salt   3 cups fresh or frozen corn
1½ Tb. sugar   3 eggs

Melt butter in saucepan; stir in flour, salt, sugar, and onion. Cook
until it bubbles; add milk and cook until thick. Stir in corn (chopped
makes a finer textured pudding, but whole is fine to use). Beat
eggs until frothy; stir into corn mixture. Pour in a buttered 1½
quart casserole and place in pan of hot water. Bake in a 350° oven
for 45 minutes, or until a knife comes out clean.

MRS. GEORGE COOK

CORN CASSEROLE

Serves: 6   Oven: 350°

½ cup butter   2 eggs, well beaten
½ cup sugar   1½ tsp. baking powder
1 Tb. flour   2 12-oz. cans whole kernel
½ cup evaporated milk   corn, drained

TOPPING:

1 Tb. butter, melted   ½ tsp. cinnamon
¼ cup sugar

Heat ½ cup butter and ½ cup sugar in a medium size pan until
butter melts. Stir in flour and blend well; remove from heat. Gradually stir in milk; add eggs and baking powder and mix well. Fold
in corn and pour into a buttered 2 quart casserole. Bake 40 minutes,
or until a knife comes out clean when inserted near center. Brush
with melted butter; sprinkle with sugar and cinnamon.

This warms over well when baked ahead of time.

ORIENTAL STUFFED EGGPLANT

Serves: 2   Oven: 375°

2 Tb. butter
¾ lb. ground lean pork
8 water chestnuts or 1 small
   can
1 small onion, minced
1 Tb. fresh gingerroot,
   minced

2 tsp. soy sauce
½ tsp. salt
1 tsp. sugar
1 Tb. sherry
1 large eggplant
2 tsp. butter

Slowly brown pork in butter. Chop the water chestnuts finely and combine with pork, onion, soy sauce, gingerroot, salt, sugar, and sherry. Mix well. Peel eggplant and cut in half lengthwise; remove seeds. Salt and stuff each half with pork mixture. Place a pan of hot water on low rack in oven; put stuffed eggplant in flat baking dish and steam for 30 minutes at 375°. (Beef may be substituted for pork.)

MRS. WILLIAM WEBSTER

EGGPLANT CASSEROLE

Serves: 6-8   Oven: 350°

1 medium eggplant
6 Tb. margarine or bacon fat
1 large onion, chopped
16-oz. can tomatoes, drained
1 cup grated Cheddar cheese

⅓ cup bread crumbs
2 eggs, beaten
1 cup bread crumbs
¼ cup butter
Salt and pepper to taste

Peel eggplant and cut in small pieces. Boil in salted water until tender; drain and mash. Heat margarine or bacon fat in skillet; add onions and sauté until tender but not brown. Add mashed eggplant, tomatoes, cheese, and ⅓ cup bread crumbs. When boiling, add eggs. Cook and stir until eggs are done. Add salt and pepper to taste. Pour into a 2 quart baking dish. Heat 1 cup dry crumbs in ¼ cup butter in oven until golden brown to make buttered bread crumbs for topping the casserole. Bake until browned, about 1 hour at 350°.

MRS. JACK FROST

EGGPLANT SOUFFLE

Serves: 6-8   Oven: 325°

2 medium eggplant   1 cup grated Old English
1 tsp. salt   cheese
2 Tb. butter   3 eggs, separated
2 Tb. flour   Salt to taste
1 cup milk

Peel and slice eggplant; cook in salted water until tender. Drain
and then chop or mash. Make a white sauce by melting butter in
a pan; adding flour, and gradually adding milk; cooking until thickened. While still hot, stir in cheese. Beat egg yolks lightly and fold
into sauce; add salt to taste; stir in eggplant. Beat egg whites until
stiff and fold into eggplant mixture. Put into a greased 2 quart
casserole and set in a pan of warm water. Bake about 1 hour, or
until set, in a 325° oven.

This is very light and would be good served with a spicy meat dish.

MRS. JOSEPH B. HURST

RATATOUILLE (EGGPLANT CASSEROLE)

Serves: 6   Oven: 400°

1 medium eggplant   1 tsp. salt
¼ cup olive oil   ⅛ tsp. pepper
1 lb. zucchini   1½ cups chopped onion
¼ tsp. thyme   2 tomatoes, peeled and
¼ tsp. oregano   chopped
¼ tsp. rosemary   1 cup chopped bell pepper
¼ tsp. basil   ½ cup chopped celery
¼ tsp. M.S.G.   Grated Cheddar cheese
2 cloves garlic, mashed   Bread crumbs

Peel and cube eggplant; sauté lightly in oil; set aside and drain on
paper towels. Scrub zucchini well and slice; sauté in oil and drain
on paper towels. Mix all spices together. Place eggplant in a 2
quart casserole; sprinkle with a little of the spice mixture. Add
zucchini and a sprinkling of spices. Add remaining chopped vegetables in layers, using the remaining spices. Cover and bake for 45
minutes at 400°. Remove from oven, top with grated cheese and
bread crumbs. Return to oven until cheese melts.

MRS. RICHARD NORTON

FRESH MUSHROOMS

Serves: 3-4

8-oz. pkg. fresh mushrooms   2 Tb. Worcestershire sauce
1 cup water   Dash of salt and pepper
2 Tb. soy sauce   1 Tb. butter

Rinse mushrooms and remove stems; put in medium saucepan with
water, spices, and butter. Cook uncovered over low heat for 30
minutes. To hold or reheat, cover to avoid shrinkage.

Excellent served with duck or steak.

OLIVIA BRADY

GARLIC CHEESE GRITS

Serves: 6   Oven: 350°

6-oz. tube Jalapeno cheese   1 tsp. salt
6-oz. tube garlic cheese   1 cup uncooked grits
4 cups water   ¼ cup butter

Slice or tear cheese into small pieces. Bring salted water to a boil; slowly add grits. Bring to a second boil; reduce heat and cook over medium heat for 4 to 5 minutes, stirring often. Add cheese and butter to grits, stirring until melted and blended. Pour into an ungreased 1½ quart casserole; bake uncovered for 30 minutes at 350°.

Delicious with steak.

MRS. JAMES H. ATKINS

MUSHROOM CASSEROLE

Serves: 4   Oven: 350°

2 beef bouillon cubes   1 lb. fresh mushrooms,
¼ cup hot water   washed, dried, sliced
2 Tb. flour   ½ cup bread crumbs
¾ tsp. salt   ½ cup Parmesan cheese
Pepper to taste   ¼ cup melted butter
½ cup light cream

Dissolve bouillon cubes in water; set aside to cool. Put flour, salt, and pepper in small saucepan and very slowly add cream, mixing thoroughly to keep from lumping; add bouillon and put over low heat, stirring constantly until thick. Pour over mushrooms in a 1½ quart casserole. Top with bread crumbs, cheese, and butter; bake 30 minutes at 350°.

MRS. JAMES CROTTY

CRANBERRY ONIONS

Serves: 4   Oven: 400°

4 large white onions   ½ tsp. whole thyme
1 cup cranberries, cut in half   ¼ cup melted butter
½ cup finely diced celery   1 bouillon cube
½ cup sugar   ⅔ cup boiling water (use
¼ cup raisins   water from cooking onions)
2 Tb. walnuts

Peel and cut out center of onions. Cook onions in boiling salted water for 10 minutes. Combine cranberries, celery, sugar, raisins, walnuts, thyme, butter, and toss. Place onions in baking dish. Spoon cranberries into onion cavities. Dissolve bouillon cube in water. Pour over onions. Bake at 400° for about 1 hour.

MRS. W. DAN COTTON

COUNTRY NOODLE CASSEROLE

Serves: 12   Oven: 350°

½ lb. sliced bacon
16-oz. pkg. very fine egg
  noodles
3 cups cottage cheese
3 cups dairy sour cream
2 cloves garlic, crushed
2 onions, minced
2 Tb. Worcestershire sauce

Dash liquid hot pepper
  seasoning
4 tsp. salt
3 Tb. horseradish
1 cup grated Parmesan
  cheese
Extra sour cream

Fry bacon until crisp; drain on paper towels and crumble. Cook noodles in boiling salted water until tender, according to package directions; drain well. Mix all remaining ingredients, except Parmesan cheese and extra sour cream, in a large bowl. Add noodles and bacon and toss with two forks until well mixed. Turn into a deep 3½ quart buttered casserole. Cover and bake in a 350° oven for 30 to 40 minutes, or until heated through. Remove cover, sprinkle surface with ¼ cup Parmesan cheese, broil until golden. Serve remaining Parmesan to sprinkle over each portion, and extra sour cream if you wish.

This dish may be prepared ahead of time and cooked just before serving.

MRS. H. WILLIAM GOODMAN

BAKED ONIONS

Serves: 6   Oven: 350°

6 yellow onions, thinly sliced
3¾-oz. bag potato chips,
  crushed
½ lb. Wisconsin mild cheese,
  grated

2 cans cream of mushroom
  soup
1 cup milk
⅛ tsp. cayenne pepper

Place alternate layers of onions, potato chips and cheese in a buttered 1½ quart casserole. Pour soup mixed with milk over all. Sprinkle pepper over the top and bake uncovered at 350° for 1 hour.

MRS. JAMES B. SPEED
FORT SMITH, ARKANSAS

BAKED ONIONS PARMESAN

Serves: 4   Oven: 350°

20 small whole white onions
1 can cream of celery soup,
  undiluted

½ tsp. salt
½ cup grated Parmesan
  cheese

Peel onions and place in a 1½ quart casserole. Pour soup over onions; add salt and sprinkle with cheese. Cover and bake at 350° for 1 hour.

Canned onions may be substituted and the baking time shortened to 30 minutes.

FRIED ONION RINGS

Serves: 4-6

1 large Bermuda onion	1 egg yolk
(¾ lb.)	⅔ cup milk
1 cup sifted flour	1 Tb. salad oil
1¾ tsp. salt	1 egg white
1½ tsp. baking powder	Shortening for frying

Peel onion; slice about ¼ inch thick and separate into rings; cover with cold water for 30 minutes; drain on paper towels. Meanwhile, prepare batter by sifting flour, salt, and baking powder together in a medium size bowl; set aside. Beat egg yolk slightly; add milk and oil. Add to flour mixture and stir until smooth. (The mixture will be thick.) Beat egg white until soft peaks form; fold into batter. Heat 1 inch of shortening in a heavy skillet until medium hot. Dip onion rings into batter, allowing excess to drop off; fry until golden. Drain on paper towels; keep warm while frying rest.

MRS. DON THOMPSON

OKRA AND TOMATOES

Serves: 6

1 large onion, chopped	2½ cups fresh tomatoes, or a
2 ribs celery, chopped	16-oz. can tomatoes and
1 Tb. bacon grease	their liquid
1 lb. fresh okra, sliced	¼ tsp. curry powder
1¼ tsp. salt	(heaping)
½ tsp. paprika	2 tsp. brown sugar

Sauté onion and celery in bacon grease. Add okra and cook 5 minutes. Add remaining ingredients, cover, and cook until tender, about 30 minutes.

OKRA FRITTERS

Serves: 6-8

1 cup flour	2 eggs, beaten
3 tsp. baking powder	⅓ cup milk
½ tsp. salt	5 cups thinly sliced okra

Sift dry ingredients together. Combine eggs and milk and add to dry mixture; stir until smooth. Add okra. Spoon by heaping tablespoons into deep fat and fry until crisp. Serve with melted butter.

FRENCH PEAS

Serves: 3

3 large lettuce leaves
3 lbs. fresh shelled peas, or a
  10-oz. pkg. frozen peas
1 tsp. sugar

½ tsp. salt
Pepper
2 Tb. butter

Line a skillet with lettuce leaves. Add peas and sprinkle with sugar, salt, and pepper. Dot with butter; top with lettuce leaf. Cook tightly covered, 10 to 15 minutes, or until tender.

BLACKEYED PEAS CREOLE

Serves: 8

2 strips bacon
1 cup onion, chopped
1 cup bell pepper, chopped
1 cup celery, chopped
20-oz. can tomatoes
1 Tb. sugar

1 large bay leaf
½ tsp. sweet basil
Salt and fresh ground pepper
  to taste
2 pkgs. frozen blackeyed peas

Fry bacon until crisp; remove from fat and drain. Brown the onion, green pepper, and celery in fat; add crumbled bacon and tomatoes, sugar, bay leaf, sweet basil, salt, and pepper. Simmer for 5 minutes. Add 2 packages frozen blackeyed peas to the above without thawing. Cook slowly for 1½ to 2 hours, adding water when necessary.

MRS. ROBERT CRESS

MARINATED BLACKEYED PEAS

Serves: 8-10

3 16-oz. cans blackeyed peas
1 cup salad oil
½ cup wine vinegar
1 garlic bud
½ cup onions, sliced

½ tsp. salt
Cracked pepper to taste
1 tsp. chili powder
1 cup stuffed green olives,
  sliced (optional)

Drain peas; add remaining ingredients. Refrigerate in covered container for at least 24 hours, remove garlic bud. Will keep for 2 weeks.

This is a particularly appropriate dish for New Year's Day and is easy to prepare days ahead.

MRS. DON F. HAMILTON

PARTY CHEESE POTATOES

Serves: 12-14   Oven: 350°

3 cups medium white sauce
1½ cups grated American
  cheese
¾ cup grated Parmesan
  cheese
Dash cayenne pepper
Salt to taste

½ tsp. powdered thyme
8 cups cooked potatoes, sliced
2 4-oz. cans mushrooms,
  drained
2 Tb. butter
½ cup bread crumbs

Prepare white sauce; stir in cheeses and seasonings. Combine with potatoes and mushrooms. Put in 2½ quart casserole; sprinkle with buttered bread crumbs. Bake 35 to 40 minutes at 350°, until golden brown and bubbly.

This is an especially good recipe for entertaining; the seasonings make it different from ordinary au gratin potatoes.

MRS. PATRICK JACOBS
TULSA, OKLAHOMA

POTATOES ANNA

Serves: 6   Oven: 425°

½ cup soft butter
2 lbs. potatoes, pared and
  thinly sliced

1 tsp. salt
⅛ tsp. pepper

Preheat oven. Grease an 8-inch covered skillet with 3 tablespoons butter. Gently toss potatoes with salt and pepper. Layer a third of the potatoes, circular fashion, around bottom and sides of skillet. Dot with butter. Repeat twice. Cook potatoes 3 minutes over high heat. Then bake, covered, 30 minutes. Remove cover, bake 5 minutes longer. Let stand 5 minutes. Invert on plate.

POTATO CASSEROLE

Serves: 6   Oven: 350°

3 large potatoes
¼ cup margarine
1 cup grated sharp cheese
1 cup sour cream
½ cup milk

⅓ cup green onion and tops
Salt and white pepper to
  taste
¼ cup chopped pimiento
(optional)

Boil potatoes in jackets until almost done; chill until very cold; peel and shred with a grater. Melt margarine in double boiler; add cheese, a small amount at a time. Mix together the sour cream and milk; add to cheese mixture. Add onions and stir; add salt and pepper to taste. Add the shredded potatoes. Put in casserole; bake at 350° for 45 minutes, uncovered.

MRS. GEORGE FARR
JACKSON, MISSISSIPPI

POTATO-LEEK CASSEROLE

Serves: 4-6   Oven: 350°

4 large potatoes   ½ tsp. salt
6 leeks   ¼ tsp. pepper
¼ cup butter   ⅔ cup grated sharp Cheddar
2 Tb. flour   cheese
2 cups milk

Peel and slice potatoes thinly. Spread half the potato slices evenly
in a well greased casserole. Slice leeks thinly and arrange over the
potatoes. Cover with remaining potato slices. In a heavy saucepan,
melt the butter. Blend in flour and gradually stir in milk; blend
well. Bring to a boil; remove from heat. Add salt, pepper, and ⅓
cup cheese; mix well. Pour evenly over the potatoes, cover, and
bake at 350° for 45 minutes. Remove cover, garnish with remaining cheese, dot with butter, and bake an additional 15 minutes, or
until lightly browned.

POTATO PANCAKES WITH APPLESAUCE

Serves: 8   Oven: 250°

6 medium size baking   ⅓ cup flour
   potatoes   1 tsp. salt
2 eggs   8 Tb. bacon fat or lard
¼ cup finely grated onion   Applesauce

Peel the potatoes and as you proceed drop them into cold water to
prevent their discoloring. In a large mixing bowl, beat the eggs
enough to break them up, add the onion and gradually beat in the
flour and salt. One at a time, pat the potatoes dry and grate them
coarsely into a sieve or colander. Press each potato down firmly
into the sieve to squeeze out as much moisture as possible, then
immediately stir it into the egg and onion batter. Preheat the oven
to 250°. In a heavy 8 to 10 inch skillet melt bacon fat over high
heat until it splutters. Pour in ⅓ cup of the potato mixture and,
with a spatula, flatten it into a pancake about 5 inches in diameter.
Fry it over moderate heat for about 2 minutes on each side. When
the pancake is golden brown on both sides and crisp around the
edges, transfer it to a heated, oven-proof plate and keep it warm
in the oven. Continue making similar pancakes with the remaining
batter, adding more fat to the pan when necessary to keep it at a
depth of ¼ inch. Serve the pancakes as soon as possible with
applesauce.

HANS BACH

SCALLOPED POTATOES

Serves: 4-6   Oven: 350°

2 Tb. butter	Salt and pepper
2 Tb. flour	½ onion, chopped fine
1½ cups milk	2 slices Velveeta cheese,
6 medium potatoes, peeled	grated or cut small
and sliced	

Grease a 1½ quart casserole. Make a thin white sauce by melting butter in a saucepan; add flour and gradually add milk, salt, and pepper, stirring constantly. Alternate layers of potatoes, onions, and cheese, adding white sauce after each layer, ending with potato layer. If you cannot see the white sauce through top layer of potatoes, add milk until you can. Cover and cook at 350° for 1 hour and 15 minutes; remove cover and cook for 30 minutes at 400°. Should be nicely browned when done.

MRS. HENRY G. HOLLENBERG, JR.

TWICE BAKED POTATOES WITH CORN

Serves: 8   Oven: 350°

4 medium baking potatoes	Milk or cream to soften
1 tsp. salt	potatoes
½ tsp. pepper	12-oz. can whole kernel corn,
1 Tb. frozen chives	drained
¼ cup butter	Velveeta cheese for garnish

Bake potatoes in a 350° oven for about 1½ hours, or until done. While hot, halve potatoes and scoop pulp out, placing it in mixing bowl. Beat in salt, pepper, chives, butter, and enough milk to soften. After potatoes are mashed well, fold in corn with a spoon. Place filling back in shells; garnish with grated cheese. Return to a 325° oven for about 20 minutes, or until cheese is melted. A small amount of crumbled bacon may be added to mixture if desired. May be prepared several days ahead; may be frozen until ready for use.
Variation: Substitute one can crab meat for corn.

MRS. JACK FROST, JR.

CANDIED YAMS

Serves: 4-6   Oven: 400°

4 medium sweet potatoes	6 Tb. butter
1 cup sugar	2 to 3 slices lemon
Dash salt	1 Tb. flour
1 tsp. cinnamon or nutmeg	¼ cup water

Peel and cut potatoes as for thick french fries. Place in 8 x 12 x 2-inch dish. Cover potatoes with sugar and salt; sprinkle cinnamon or nutmeg over the sugar; cover with pieces of butter. Twist lemon slices over this and place peel in with potatoes. Sift flour evenly over the potatoes; add water. Bake in 400° oven for 1 hour, or until potatoes are done and sugar and butter have made a thick syrup. Baste potatoes frequently with syrup. Serve immediately.

MRS. R. E. JACK BUSH, SR.

SWEET POTATO AND APPLE CASSEROLE

Serves: 8   Oven: 350°

6 medium baking apples   Salt to taste
½ cup maple syrup   4 medium sweet potatoes
½ cup brown sugar   1 cup chopped pecans
½ cup butter

Pare and slice apples; place in saucepan and cover with maple syrup.
Add brown sugar and butter. Cook until tender; add salt to taste.
Bake sweet potatoes in their jackets until done; peel and slice.
Place apples and potatoes in four layers in a greased 2 quart casserole, beginning with potatoes and ending with apples. Top with
pecans. May be made ahead and heated in a 350° oven until very
hot, about 30 to 45 minutes. (Always bake sweet potatoes to retain
their best flavor.)

MRS. DON F. HAMILTON

CHINESE FRIED RICE

Serves: 8-12

¼ cup salad oil   5-oz. can water chestnuts,
Scallions (1 bunch), chopped   sliced
3 cups Minute Rice   ¼ cup soy sauce
1 bell pepper, sliced   16-oz. pkg. frozen peas
2 cups chicken broth   4 eggs, scrambled dry
4-oz. can mushrooms

Heat oil in large heavy skillet and cook rice, green pepper, and scallions for 5 minutes, stirring occasionally. Add broth, mushrooms,
water chestnuts, and soy sauce. Cover and simmer about 15 minutes, until liquid cooks down. Add frozen peas and eggs last 5 minutes. Peas should stay whole and firm. Add more liquid if necessary to keep mixture moist.

*Optional: 2 cups chicken, shrimp, or pork may be added for main
dish.*

MRS. HENRY W. RUSSELL

CURRIED RICE

Serves: 8

2¼ cups long grain white rice   3 tsp. salt
9 Tb. butter   4½ cups chicken broth
2 tsp. curry powder

In heavy pan, cook rice in butter until golden, stirring constantly.
Add curry powder, salt, and chicken broth; bring to boil. Cover and
cook about 14 to 20 minutes over low heat until rice is tender and
liquid is absorbed.

MRS. F. WILLIAM TERRY, JR.

DIANE'S RICE PILAF

Serves: 6-8

6 Tb. butter
2 cloves garlic, minced
1 yellow onion, finely
  chopped
1½ cups long grain rice,
  uncooked

⅓ cup pine nuts
2½ cups chicken stock
  (12½-oz. can Wolferman's
  and 1 cup chicken broth)
1 tsp. freshly ground white
  pepper

Melt butter in a frying pan; add garlic and onion and stir over low
heat until transparent. Add rice and stir until well coated; add pine
nuts and mix well. Add chicken stock and pepper; cook over moderate heat until the mixture comes to a boil. Reduce heat, cover
tightly, and simmer for 25 minutes. Fluff with two forks. Serve
and wait for the comments.

MRS. WILLIAM CASTLES
TULSA, OKLAHOMA

HERB RICE

Serves: 4

1 cup raw rice
1 tsp. salt
½ tsp. rosemary
½ tsp. marjoram

½ tsp. thyme
2 chicken bouillon cubes
1 Tb. butter
2 cups water

Combine all ingredients in a pan and bring to a boil. Stir, cover,
and cook over very low heat for 14 minutes, or until rice is tender
and water is absorbed. You may use less water if you prefer a
firmer texture.

This is particularly tasty with game or poultry.

MRS. WATKINS CROCKETT, JR.
NASHVILLE, TENNESSEE

MARIE SCHULTE'S RICE CASSEROLE

Serves: 8-10   Oven: 350°

2 cups cooked white rice
½ cup grated Monterey Jack
  cheese
1 cup sour cream

1 can regular green chili
  peppers, chopped
Parmesan cheese

In a 1½ quart round casserole that has been greased with margarine, put a layer of rice, a layer of cheese and a layer of sour cream
that has been mixed with the chili peppers; repeat. Sprinkle top
with Parmesan cheese. Bake 20 to 25 minutes at 350°, uncovered.

MARIE SCHULTE

RICE O'BRIEN

Serves: 6

1 cup raw rice	1 cup chopped green onion
2 cups water	1 cup chopped bell pepper
3 chicken bouillon cubes	1 cup diced celery
1 tsp. salt	1 cup sliced ripe olives
¼ cup butter	6 Tb. chopped pimientoes

Cook rice in water flavored with bouillon cubes and salt. Meanwhile, melt butter in a large skillet; add onion, pepper, celery, and sauté until just tender. Add olives and pimientoes; fold in rice. Serve immediately.

MRS. CY SANDERS

RICE POTPOURRI

Serves: 8 **Oven: 350°**

½ cup butter	Salt and pepper to taste
1 large bell pepper, chopped	1 can mushroom soup, diluted
1 large onion, chopped	with 1 can water
1 tsp. leaf sweet basil	1 cup raw rice
1 tsp. leaf marjoram	¼ lb. Cheddar cheese, grated
¼ tsp. curry powder	Bread crumbs

Melt butter in a skillet; add and sauté bell pepper and onion. Crush sweet basil and marjoram and add to mixture, along with curry powder, salt, and pepper. Add diluted soup and cook until onion and pepper are tender. Cook rice according to package directions; fold into vegetable mixture. Put mixture into a 2 quart casserole; top with cheese and bread crumbs. Heat in 350° oven for about 30 minutes, uncovered.

MRS. TED R. ROGERS

RICE RING WITH WATER CHESTNUTS AND MUSHROOMS

Serves: 10

16 oz. white rice	1 cup chopped parsley
1½ cups butter	2 4-oz. cans mushrooms,
2 bell peppers, minced	drained
1 bunch green onions, finely	2 cans water chestnuts,
chopped (tops and stems)	drained and sliced
2 cups chopped celery	Dash of soy sauce

Cook rice according to directions on box; cool. Sauté celery, parsley, peppers, onions, and mushrooms in 1 cup butter until soft. Put ½ cup butter in a pan; add water chestnuts and soy sauce; cook 10 minutes. Fold all ingredients into cold rice. Put strips of oiled, waxed paper in a ring mold; pack in rice. Steam in or over hot water until thoroughly heated. May be made a day ahead and heated before serving.

MRS. JACK DEACON
JONESBORO, ARKANSAS

RICE SURPRISE

Serves: 8   Oven: 350°

1 cup rice
Chicken broth
1 cup sour cream
1½ Tb. Jalapeno peppers,
seeded and minced
1½ Tb. Jalapeno juice

⅓ cup creamy Italian
dressing
1 can water chestnuts,
drained and sliced
1 lb. Monterey Jack cheese,
grated

Cook rice according to package directions, substituting chicken broth for water. Combine all ingredients except cheese. Pour one-half of the mixture into a 2 quart casserole; top with one-half of cheese. Repeat layer. Bake uncovered in a 350° oven for 30 minutes. (If you like very hot food, you may increase the quantity of Jalapenos.)

MRS. LEWIS BLOCK, JR.

WILD RICE CASSEROLE

Serves: 8   Oven: 325°

1½ cups raw wild rice
4 Tb. butter
2 Tb. chopped parsley
4-oz. can sliced mushrooms,
drained
½ bell pepper, chopped

1 small onion, chopped
2 cans chicken broth
1 can water
1 clove garlic, minced
Salt and pepper to taste

Brown rice in butter until golden brown. Mix with all other ingredients. Pour into a 2 quart casserole and bake 1 hour at 325°, uncovered.

Variation: Substitute Uncle Ben's mixture of wild and long-grained rice for wild rice.

MRS. JAMES V. FLACK, JR.

WINE RICE

Serves: 8

1 cup raw rice
1 cup chopped fresh tomatoes
½ cup chopped onion
1 lb. fresh mushrooms, sliced
Chicken broth
½ cup red wine

2 tsp. salt
¼ tsp. pepper
1 cup tiny green peas, heated
and drained
½ cup butter
¼ to ½ cup Parmesan cheese

Place rice, tomatoes, onion, and mushrooms in a large skillet. Add amount of chicken broth equal to amount of liquid called for on rice package, less ½ cup; add wine, salt, and pepper; mix well. Cover and simmer for 30 to 40 minutes, or until liquid is absorbed and rice is tender. Stir in peas and butter; sprinkle with cheese and serve immediately.

MRS. GUS WALTON, JR.

WILD RICE POTPOURRI

Serves: 6   Oven: 350°

1 cup wild rice   4-oz. can sliced mushrooms,
2 Tb. butter   drained
2 ribs celery, finely chopped   ½ lb. processed American
1 small onion, finely chopped   cheese, diced
½ bell pepper, chopped   ½ cup light cream

Cook rice according to directions on package. (Then steam the
rice in a collander over boiling water with a towel over the top;
this really makes it dry and fluffy.) Melt butter in a skillet; add
and sauté the celery, onion, and green pepper; add to rice. Add
mushrooms and cheese to rice mixture. Turn into a greased 1½
quart casserole; pour cream over rice. Bake uncovered for 30 minutes. (By withholding the cream until casserole is to be baked, this
dish may be prepared in advance and frozen.)

*Serve with broiled chicken, roast, turkey, duck, or one of our dove
casseroles.*

MRS. A. HOWARD STEBBINS, III

SPINACH MADELAINE

Serves: 6   Oven: 350°

2 pkgs. frozen chopped   ½ tsp. black pepper
   spinach   ¾ tsp. celery salt
4 Tb. butter   ¾ tsp. garlic salt
2 Tb. flour   ½ tsp. salt
2 Tb. chopped onion   6-oz. roll Jalapeno cheese
½ cup evaporated milk   1 tsp. Worcestershire sauce
½ cup spinach liquid   Red pepper to taste

Cook spinach according to directions on package. Drain and reserve
liquid. Melt butter in saucepan over low heat. Add flour stirring
until blended and smooth but not brown. Add onion and cook until
soft but not brown. Add spinach liquid and milk slowly, stirring
constantly to avoid lumps. Cook until smooth and thick, continue
stirring. Add seasonings and cheese which has been cut into small
pieces; stir until melted. Combine with cooked spinach. This may
be served immediately or put into a casserole topped with buttered
bread crumbs. The flavor improves if the latter is done and kept
in the refrigerator overnight. This may also be frozen.

*This is great used as a dip. Heat in a pan and pour into a chafing
dish. It will serve 20.*

MRS. LEMUEL CLEMENT
NORTH LITTLE ROCK, ARKANSAS

ARKANSAS SPINACH ROCKEFELLER

Serves: 4   Oven: 350°

1 box frozen chopped	2 Tb. butter
spinach	1 tsp. Louisiana Hot Sauce
½ cup milk	1 tsp. salt
½ cup cubed sharp cheese	1 egg, beaten
Juice of 1 lemon	4 Tb. Parmesan cheese
6 green onions, chopped	

Cook spinach as directed on box, omitting salt; squeeze all liquid out. Put in saucepan with remaining ingredients, except egg and Parmesan cheese. Heat until cheese is melted; cool and mix with beaten egg. Fill four buttered ramekins or a 1 quart casserole. Top with Parmesan cheese; bake in 350° oven for 20 minutes, uncovered.

MRS. JAMES A. COYNE, JR.
ROLAND, ARKANSAS

CREAMED SPINACH

Serves: 6-8   Oven: 350°

1 lb. fresh spinach	2 Tb. butter, melted
1 cup medium cream sauce	2 Tb. Parmesan cheese
Salt and pepper to taste	½ cup Hollandaise sauce
Dash wine vinegar	

Pick and wash spinach; boil in salted water for 3 minutes. Drain all liquid from spinach and mix with cream sauce, wine vinegar, salt and pepper, and melted butter. Place in a 1½ quart casserole; cover with Hollandaise and sprinkle with Parmesan cheese; heat in 350° oven for 10 minutes. This can be made ahead and refrigerated.

MRS. GENE MASON

SPINACH AND CHEESE CASSEROLE

Serves: 4-6   Oven: 325°

3 eggs, beaten	2 cups Cheddar cheese,
2 Tb. flour	grated
10-oz. pkg. frozen, chopped	½ tsp. salt
spinach, thawed and	½ tsp. garlic salt
drained	1 tsp. onion salt
2 cups cottage cheese	1 Tb. lemon juice

Beat eggs and flour until smooth. Mix in all other ingredients. Pour into a well greased 9 x 13-inch casserole; bake at 325° for 60 to 70 minutes. May be made a day ahead and cooked before serving.

MRS. HESTER MEYER

SPINACH RAREBIT

Serves: 6-8   Oven: 350°

2 10-oz. pkgs. frozen chopped spinach
10-oz. pkg. frozen Welsh Rarebit (Stouffer's)
8 slices bacon

5-oz. can water chestnuts, drained and sliced
½ of a 3½-oz. can french fried onion rings

Cook and drain spinach. Thaw Welsh Rarebit. Cook bacon crisp; drain and crumble. Combine spinach, water chestnuts, ⅓ of Welsh Rarebit in baking dish. Top with crumbled bacon. Spread remaining rarebit evenly over all; top with onion rings. Bake uncovered in a 350° oven for 15 minutes.

MRS. GEORGE MCLEOD

SPINACH QUICHE

Serves: 8-10   Oven: 325°

10-inch pie shell, unbaked
2 10-oz. pkgs. frozen spinach
3 Tb. butter
3 eggs
1½ cups milk

2 tsp. garlic salt
½ tsp. basil
Grated nutmeg
Pepper to taste
Parmesan cheese—optional

Cook spinach until melted; drain and add butter. Beat eggs with milk; mix with spinach and add garlic salt, basil, nutmeg and pepper. Pour into pie shell; bake for 45 minutes to 1 hour, or until set. May be served hot, warm or cold. Parmesan cheese may be sprinkled on top before baking if desired.

MRS. BOOKER WORTHEN

SPINACH RICE CASSEROLE

Serves: 8   Oven: 350°

2 10-oz. pkgs. frozen chopped spinach
4 eggs
1 cup milk
1 tsp. onion juice
1 tsp. Worcestershire sauce

2 tsp. salt, or to taste
¾ lb. Cheddar cheese, shredded
3 cups cooked rice
¼ cup melted butter

Cook and drain spinach. Beat eggs and stir in milk, onion juice, Worcestershire, and salt. Add cheese and fold in spinach, rice, and butter. Pour into a greased 2 quart casserole and bake in a 325° oven for 30 minutes, or until thoroughly heated.

MRS. ROBERT G. CARNAHAN

ACORN SQUASH WITH CRANBERRIES

Serves: 4   Oven: 350°

2 acorn squash
1 cup frozen or fresh cranberries
½ cup brown sugar

2 Tb. melted butter
½ tsp. cinnamon
¼ to ½ tsp. hot pepper
  seasoning (liquid)

Cut squash in half lengthwise; remove seeds and cut a slice from the bottom so they will sit steadily. Combine cranberries, brown sugar, butter, cinnamon, and liquid hot pepper; fill squash with this. Place in baking dish and surround with one inch hot water. Bake in 350° oven until squash is done.

CORDELL S. DOUGHERTY

BAKED ACORN SQUASH

Serves: 6

3 medium acorn squash
⅓ cup butter
Salt

6 tsp. sherry
Nutmeg
4 tsp. brown sugar

Cut squash in half lengthwise and remove seeds. Rub well inside and out with butter. Fill cavities with remaining ingredients evenly divided between squash. Bake in 350° oven for 50 minutes or until tender. Squash may also be baked with just butter and salt and then filled with creamed meats or vegetables.

MRS. MIKE MEHAFFY

BAKED SQUASH WITH BACON

Serves: 6-8   Oven: 350°

8 to 10 medium squash
4 to 6 slices raw bacon

1½ Tb. instant minced onions
Salt and pepper to taste

Wash squash; cut in half lengthwise; place in shallow baking dish. Cut bacon into small strips crosswise. Put onion, salt, pepper, and bacon on squash; add 1 inch of water to baking dish. Place in 350° oven for 30 minutes.

MRS. HOUCK REASONER

YELLOW SQUASH CASSEROLE

Serves: 8-10   Oven: 350°

4 cups cooked squash
½ onion, chopped
½ bell pepper, chopped
2 eggs, beaten

½ cup milk
¾ cup grated Cheddar cheese
1 cup cracker crumbs
Salt and pepper to taste

Cool squash; mash. Sauté onion and green pepper in butter until tender. Mix with all other ingredients, reserving a small amount of cheese and cracker crumbs for garnish. Put in a greased 2 quart casserole, garnish with cheese and crumbs. Bake at 350° for 45 minutes, uncovered.

This may be prepared ahead and also freezes well.

MRS. KENT VESTAL

SQUASH CASSEROLE

Serves: 8   Oven: 350°

½ cup butter
1 pkg. Pepperidge Farm corn
  bread dressing
1 can cream of chicken soup

3 cups cooked and mashed
  squash
1 small jar chopped pimiento
1 small onion, chopped

Melt butter and pour over dressing; put ½ of this mixture in the bottom of a 2 quart casserole. Mix all other ingredients and put on top of dressing. Add the rest of the dressing and bake 1 hour at 350°, uncovered.

MRS. BERNICE HOLDER

PLANTATION SQUASH

Serves: 12   Oven: 325°

12 medium yellow squash
2 pkgs. frozen chopped
  spinach
3-oz. pkg. cream cheese,
  softened
3 well beaten eggs
6 Tb. melted butter

1 heaping Tb. sugar
½ tsp. seasoned salt
½ tsp. onion salt
1 Tb. cracked black pepper
1 cup Ritz cracker crumbs
Paprika
1 cup crumbled crisp bacon

Scrub squash; cut green stem away. Cook whole in boiling water just until tender, testing with a fork. Cut in half and scoop out pulp with a spoon and place pulp in a large bowl. Boil spinach in lightly salted water until tender; drain well in a colander; add to pulp. Add cream cheese to warm squash-spinach mixture. Add all except last three ingredients to mixture and mix well. Lightly salt squash shells and fill with mixture, mounding the top; garnish each with crumbs, paprika, and bacon. Place on a lightly greased sheet or in a shallow casserole. Cover with foil and bake at 325° for 30 minutes or until hot. May be prepared a day ahead.
Men love it!

MRS. DAVID SNOWDEN

RED HOT SQUASH CASSEROLE

Serves: 4   Oven: 350°

6 to 8 medium yellow squash,
  sliced
1 large onion, chopped
1 tsp. salt
1 tsp. sugar

¼ lb. Velveeta cheese
2 Tb. milk
1 or 2 Jalapeno peppers,
  seeded and minced
Paprika

Boil squash and onion in water with salt and sugar until done. Drain well in a colander and pour into a 1 quart casserole. Make a sauce of cheese and milk; pour over squash; add peppers; mix well. Garnish with paprika. Heat in 350° oven uncovered for 20 to 30 minutes, or until thoroughly hot.

MRS. ROBERT HICKMAN

BAKED TOMATOES VERDIS

Serves: 8   Oven: 400°

8 medium tomatoes   3 Tb. butter
2 medium carrots   1 egg, beaten
1 small bell pepper   1 cup dried bread crumbs
1 onion   ½ cup milk
3 large celery ribs   ½ tsp. salt
3 cups fresh spinach   ⅛ tsp. pepper
3 sprigs parsley   Swiss cheese, grated

Select firm tomatoes. Slice out stem end and scoop out seeds and pulp. Chop up remaining vegetables and simmer, covered, in butter until browned. Add remaining ingredients and mix thoroughly. Fill tomatoes and sprinkle with cheese. Place in buttered pan and bake uncovered at 400° for 20 minutes, or until tomatoes are tender.

MRS. W. M. POWELL

STUFFED TOMATOES HOLLANDAISE

Serves: 4   Oven: 350°

4 medium tomatoes   1 pkg. frozen French style
1 cup Hollandaise sauce   green beans
4 slices bacon, cooked crisp Salt and pepper to taste

Early in the day, or even the night before, prepare tomatoes by peeling and removing about ½ of the pulp. Prepare Hollandaise sauce ahead. Cook beans according to package directions; drain well; season to taste with salt and pepper. Add sauce to beans; mix well. When ready to serve, assemble by filling each tomato with the hot bean mixture; top with crumbled bacon, and heat in oven about 10 minutes.

A colorful, tangy way to serve tomatoes.

MRS. JAMES M. DUNAWAY

GRILLED TOMATOES WITH ROSEMARY

Serves: 4

4 firm tomatoes   Salt and freshly ground
2 cloves garlic   pepper to taste
2 tsp. fresh or 1 tsp. dried Olive oil
   rosemary

Preheat broiler to high. Rinse and dry tomatoes carefully; do not core or peel them. Split tomatoes in half as close to center as possible; arrange on a baking dish. Cut the garlic into thin slivers; insert the slivers at various points over the cut surface of the tomatoes. Chop the rosemary coarsely and sprinkle on tomatoes; sprinkle with salt and pepper and dribble the olive oil over all. Run the tomatoes under the broiler, 4 to 5 inches away, and let them broil 3 minutes or longer (until garlic is browned and tomatoes are soft but firm). Remove pieces of garlic and serve hot.

Variation: Basil, thyme, Parmesan cheese, oregano, or dry sherry may be substituted for the rosemary.

MRS. JOHN V. SATTERFIELD, III

TOMATOES STUFFED WITH FRESH CORN

Serves: 8   Oven: 350°

8 tomatoes
8 ears of corn, medium size
  or 4 cups canned or frozen
  corn
½ cup butter
¼ cup bell pepper, chopped

¼ cup onion, chopped
1 small jar chopped pimiento
2 Tb. parsley, chopped
1 cup Cheddar cheese, grated
Salt and pepper to taste

Skin and seed tomatoes. Salt cavities well and invert on a paper towel. Cook corn on cob, cool and then cut from cob. Melt butter in skillet; sauté onion and bell pepper until onion is tender. Add corn, parsley, and pimiento, cooking for several minutes. Add cheese and stir until cheese melts. Salt and pepper to taste. Stuff tomatoes with corn. Place in baking dish; before baking add water only to cover bottom. Cover and bake for 30 minutes at 350°. These may be made a day ahead, but bring to room temperature before baking. For a different, delicious taste put these tomatoes in a foil baking dish with a foil tent and put on grill while you grill steaks.

MRS. GEORGE L. COOK

ITALIAN ZUCCHINI

Serves: 4

¼ cup bacon drippings or
  salad oil
½ lb. zucchini, sliced ¼ inch
  thick
10-oz. pkg. frozen Italian
  green beans

1 small onion, sliced
1 small clove garlic, crushed
¼ cup water
1 Tb. soy sauce
2 Tb. toasted slivered
  almonds

Heat oil in skillet; add zucchini, beans, onion, and garlic, tossing to mix. Pour in water. Cover and cook just until tender, about 8 to 10 minutes. (If too much liquid, uncover for a few minutes to cook away some juice.) Stir in soy sauce. Before serving, top with almonds.

Variation: Substitute cucumber for zucchini.

MRS. DON F. HAMILTON

ZUCCHINI SQUASH WITH SOUR CREAM

Serves: 4

2 Tb. butter
½ tsp. salt
¼ tsp. paprika

1 lb. zucchini squash
1 tsp. sugar
2 Tb. sour cream

Melt butter; add salt and paprika; add squash, washed and grated in long strips. Cook 5 minutes; add sugar; cover and cook 2 minutes; add sour cream; heat thoroughly and serve.

MRS. GEORGE PURYEAR
JONESBORO, ARKANSAS

MIMI'S CASSEROLE OF ZUCCHINI, EGGPLANT, AND TOMATOES

Serves: 10   Oven: 350°

1½ lbs. eggplant, cut in   8-oz. can tomato puree
   1-inch pieces   1 tsp. salt
¾ lb. zucchini   Freshly ground pepper
½ cup corn oil   ½ tsp. salad herbs
½ cup butter   4 Tb. chopped parsley
1 large clove garlic, diced   1 cup croutons

Peel eggplant if you wish. (Tender young eggplants do not need peeling.) Scrub zucchini; dice both vegetables. Mix the oil and butter; pour half of mixture into a large skillet; add garlic, and sauté for 1 minute. Add the eggplant and zucchini, about ⅓ at a time and sauté quickly. Add remaining oil if needed. Do not brown, but cook until partially softened. Have a shallow casserole ready. Pour half the tomato puree in the bottom of casserole and season with salt, pepper, and salad herbs. Add vegetables and top with tomato puree; sprinkle croutons over all. Bake in 350° oven for 40 minutes, uncovered; serve immediately.

MRS. JAMES VERNON FLACK, JR.

ZUCCHINI AU OEUFS

Serves: 4-6   Oven: 350°

1 lb. zucchini squash   5 eggs
1 medium onion, chopped   Salt and pepper to taste
1 large bell pepper, chopped   Grated Cheddar cheese
½ cup salad oil

Scrub squash well and slice into ⅛-inch pieces. Cook squash, onion, and pepper in oil in a large skillet until tender; remove from heat. Beat eggs and add to vegetables; add salt and pepper to taste. Pour into a 1½ quart greased casserole and bake uncovered at 350° for about 20 minutes. Garnish with cheese and return to oven for 10 minutes, or until cheese melts and knife inserted near center comes out clean.

MRS. GEORGE PURYEAR
JONESBORO, ARKANSAS

GARDEN VEGETABLE SKILLET

Serves: 6

½ cup butter
1 cup thinly sliced onion
1 clove garlic, finely chopped
2 zucchini, cut in ½-inch
  slices
1 small eggplant, peeled and
  cut into ½-inch slices

½ cup flour
2 small bell peppers, cut
  into strips
2 tomatoes, cut into wedges
1 tsp. salt
¼ tsp. oregano
⅛ tsp. cracked pepper

In a large covered skillet, melt the butter. Sauté onions and garlic until onions are limp. Dip zucchini and eggplant in flour to coat lightly. Add to onions along with green peppers. Cover and simmer 30 minutes. Add tomatoes, salt, oregano, and pepper. Cook an additional 15 minutes.

MRS. DON THOMPSON

SALADS AND

DRESSINGS

MARINATED ASPARAGUS SALAD

Serves: 4-6

⅔ cup olive or salad oil
⅓ cup tarragon vinegar
2 Tb. sweet pickle relish
1 Tb. minced chives
2-oz. jar pimiento, chopped
2 Tb. chopped parsley

1 hard-boiled egg, finely
   chopped
¾ tsp. salt
Pepper to taste
2 14-oz. cans green asparagus
16-oz. can artichoke hearts

Gradually add oil to vinegar, beating constantly; add remaining
ingredients. Mix well and pour over drained vegetables; let stand
2 hours, drain and serve.

MRS. JAMES KALMBACH
DALLAS, TEXAS

MOLDED ASPARAGUS SALAD

Serves: 6-8

1½ Tb. unflavored gelatin
¼ cup cold water
¾ cup asparagus juice
½ cup cream, whipped
½ cup mayonnaise
14-oz. can cut asparagus,
   drained

¼ to ½ cup slivered almonds
Garlic salt
Dash of Worcestershire
   sauce
Dash of Accent
½ tsp. salt
Juice of ½ lemon

Soak gelatin in cold water, dissolve in boiling asparagus juice. Let
begin to set. Fold in whipped cream, mayonnaise, asparagus, almonds, and seasonings. Pour into molds.

MRS. C. RAY WILLIAMS

SWEET AND SOUR ASPARAGUS

Serves: 8

2 14-oz. cans asparagus
⅔ cup white vinegar
½ tsp. salt
½ cup sugar
3 sticks whole cinnamon

1 tsp. whole cloves
1 Tb. celery seed
½ cup water
8 lettuce leaves
Grated hard-boiled eggs

Drain asparagus and place in shallow dish. Bring to boil—vinegar,
salt, sugar, cinnamon, cloves, celery seed, and ½ cup water. Pour
boiling liquid over asparagus and refrigerate at least 24 hours.
Serve on lettuce leaves with grated hard-boiled eggs to garnish.

MRS. BOYCE LOVE

AVOCADO MOUSSE

Serves: 6-8

1 Tb. gelatin
½ cup cold water
½ cup boiling water
2½ cups mashed avocado
 (4-5 medium avocados)
3 Tb. parsley, minced fine
1 Tb. lemon juice

½ tsp. onion juice
1 tsp. Worcestershire sauce
1 tsp. salt
½ cup cream, whipped
½ cup mayonnaise
Water cress

Soak the gelatin in cold water, dissolve in boiling water. Let stand until cool. Mash avocados with a silver fork. Add parsley, lemon and onion juices, Worcestershire sauce, and salt. Whip cream stiff, fold in mayonnaise; add dissolved gelatin. Combine this with avocado mixture; pour into a one quart mold rinsed out with cold water. Chill until firm. Unmold salad on platter and surround with water cress.

Serve plain or with tomato quarters and sliced hard-boiled eggs, or sections of grapefruit and orange sections.

MRS. JAMES PENICK, JR.

AVOCADO AND GRAPEFRUIT SALAD

Serves: 8

3-oz. pkg. lime gelatin
¾ cup hot grapefruit juice
1 avocado
13-oz. pkg. cream cheese
¼ tsp. monosodium
 glutamate

1 tsp. celery, chopped
1 cup mayonnaise
Dash salt
1 cup grapefruit sections,
 drained

Mix gelatin and grapefruit juice; stir until dissolved. Mash avocado; blend in cream cheese. Add monosodium glutamate, celery, mayonnaise, and salt. Add to gelatin mixture; fold in grapefruit sections. Pour into mold; refrigerate until set.

MRS. RALPH DOWNS

SWEDISH BEAN SALAD

Serves: 6

16-oz. can French string
 beans, drained
1 sliced cucumber
8 green onions, sliced thin
1 tsp. fresh dill weed

½ cup sour cream
¼ cup mayonnaise
Salt, white pepper, and
 seasoning to taste

Mix all ingredients and add salt, white pepper and seasoning to taste. Chill overnight.

MRS. CHARLES McKENZIE

HOT BEAN SALAD

Serves: 6   Oven: 450°

16-oz. can kidney beans,   ¼ cup thinly sliced green
   drained   onions
1 cup thinly sliced celery   ½ tsp. salt
4 oz. sharp cheese, diced or   ½ cup mayonnaise
   shredded   ⅓ cup Ritz cracker crumbs
⅓ cup sweet pickle, chopped

Combine all ingredients except crumbs. Sprinkle crumbs on top.
Bake at 450° for 10 minutes or until bubbly. This may be prepared
as much as two days ahead; omit crumbs until ready to serve. It
will freeze.

MRS. J. DANIEL ROEBUCK

SWEET-SOUR BEAN SALAD

Serves: 8

16-oz. can cut green beans   ¾ cup sugar
16-oz. can cut yellow beans   ⅔ cup cider vinegar
16-oz. can kidney beans   ⅓ cup salad oil
1 small bell pepper, chopped   1 tsp. salt
1 small onion, chopped   ½ tsp. pepper
3 ribs celery, chopped

Combine all beans, pepper, onion, and celery. Mix remaining ingredients; add to vegetable mixture. Refrigerate overnight.

MRS. JOHN W. REX
OKLAHOMA CITY, OKLAHOMA

BEET RING MOLD

Serves: 8

2 3-oz. pkgs. lemon gelatin   1 cup India relish
1 pkg. unflavored gelatin   1 cup celery, chopped
2 cups boiling water   1½ cups onion, minced
2 cups iced water   2 cups salad olives, chopped
Juice of 2 lemons   1 cup sour cream
4 cups diced beets   3 oz. Roquefort cheese

Mix both gelatins with boiling water; add iced water and lemon
juice; stir. Add remaining ingredients; refrigerate until firm.
Serve with sour cream mixed with Roquefort cheese.

MRS. NEIL PARK

ZESTY BROCCOLI MOLD

Serves: 10-12

4 hard-boiled eggs, chopped	¼ cup cold water
2 10-oz. pkgs. frozen chopped	1¾ tsp. salt
broccoli, cooked and drained	2 Tb. lemon juice
1 envelope gelatin	4 Tb. Worcestershire sauce
1 cup beef consomme,	Dash of Tabasco
undiluted	¾ cup mayonnaise

Cook eggs and broccoli ahead of time. Soften gelatin in cold water and dissolve in heated consomme. Combine drained broccoli and chopped eggs. Add other ingredients. Add mayonnaise last so it will not curdle. Mix well. Pour into one lightly oiled ring mold or into individual molds. Refrigerate.

Serve with Creamy Dressing, see index.

MRS. WALTER RIDDICK, JR.

BROCCOLI VINAIGRETTE

Serves: 8

2 lbs. fresh or frozen broccoli	½ cup minced bell pepper
2 cups oil and vinegar	¼ cup snipped parsley
dressing	¼ cup capers
½ cup chopped dill pickle	Pimiento (optional)
relish	

Cook broccoli until barely tender; drain. Put remaining ingredients in jar; shake until well mixed. Pour over broccoli in flat dish. Chill a few hours or overnight. Garnish with strips of pimiento.

MRS. DON THOMPSON

BRUSSELS SPROUTS SALAD

Serves: 8

16-oz. can French-style	Garlic salt to taste
string beans	Salt and pepper to taste
16-oz. can artichokes	2-oz. jar pimientos
10-oz. box frozen brussels	1 bottle Italian dressing
sprouts, barely cooked	

Mix all ingredients; refrigerate for several hours or overnight.

MRS. JAMES V. FLACK, JR.

CAESAR SALAD

Serves: 4

1 clove garlic, pressed	2 tsp. capers
⅓ cup olive oil	6 Tb. Parmesan cheese
Anchovy paste	1 slice bread, cubed, toasted,
1 egg, beaten slightly	and tossed in garlic butter
Juice of 1 lemon	4 strips crisp bacon,
2 Tb. wine vinegar	crumbled
1½ tsp. Worcestershire sauce	1 head lettuce or mixture of
Salt and pepper to taste	favorite salad greens

Mix garlic with olive oil and let stand for at least 1 hour. Rub wooden bowl with anchovy paste. Add egg. Add olive oil and garlic and stir GENTLY. Pour in lemon juice and vinegar and stir GENTLY. (Always mix egg and olive oil before adding lemon juice.) Add Worcestershire, salt, pepper, capers, and cheese. Prepare croutons and bacon. Tear salad greens and put in bowl. Sprinkle croutons and bacon on top of lettuce. Toss and serve.

CANLIS SPECIAL SALAD

Serves: 4-6

2 Tb. olive oil	½ cup Romano cheese,
Salt to taste	grated
1 large garlic clove	1 lb. bacon, fried crisp and
2 tomatoes, peeled and cut in	chopped
eighths	1 recipe Canlis Special
2 medium heads romaine,	Dressing, see index
sliced in 1-inch strips	1 cup croutons
¼ cup green onion, chopped	

In large wooden bowl put olive oil and salt; rub bowl firmly with garlic; remove garlic. Add tomatoes, romaine, onions, cheese, and bacon. When ready to serve drizzle Canlis Special Dressing (see index) over salad; add croutons last. Toss to mix well. Serve at once.

MRS. JOHN A. RIGGS, III

CAULIFLOWER SALAD

Serves: 4-6

1 large cauliflower	1 clove garlic, finely chopped
Cold, salted water	2 Tb. finely chopped capers
6 anchovy fillets, finely	½ cup olive oil
chopped	2 Tb. wine vinegar
3-oz. can ripe olives, sliced	Salt and lemon-pepper or
6 Tb. finely chopped parsley	fresh ground pepper

Break cauliflower in flowerlets. Place in bowl of cold, salted water until ready to use. Drain well. Mix anchovies, olives, parsley, garlic, and capers with oil and vinegar; add cauliflower and season to taste.

MRS. EUGENE MASON

CAULIFLOWER SLAW

Serves: 8

1 large head cauliflower	½ cup French dressing
¼ cup minced green onion	2 tsp. caraway seed
½ cup celery leaves	Salt to taste.
1 cup sour cream	

Slice cauliflower thin and combine with other ingredients. Refrigerate.

Make at least one day ahead.

MRS. GEORGE ROSE SMITH

COTTAGE CHEESE SALAD

Serves: 12

¾ cup cubed cucumber	1½ cups cubed tomato
½ cup red cider vinegar	1 Tb. onion juice or grated
1 qt. small curd cottage	onion
cheese	Salt and cayenne to taste
1 cup diced celery	4 Tb. mayonnaise
½ cup diced bell pepper	12 lettuce leaves

Marinate cucumber in vinegar for 10 minutes. Drain well and discard vinegar. Drain off any excess liquid from cottage cheese. Combine cucumber, cottage cheese, celery, green pepper, tomato, onion, salt, cayenne, and mayonnaise. Taste and adjust seasonings. Chill. Place each serving on lettuce leaf just before serving.

MRS. W. MAGE HONEYCUTT

DILLED CUCUMBERS IN SOUR CREAM

Serves: 4

2 cucumbers	2 tsp. lemon juice
1 cup sour cream	¾ tsp. salt
½ tsp. dried dill weed	Boston lettuce leaves

Peel cucumbers; cut in ¼-inch slices; cut each slice in quarters. Toss with sour cream, dill, lemon juice, and salt. Refrigerate 1 hour; stirring occasionally. Serve on lettuce leaves.

MRS. CLIFF WOOD

GREEN SALAD

Serves: 4

1 cucumber	Garlic salt to taste
1 cup fresh mushrooms	Salad greens
1½ Tb. lemon juice	Pepper to taste
1½ Tb. tarragon vinegar	½ cup olive oil

Thinly slice the cucumber and fresh mushrooms into salad bowl. Add lemon juice, tarragon (or wine) vinegar and garlic salt. Let stand. Dry crisp salad greens carefully. Tear and add to bowl. Use more garlic salt and freshly ground pepper. Pour olive oil over greens and toss well.

MRS. BOOKER WORTHEN

ITALIAN SALAD

Serves: 6

2 cups raw cauliflower	½ to 1 cup green onions,
2 cups cherry tomatoes	chopped
2 cups zucchini squash	Italian dressing

Break cauliflower in pieces; cut cherry tomatoes in half; slice zucchini; chop green onions; mix. Add Italian dressing; chill until ready to serve.

KRAUT SALAD

Serves: 10-12

2 14-oz. cans kraut, drained	1 cup chopped onion
7-oz. can sliced pimiento	⅓ cup water
1 cup chopped bell pepper	⅔ cup vinegar
1 cup chopped celery	⅓ cup salad oil
8½-oz. can water chestnuts, sliced	1¼ cups sugar

Mix the vegetables in a bowl. Boil the water, vinegar, oil and sugar; pour over the vegetables. Put in large jar or tightly covered container. Refrigerate for 24 hours, shaking occasionally. Keeps indefinitely.

MRS. EUGENE MASON

DILLED MACARONI SALAD

Serves: 8

8-oz. pkg. macaroni
1 cup mayonnaise
2 Tb. vinegar
1¼ tsp. salt
½ tsp. dill weed
⅛ tsp. pepper

1 cup coarsely chopped celery
½ cup coarsely chopped
  bell pepper
2 Tb. chopped onion
2 Tb. chopped pimiento

Cook macaroni as label directs; drain. In large bowl, combine mayonnaise, vinegar, salt, dill, and pepper; add macaroni, celery, green pepper, onion, and pimiento. Toss well; cover and refrigerate several hours. Serve in bowl lined with lettuce leaves.

MRS. H. WILLIAM GOODMAN

WILSON'S PANTRY SALAD

14-oz. can artichoke hearts,
  halved
14-oz. can hearts of palm,
  sliced
2-oz. jar pimiento
3-oz. can pitted ripe olives,
  sliced

4 green onions, chopped
2 10½-oz. cans asparagus
  tips
1 bottle Herb and Garlic
  dressing
Parmesan cheese
Toasted slivered almonds

Marinate first 6 ingredients in dressing. Toss lightly. Serve on bed of lettuce sprinkled with Parmesan cheese and almonds.

MRS. JIM WILSON

PEAS A LA DURKEES

Serves: 8

3 3-oz. pkgs. cream cheese
10-oz. bottle Durkees
1 envelope gelatin
½ cup water

17-oz. can tiny peas
14½-oz. can cut asparagus
2-oz. jar pimiento
1 cup celery, diced

Soften cheese; mix with Durkees. Soak gelatin in water. Drain peas; heat juice; add gelatin to drained juice; add to cheese mixture. Add remaining vegetables; mix well; pour in mold. Refrigerate until set.

MRS. HARRY B. WALL

GREEN PEA SALAD

Serves: 6

4 chopped hard-boiled eggs
2 16-oz. cans tiny green peas
1 medium onion, minced
2 Tb. mayonnaise, heaping
Dash sweet pickle relish

1¼ Tb. chili sauce
¼ tsp. vinegar
Salt and pepper
1 clove garlic, mashed

Mix ingredients together carefully; refrigerate for 2 hours before serving.

MRS. PAT MEHAFFY

POTATO SALAD

Serves: 24

12 medium red potatoes,
    boiled and diced
10 hard-cooked eggs, grated
1 red onion, diced
2-lb. carton cottage cheese
2 tsp. salt

1½ tsp. celery seed
2 Tb. prepared mustard
¾ cup Durkees
1½ pts. mayonnaise
Paprika

Slightly mash potatoes with pastry blender. Add eggs, onion, and cottage cheese; refrigerate overnight to allow flavor to penetrate. Add remaining ingredients; sprinkle with paprika.

GERMAN POTATO SALAD

Serves: 6

5 to 6 medium potatoes
1 medium onion, sliced
½ cup chopped celery
2 hard-boiled eggs
6 slices bacon, fried and diced

6 Tb. bacon drippings
¼ cup sugar
½ tsp. dry mustard
½ cup vinegar

Boil the potatoes and slice them while still hot. Add onion, celery, eggs, and bacon. Leave bacon drippings in skillet and add sugar, mustard, and vinegar. Heat and pour over potato mixture. Serve hot.

MRS. MIKE MEHAFFY

HOT POTATO SALAD

Serves: 6-8   **Oven: 350°**

6 potatoes	1 Tb. celery seed
1 small onion, chopped	3-oz. jar Spanish olives,
6 slices bacon	sliced
Mayonnaise or salad dressing	½ lb. mild cheese
to moisten	Sugar, salt, and pepper (dash
1 Tb. Worcestershire sauce	of each)

Boil potatoes until done. Cook onion and bacon together. Add this and drippings to cooked, diced potatoes. Add enough mayonnaise or salad dressing to moisten; then Worcestershire sauce and celery seed. Add olives that have been sliced and cheese that has been cut into small pieces. Add dash of sugar, salt, and pepper. Place in oblong baking dish and heat until cheese melts (about 30 to 40 minutes) in 350° oven.

This may be prepared a day ahead or even prepared and frozen.

MRS. JACK FROST, JR.

RICE SALAD

Serves: 8

2 cups cooked rice	1 Tb. grated onion
4 hard-boiled eggs, diced	Salt and pepper to taste
½ bell pepper, minced	Dash red pepper
½ to 1 cup celery, diced	2-oz. jar pimiento
¼ to ½ cup sweet pickle	½ tsp. mustard
relish	Mayonnaise to taste

Combine all ingredients; mix thoroughly; refrigerate until chilled.

MRS. WARREN JENNINGS
DEWITT, ARKANSAS

GERMAN SLAW

Serves: 12-15

1 head cabbage, chopped	¾ cup salad oil
1 bell pepper, chopped	1 cup vinegar
1 onion, chopped	1 cup sugar
3 ribs celery, chopped	1 tsp. celery seed
2 carrots, chopped	

Combine vegetables. Bring remaining ingredients to boil; pour over vegetables. Refrigerate at least 4 hours.

MRS. BOYCE LOVE

TABBOOLI

Serves: 8

1½ cups bulgar wheat
7 cups boiling water
1 cup parsley, chopped
¼ cup fresh mint, minced
¼ cup green onions, chopped
3 Tb. bell pepper, chopped

2 tomatoes, peeled and
  chopped
½ cup lemon juice
¼ cup olive oil
2 Tb. salt
Ground pepper to taste

Put wheat in bowl; pour water over it; cover; let stand several hours or overnight until water is absorbed and wheat is tender and fluffy. Put in strainer; shake off excess water. Stir in vegetables and mint. Mix lemon juice, oil, salt, and pepper; mix with wheat mixture. Serve as cold as possible.

MRS. ALSTON JENNINGS

TOMATO ASPIC

Serves: 4

1 envelope unflavored gelatin
1¾ cups V-8 juice
¼ tsp. salt
⅛ tsp. pepper
1 tsp. Worcestershire sauce

Tabasco to taste
1 Tb. dried onion flakes
1 Tb. lemon juice
14-oz. can artichoke hearts
Salad greens

Sprinkle gelatin in ½ cup cold V-8 juice to soften. Add 1¼ cups very hot V-8 juice and stir gelatin until it is thoroughly dissolved. Stir in salt, pepper, Worcestershire sauce, Tabasco, onion flakes, and lemon juice. Fold in artichoke hearts which have been rinsed and cut into small pieces, removing any tough fibers. Turn into a 2 or 3 cup mold or individual molds and chill until firm. Unmold on salad greens. This is excellent served with Cottage Cheese Dressing, see index.

This recipe is easily doubled.

MRS. JAMES B. KALMBACH
DALLAS, TEXAS

TOMATOES STUFFED WITH GARDEN VEGETABLES

Serves: 6

6 medium tomatoes
½ cup green onions, chopped
½ cup bell pepper, chopped
½ cup carrots, diced

¾ cup celery, diced
½ cup radishes, diced
1 cup French dressing
Salt to taste

Peel tomatoes; scoop out center; invert on plate; refrigerate. Marinate remaining vegetables in dressing for at least 1 hour. When ready to serve, salt inside of tomato; fill with vegetable mixture. Serve on lettuce.

TOMATOES BABICHE

Serves: 6

6 medium tomatoes
Salt and pepper to taste
6-oz. jar marinated artichoke
  hearts, drained
3 3½-oz. jars cocktail mushrooms, drained

½ cup mayonnaise
⅓ cup sour cream
1 tsp. curry powder
1 tsp. lemon juice
1 Tb. instant minced onion
Paprika

Peel each tomato; scoop out center, leaving a ¼-inch shell; sprinkle generously with salt and pepper. Fill each one with artichoke hearts and mushrooms; refrigerate. In a bowl combine mayonnaise, sour cream, curry, lemon juice, and onion; refrigerate. Just before serving, top each tomato with curry mixture; sprinkle with paprika. Place remaining curry mixture in bowl on platter; surround with tomatoes.

MRS. ALSTON JENNINGS

TOMATOES VINAIGRETTE

Serves: 3-4

8 thick tomato slices
1 cup salad oil
8 Tb. wine vinegar
2 tsp. oregano
1 tsp. salt

2 garlic cloves, pressed
½ tsp. pepper
½ tsp. dry mustard
Parsley

Arrange tomatoes in bottom of flat dish. Mix remaining ingredients except parsley and pour over tomatoes. Cover; refrigerate 2 to 3 hours or overnight, spooning dressing over occasionally. At serving time, sprinkle with parsley.

MRS. DAVID HUBENER

TOMATO-COTTAGE CHEESE LOAF

Serves: 6

2 envelopes gelatin
½ cup cold water
2 cups tomato juice
Lemon juice
Sugar
Salt
Worcestershire sauce

1 envelope gelatin
¼ cup cold water
1 cup scalded milk
1 lb. cottage cheese
1½ tsp. grated onion
Salt and pepper

Soften 2 envelopes gelatin in cold water. Heat with tomato juice and season to taste with lemon juice, sugar, salt, and Worcestershire sauce. Soften 1 envelope gelatin in cold water. Add scalded milk. Cool and fold in cottage cheese. Add grated onion, salt, and pepper. Pour ½ of tomato juice in loaf pan and refrigerate until set. Put cottage cheese mixture on top of that and set. Pour remaining tomato juice on top and set again.

MRS. LAMAR COLLIER

WILTED LETTUCE

Serves: 4

1 large head romaine lettuce	Onion salt to taste
Onion slivers to taste	2 to 2½ Tb. sugar
3 to 4 Tb. cider vinegar	4 slices bacon
Garlic salt to taste	Croutons (optional)

Tear lettuce; add onion, vinegar, and seasonings. Just before serving, fry bacon; pour hot bacon grease over lettuce. Serve immediately. May add seasoned croutons, if desired. The amount of bacon you use will be determined by the size of the head of lettuce; you want enough grease to cover amply, but not an excess.

MRS. WILLIAM L. TEDFORD, JR.

COTTAGE CHEESE APRICOT SALAD

Serves: 8

3-oz. pkg. lemon gelatin	½ cup coarsely chopped
1 cup boiling water	walnuts or pecans
1 cup apricot juice	½ cup maraschino cherries
12-oz. carton cream-style	1 cup canned apricots, peeled
cottage cheese	and sliced
1 cup cream, whipped	

Dissolve gelatin in boiling water. Add juice. Chill until jelly-like consistency. Fold in remaining ingredients. Chill.

This may also be prepared by putting cottage cheese and apricots in a blender and blending before adding to gelatin mixture.

MRS. C. RAY WILLIAMS

BING CHERRY SALAD WITH COCA-COLA

Serves: 10-12

2½ cups bing cherries, pitted	2 6-oz. Coca-Colas
1 cup crushed pineapple	1 cup chopped nuts
2 cups fruit juice	12-oz. pkg. cream cheese
2 3-oz. pkgs. cherry gelatin	

Drain juice from cherries and pineapple. Two cups of juice are needed; add water to make this amount, if necessary. Bring juice to a boil and pour over gelatin, stirring until completely dissolved. When cool, add Coca-Cola; stir and chill in refrigerator until partly congealed. Add drained cherries, pineapple and nuts, and pour into heart-shaped mold or individual heart molds. When firm, unmold on salad greens and serve with a piping of cream cheese around the edge of the heart. This is done with a pastry tube.

MRS. A. HOWARD STEBBINS, III

BRIDE'S SALAD

Serves: 12-14

2 egg yolks
¼ cup sugar
¼ cup cream
Juice of 2 lemons
⅛ tsp. salt
6 pineapple slices, cut in
    pieces

2 cups pitted Queen Anne
    cherries
½ lb. green grapes
1 cup almonds, shredded
1 cup cream, whipped
½ lb. cream cheese, cut in
    small pieces

Put first five ingredients in pan and cook slowly, stirring often until thick. Put in large bowl and refrigerate until chilled. Add remaining ingredients and stir gently, but thoroughly. Chill for 24 hours. Serve on lettuce leaves with or without mayonnaise.

MRS. JAMES WOOD CHESNUTT
HOT SPRINGS, ARKANSAS

CRANBERRY SALAD

Serves: 12

2 3-oz. pkgs. raspberry
    gelatin
½ pkg. gelatin
16-oz. can whole berry cran-
    berry sauce

2 cups boiling water
20-oz. can crushed pineapple
    (do not drain)
½ to 1 cup broken pecans
½ cup celery (optional)

Mix gelatins together; add boiling water. Add cranberry sauce; stir until dissolved. Add pineapple with juice, pecans and celery. Pour in mold and refrigerate.

MRS. R. E. JACK BUSH, SR.

CRANBERRY CASHEW SALAD

Serves: 4-5

1½ Tb. unflavored gelatin
¼ cup cold water
2 cups whole cranberries
1 cup water
1 cup sugar

¼ cup salted cashew nuts,
    chopped fine or ground
½ cup chopped apples
½ cup diced celery
Lettuce

Soak gelatin in ¼ cup cold water. Cook the cranberries with 1 cup water and sugar. Bring to boil and continue to cook at medium boil until the cranberries pop. Fold the gelatin soaked in water to the hot mixture. Cool. Add cashew nuts, apples and celery. Turn into 4 or 5 individual molds or one medium sized mold and chill. Serve on lettuce.

MRS. WILLIAM BURKE BRADY

FRUIT SALAD

Serves: 8-10

16-oz. can fruit cocktail
13¼ oz. chunky pineapple
3 red apples, finely diced
3 oz. miniature marsh-
  mallows
½ cup sugar
2 Tb. flour

Juice of 1 lemon
Juice from pineapple
1 egg yolk
1 tsp. dry mustard
Cheddar cheese, grated
Coconut, shredded

Drain juice from fruit cocktail; drain and reserve juice from pine-apple. Mix fruits and add apples and marshmallows. Set aside. Make a sauce by combining sugar, flour, lemon and pineapple juice, egg yolk, and dry mustard in the top of a double boiler. Cook, stirring constantly until thickened; let cool. Pour over the fruit and mix gently; chill. Top each serving with cheese and coconut.

MRS. CLARK HILL

FROZEN FRUIT SALAD

Serves: 12-14

11-oz. cream cheese
½ pt. heavy cream
½ cup fruit juice from fruit
  cocktail
½ cup sugar
16-oz. can fruit cocktail,
  drained

2 bananas, sliced
1 cup miniature marsh-
  mallows
10-oz. pkg. frozen straw-
  berries or raspberries,
  drained

Cream cheese in mixer; add cream (unwhipped), fruit juice and sugar. Mix until blended.

Place drained fruit cocktail, sliced bananas, marshmallows and drained strawberries in oblong pan (13¼ x 9½ x 2-inch); pour dressing over fruit. Stir until well mixed. Place in freezer until frozen.

MRS. FRANK BAUER, JR.

GREEN AND GOLD SALAD

Serves: 4-6

Lettuce
1 cucumber, sliced
2 small avocados, sliced and
  peeled

Pineapple stick, fresh or
  canned
11-oz. can mandarin oranges
2 bananas

Put washed, drained, and chilled lettuce on a salad platter. Place the sliced cucumbers, avocados, and pineapple sticks around. Sprinkle the oranges and bananas on top of that. Refrigerate. Serve with Curry Dressing, see index.

MRS. ROBERT FISHER
BRONXVILLE, NEW YORK

24-HOUR LEMON PUDDING SALAD

Serves: 8

16-oz. can fruit cocktail
16-oz. can sliced pineapple
1 lb. white seedless grapes
6¼-oz. pkg. miniature
   marshmallows

3 egg yolks
¼ cup heavy cream
¼ cup lemon juice
¼ to ½ cup sugar
1 cup cream, whipped

Drain fruit; set aside. Mix egg yolks, ¼ cup cream, lemon juice, and sugar; cook until thick, stirring constantly. Cool. Add whipped cream; add fruit and marshmallows; refrigerate 24 hours.

MRS. RAYMOND MORRIS

ORANGE SALAD

Serves: 9

6-oz. pkg. orange gelatin
2 cups boiling water
¾ cup orange juice
8¼-oz. can crushed pine-
   apple, undrained

2 11-oz. cans mandarin
   oranges, drained
½ to ¾ cup pecans, chopped
9 lettuce leaves, drained

Mix gelatin with water and juice; add pineapple and oranges. Pour into 8 x 8 x 2-inch pan; sprinkle top with pecans; chill until set. Cut into 9 squares; serve on lettuce.

Good with duck.

MRS. JERRY LIGHT

ORANGE SPINACH TOSS

Serves: 4

4 cups spinach leaves, torn
3 oranges, peeled and
   sectioned (may substitute
   mandarin oranges)

4 slices crisp, crumbled bacon
¼ to ½ cup chopped peanuts
1 envelope French dressing
   mix (prepared as directed)

In salad bowl, combine spinach, oranges, bacon and peanuts. Mix and pour dressing over mixture. Serve immediately.

MRS. ROBERT CARNAHAN

PEACH PICKLE SALAD

Serves: 10-12

3-oz. pkg. lemon gelatin
3-oz. pkg. orange gelatin
1 cup hot water
3 cups juice from fruits
17-oz. can bing cherries

8¼-oz. can crushed pineapple
1 lb., 13 oz. can spiced
   peaches
1 cup broken pecans

Dissolve both packages of gelatin in hot water. Stir in juice from the fruits. Cool. Add fruit and pecans. Allow to congeal in refrigerator. Serve with mayonnaise.

OVERTON WARD
NASHVILLE, TENNESSEE

STRAWBERRY SALAD

Serves: 8

2 3-oz. pkgs. strawberry
gelatin
2 cups boiling water
2 10-oz. pkgs. frozen strawberries

16-oz. can crushed pineapple,
drained
2 bananas, diced
1 cup sour cream

Dissolve gelatin in water; add strawberries; stir until melted; add pineapple and bananas. Pour ½ mixture in 8 x 8 x 2-inch pan; chill until firm. Spread sour cream over chilled mixture; add remaining gelatin mixture; chill until firm.

MRS. PETER J. POWELL

RED CAVIAR MOLDS

Serves: 10-12

1 Tb. gelatin
¼ cup cold water
1 cup boiling water
1 small onion, grated
½ tsp. salt
½ tsp. pepper

½ cup cream, whipped
½ cup mayonnaise
Juice of ½ lemon
4-oz. jar red caviar
Salad oil

Dissolve gelatin in cold water; add boiling water, onion, salt, and pepper. Stir until gelatin is dissolved. Refrigerate until gelatin begins to thicken. Combine whipped cream, mayonnaise, and lemon juice; add gelatin mixture; gently fold in caviar. Fill molds or muffin tins that have been greased with salad oil. May be served as a salad or as a first course.

MRS. ALSTON JENNINGS

CUCUMBERS STUFFED WITH HAM

Serves: 4

2 cucumbers
French dressing
2 cups diced, cooked ham
2 Tb. cream cheese

4 Tb. light cream
Horseradish to taste
Pepper to taste
Shrimp (optional)

Peel cucumbers, cut in half lengthwise; scoop out seeds, leaving boat-shaped cases. Marinate cucumbers in dressing for at least 1 hour. Combine cream cheese, cream, horseradish, and pepper; add ham; fill cucumbers with mixture. Garnish with shrimp.

MRS. ROBERT FISHER
BRONXVILLE, NEW YORK

LAMB AND CUCUMBER ASPIC

Serves: 12-14

½ lamb shoulder
1 Tb. salt
1 onion, diced
3 Tb. gelatin
½ cup cold water
3 cups hot stock
2 Tb. vinegar
1½ tsp. Worcestershire sauce

Juice of 2 lemons
½ tsp. salt
Cayenne to taste
1 bell pepper, chopped
2-oz. jar pimiento
4 hard-boiled eggs, sliced
1 cucumber, sliced
Ripe and green olives

Place lamb shoulder in pan; cover with water; add onion and salt; cook covered until tender. Cool. Reserve broth (you should have 3 cups); cool; skim fat off top. Separate meat and fat from bone; cut in even pieces. Place meat in mold. Soften gelatin in water; add stock; stir until gelatin is dissolved. Add vinegar, Worcestershire, juice of lemons, salt, cayenne, green pepper, and pimiento. Pour over meat. Chill until partially set. Garnish with eggs, cucumber, and olives. Chill overnight. Serve with homemade mayonnaise.

MRS. AUGUSTUS FULK, III

SHRIMP AND ARTICHOKE SALAD

Serves: 4-6

⅔ cup catsup
⅓ cup wine vinegar
1 cup salad oil
Salt and pepper to taste
Dash sugar

14-oz. can artichoke bottoms
1 lb. shrimp, cooked and
  cleaned
Mayonnaise
Lettuce leaves

In jar combine catsup, vinegar, salad oil, salt, pepper, and sugar. Drain artichoke bottoms; put in jar for about 6 hours. Arrange artichoke bottoms on bed of lettuce; top with shrimp and mayonnaise.

MRS. JOSEPH WARD

SWEETBREAD SALAD WITH GRAPES

Serves: 8

3 lbs. sweetbreads
½ cup French dressing
3 cups seedless grapes

2 cups celery, minced
1½ cups mayonnaise
Salt to taste

Cook sweetbreads according to any recipe; drain and cool. Cut in pieces the size of grapes; cover with French dressing; chill. Combine grapes, celery, mayonnaise, and salt. Mix gently with sweetbreads; add more mayonnaise if necessary. Chill and serve.

CORDELL S. DOUGHERTY

SHRIMP MOLD

Serves: 4-6

10½-oz. can shrimp soup
1 envelope gelatin
½ cup cold water
½ cup minced celery
½ cup minced cucumber

¼ cup mayonnaise
3 Tb. lemon juice
1 lb. cooked shrimp
Lettuce leaves
Homemade mayonnaise

Soften gelatin mixture in water. Set in pan of hot water to dissolve. Combine soup, gelatin, celery, cucumber, mayonnaise, and lemon juice; add shrimp. (You may substitute crab meat or lobster.) Pour into mold. Chill. Serve on lettuce with homemade mayonnaise.

MRS. FRANK ELLIS MCGEHEE

TUNA SALAD LOAF

Serves: 6-8

1 Tb. unflavored gelatin
¼ cup cold water
¾ cup hot water
2 Tb. lemon juice
1 tsp. prepared mustard

¼ tsp. salt
¼ tsp. paprika
2 7-oz. cans tuna fish
1 cup celery, chopped
½ cup cream, whipped

Soften gelatin in cold water; add hot water; stir until dissolved. Add lemon juice, mustard, salt, and paprika. Chill until partially set. Add tuna, celery, and whipped cream. Pour into mold; refrigerate until set. Serve with cucumber sauce.

CUCUMBER SAUCE:

1 cup mayonnaise
½ cup cucumber, finely
  chopped
2 Tb. bell pepper, chopped

1 tsp. tarragon vinegar
½ tsp. salt
Dash cayenne pepper

Combine all ingredients.

MRS. ROBERT LINDSEY

PRESSED VEAL

Serves: 14

3 lbs. lean veal, cubed	Salt and pepper to taste
(or 5-lb. chicken)	1 cup mayonnaise
1 bunch celery	Worcestershire sauce to taste
1 onion	Lemon juice to taste
Salt	Tabasco to taste
6 hard-boiled eggs	½ pt. sour cream
1 envelope unflavored gelatin	Horseradish to taste

In pan cover veal or chicken with cold water; add 2 ribs of celery, onion, and salt; cover and simmer until tender; save the broth (you should have 2 cups). Put veal through a food mill using a coarse plate; grind uncooked celery; rice the eggs; mix with veal. Soften gelatin in ½ cup warm broth; stir until dissolved; add to meat and egg mixture. Add 1½ cups more broth, salt and pepper, mayonnaise. Worcestershire, lemon juice, Tabasco; mix well; put in oiled 10-inch tube pan; refrigerate. Serve with sour cream mixed with horseradish.

MRS. GORDON RATHER, SR.

DRESSINGS

CANLIS SPECIAL DRESSING

Serves: 4-6

⅓ cup olive oil	¼ tsp. pepper
⅓ cup lemon juice	¼ tsp. oregano
¾ cup fresh mint, chopped,	1 egg
or ¼ tsp. dry mint	

In small bowl combine all ingredients except the egg. Place egg in boiling water; turn off heat and let stand for 1 minute. Break coddled egg into oil mixture; whip vigorously.

MRS. JOHN A. RIGGS, III

COTTAGE CHEESE DRESSING

Yield: 2 cups

16-oz. carton cottage cheese	2-oz. wedge blue cheese

Mix wedge of blue cheese (room temperature) with cold cottage cheese and chill until needed.

Good with Tomato Aspic.

MRS. JAMES B. KALMBACH
DALLAS, TEXAS

CREAMY DRESSING

Yield: 4 cups

1 pt. heavy cream	1 cup mayonnaise
½ cup Durkees dressing	1 cup sour cream

Blend all four ingredients in a blender for a minute or so. Chill and serve.

This is excellent with the Zesty Broccoli Mold.

MRS. GEORGE COOK

HILDA'S CREAM DRESSING

Yield: 2 cups

2 Tb. flour	Juice from 1 orange
1 egg	Juice from 1 lemon
½ cup sugar	½ pt. cream, whipped
1 cup pineapple juice	

Mix flour, egg and sugar. Gradually add juices and cook until thick. Chill. When cold fold in whipped cream. This will keep refrigerated in a covered jar for three weeks.

MRS. SMITH DAVIS

CURRY DRESSING

Serves: 4-6

½ cup mayonnaise	½ tsp. curry powder
½ cup sour cream	2 Tb. French olive oil
½ cup chutney	1 Tb. red wine vinegar

Several hours before serving, place all ingredients in blender and blend until smooth. Serve chilled.

Good with Green and Gold Salad.

MRS. ROBERT FISHER
BRONXVILLE, NEW YORK

FRENCH DRESSING

Yield: 1 cup

¼ cup vinegar	1 tsp. dry mustard
¾ cup olive oil	1 tsp. sugar
(no substitute)	1 pod garlic (optional)

Mix ingredients together. If you want a garlic dressing, add 1 pod of squeezed garlic to dressing.

MRS. NEIL PARK

GERMAN SALAD DRESSING

4 Tb. salad oil	1 Tb. mayonnaise
½ medium onion, finely chopped	1 tsp. chopped parsley
	2 egg yolks
5 dashes Maggi seasoning	1 dash pepper
1 Tb. vinegar	Evaporated milk

Add ingredients in above order, then stir in evaporated milk until desired thickness. Refrigerate.

Delicious on tossed green salads.

MRS. ROBERT GORDON CARNAHAN

GLENLEIGH TAVERN DRESSING

Yield: ½ cup

¼ cup olive oil	¼ tsp. dry mustard
¼ cup corn oil	¼ tsp. cayenne
2 Tb. vinegar	¼ tsp. curry powder
1 Tb. lemon juice	1 tsp. dried minced onion
½ tsp. salt	½ tsp. dried crushed
¼ tsp. paprika	tarragon

Mix all ingredients in a jar and shake well.

MRS. DON HAMILTON

GREEN GODDESS DRESSING

Yield: 2¼ cups

3 Tb. green onions and some tops, finely chopped	Dash salt and cracked pepper
3 Tb. chopped parsley	1 cup mayonnaise
1 Tb. lemon juice	1 cup sour cream
1 Tb. tarragon vinegar	1 Tb. anchovy paste (optional)

Mix all ingredients and chill.

MRS. TYNDALL DICKINSON

EASY BLENDER MAYONNAISE

Yield: 1 cup

1 whole egg	1 Tb. lemon juice
¼ tsp. dry mustard	1 cup salad oil
½ tsp. salt	

Break egg into blender jar. Add the mustard and salt. Cover and blend at top speed for 30 seconds, or until mixture is thick and foamy. Pour in the lemon juice and blend for 10 seconds. Uncover jar, and blending at high speed, pour the oil into the center of the egg mixture in a very thin stream of droplets. It is important that the oil be added slowly. The sauce will begin to thicken after ½ cup of oil has been added. If it becomes too thick, blend in a few drops of lemon juice or remove the mixture from the blender jar and add the remainder of the oil by hand with a wire whisk. Taste and correct the seasonings if necessary.

MRS. PHILIP ANDERSON, JR.

MAIN CHANCE LOW CALORIE DRESSING

Yield: 2 cups

1 cup parsley, chopped
8 green onions, chopped
2 tsp. dry mustard
1 tsp. horseradish
1 tsp. Worcestershire sauce
½ cup safflower oil

½ cup mineral oil
⅓ cup tarragon vinegar
2 eggs, beaten
1 tsp. Accent
Vegisalt or salt to taste

Combine all ingredients.

MRS. EUGENE LEWIS, JR.

NECTAR DRESSING

3-oz. pkg. cream cheese
2 Tb. honey or 3 Tb. sugar
1½ Tb. lemon juice
Grated rind of 1 lemon

¾ tsp. salt
⅛ tsp. cayenne
¼ cup salad oil.

Beat cheese, honey, lemon juice, and seasonings until smooth. Add 1 tablespoon oil at a time, beating well after each addition. Chill.

This is best the same day it is made.

MRS. DREW LANDER

OIL AND VINEGAR SALAD DRESSING

Yield: 1 cup

⅓ cup tarragon wine vinegar
⅔ cup olive oil
2 medium cloves of garlic
1 tsp. salt

1 Tb. coarse or fresh ground
    black pepper
1 Tb. tarragon

Mix all ingredients in a jar or bowl. This can be stored unrefrigerated. Before serving, shake well.

ARCHIBALD TAYLOR

BELL'S ROQUEFORT DRESSING

Yield: 2 cups

10 oz. Roquefort cheese
    (crumbled)
1 cup onion, chopped
1 cup celery, chopped

½ cup salad oil
½ cup vinegar
3 Tb. sugar
4 to 5 Tb. mayonnaise

Mix all ingredients and place in refrigerator at least overnight to thicken.

MRS. WYLIE FORD
FORT SMITH, ARKANSAS

FROZEN ROQUEFORT DRESSING

Serves: 6-8

¼ lb. French Roquefort   1 cup heavy cream
   cheese   Salt, pepper, and paprika to
1 Tb. white wine vinegar   taste

Mash cheese to a paste with vinegar. Whip cream; add seasonings.
Gradually fold in cheese paste. Freeze. When ready to use, cut in
squares and place on salad; it softens quickly.

CORDELL S. DOUGHERTY

ROQUEFORT CHEESE SALAD DRESSING

Yield: 1 cup

¼ cup wine vinegar   1 tsp. dry mustard
¾ cup salad oil   1 clove garlic (pressed)
2 tsp. salt   ¾ tsp. hot sauce
1 tsp. pepper   4 oz. Roquefort cheese
1 tsp. Worcestershire sauce

Put all ingredients in blender and mix thoroughly. May be stored
in refrigerator indefinitely. Dressing is salty and salad will need
little, if any, salt.

MRS. BART ROACH

POPPY SEED DRESSING

Yield: 3 cups

1½ cups sugar   1 Tb. onion juice
2 tsp. dry mustard   2 cups salad oil
2 tsp. salt   3 Tb. poppy seeds
⅔ cup vinegar

Mix sugar, mustard, salt, and vinegar. Add onion juice (grate onion
on fine side of grater) and stir it in thoroughly. Add oil slowly,
beating constantly and continue to beat until thick. Add poppy
seeds and beat for a few minutes. Store in a cool place or in the
refrigerator, but not near the freezing coil. Make this in electric
mixer on medium speed.

This sometimes separates after a few days of storage. Stir it slowly
and it will again blend together.

*It is delicious on all fruit salads, but has a special affinity for
grapefruit.*

MRS. FRANK BAUER, JR.

NANCY'S RUSSIAN DRESSING

Yield: 2½ cups

1 cup salad oil
1 cup catsup
⅓ cup sugar
3 Tb. vinegar
1 Tb. onion, chopped

3 Tb. bell pepper, chopped
   fine
1 tsp. celery seed
1 tsp. salt
¼ tsp. pepper

Mix and shake well in jar. Chill.

MRS. J. W. GUTHRIE
OKLAHOMA CITY, OKLAHOMA

SOUR CREAM DRESSING

Yield: 2 cups

8 oz. sour cream
¾ cup mayonnaise
1¾ tsp. garlic salt
1½ tsp. coarsely cracked
   black pepper

3 Tb. Parmesan cheese,
   grated
3 Tb. milk
Buttermilk, optional

Mix all ingredients. May use 1½ tablespoons buttermilk and 1½ tablespoons milk; use more milk as needed to thin dressing to desired consistency. Recipe may be multiplied by 10 to yield 1¾ gallons, using the buttermilk and milk.

RED APPLE INN
EDEN ISLE, ARKANSAS

THOUSAND ISLAND DRESSING

Yield: 2½ cups

1 cup mayonnaise
1 tsp. paprika
¼ cup catsup or chili sauce
2 Tb. vinegar
½ cup celery, chopped

½ cup stuffed olives, sliced
1 small onion, chopped
2 Tb. minced parsley
3 hard-boiled eggs, coarsely
   diced

Combine all ingredients. Chill.

MRS. JACK FROST, JR.

SAUCES AND

ACCOMPANIMENTS

BASIC WHITE SAUCE

Yield: 2 cups

MEDIUM WHITE SAUCE:

¼ cup butter   ⅛ tsp. pepper
¼ cup unsifted flour   2 cups milk
1 tsp. salt

In heavy saucepan, heat butter till melted; remove from heat and add flour, salt and pepper, stirring constantly until smooth texture. Add milk slowly, stirring constantly, and return to medium heat. Bring to a boil and cook one minute, stirring constantly.

THIN WHITE SAUCE:

Reduce butter and flour to 2 Tb. each, following above directions. Use for soups.

THICK WHITE SAUCE:

Increase butter and flour to 6 Tb. each, following above instructions.

EXTRA THICK WHITE SAUCE:

Increase butter and flour to 8 Tb. each, this is for a soufflé base.

MEAT SAUCES

BASIC BROWN SAUCE

Yield: 1¾ cups

¼ cup butter   6 Tb. flour
2 cups brown stock or   Salt and pepper
   bouillon

Melt butter in heavy saucepan; remove from heat, stir in flour. Return to moderately low heat; stir until brown but not burned. Remove again and add bouillon. Stir and cook 2-3 minutes until thickened.

BASIC TOMATO SAUCE

3 Tb. olive oil   2 cups water or beef broth
2 cups chopped onion   1 bay leaf
3 cloves garlic, minced   ½ tsp. salt
3½ cups Italian tomatoes,   ¼ tsp. pepper
   undrained   ½ tsp. oregano or ¼ tsp.
2 6-oz. cans tomato paste   each, oregano and basil

Sauté onion and garlic in oil until soft and yellow. Add other ingredients except herbs and simmer for 2 hours, uncovered, stirring occasionally, adding water if necessary. Add herbs and continue cooking 15 minutes. Remove bay leaf.

MRS. W. MAGE HONEYCUTT

BEARNAISE SAUCE

Yield: 1 cup

½ cup tarragon vinegar   ½ tsp. dried tarragon
¼ cup dry white wine   3 egg yolks
1 Tb. minced green onion   ½ cup butter (no substitute)

In heavy saucepan combine first 4 ingredients. Over medium heat, bring to a boil and cook 10 minutes. Pour through a strainer into a double boiler and add yolks, beating with a wire whisk. Beat constantly over hot water until thick. Add butter, one tablespoon at a time mixing well. Keep warm over low heat.

BORDELAISE SAUCE FOR STEAK

Yield: 2 cups

¼ cup butter   2 bay leaves
2 shallots, finely chopped   3 Tb. flour
2 cloves garlic, finely chopped   ½ tsp. meat extract
2 slices onion   1 cup bouillon
2 small carrots, sliced   1 cup Burgundy
2 sprigs parsley   2 Tb. parsley, finely chopped
10 whole peppercorns   ¼ tsp. salt
2 whole cloves   ⅛ tsp. pepper

In hot butter, sauté shallots, garlic, onion, carrot, parsley, peppercorns, cloves and bay leaves about 3 minutes. Remove from heat; stir in flour, cook until slightly brown, about 5 minutes. Add meat extract, bouillon and ¾ cup Burgundy, bring to a boil, stirring constantly. Reduce heat, simmer 10 minutes. Strain, add parsley, salt, pepper and remaining wine. Reheat when needed.

This is good served over slices of beef tenderloin and wild rice.

MRS. BART ROACH, JR.

CARRIE'S BARBECUE SAUCE

Yield: 1½ cups

¼ cup Worcestershire sauce   1 Tb. prepared mustard
¼ cup A-1 sauce   ½ can tomato soup
Juice of 1½ lemons   ¾ stick butter
⅛ tsp. garlic powder   Salt and pepper to taste

Combine all ingredients, cook for one hour. This recipe will freeze.

MRS. EDWARD L. BEARD

FIREPIT STEAK SAUCE

⅓ cup soy sauce
½ cup salad oil
½ cup wine vinegar
½ cup fresh lemon juice

1 tsp. dry ginger
½ tsp. Accent
2 cloves garlic
Fresh cracked pepper

Bring combined ingredients to a boil; simmer 10 minutes, then baste as steaks are grilling.

MRS. J. L. LANE
ALEXANDRIA, VIRGINIA

HORSERADISH SAUCE

8-oz. jar apple jelly
8-oz. jar pineapple preserves
6-oz. jar horseradish

6-oz. jar mustard
Salt and pepper to taste

Put in blender, blend well. Serve with ham or cold meat.

MRS. BART ROACH, JR.

MORNAY SAUCE

Yield: 2½ cups

1 egg yolk
¼ cup heavy cream
2 cups medium white sauce

½ cup grated Gruyere or
Parmesan cheese

Blend egg yolk, cream and add hot medium white sauce. Stir and cook for ½ minute. Add grated cheese, cook only until cheese melts. Do not boil.

MUSHROOM SAUCE

Yield: 3 cups

½ lb. mushrooms, drained
4 Tb. butter
4 Tb. flour
1½ cups chicken broth

½ cup mushroom broth
¼ cup heavy cream
½ tsp. lemon juice
Salt and pepper to taste

Blend all ingredients except cream and lemon juice; heat. Just before serving add cream and juice, heat through.

MRS. A. H. STEBBINS, III

MUSTARD SAUCE

Yield: 2½ cups

4-oz. can dry mustard, sifted	1 cup sugar
1 cup malt vinegar	2 beaten egg yolks

Mix first two ingredients, let stand for several hours or overnight. Add sugar, stir until smooth. Put over low heat, add yolks, stir until thick. Refrigerate.

Especially good on baked ham.

MRS. JACK T. LYNN

RAISIN SAUCE

Yield: 2½ cups

½ cup seeded raisins	1 tsp. cornstarch
¼ cup chopped citron	1 Tb. butter
1 cup boiling water	½ tsp. lemon juice
¾ cup sugar	

Simmer raisins, citron in boiling water until tender. Sift sugar and cornstarch together; add to raisin mixture; mix well, continue cooking 10 minutes. Add butter, lemon juice; mix well.

Delicious with baked ham.

MRS. J. L. LANE
ALEXANDRIA, VIRGINIA

RUM SAUCE

Serves: 4

4 Tb. sugar	4 rings canned pineapple
1 oz. orange juice	1 oz. rum
½ cup less 1 Tb. brown sugar	

Cook white sugar in pan over low heat until light caramel color, stirring constantly. Add orange juice, brown sugar, stirring until it boils. Marinate pineapple in rum overnight, then add to sauce. Serve over chicken breasts.

VEGETABLE SAUCES

DRESSING FOR BROCCOLI OR ASPARAGUS

½ cup butter, melted	¼ tsp. dry mustard
1½ cups mayonnaise	¼ tsp. cayenne pepper
2 Tb. horseradish	½ tsp. salt
1 tsp. instant minced onion	½ tsp. vinegar

Mix ingredients, heat and serve over cooked vegetables.

HOLLANDAISE SAUCE

Yield: 1⅓ cups

½ to 1 cup butter, melted	⅛ tsp. pepper
3 egg yolks	1 Tb. water, hot
½ tsp. salt	2 Tb. lemon juice

Melt butter over hot water. Combine next 3 ingredients in blender. Set on low speed for 3 or 4 seconds. Turn to high speed and add water and lemon juice in fine stream while blender is on until mixed, about 3 seconds. Continue to blend on high speed and add butter in a fine stream. Serve at once.

Variations:

Curry—To ¾ cup sauce add 1 tsp. curry powder; good over fish and egg dishes.

Orange—To ¾ cup sauce add 2 Tb. orange juice and ½ tsp. rind; good over asparagus and green beans.

Bearnaise—To ¾ cup sauce, add ⅓ cup tarragon vinegar, ⅓ cup dry white wine, 2 tsp. minced green onion, omitting water and lemon juice.

VINAIGRETTE SAUCE

1 cup olive or salad oil	½ tsp. pepper
⅓ cup wine vinegar	½ tsp. dry mustard
2 tsp. crushed oregano leaves	2 cloves garlic, crushed
1 tsp. salt	

Combine oil and vinegar; add other ingredients and mix well. Refrigerate and serve over salad or cold vegetables.

FISH SAUCES

CURRIED SHRIMP SAUCE

¼ cup butter	1½ cups cooked shrimp,
¼ cup flour	chopped
3 Tb. catsup	2 tsp. curry powder
1½ cups milk	1 tsp. salt
1½ Tb. sherry	Paprika
	Red pepper

Make cream sauce of first 4 ingredients. Add shrimp and remaining ingredients. Heat through. Serve over rice, dry toast points, omelet or vegetables.

MRS. J. BRIAN FRAZIER

TARTAR SAUCE

1 cup homemade mayonnaise	1 small onion, chopped fine
1 dill pickle, chopped fine	Juice of ½ lemon

Mix, chill and serve.

MRS. ED I. McKINLEY, JR.

SEAFOOD COCKTAIL SAUCE

Yield: 1½ cups

1 cup mayonnaise
½ tsp. salt
Pepper to taste
¼ tsp. paprika
¼ cup India relish
1 hard-cooked egg, chopped
1 cup chili sauce

½ tsp. minced chives
¼ bell pepper, chopped
½ pimiento, chopped
1 Tb. celery, chopped
Mustard to taste
Dash of hot sauce
1½ tsp. A-1 sauce

Mix all ingredients together, let flavors blend. Also good as dip for fresh vegetables and dressing for tossed salad.

SHRIMP AND MUSHROOM SAUCE

Serves: 6-8

2 10-oz. cans shrimp soup
½ lb. fresh mushrooms,
   sliced
2 Tb. butter

⅓ cup heavy cream
⅓ cup dry sherry
1 cup cooked shrimp, diced
2 Tb. chopped fresh parsley

Heat soup, stirring constantly with wooden spoon. Sauté mushrooms in butter for 5 minutes or until tender. Add mushrooms and remaining ingredients to soup, reheat but do not allow to boil.

Serve over grits souffle or omelet.

MRS. FRED W. TERRY

DESSERT SAUCES

BRANDY PUDDING SAUCE

1 cup butter
2 cups powdered sugar
2 egg whites

5 Tb. brandy
¼ cup boiling water

Cream butter and sugar; add unbeaten egg whites, one at a time. Add brandy then water. Place bowl in hot water, stir constantly until smooth and satiny.

MRS. G. TED CAMERON

BUTTERSCOTCH SAUCE

Yield: 1 pint

1¼ cups dark brown sugar
⅔ cup light corn syrup
4 Tb. butter

3½-oz. can evaporated milk
1 tsp. vanilla

Cook first 3 ingredients in double boiler until thick. When mixture begins to cool, stir in vanilla and milk. This takes about 15 minutes.

Keeps well in refrigerator.

MRS. J. L. LANE
ALEXANDRIA, VIRGINIA

FUDGE SAUCE

Yield: ¾ cup

1 cup sugar	1 pinch salt
4 Tb. cocoa	1 tsp. vanilla
1 Tb. flour	½ cup chopped pecans
½ cup milk	(optional)

Mix all ingredients except pecans and vanilla. Boil for 2 minutes only, stirring constantly. Add vanilla, nuts, serve warm. Store in refrigerator, reheat over hot water.

MRS. CHRISTOPHER KELLER, JR.

FUDGE SUNDAE

5½-oz. can evaporated milk	½ cup sugar
2 1-oz. squares unsweetened	2 Tb. butter or margarine
chocolate	

Cook in double boiler, stirring constantly until sauce thickens, about 20 minutes. Especially good served over peppermint ice cream. Will keep for days in the refrigerator.

MRS. JOHN W. REX
OKLAHOMA CITY, OKLAHOMA

HARD SAUCE

Yield: ½ cup

⅓ cup butter	1 tsp. vanilla or 2 Tb. brandy
1 cup powdered sugar	or rum
½ tsp. lemon extract	

Cream butter, add sugar and flavorings, blend.

LEMON SAUCE

Serves: 10

1 cup sugar	Juice of 2 lemons and grated
1 Tb. cornstarch	rind
½ tsp. salt	1 cup water
3 whole eggs	2 Tb. butter

Mix dry ingredients; add slightly beaten eggs, lemon juice, grated rind and water. Cook in double boiler until thick, stirring constantly. Add butter, cool.

(Small amount of whipped cream may be added when cool instead of using water.)

RASPBERRY SAUCE

Yield: 2 cups

2 tsp. cornstarch
¼ cup sugar
½ cup currant jelly

10-oz. pkg. frozen rasp-
berries, thawed

In saucepan, combine cornstarch, and sugar; stir in jelly and raspberries. Cook over medium heat, stirring constantly until thick and
clear. Can be forced through a sieve to remove seeds.

MRS. A. M. FULK, III

RUM BUTTER SAUCE

Yield: ½ cup

3 oz. butter
3 oz. brown sugar
2 oz. or ¼ cup DARK rum

Little grated lemon or orange
rind
Squeeze of lemon juice

Cream butter; beat sugar in by degrees with rind and juice. Add
rum to flavor well. (Use only dark rum.)

Serve with rich fruit puddings, mince and apple pies or baked
bananas.

MRS. CHARLES McDADE

VANILLA SAUCE

1 cup sugar
1 Tb. flour
1 cup boiling water

Pinch of salt
½ tsp. vanilla
3 Tb. butter

Mix sugar and flour. Add remaining ingredients and cook over
medium heat to desired thickness.

ACCOMPANIMENTS

CURRIED FRUIT

Serves: 10-12

Oven: 325°

16-oz. can each: pears, peach
halves, and pineapple
chunks
½ cup sliced cherries
3 sliced bananas

⅓ cup butter
¾ cup brown sugar
2 tsp. curry powder
1 tsp. ginger

Drain fruit and place in large casserole. Melt butter and add sugar
and spices, mixing well. Pour butter mixture over fruit. Bake
covered in a 325° oven for one hour.
Serve hot.

MRS. DON HAMILTON

HOT FRUIT

Serves: 8-10   Oven: 350°

16-oz. can apricots   1 cup applesauce
16-oz. can pears   10-oz. pkg. frozen raspberries
16-oz. can black cherries   2 Tb. frozen orange juice
  (pitted)   concentrate
16-oz. can pineapple chunks   ¼ cup honey

Drain fruit and arrange in a 2-quart casserole. Mix honey and orange juice concentrate and pour over top. Heat in 350° oven for 20 minutes.

MRS. JACK BEW

RELISHES

STERILIZING JARS

Fill glasses or jars three-fourths full of water and place them a distance apart in a shallow pan partly filled with water. May place lids lightly on jars to sterilize both at once. Simmer for 15-20 minutes. Keep hot until ready to fill.

STRAWBERRY PRESERVES

Yield: 5 cups

4 cups cleaned strawberries   5 cups sugar
2 Tb. lemon juice

Put berries and lemon juice, reconstituted will do, in a deep pot. Boil about 5 minutes, longer if berries are very juicy. Pour in sugar; simmer 10 minutes, skimming foam all the time. Pour into shallow pan and cool to room temperature. Pour into sterile jars and seal. Do not double recipe.

MRS. HAROLD HEDGES

CRANBERRY JELLY

Yield: 3 cups

1 lb. cranberries   2 cups sugar
2 cups cold water

Boil cranberries in water until skins pop open, about 5 minutes; press through a sieve. Add sugar and bring to hard boil, skimming thick foam. Boil rapidly for 3 minutes, stirring occasionally. Pour immediately into sterilized, hot jars.

MRS. HARRY PARKIN

CRANBERRY PORT JELLY

Yield: 8 jars

3 cups cranberry cocktail
juice
7 cups sugar
¼ tsp. cinnamon

¼ tsp. cloves
1 cup port wine
6 oz. liquid fruit pectin

Combine first 4 ingredients; mix; stir over high heat until sugar is dissolved. Boil hard for 1 minute, stirring constantly. Remove; stir in wine and pectin; skim; pour into hot, sterile jars.

MRS. JOHN J. TRUEMPER, JR.

PORT WINE JELLY

Yield: 4 cups

3 cups sugar
2 cups port wine

3 oz. liquid fruit pectin

Place sugar and wine in top of double boiler over rapidly boiling water. Stir until dissolved, about 2 minutes. Remove from heat and stir in pectin immediately, mixing well. Skim off any foam. Pour into hot, sterilized jars and seal with ⅓ inch melted paraffin.
Serve with meat or mixed with cream cheese and serve on biscuits.

MRS. J. E. LIGHTLE, JR.
SEARCY, ARKANSAS

BRANDIED APRICOT JELLY

3½ cups sugar
1½ cups apricot nectar
½ cup brandy

2 Tb. lemon juice
3 oz. liquid pectin
Paraffin

In top of double boiler, over rapidly boiling water, combine sugar, nectar, brandy, and lemon juice; stir until sugar is dissolved, approximately 2 minutes. Remove from heat; stir in pectin at once; mix well; skim off any foam; pour into hot, sterile jars. Cover at once with ⅓-inch of melted paraffin.
Try this with duck or chicken.

MRS. JOHN J. TRUEMPER, JR.

PEPPER JELLY

Yield: 4 cups

2 cups ground sweet and hot
peppers, mixed in any
amount desired for hotness

¾ cup vinegar
1 box Sure-Jell
3½ cups sugar

Mix ground peppers with vinegar in a 3 quart pan. Add Sure-Jell and bring to a rolling boil. Add sugar and boil hard for one minute, stirring constantly. Pour into hot, sterile jelly glasses and seal with paraffin.

MRS. W. J. JERNIGAN, SR.

QUICK PICKLED PEACHES

Yield: 1 quart jar

2 1-lb. 13-oz. cans cling peach halves	½ cup cider vinegar
	3 sticks cinnamon
¾ cup packed brown sugar	1 Tb. whole cloves

Drain syrup from peaches. Combine syrup, sugar, vinegar, and spices. Simmer 5 minutes and pour mixture over peaches. Stick one whole clove in each peach half and let stand for several days in refrigerator. Gently shake the jar several times during this period.

MRS. WILL T. DOROUGH
SWEET HOME, ARKANSAS

BREAD AND BUTTER PICKLES

Yield: 3-4 pts.

12 medium cucumbers	1 tsp. ginger
6 small onions	1 tsp. cornstarch
½ cup rock salt	2 tsp. celery seed
1½ qts. ice water	2 tsp. mustard seed
2 cups sugar	½ tsp. tumeric
2 cups cider vinegar	½ tsp. black pepper

Slice cucumbers and onions very thin (¼ inch or less). Soak for two hours in brine made up of salt and ice water to cover. Drain and rinse lightly. Meanwhile combine remaining ingredients in kettle (not copper or iron) and boil one minute. When ready, add the soaked and drained cucumbers and onions and cook until beginning to boil. Pack into hot, sterile jars and seal.

MRS. JAMES VERNON FLACK, JR.

KOSHER DILL PICKLES

Yield: 6-8 qts.

20 to 25 small cucumbers	1 red pepper
⅛ tsp. powdered alum	1 qt. cider vinegar
1 clove garlic	1 cup salt, not iodized
2 Tb. dill seed or 1 head and stalk fresh dill	3 qts. water

Wash cucumbers well; soak in cold water overnight. Next day, pack in hot, sterilized jars. To each quart jar add the above amount alum, garlic, red pepper, dill seed, or head with piece of the stalk of dill. Combine vinegar, salt, and, water; boil; pour over cucumbers. Seal. Let rest several weeks. Place in refrigerator to crisp.

MRS. JAMES MITCHELL COCKRILL

PICKLED EGGPLANT

Yield: 3-4 pts.

2 lbs. eggplant, peeled and
cut into 1-inch cubes
1 cup celery, thinly sliced
1 large onion, thinly sliced
⅓ cup salt
1 bell pepper, seeded and
cut into strips

1 red pepper, seeded and
cut into strips
Ice cubes
1½ cups sugar
1 Tb. dill seeds
1½ cups cider vinegar
4 cloves garlic, halved

Combine eggplant, celery, onion, green pepper, red pepper, and salt
in a large bowl. Place a layer of ice cubes on top; cover; let stand
3 hours; drain well. Combine sugar, dill seeds, and vinegar in a
large saucepan; bring to boil, stirring constantly; stir in vegetables.
Bring to boil again, stirring occasionally; remove from heat. Ladle
into large covered container; add garlic; refrigerate. If you cannot
find red peppers, let a green one stand out for 2 or 3 days until it
turns red.

MRS. JOHN J. TRUEMPER, JR.

PICKLED MUSHROOMS AND ARTICHOKES

Yield: 3 12-oz. jars

12 oz. canned mushroom caps
(not cooked in butter)
14-oz. can artichoke hearts
¾ cup salad oil
⅓ cup lemon juice

¼ cup chopped fresh parsley
1 clove garlic, crushed
1 tsp. salt
½ tsp. ground pepper

Drain mushrooms and artichokes; pack in hot sterilized jars. Cover
with marinade made by combining rest of ingredients. Seal tightly.
Store at least 2 days before using. Keeps indefinitely in refrigerator.

MRS. JOHN J. TRUEMPER, JR.

DESSERTS

APPLE CRISP

Serves: 8   Oven: 350°

8 apples, peeled and sliced   1 tsp. lemon juice
½ cup sugar   1 cup sugar
½ tsp. cinnamon   ¾ cup flour
½ tsp. nutmeg   ½ cup butter, softened
½ cup water

Put apples in bottom of large baking dish. Combine sugar, cinnamon, and nutmeg; sprinkle on top of apples. Combine water and lemon juice; pour over apples. Combine sugar, flour, and butter; crumble over apple mixture. Bake at 350° for 30 minutes.

MRS. HARRY B. WALL

BAKED APPLES SUPREME

Serves: 6   Oven: 375°

6 medium apples (Jonathan)   1 cup pecans, coarsely
12 Tb. brown sugar   chopped
Dash of cinnamon   1 cup raisins
Dash of ginger (optional)   2 or more cups water, boiling
3 Tb. butter

Wash and core apples; place apples in baking dish. Cover bottom of baking dish with boiling water; fill each apple cavity with 2 tablespoons sugar, dash of cinnamon and ginger and ½ teaspoon butter. Bake covered for 30 minutes at 375° or until apples are soft. Baste occasionally with liquid in pan. When apples are done, remove them; pour remaining liquid into a saucepan; add raisins and nuts. Gently boil until syrup thickens. Pour over apples. Serve hot or cold with whipped cream.

MRS. EMMETTE P. ALLEN
BROOKHAVEN, MISSISSIPPI

BANANAS BURGUNDY

Serves: 4-6

8 to 10 bananas   ½ cup Burgundy wine
3 cups sugar   1 Tb. ground cloves
1½ cups wine vinegar   2 tsp. ground cinnamon

Select bananas that are on the slightly green side, allowing approximately two per person. Peel and cut into two-inch pieces; drop into boiling mixture listed above. Cook two minutes on top of stove, uncovered. Serve immediately.

This mixture keeps indefinitely under refrigeration. It may be used as a vegetable or dessert.

An exotic way to serve bananas; delicious served over ice cream.

MRS. LEONARD BELLINGRATH

BANANAS FOSTER

Serves: 6-8

6 large all yellow bananas	½ cup butter
Fresh lemon juice	½ tsp. cinnamon
1 cup brown sugar	

Peel and halve bananas lengthwise. Brush with lemon juice. Melt sugar and butter in chafing dish (or saucepan). Add bananas. Cook until tender. Add cinnamon. Serve hot over vanilla ice cream if desired.

Variation: 1 Tb. banana liqueur and 2 Tb. light rum may be added just before serving.

MRS. FRANK MACKEY, JR.

SPICED FRUIT COMPOTE

Serves: 12

2 large oranges	1½ cups orange juice
17-oz. can apricots, drained	½ cup sugar
2 large cans pear halves, drained	3 cinnamon sticks
	15 whole cloves
½ tsp. salt	¼ tsp. ginger

Peel oranges; section oranges and place in a large bowl. Add drained apricots and pears. Simmer salt, orange juice, sugar, cinnamon sticks, cloves and ginger in a saucepan over medium heat for 5 minutes. Pour at once over fruit. Refrigerate covered, at least overnight.

A delightful accompaniment to brunch.

MRS. G. BURNS NEWBILL
BENTON, ARKANSAS

CHERRIES SUPREME

Serves: 6

2 16-oz. cans black cherries, drained and pitted	6 Tb. whiskey
	½ cup sour cream
2 10-oz. jars currant jelly	Cherry Marnier (optional)
Juice of 2 lemons	

Mix together jelly, lemon juice and whiskey in a bowl. Stir in drained cherries and refrigerate at least overnight. Serve garnished with sour cream flavored with Cherry Marnier, if desired.

This dessert will keep for some time and is beautiful when served in clear bowls.

MRS. ROBERT D. LOWRY

CHERRIES JUBILEE

Serves: 12   Oven: 350°

2 cans black bing cherries,   ¼ tsp. cinnamon
   pitted and drained   1 cup bourbon
10½-oz. jar red currant jelly   12 large ice cream balls
¼ cup lemon juice

Drain cherries; beat jelly, lemon juice, and cinnamon in an oven-proof casserole until well mixed. Stir in cherries and heat in a 350° oven for 10 to 15 minutes. Remove hot cherries from oven; pour ¾ cup bourbon into casserole. Place serving ladle in casserole to warm ladle. Remove, pour ¼ cup bourbon in ladle and light with a match. Pour burning ladle of whiskey into casserole to ignite cherries. After flames are extinguished, serve cherries over ice cream balls in individual dishes.

The ice cream balls may be placed in a large bowl and the cherries in a chafing dish if you prefer to flame the dessert at the table. Have individual serving bowls ready.

MRS. JAMES B. KALMBACH
DALLAS, TEXAS

JAPANESE ORANGE DESSERT

Serves: 8-10

1 egg, beaten   11-oz. can mandarin oranges,
3 Tb. lemon juice   drained
3 Tb. sugar   1 cup bananas, sliced
½ cup cream, whipped   ½ cup toasted, slivered
1 cup marshmallows, small   almonds

Combine egg, lemon juice, and sugar in top of double boiler and cook over boiling water until thick (about 5 minutes). Cool. Stir in whipped cream, marshmallows, oranges, and bananas. Chill. Before serving, stir in almonds.

This can be served many ways—in parfait glasses; over pound cake; or best, over lemon custard ice cream in meringue shells.

MRS. WILLIAM A. SAUNDERS, JR.

ORANGE-MACAROON PUDDING

Serves: 8

½ lb. marshmallows   1 pint cream, whipped
1 cup orange juice   ½ lb. macaroons

Dissolve marshmallows in orange juice in top of double boiler over boiling water. Cool until cold. Fold in whipped cream (or substitute non-dairy whipped topping). Toast and grind macaroons. Place a layer of crumbs on bottom of mold or serving dish; cover with pudding; top with remaining crumbs. Chill. May be prepared a day ahead.

MRS. JAMES T. DYKE

LES ORANGES AUX LIQUEURS

Serves: 4

8 large seedless oranges
½ cup powdered sugar
2 Tb. cognac

3 Tb. Grand Marnier
3 Tb. Kirschwasser

Peel oranges, removing all the white membrane. Section them by running a sharp knife on either side of the connecting tissues. Keep the flesh intact. Squeeze juice from connecting tissues. Sprinkle the juicy sections with powdered sugar and refrigerate for an hour or longer. Sprinkle with liqueurs and toss lightly with a fork and spoon. Serve on chilled dessert plates.

Variation: Other fruits and berries, such as peaches, strawberries and raspberries alone or in combination, may be prepared the same way.

MRS. JOHN V. SATTERFIELD, III

FRESH FRUIT SHORTCAKE

Serves: 6   **Oven: 375°**

PASTRY:

2 cups flour
¼ tsp. salt
⅓ cup sugar

¾ cup shortening
1 egg, beaten
1 Tb. water

Stir flour, salt and sugar together. Cut in shortening with pastry blender or two knives until size of small peas. Blend egg and water. Stir into flour-shortening mixture until smooth. Form into 2 balls. Roll out on slightly floured board into 2 rectangles 9 x 12-inch. Cut into 12 strips 2 x 4-inch. Place on ungreased cookie sheet and bake at 375° for 8 minutes or until light brown. Cool.

PEACH FILLING:

6 to 9 large ripe peaches
½ cup orange juice
¾ cup sugar

1 pt. cream, whipped
¼ cup sugar

Dip peaches in boiling water for 30 seconds. Hold under cold water and slip off skins. Slice. Mix gently with orange juice and sugar. Cover and refrigerate until serving time. Drain off juice. Whip cream in chilled bowl; add ¼ cup sugar to cream.

TO ASSEMBLE SHORTCAKE:

Lay one strip of pastry on dessert plate. Spread with whipped cream. Place 4 or 5 peach slices in a row on cream. Top with second strip of pastry, whipped cream and sliced peaches.

Variation: Other fresh fruits may be used, omitting the orange juice.

MRS. R. E. JACK BUSH, SR.

CRUMBLED PEARS

Serves: 6   Oven: 325°

6 large fresh pears
2 Tb. lemon juice
½ cup honey
¼ cup melted butter

2½ cups graham cracker
crumbs
1 tsp. grated lemon rind
Sugar

Pour melted butter in pyrex dish; peel and core pears; dip in lemon juice and in honey. Roll in crumbs, place in casserole. Mix lemon rind in a little sugar and place a dab in center of each pear. Bake 325° till tender, 20 to 25 minutes. Serve hot with lemon sauce.

LEMON SAUCE:

1 lemon, juice and grated
rind
1 Tb. flour
2 egg yolks, beaten

2 Tb. butter
½ cup sugar
½ cup boiling water

Place all ingredients in top of double boiler and cook over hot water until thick. Serve over crumbled pears.

MRS. J. L. (PENIE) LANE
ALEXANDRIA, VIRGINIA

PEACH MOLD

Serves: 8

3-oz. pkg. orange gelatin
1 cup hot peach juice
1 cup peaches, sliced
½ cup heavy cream

½ cup Port, or Marsala, or
peach liqueur
Sliced or frozen peaches
Sweetened whipped cream

Dissolve gelatin in hot peach juice; cool to lukewarm; place drained peaches in gelatin mixture; add wine and place in blender. Cover and beat at low speed then high speed until smooth. Add cream (not whipped) and whip a few seconds only. Pour in a 2 quart mold or individual molds and refrigerate. Unmold and garnish with sliced peaches and sweetened whipped cream.

MRS. HAROLD HEDGES

APRICOT ICE

Serves: 6

17-oz. can apricot halves
1 cup water
Juice of 2 lemons

1 cup water
1 cup sugar
½ cup light corn syrup

Drain and crush apricots; save juice. Add 1 cup water and lemon juice to apricot juice, and mix with crushed apricots. Boil 1 cup water and sugar for 5 minutes; add corn syrup. Stir sugar mixture into apricot mixture. Freeze. Stir once when half frozen to make a smoother ice.

MRS. RALPH DOWNS

CREPES WITH SOUR CREAM AND STRAWBERRIES

Serves: 6-8

CREPES:

Yield: 16 crepes

1 cup flour, sifted
2 Tb. sugar
1 ¼ tsp. baking powder
½ tsp. salt

2 eggs, beaten slightly
1 ¼ cups milk
3 Tb. salad oil

Combine flour, sugar, baking powder and salt in mixing bowl. Add eggs, milk and oil to dry ingredients. Mix only until moistened. Pour ¼ cup batter for each crepe into hot—either well greased or non-stick pan and cook until top is full of bubbles, edges dry and underside browned. Turn and brown other side. Place on waxed paper. Crepes may be made ahead and frozen with wax paper between them.

FILLING:

1 cup sour cream
1 ½ Tb. sugar
1 Tb. Grand Marnier liqueur
2 Tb. butter

2 cups sweetened sliced
strawberries, fresh or
frozen
Powdered sugar

Prepare pancakes ahead of serving time. Combine sour cream, sugar, and Grand Marnier. Spread pancakes with equal amounts of sour cream mixture and a few sliced strawberries. Roll up and arrange in long, shallow dish. Cover and refrigerate until serving time.

To heat, melt butter in chafing dish or crepe pan over high heat. Heat pancake rolls carefully. Add remaining strawberries. Heat only until completely warmed. Place 2 or 3 crepes on dessert plate and garnish with powdered sugar.

MRS. DON THOMPSON

LEMON ICE CREAM

Serves: 12-14

11 cups light cream
Juice of 8 lemons
4 cups sugar

2 tsp. lemon extract
1 Tb. grated lemon rind

Mix all ingredients thoroughly; freeze in your freezer, stirring once when partially frozen or freeze in your ice cream freezer.

MRS. MIKE MEHAFFY

STRAWBERRY SQUARES WITH CLARET SAUCE

Yield: 12-16 squares   Oven: 350°

CRUST:

1 cup flour	½ cup chopped pecans
¼ cup brown sugar	½ cup margarine, melted

Sift together flour and brown sugar; add chopped pecans and margarine. Spread evenly in shallow pan. Toast crumbs 20 minutes in 350° oven. Stir occasionally while baking. Sprinkle ⅔ of crumbs evenly in 9 x 13 x 2-inch baking pan; press crumbs against bottom of dish to form crust.

FILLING:

2 egg whites	2 cups sliced berries if fresh,
⅔ cup sugar if using frozen berries, or 1 cup sugar if using fresh berries	or 10-oz. pkg. frozen berries, mostly thawed
2 Tb. lemon juice	½ pt. cream, whipped

Combine egg whites, sugar, lemon juice and berries. Beat at high speed with electric mixer until high peaks form—about 10 minutes. Fold in whipped cream. Spoon over crust in pan. Top with remaining crumbs. Freeze 6 hours or overnight.

SAUCE:

1 cup sugar	⅓ cup claret wine
¼ cup water	

Boil sugar and water slowly for 8 minutes. Add ⅓ cup claret wine. Put a spoonful of sauce on each square, then pass more sauce.

MRS. EDWIN L. BAXLEY

GRANNY PARKIN'S ICE CREAM

Serves: 12-14

4 eggs	1 pt. light cream
1½ cups sugar	2 tsp. vanilla
1 qt. heavy cream	

Mix sugar and eggs in large mixing bowl; add creams, and vanilla. Add fruit or chocolate if desired, see variations. Stir until well blended. Pour mixture in ice cream freezer. Place freezer can in ice cream freezer and pack with ice to which one cup of ice cream salt has been added at different levels. If freezer is electric, run for 20 to 30 minutes. Ice cream should be soft but not runny. Place in containers and freeze; makes approximately one gallon.

Variations: Peach Ice Cream—*Peel and mash, or blend 7 medium peaches; add ½ cup sugar.*
Strawberry Ice Cream—*Wash, top and mash, or blend, 1 quart fresh strawberries; add ½ cup sugar.*
Chocolate Ice Cream—*16-oz. can chocolate syrup.*

CARAMEL ICE CREAM DESSERT

Serves: 16   **Oven: 400°**

CRUST:

2 cups flour   1 cup margarine, melted
½ cup oatmeal   1 cup chopped pecans
½ cup brown sugar

Combine all ingredients and crumble on a cookie sheet. Bake at 400° for 15 to 20 minutes, stirring to brown evenly. Press ½ of the crumbs on the bottom of a 9 x 13-inch pan.

FILLING:

Caramel sauce or jar of   ½ gal. vanilla ice cream
   caramel ice cream topping

Layer ice cream and caramel sauce on top of crumb crust. Sprinkle the top with remaining crumbs. Freeze. Cut in squares and top with caramel sauce.

MRS. RICHARD B. HARDIE

ICE CREAM BOMBE

Serves: 12

½ gal. coffee ice cream   ½ pt. cream, whipped
14-oz. can condensed milk   ¼ cup sugar
4 to 8 oz. coconut   Rum or Drambuie (optional)
6 oz. crunchy peanut butter   Bitter chocolate square
½ gal. chocolate ice cream

Soften coffee ice cream; mold coffee ice cream in an angel food cake pan. Freeze until firm. Mix condensed milk, coconut and peanut butter. Spread mixture over coffee ice cream. Soften chocolate ice cream; fill pan to top with chocolate ice cream. Freeze until hard. Unmold by placing briefly in hot water. Whip cream and add sugar; add about 3 tablespoons rum or Drambuie, if desired. Ice cake with whipped cream and replace in freezer. Garnish with shaved bitter chocolate.

Bombe is very, very rich.

MRS. WILLIAM B. BISHOP

CHOCOLATE POT DE CREME

Serves: 4

6-oz. pkg. semi-sweet chocolate chips
1 ¼ cups light cream, heated
to boiling

Dash salt
1 egg
1 tsp. vanilla
Sweetened whipped cream

Put chocolate pieces in blender container. Pour hot cream over chocolate. Run blender until chocolate is liquefied. Add salt, egg and vanilla. Cover and run until smooth. Pour into traditional cups, demi-tasse cups or custard cups. Chill at least three hours. Servings should be small as this is very rich. Garnish with a small spoonful of whipped cream, or sour cream may be used.

MRS. BART ROACH

FRENCH MINTS

Serves: 15

1 cup butter
2 cups powdered sugar, sifted
4 eggs
4 squares unsweetened chocolate, melted

2 tsp. vanilla
½ tsp. pure peppermint
extract (drug store)
Vanilla wafer crumbs
15 cherries

Cream butter and sugar in mixer; add eggs one at a time, beating well after each addition. Add melted chocolate and flavorings. Sprinkle crushed vanilla wafers in bottom of 15 paper cupcake cups; fill with mixture; put additional crumbs on top. Top with a cherry. Freeze.

Serve right out of freezer. Makes a small serving but very rich. This is a good dessert to pass on a tray, removing each mint from paper cup and serving on a paper doily; especially good for buffet service when only one plate is used.

MRS. GORDON RATHER

CHOCOLATE ICE BOX DESSERT

Serves: 12-14

1 dozen lady fingers
4 squares bitter chocolate
1 cup sugar
¼ cup water
5 eggs, separated

¾ pt. cream, whipped
½ cup chopped nuts
1 box chocolate cookies,
crushed
Whipped cream

Line sides of a spring-form pan with split lady fingers; combine chocolate, sugar and water in top of a double boiler; heat until mixture is melted and smooth. Add well beaten egg yolks; cook until thick; cool. Beat egg whites until stiff; fold into cooled chocolate mixture. Whip cream and fold into chocolate mixture. Pour one-half of the filling in the spring-form pan; sprinkle with crushed chocolate cookies; pour remaining filling on top. Refrigerate for 24 hours. Garnish with whipped cream.

MRS. ED I. McKINLEY, JR.

CHOCOLATE ICE CREAM DESSERT

Serves: 8   Oven: 400°

CRUST:

½ cup butter	¼ cup brown sugar
1 cup sifted flour	½ cup chopped pecans

Mix all ingredients for crust with fork or pastry blender. Crumble in large oblong pan. Bake 15 minutes, or until brown, in 400° oven, stirring occasionally. Take from oven and press against sides and bottom of 9-inch pie pan, reserving a small amount to sprinkle over top of pie. (Recipe may be doubled and used in 13 x 9-inch pan.) Cool.

FILLING:

1 pt. chocolate ice cream*	½ cup chopped pecans,
1 pt. vanilla ice cream*	toasted
½ pt. cream, whipped	Chocolate sauce
3 Tb. sugar	

Soften ice cream (may be done in mixer). Spread a layer of chocolate ice cream, ¼ cup pecans, a layer of vanilla ice cream and the remaining pecans. Top with sweetened whipped cream and sprinkle with reserved crust crumbs. Freeze. Top with chocolate sauce if desired.

*Any flavor of ice cream may be substituted, or frozen fruit may be used in place of nuts in filling.

Good to fix ahead; keeps well in freezer.

MRS. KENT VESTAL

MIDGE'S PARTY TORTE

Serves: 8-10

16 oz. thin chocolate wafers, crushed	3 cups cream, whipped
½ cup margarine, melted	¾ cup maraschino cherries, chopped
3 cups powdered sugar	½ cup pecans, chopped
½ cup soft butter	3 bananas, mashed
3 eggs, well beaten	

Mix wafer crumbs with ½ cup melted margarine and press into a 9½ x 13 x 2-inch pan, reserving some crumbs to sprinkle on top. Mix powdered sugar, butter and eggs thoroughly; pour over crust. Whip cream and spread on egg mixture. Drain cherries and cut fine. Mix with chopped nuts and spread over whipped cream. Spread mashed bananas over cherries and nuts. Top with remaining wafer crumbs. Freeze overnight.

MRS. JAMES E. MADIGAN

CHOCOLATE IGLOO DESSERT

Serves: 10-12   Oven: 350°

1 Tb. gelatin	3 eggs, separated
¼ cup cold water	1 tsp. vanilla
⅓ cup sugar	⅓ cup sugar
¼ tsp. salt	1 pkg. devil's food cake mix
1¾ cups milk	1 cup whipping cream
1 pkg. Baker's German Sweet	2 Tb. sugar
Chocolate	

Soften gelatin in cold water. Combine ⅓ cup sugar, salt and milk in medium saucepan. Add chocolate and cook over medium heat, stirring constantly until chocolate is completely melted. Blend mixture well with egg beater. Add small amount of hot mixture to slightly beaten yolks, stirring vigorously. Gradually add remaining hot mixture while stirring. Return to saucepan and cook over low heat until slightly thickened. Remove from heat; add softened gelatin and stir until dissolved. Pour into bowl and chill until partially set.

Stir vanilla into egg whites and beat until foamy. Add ⅓ cup sugar, 2 tablespoons at a time while beating until stiff peaks form. Fold into chilled chocolate mixture. Spoon into a 1½ quart mixing bowl and chill until firm. About 2½ hours.

Prepare cake according to directions for 8-inch layers. Cool. Freeze one layer for later use. Loosen mold at top edge with sharp knife. Place in bowl of warm water for a few seconds. Remove from water and shake bowl to loosen. Place edge of bowl one inch in from edge of cake layer to unmold on cake. Whip cream, adding sugar just before stiff and "ice" mold and cake. Cake must be assembled at the last minute and served immediately. Garnish with chocolate curls.

Nice for a dessert party!

MRS. GIL BUCHANAN

ALMOND LOG

Serves: 6

½ cup butter	½ cup chopped almonds,
1 cup brown sugar	toasted
1 egg	½ cup chopped pecans,
5 Tb. flour	toasted
½ tsp. almond extract	Unsweetened whipped cream

Cream butter until it is light. Gradually add brown sugar. Beat until smooth and light. Beat in egg and flour. Flavor mixture with almond extract and stir in chopped and toasted almonds and pecans. Shape the mixture into a log in foil and freeze for at least 3 hours (more preferred). Serve it in slices and top with unsweetened whipped cream.

MRS. JAY FRENCH HILL

CHOCOLATE ROLL

Serves: 14-16   Oven: 350°

5 egg yolks   1 pt. cream, whipped
1 cup powdered sugar   Chocolate sauce (recipe
3 Tb. cocoa   follows)
5 egg whites

Beat egg yolks until thick. Add sugar and beat thoroughly. Add cocoa, fold in stiffly beaten egg whites. Spread on buttered and floured cookie sheet. Bake at 350° for 10 to 15 minutes. Cool 5 minutes before turning out on floured cloth. Cover with damp cloth. When cool spread with whipped cream and roll (like a jelly roll). Serve with hot chocolate sauce. The roll can be frozen and used at a later date.

CHOCOLATE SAUCE:

1 cup sugar   1½ oz. bitter chocolate,
½ cup water   melted
¼ tsp. cream of tartar   ¼ tsp. vanilla

Boil sugar, water, and cream of tartar for 5 minutes. Pour slowly over melted chocolate and stir. Cool slightly and add vanilla. Serve hot.

MRS. E. A. CULBERTSON
MIDLAND, TEXAS

FONDUE AU CHOCOLAT

Serves: 6

9 oz. milk chocolate   Assorted fruit, such as
⅓ cup heavy cream   strawberries, grapes, apple
2 Tb. kirsch or brandy   wedges, bananas, or orange
½ Tb. instant coffee   sections
Pinch of cinnamon or clove   Pieces of angel food or pound
⅓ cup crushed almonds   cake
    (optional)

Break chocolate into pieces and put in chafing dish or fondue pot over low heat. Add cream and stir until mixture is melted and smooth. Add remaining ingredients, except fruit or cake, and continue stirring. Place pot on candle warmer or **very low** alcohol or Sterno flame. Make sure fruit is dry; dip pieces of fruit or cake into chocolate using fondue forks.

Variation: Bittersweet chocolate may be substituted for milk chocolate.

COFFEE TORTONI

Serves: 6-8

1 egg white
1 Tb. instant coffee
⅛ tsp. salt
2 Tb. sugar
1 cup cream, whipped

¼ cup sugar
1 tsp. vanilla
1 Tb. creme de cocoa
½ cup toasted almonds, chopped

Combine egg white, coffee and salt; beat until stiff, gradually add 2 tablespoons sugar. Beat until stiff and satiny. Whip cream, add ¼ cup sugar and vanilla. Combine with other mixture. Add creme de cocoa and fold in nuts. Pour into individual molds or sherbet glasses. Freeze. Sprinkle top with almonds.

When doubling recipe, add 1 extra egg white. Cut down on sugar, using only ⅛ cup, as creme de cocoa makes it sweet enough.

MRS. VIRGINIA P. SINCLAIR
SAN ANTONIO, TEXAS

ANGEL DELIGHT DESSERT

Serves: 12   Oven: 350°

CRUST:

4 egg whites
¼ tsp. cream of tartar

1 cup sugar

Beat egg whites till foamy; add cream of tartar and beat until stiff. Add sugar slowly and beat until absorbed. Spread mixture in a 7 x 12-inch baking dish, pushing up around the edges, leaving a thin layer on the bottom of the pan. Bake at 350°, on middle rack of oven, for 60 minutes. Cool to room temperature.

FILLING:

2 cups milk
4 egg yolks, beaten
3½ Tb. flour
¾ cup sugar

1 tsp. vanilla
½ cup chopped pecans
½ pt. cream, whipped

Heat milk; add 2 tablespoons of hot milk to egg yolks. Mix flour and sugar together and add to yolk mixture. Add flour and yolk mixture to the remainder of hot milk and cook in double boiler or over very low heat until very thick. Add vanilla and set aside.

Remove any excess brown from the meringue and crumble it in the pecans. Pour the cooled pudding in the crust, spread with whipped cream and top with crust-nut mixture. Refrigerate overnight.

May not be frozen and should be prepared a day ahead.

MRS. ED LIGON, JR.

MERINGUE SHELLS

Yield: 12   Oven: 275°

3 egg whites	1 tsp. vanilla
¼ tsp. cream of tartar	1 cup sugar
Dash of salt	

Separate 3 eggs while still cold; bring egg whites to room temperature so they will whip to their fluffiest. Add cream of tartar, salt and vanilla. Beat till frothy. Gradually add sugar; continue beating to very stiff peaks. Meringue should be glossy, not dry. Cover baking sheet with plain ungreased paper or foil. Draw twelve circles, 2 inches in diameter; spread each with ¼ cup meringue. Using back of spoon, shape inside of meringue shell, mounding around the edges to make soft peaks. Bake in very slow oven (275°) for one hour. Fill meringues with ice cream and sauce, fresh fruits, or a cream filling. These can be made ahead and stored in a tin.

MRS. FRANK BAUER, JR.

CREAM PUFFS

Yield: 10-12   Oven: 400°

PUFFS:

½ cup butter	4 eggs
1 cup boiling water	Pinch of salt
1 cup flour	

Melt butter in water; add flour all at once; beat well; cook over moderate heat for 1 or 2 minutes, or until mixture mounds. Remove from heat; add eggs one at a time, beating well after each addition; add salt. Grease cookie sheet; dust with flour; drop a tablespoonful of dough on cookie sheet for each puff; do not add to it. Bake at 400° for 10 to 15 minutes; reduce heat to 250°; bake for another 45 minutes. Remove from oven; cut off tops; remove any soft dough on inside of puff.

FILLING:

½ cup flour	2 cups milk
¾ cup sugar	2 eggs, beaten
Pinch of salt	1 tsp. vanilla

Mix flour, sugar, and salt together in top of double boiler; gradually add milk, stirring constantly. Add eggs; cook slowly until thick; cool; add vanilla. Fill each puff with filling; refrigerate.

These puffs are delicious served for luncheon buffet filled with chicken, ham or sea food salad.

MRS. MALLORY CRANK

FORGOTTEN TORTE

Serves: 10   **Oven: 450°**

6 egg whites
½ tsp. cream of tartar
¼ tsp. salt
1½ cups sugar
1 tsp. vanilla

⅛ tsp. almond extract
Red food color
1 cup cream, whipped
1 Tb. powdered sugar

About 2 hours before the overnight baking, place egg whites in a large bowl and let stand to reach room temperature. Heat oven to 450°; butter only the bottom of a 9-inch tube pan. Add cream of tartar and salt to whites. Beat at medium speed with electric mixer until foamy. Gradually add sugar, a little at a time, beating well after each addition. Add vanilla and almond extracts, a few drops of red food coloring and continue beating until meringue forms stiff, glossy peaks. Spread mixture evenly in prepared tube pan. Place pan in oven. Close oven door. TURN OFF HEAT IMMEDI-ATELY. Let stand overnight or longer. A few hours before serving, loosen edges of torte and turn out on serving plate. Torte will settle a bit. Whip cream and add powdered sugar. Frost torte with cream. Refrigerate. Top with one of the following:

FRUIT TOPPING:

Defrost one pound package frozen strawberries or raspberries. Spoon over slices of torte on dessert plates.

MRS. W. BIGELOW ROBINSON

PEACH MELBA TOPPING:

10-oz. pkg. thawed rasp-
berries
1 Tb. cornstarch

1 Tb. sugar
12-oz. pkg. thawed peaches

Put raspberries, cornstarch, and sugar in a saucepan and cook until clear, stirring constantly. Strain if desired. Put in refrigerator. Before serving add peaches. Spoon over slices of torte.

MRS. MARY B. ELLIS
CAMDEN, ARKANSAS

TOFFEE TOPPING:

Crush 10 to 12 Heath bars in the blender. After frosting the torte with whipped cream, sprinkle candy crumbs all over. Refrigerate until ready to serve.

MRS. WILLIAM EADS, JR.
FORT SMITH, ARKANSAS

BAKED CUSTARD WITH RASPBERRIES

Serves: 4   Oven: 350°

1 egg
¼ cup sugar
⅛ tsp. salt
1 cup scalded milk

¼ tsp. vanilla
1 pkg. frozen raspberries, thawed

Beat egg, sugar and salt together. Stir in milk and vanilla. Pour into individual baking cups. Set cups in a baking dish with 2 inches water in it. Bake at 350° for 45 to 50 minutes or until knife comes out clean. Cool in refrigerator, unmold and drizzle with berries and juice.

Easy, refreshing and delicious!

BOILED CUSTARD

Serves: 6

2 tsp. cornstarch
1 cup sugar
1 qt. milk

3 eggs
1 Tb. butter
1 tsp. vanilla

Mix cornstarch and sugar in top of double boiler; add milk and well beaten eggs. Place over boiling water. Cook 10 to 12 minutes or until mixture coats a spoon. Remove from heat; add butter and stir vigorously for a few minutes. Add vanilla. Stir until mixed. Chill. If there are any small lumps, pour mixture through a strainer before chilling.

Delightful served by itself or with a small meringue shell floating in it.

MRS. WILLIAM A. SAUNDERS, JR.

SHERRY COOLER

Serves: 6-8

2 Tb. gelatin
1 cup cold water
1 cup boiling water
1 cup sugar

3 Tb. lemon juice
1½ cups sherry
1 lemon, cut in thin slices

Soak gelatin in cold water; dissolve sugar and soaked gelatin in boiling water. Add sherry and lemon juice. Pour in a 2 quart serving bowl (glass is pretty). Float thin lemon slices on top. Chill until set. (If made a day ahead, cover with plastic wrap to preserve flavor.) Serve from bowl. Top with whipped cream. Also, delightful topped with boiled custard and whipped cream.

A light and refreshing dessert!

MRS. JOSEPH MULLEN

CHARLOTTE RUSSE

Serves: 8

1 pkg. gelatin	¼ cup sugar
¼ cup cold water	Dash of salt
3 eggs, separated	1 pt. cream, whipped
¼ cup sugar	12 ladyfingers, split
¼ cup sherry	Maraschino cherries

Soften gelatin in water; warm over low heat until completely dissolved. Beat egg whites until stiff; beat yolks until thick and lemon colored. Add ¼ cup sugar to yolks, then sherry; beat well. Add ¼ cup sugar to whites; beat well. Add gelatin and salt to yolk mixture; fold in whites; fold in whipped cream. Line mold with ladyfingers; pour cream mixture into bowl immediately. Garnish with cherries; refrigerate until set.

MRS. WILLIAM BELL ROBERTS
ATLANTA, GEORGIA

QUICK AND DELICIOUS

STRAWBERRIES DRAMBUIE

Serves: 6-8

1 pt. strawberries, whole	1 Tb. Drambuie
1 cup cream, whipped	Nutmeg or finely ground
¼ cup sugar	nuts

Place strawberries in champagne glasses; whip cream with sugar; fold Drambuie into sweetened cream and put a large spoonful of cream mixture on strawberries. Garnish each with a pinch of nutmeg or nuts.

MRS. GEORGE STEWART

LEMON-BERRY CREAM

Lemon thin cookies	Whipped cream or non-dairy
Rich vanilla pudding	whipped topping
Strawberries, fresh or frozen	Toasted almonds

Use crystal sherbet stems. Layer the above in order given. Refrigerate several hours or overnight before serving.

MRS. CHARLES HORTON
MIAMI, FLORIDA

CHOCOLATE-MENTHE DREAM

Ladyfingers, split	3 Tb. creme de menthe
½ pt. cream, whipped	Chocolate sauce

Line pan with split ladyfingers; whip cream; fold creme de menthe into cream; spread on top of ladyfingers; top with chocolate sauce. Chill at least 4 hours.

MRS. DREW LANDER

PEACH ANGEL

Toasted angel food cake   Sour cream
  slices   Orange brandy
Frozen peaches, thawed

Place toasted angel food cake slice on dessert plate; add peaches; top with a spoonful of sour cream; pour over this a touch or more of orange brandy.

MRS. DREW LANDER

STRAWBERRY PIE

Serves: 6-8
  8-in. pie shell, baked   1 lb. pkg. frozen sweetened,
  3-oz. pkg. strawberry gelatin   sliced strawberries,
  1 cup boiling water   unthawed
  ½ cup cream, whipped

Dissolve gelatin in water. Add unthawed strawberries; break up berries with a fork. As berries thaw, gelatin thickens. When partially set, pour into cooled pie shell. Garnish with whipped cream before serving.

MRS. CHARLES R. MCDADE

LEMON ICE BOX PIE

Serves: 6-8
  6-oz. can frozen lemonade,   5-oz. carton non-dairy
    thawed   whipped topping
  14-oz. can sweetened con-   9-in. graham cracker crust
    densed milk

Stir condensed milk and lemonade until blended; fold in whipped topping (or whipped cream); pour into graham cracker crust. Chill at least 2 hours before serving.

MRS. ALLAN DISHONGH

FUDGE SUNDAE PIE

Serves: 8
  1 graham cracker or vanilla   ¼ cup milk
    wafer crust   1 qt. ice cream, softened
  6-oz. pkg. chocolate chips   ½ pt. cream, whipped
  16 marshmallows   ¾ cup pecans, chopped

For fudge sauce, melt chocolate chips, marshmallows and milk in top of double boiler. Set aside to cool.

Fill crust with softened ice cream. Cover with fudge sauce, whipped cream and pecans. Freeze.

Can make ahead and keep on hand for emergency dessert.

MRS. J. W. GUTHRIE
OKLAHOMA CITY, OKLAHOMA

LEMON ICE CREAM PIE

Serves: 8   Oven: 300°

GINGERSNAP CRUST:

    35 gingersnaps, crushed   1 Tb. powdered sugar
    ½ cup margarine, melted

Add melted butter and sugar to gingersnap crumbs. Mix well.
Press firmly into a 9-inch pie pan. Bake 5 minutes in 300° oven.
Cool.

FILLING:

    1 qt. lemon ice cream   Strawberries
    ½ pt. cream, whipped

Spread ice cream in pie crust. Cover pie with foil and place in deep
freeze. To serve, cut in wedges and top with whipped cream and a
few sweetened strawberries.

                            MRS. J. L. (PENIE) LANE
                            ALEXANDRIA, VIRGINIA

FROZEN BERRY CREAM

Serves: 6

    2 cups berries, washed   1 tsp. vanilla
    ½ cup sugar   Pinch of salt
    1 cup cream, whipped

Mash berries (blackberries, blueberries, or strawberries) and sugar
together with a fork. Fold in whipped cream with vanilla and salt.
Place in refrigerator tray. Freeze until firm—not solid—about 5
hours.

                            MRS. WARREN JENNINGS
                            DeWITT, ARKANSAS

FROZEN WHIPPED CREAM

Serves: 6-8

    1 pt. cream, whipped   1 Tb. vanilla
    ¼ cup sugar   1 cup pecans, ground

Mix together in square pan and freeze. Serve with your favorite
sauce.

Chocolate sauce is delicious.

                            MRS. HIRAM COOPER

FRESH FRUIT ICE

Serves: 10

3 cups water	1½ bananas, mashed
1½ cups sugar	1 qt. strawberries, pureed
11-oz. can crushed pineapple	Juice of 2 lemons

Boil water and sugar until sugar is dissolved. Cool; add remaining ingredients. Freeze. Serve slightly thawed.

Proportions of fruits may be changed to suite taste.

MRS. LARRY BURROW

REFRESHING DESSERTS

Cut top off a fresh orange (reserve top) ; scoop out orange sections ; fill orange shell with orange sherbet ; put top on and place in freezer until ready to serve. Garnish with a sprig of fresh mint.

MRS. J. L. (PENIE) LANE
ALEXANDRIA, VIRGINIA

Slice lime sherbet into 2-inch squares ; put a dash of whipped cream on top with a strawberry in the center. Freeze until ready to serve.

MRS. J. L. (PENIE) LANE
ALEXANDRIA, VIRGINIA

Soften ½ gallon of orange sherbet enough to stir in ½ cup chopped black walnuts. Freeze until about 15 minutes before serving. Pass a pitcher containing about ½ cup bourbon and drizzle over sherbet.

Do not substitute English walnuts and do not try it with wine.

MRS. GEORGE ROSE SMITH

PIES

HINTS FOR PIECRUST MAKING

Too much flour makes piecrust tough.

Too much shortening makes it dry and crumbly.

Too much liquid makes it heavy.

Pie dough may be made in advance, wrapped in wax paper and stored in the refrigerator. Chilled dough handles more easily.

All materials used should be as cold as possible. The liquid should be iced. Pie dough should be handled lightly and as little as possible. If a crust is to be baked without any filling, prick the bottom and sides with a fork and bake in a 450° oven for 10 to 12 minutes.

PERFECT PASTRY

Yield: 2 9-inch piecrusts

¾ cup shortening	¾ tsp. salt
2 cups flour	5 Tb. ice water

Cut shortening into flour and salt mixture with a pastry blender or two knives until the consistency of coarse meal. Do not overmix. Add water and stir until mixed. Place dough in refrigerator one hour before rolling out crust.

ELLA GARDENHIRE
CAMDEN, ARKANSAS

STIR-N-ROLL PIE CRUST

Yield: 9-inch pie crust

1⅓ cups flour	⅓ cup salad oil
1 tsp. salt	3 Tb. cold milk

Mix flour and salt. Pour oil and milk into one measuring cup. Do not stir; add all at once to flour. Stir until mixed. Roll between 2 pieces of wax paper.

MRS. JACK SMITH

GRAHAM CRACKER CRUST

18 graham crackers, crushed	½ cup butter, melted
⅓ cup sugar	Dash of cinnamon (optional)

Mix all ingredients together and press into 8-inch pie pan.

CRACKER PECAN PIE

Serves: 6-8   Oven: 350°

3 beaten egg whites	1 tsp. vanilla
1 cup sugar	14 Ritz crackers, crushed
½ tsp. baking powder	½ pt. cream, whipped
½ cup chopped pecans	

Beat egg whites until stiff; add sugar slowly. Fold in baking powder, pecans, vanilla and crackers. Bake in greased 9-inch pie pan for 45 minutes at 350°. When cool, slice and serve with whipped cream.

Variation: May be made with soda crackers or graham crackers.

MOCHA TOPPING (Optional):

½ pt. cream, whipped	2 Tb. sugar
1 tsp. instant coffee	Chocolate curls

Whip cream; add coffee and sugar gradually. Spread over baked Cracker Pecan Pie; chill. Top with chocolate curls.

MRS. BART ROACH

BUTTERSCOTCH NUT PIE

Serves: 8   Oven: 375°

CRUST: 9-inch

⅓ cup butter	1 egg yolk
3 Tb. sugar	1 cup flour

Soften butter with sugar and egg yolk just until blended. Add flour. Mix until dough forms. Place ¼ cup dough in small pan for crumb topping. Press remaining mixture evenly over bottom and sides of pie pan. Flute edges. Bake crust at 375° for 12 to 15 minutes. Bake crumbs for topping for 10 to 12 minutes. Cool.

FILLING:

1-oz. pkg. gelatin	½ cup nuts, chopped
¼ cup water, cold	½ tsp. rum flavoring
6-oz. pkg. butterscotch bits	4 egg whites
3-oz. pkg. cream cheese	¼ cup sugar
½ cup milk	2 Tb. nuts, chopped
3 egg yolks	

Soften gelatin in cold water. Dissolve over boiling water. Stir in butterscotch bits and cheese. Remove from heat. Add milk, egg yolks, nuts and flavoring; beat well. Chill until very thick, but not set. Beat egg whites until soft mounds form. Add sugar gradually; beat until stiff. Fold into butterscotch mixture. Pour into prepared crust. Sprinkle with crumbs and 2 tablespoons chopped nuts. Chill at least 2 hours.

BRANDY ALEXANDER PIE

Serves: 6-8

9-inch pie crust, baked	4 eggs, separated
1 envelope unflavored gelatin	¼ cup cognac
½ cup cold water	⅓ cup creme de cacao
⅔ cup sugar (to be used ⅓ at a time)	2 cups whipped cream (to be used 1 cup at a time)
⅛ tsp. salt	Chocolate curls for garnish

Sprinkle the gelatin over the cold water in a saucepan. Add ⅓ cup of sugar, salt and egg yolks. Stir to blend. Heat over low heat, stirring, until gelatin dissolves and mixture thickens. DO NOT BOIL. Remove from heat and stir in cognac and creme de cacao. Chill until mixture starts to mound when tipped from a spoon (25-45 minutes). Stir occasionally while chilling. Beat the egg whites until stiff. Gradually beat in the remaining sugar and fold gently into the thickened mixture. Whip one cup of the cream and fold into mixture. Turn into crust. Chill 6 to 8 hours or overnight. Whip the second cup of cream and spread over top of pie. Garnish with chocolate curls. Delicious without whipped cream on top.

MRS. GRIFFIN SMITH

CHESS MERINGUE PIE

Serves: 6-8   Oven: 350°

9-inch pie crust, unbaked   ⅓ cup butter, melted
5 eggs (separate 2 whites for   1 cup sugar
  top)   1 Tb. corn meal
⅛ tsp. salt   4 Tb. sugar
2 Tb. heavy cream

Beat eggs and egg yolks. Add salt, cream, melted butter, 1 cup
sugar and corn meal. Mix well. Pour in unbaked pie shell. Bake at
350° until almost set (about 30 minutes). Beat 2 egg whites stiff
and add 4 tablespoons sugar. Spread on top of pie. Bake until
lightly browned.

MRS. CHARLES OLIVER

KENTUCKY DERBY PIE

Serves: 8   Oven: 350°

9-inch pie shell, unbaked   6-oz. pkg. semi-sweet
2 eggs   chocolate chips
1 cup sugar   1 cup pecans, chopped
½ cup flour   1 tsp. vanilla
½ cup butter, melted

Beat eggs; add sugar, flour and melted butter. Stir until blended.
Add chips, nuts and vanilla. Pour into unbaked pie shell. Bake in
350° oven for 45 minutes.

Prepare at least 6 hours before serving; may be prepared the day
before but do not refrigerate before serving.

MRS. E. KEARNEY DIETZ

CREME DE MENTHE PIE

Serves: 6-8

CRUST:
15 chocolate cookies, crushed   ½ cup butter, melted
Mix cookie crumbs with melted butter and press into a 9 or 10-inch
pie pan.

FILLING:
24 marshmallows, large   ½ pt. cream, whipped
4 Tb. milk   1 chocolate bar, small
4 Tb. creme de menthe, green
Melt marshmallows and milk in double boiler. Cool. Add creme de
menthe and fold in whipped cream. Pour into prepared cookie crust
and refrigerate overnight. Shave chocolate bar on top before
serving.

MRS. JOEL LEDBETTER, SR.

FRENCH CHOCOLATE PIE

Serves: 8   Oven: 300°

SHELL:

2 egg whites	½ cup sugar
⅛ tsp. salt	½ tsp. vanilla
⅛ tsp. cream of tartar	½ cup pecans, chopped

Beat egg whites with salt and cream of tartar until foamy. Add sugar gradually, beating until very stiff. Fold in vanilla and nuts. Spread in a 9-inch pie pan (which has been greased and floured). Bake for 50 to 55 minutes at 300°.

COOKED FILLING:

½ cup margarine	1 tsp. vanilla
¾ cup sugar	2 egg yolks
1½ squares bitter chocolate, melted, cooled	2 whole eggs
	½ pt. cream, whipped

Cream margarine. Gradually add sugar and blend in chocolate and vanilla. Beat until smooth at medium speed of electric mixer. Add yolks and whole eggs, one at a time. Beat 4 minutes after each addition, 15 minutes total. Spread in cooled pie shell. Top with slightly sweetened whipped cream.

Best served after several hours refrigeration.

MRS. WILLIAM R. OVERTON

QUICK FILLING:

1 pkg. German Sweet Chocolate	1 tsp. vanilla
3 Tb. water	1 cup cream, whipped

Melt chocolate in water over low heat, stirring constantly. Cool till thickened. Add vanilla; fold in whipped cream. Spread in meringue shell. Chill 2 hours.

MRS. MIKE MEHAFFY

TOASTED COCONUT PIE

Serves: 8   Oven: 350°

9-inch pie crust, unbaked	4 tsp. lemon juice
3 eggs, beaten	1 tsp. vanilla
1½ cups sugar	1⅓ cups flaked coconut
½ cup butter	Whipped cream

Combine ingredients except cream. Pour into pastry shell. Bake 40 to 45 minutes in 350° oven. Cool. Top with whipped cream.

MRS. J. W. GUTHRIE
OKLAHOMA CITY, OKLAHOMA

CHOCOLATE PECAN PIE

Serves: 8   Oven: 375°

9-inch pie crust, unbaked   3 eggs, slightly beaten
2 squares bitter chocolate   1 tsp. vanilla
3 Tb. butter   1 cup coarsely chopped
1 cup light corn syrup   pecans
¾ cup sugar   ½ cup cream, whipped

Melt chocolate and butter over hot water. Combine syrup and sugar
in saucepan. Bring to boil over high heat, stirring until sugar is
dissolved. Boil 2 minutes. Add chocolate mixture. Pour slowly over
eggs, stirring constantly. Add vanilla and nuts. Stir to mix well.
Pour into unbaked pie shell. Bake at 375° for 45 to 50 minutes.
Cool. Top with unsweetened whipped cream.

MRS. J. L. (PENIE) LANE

CHOCOLATE SUNDAE PIE

Serves: 6-8

CRUST:

24 to 30 vanilla or chocolate   ¼ cup melted margarine
  wafers, crushed

Mix wafer crumbs with melted margarine; press into a 9-inch pie
pan.

FILLING:

1 envelope unflavored gelatin   ¼ tsp. salt
¼ cup cold water   1½ tsp. vanilla
1 cup milk, scalded   3 egg whites, stiffly beaten
3 egg yolks, slightly beaten   1 cup cream, whipped
½ cup sugar   1 sq. bitter chocolate, slivered

Add gelatin to cold water to soften. Set aside. Scald milk (heat in
saucepan until skim forms on top). Combine egg yolks, sugar and
salt in top of double boiler. Slowly add scalded milk. Cook in double
boiler until mixture coats spoon. Remove from heat, add softened
gelatin and stir until dissolved. Cool. Add vanilla. Fold in stiffly
beaten egg whites and whipped cream. Pour into crust. Sprinkle
with slivered chocolate. Refrigerate.

MRS. CHARLES ROBINSON

MINIATURE PECAN PIES

Yield: 24 pastries   Oven: 325°

PASTRY:

3-oz. pkg. cream cheese   1 cup flour, sifted
½ cup butter

Allow cream cheese and butter to soften at room temperature; blend. Stir in flour, chill slightly for one hour. Shape into 2 dozen 1-inch balls; place in tiny ungreased 1¾-inch muffin cups. Press dough against bottom and sides of cups.

FILLING:

¾ cup brown sugar   Dash salt
1 egg   1 cup pecans, coarsely
1 Tb. soft butter   chopped
1 tsp. vanilla

Beat together sugar, egg, butter, vanilla and salt until just smooth. Divide half of pecans among pastry-lined cups; add filling mixture and top with remaining pecans. Bake at 325° for 25 minutes or until filling is set. Cool, remove from pans.

These will freeze and also keep well for several days in a covered cake tin.

MRS. JOHN REX
OKLAHOMA CITY, OKLAHOMA

AUNT MARY'S PECAN PIE

Serves: 6-8   Oven: 400°

9-inch pie crust, baked   2 Tb. melted butter
3 eggs   1 tsp. vanilla
½ cup light corn syrup   ⅛ tsp. salt
½ cup dark corn syrup   1 cup pecans
1 cup sugar

Heat oven to 400°. Beat eggs slightly. Add other ingredients, pecans last. Pour into pie crust and bake at 400° for 15 minutes. Then bake at 350° for 30 minutes. Center of pie will be a little softer than outside.

This pie can be baked and frozen.

MRS. C. C. MOFFITT
BRINKLEY, ARKANSAS

CREAM BASE FOR CREAM PIES

Serves: 6   Oven: 350°

3 egg yolks   1 cup milk
¾ cup sugar   1 Tb. butter
2 Tb. flour, heaping   1 8-inch baked pie shell

Place yolks, sugar mixed with flour, milk and butter in top of
double boiler. Cook over boiling water, stirring constantly until
thick. Remove from heat and add selected variation from below.
Cool slightly. Pour mixture into baked pie shell. Top with meringue.

MERINGUE:

3 egg whites   ¼ tsp. cream of tartar
1 Tb. water   6 Tb. sugar
⅛ tsp. salt

Beat whites, water, salt, and cream of tartar until frothy; add sugar
½ teaspoon at a time, beating well after each addition. Spread on
slightly cooled filling and bake at 300° for 15 to 20 minutes.

Variations:

Lemon Pie—*2 lemons, juice and rind added to cream base.*

Chocolate Pie—*1 ounce melted bitter chocolate added to cream base.*

Coconut Pie—*⅔ cup flaked coconut added to cream base; ⅓ cup
coconut sprinkled on top of meringue.*

Banana Pie—*2 ripe bananas, peeled and cut into thin slices placed
on bottom of baked pie shell; pour cream base in and top with
meringue.*

MRS. JACK T. LYNN

TUTTI-FRUTTI PIE

Serves: 6-8

9-inch baked pie crust or   ⅓ cup lemon juice
  graham cracker crust   1 cup chopped pecans
1 can condensed milk   Sliced bananas
16-oz. can fruit cocktail,   Lemon juice
  drained   Whipped cream

Combine condensed milk and ⅓ cup lemon juice in a bowl; stir by
hand until thick. Add fruit cocktail and pecans. Pour into pie shell.
Slice bananas over top and sprinkle with lemon juice to prevent
them from turning brown. Top with whipped cream. Refrigerate
overnight.

MRS. JOHN BENTON DYKE

FRESH PEACH CUSTARD PIE

Serves: 6-8   Oven: 350°

9-inch pie crust, unbaked   2 eggs
2 cups peeled and sliced fresh   2 Tb. butter
   peaches   1 tsp. vanilla or almond
1 cup sugar   extract
1½ Tb. flour

Put sliced peaches and juice into pie shell. Mix all other ingredients.
Pour over peaches. Bake at 350° for 35 minutes. Turn up oven to
brown last 1 or 2 minutes. Serve warm with ice cream.

This pie cannot be prepared in advance and will not freeze.

MRS. DOUGLAS BRANDON

DUTCH APPLE PIE

Serves: 6-8   Oven: 400°

9-inch pie crust, unbaked

Refrigerate pie shell until ready for use.

TOPPING:

⅔ cup sifted flour   ⅓ cup light brown sugar,
⅓ cup margarine   fully packed

Combine flour and sugar in bowl. Cut in margarine with pastry
blender or 2 knives until mixture is consistency of coarse corn meal.
Refrigerate. Preheat oven to 400°.

FILLING:

3 cups green apples   2 Tb. flour
1 to 2 tsp. lemon juice   1 tsp. cinnamon
¾ cup sugar

Pare, core and slice apples. Sprinkle with lemon juice. Combine
sugar, flour and cinnamon. Toss with apples. Turn into pie shell.
Cover with topping. Bake 40-45 minutes.

MRS. JACK SMITH

FRESH STRAWBERRY PIE

Serves: 6-8

9-inch pie crust, baked   1 cup sugar
1½ qts. fresh strawberries   2 Tb. lemon juice
3 Tb. cornstarch   ½ pt. cream, whipped

Wash and hull berries and reserve half of the best ones. Mash
the other half, add cornstarch and sugar and cook until thick and
clear. Remove from heat and stir in lemon juice. Cool; add the
whole berries, or if too large, cut in half, but save a few for garnish-
ing. Pour into the pie shell, cover with whipped cream and garnish.

Delicious!

MRS. JOHN R. FLETCHER

SKY-HIGH LEMON ICEBOX PIE

Serves: 8

9-inch pie shell, baked
4 egg yolks
⅔ cup sugar
Pinch of salt
4 Tb. lemon juice (more for tart flavor)
Grated rind of 2 lemons

¾ Tb. unflavored gelatin
⅓ cup cold water
4 egg whites
⅔ cup sugar
½ pt. cream, whipped
Lemon slivers

Place egg yolks, ⅔ cup sugar, salt and lemon juice in top of double boiler; cook over boiling water, stirring until thick; add lemon rind and gelatin which has been soaked in cold water for 5 minutes. Let mixture cool. Beat egg whites until stiff; slowly add ⅔ cup sugar. Beat until creamy. Fold egg whites into cooled lemon mixture. Place in baked pie shell, sky-high; chill at least 6 hours or overnight. Top with whipped cream. Garnish with lemon slivers.

HOLIDAY PUMPKIN PIE

Serves: 8   Oven: 450°

PECAN LAYER FOR UNBAKED PIE CRUST:

10-inch deep pie crust, unbaked
3 Tb. butter

⅓ cup brown sugar
⅓ cup pecans, chopped

Cream butter and sugar; add pecans. Press on top of prepared pie crust. Bake at 450° for 10 minutes. Cool. Reduce oven to 350° for later use.

CUSTARD LAYER:

1 cup evaporated milk
½ cup water
3 eggs
1½ cups canned pumpkin
½ cup sugar
½ cup brown sugar

¼ tsp. salt
1½ tsp. cinnamon
½ tsp. ginger
¼ tsp. nutmeg
¼ tsp. cloves
Whipped cream, sweetened

Scald milk with water in small pan. Beat eggs in large bowl. Stir in pumpkin, sugar, brown sugar, salt and spices. Beat in milk mixture. Pour into prepared pie crust. Bake at 350° for 50 minutes, or until set but soft. Cool and garnish with whipped cream before serving.

MRS. RAYMOND C. COOK

CITRUS CHIFFON PIE

Serves: 8-10

9-inch pie crust, baked	½ cup orange juice
1-oz. pkg. gelatin	Juice of 1 lemon
¼ cup water, cold	½ tsp. salt
4 eggs, whole	1 egg white
1 cup sugar	1 tsp. vanilla
1 tsp. grated lemon rind	Whipped cream

Dissolve gelatin in water. Beat whole eggs, add ½ cup sugar, citrus juices and rind, salt and gelatin mixture. Cook to a custard. Cool. Beat egg white until frothy; slowly add to it remaining ½ cup sugar and vanilla. Fold into custard mixture. Chill until firm. Serve with whipped cream. (Sweet and Low may be substituted for sugar and non-dairy whipped topping for whipped cream.)

Ever so light—perfect for after a heavy dinner.

MRS. DREW LANDER

MILE HIGH PIE

Serves: 8   **Oven: Broil**

10-inch pie crust, baked	½ tsp. vanilla
1 pt. vanilla ice cream	¼ tsp. cream of tartar
1 pt. chocolate ice cream	½ cup sugar
8 egg whites	

Layer ice cream in pie shell. Beat egg whites with vanilla and cream of tartar until soft peaks form. Gradually add sugar, beating until stiff and glossy and sugar is dissolved. Spread meringue over ice cream to edges of pastry. Broil 30 seconds to one minute to brown meringue. Freeze at least several hours. Drizzle chocolate sauce over each serving.

CHOCOLATE SAUCE:

2 squares German Sweet	½ cup cream, heavy
Chocolate	½ cup sugar
2 squares bitter chocolate	

Cook all ingredients in a double boiler until thick, using only half of the cream. Add remaining cream to achieve pouring consistency. Serve in sauce boat.

MRS. BERNICE HOLDER

CAKES

PEGGY'S POUND CAKE

Serves: 18-20   Oven: 325°

1½ cups butter	3 cups Gold Medal Presifted
3 cups sugar	Flour (no substitute)
6 eggs	1½ tsp. vanilla
1 tsp. salt	1 cup sour cream
¼ tsp. soda	

In an electric mixer cream butter and sugar; beat until light. Add eggs one at a time, beating well after each addition. Mix dry ingredients; add gradually to creamed mixture, beating well. Add vanilla. Fold in sour cream just until mixed. Pour into two greased and floured loaf pans or one 10-inch tube pan. Bake at 325° for 1 hour and 10 to 15 minutes.

MRS. PEGGY OSLER

BUTTERMILK POUND CAKE

Serves: 18-20   Oven: 350°

1 cup Crisco shortening	1 tsp. vanilla
3 cups sugar	3 cups flour, unsifted
6 eggs, extra large	1 cup buttermilk, cultured
½ tsp. salt	½ tsp. soda

Cream shortening and sugar; add eggs separately, beating after each addition. Add salt and vanilla. Stir soda into ½ cup buttermilk and set aside to add last. Alternate flour and buttermilk to creamed mixture. Pour satiny batter into greased, floured, large round tube pan; shake until even and smooth. Bake at 350° for about 1 hour and 15 minutes; cool 5 minutes before removing from pan. Time may vary with weight of pan but this cake always appears slightly undercooked.

MRS. W. K. INGRAM
WEST MEMPHIS, ARKANSAS

ALMOND POUND CAKE

Serves: 18-20   Oven: 350°

1 cup margarine	2 cups flour, sifted
2 cups sugar	2 tsp. vanilla
5 eggs	3 tsp. almond extract

Cream margarine, sugar and one egg in large mixing bowl and beat with electric mixer for 5 to 10 minutes. Add flour and remaining eggs alternately and continue beating at low speed. Add vanilla and almond extract. Grease and flour a Bundt pan; pour batter in pan and bake at 350° for one hour. Cool in pan.

BROWN SUGAR LOAF

Serves: 18-20   Oven: 350°

3 cups flour	5 eggs
1 tsp. baking powder	1 cup milk
1 cup butter	1 tsp. vanilla
1 cup shortening	½ cup chopped nuts
1 lb. dark brown sugar	(optional)
1 cup sugar	

Sift together flour and baking powder. Set aside. Cream butter, shortening, brown sugar and sugar. Add eggs separately, beating after each addition. Add flour and milk alternately to egg and sugar mixture. Add vanilla; fold in nuts. Bake in greased and floured tube or Bundt pan for 1 hour and 15 minutes at 350°. Let cool and remove from pan. Garnish with sifted powdered sugar, if desired.

MRS. W. Y. HESTER

CHOCOLATE POUND CAKE

Serves: 18-20   Oven: 325°

1 cup butter	½ tsp. baking powder
½ cup shortening	½ tsp. salt
2½ cups sugar	4 Tb. cocoa
5 eggs	1 cup milk
3 cups flour	1 Tb. vanilla

Cream together butter and shortening. Add sugar and eggs, blending well. Sift dry ingredients together. Add alternately with milk to creamed mixture. Add vanilla; mix thoroughly. Bake in a greased and floured tube pan for 80 minutes at 325°.

CHOCOLATE ICING:

¼ cup butter	1 tsp. vanilla
2 oz. bitter chocolate	Cream to moisten
1 lb. powdered sugar	

Melt butter and chocolate. Add sugar and vanilla, adding cream as needed to achieve spreading consistency.

MRS. JAMES VERNON FLACK, JR.

TUNNEL OF FUDGE CAKE

Serves: 18-20   Oven: 350°

1½ cups butter, softened	1 pkg. Pillsbury Double
6 eggs	Dutch Fudge Buttercream
1½ cups sugar	Frosting Mix
2 cups flour	2 cups nuts, chopped

Cream butter at high speed. Add eggs separately, beating well after each addition. Gradually add sugar, continue creaming until light and fluffy. By hand, stir in flour, frosting mix and nuts until well blended. Pour into a greased and floured Bundt pan, bake at 350° for 60 to 65 minutes. Cool 2 hours. Remove from pan. Cool completely before serving.

MOMMA'S GINGERBREAD

Serves: 12   Oven: 350°

1 cup butter
2 cups sugar, scant
4 Tb. molasses
2 tsp. ginger
2 tsp. cinnamon
1 tsp. cloves, ground

1 tsp. nutmeg
Pinch of salt
2 cups buttermilk
2 tsp. soda
2 eggs, well beaten
3 cups flour, sifted

Melt butter, then add next 7 ingredients; mix well. Dissolve soda in the buttermilk, then add to other mixture. Stir well. Add beaten eggs; stir in flour. Grease and flour 9 x 12-inch pan; bake at 350° for 35 to 40 minutes. Serve hot or cold with whipped cream or lemon sauce.

LEMON SAUCE:

1 cup sugar
½ cup butter
Juice of 1 lemon

1 egg, softly beaten
½ to 1 cup boiling water

Put all ingredients in top of a double boiler and stir until thick. May be served hot or cold.

This gingerbread is company fare.

MRS. JAMES E. MADIGAN

MISSION SUNDAY FUDGE CAKE

Serves: 9   Oven: 350°

1 cup flour
½ tsp. soda
¼ tsp. salt
½ cup butter
1 cup brown sugar, firmly
  packed
3 eggs

1½ squares bitter chocolate,
  melted and cooled
½ cup buttermilk
1 tsp. vanilla
¼ cup nuts, chopped
½ cup coconut

Sift together flour, soda and salt. Cream butter and gradually add sugar. Blend well. Add eggs separately, beating after each addition. Add chocolate and beat for 1 minute. Combine buttermilk and vanilla; add alternately with dry ingredients (begin and end with dry ingredients). Fold in nuts and coconut. Bake in a greased and floured 8 x 8-inch pan at 350° for 25 to 30 minutes.

CHOCOLATE MALLOW ICING:

1 square bitter chocolate
2 Tb. butter
1½ cups powdered sugar

1 tsp. vanilla
2 to 3 Tb. cream, heavy
6 large marshmallows, diced

Melt chocolate and butter over hot water. Add powdered sugar. Blend in vanilla, cream and marshmallows. Spread over warm cake.

This is a small, but richly delicious cake.

MRS. C. RAY WILLIAMS

CORDELL'S CAKE

Serves: 12-14   Oven: 350°

¾ cup shortening
1½ cups sugar
3 eggs, beaten
1¾ cups Gold Medal All
  Purpose Flour
½ tsp. baking powder
½ tsp. soda
½ tsp. salt

¾ tsp. nutmeg
1 tsp. cinnamon
2 Tb. Droste cocoa
¾ cup buttermilk
1 tsp. vanilla
1 tsp. lemon extract
½ cup coarsely chopped
  pecans, toasted

Cream shortening, add sugar gradually; cream thoroughly. Blend in 3 well beaten eggs. Sift flour once before measuring. Sift together flour, baking powder, soda, salt, spices and cocoa. Add to creamed mixture, alternating with buttermilk. Blend in flavorings and nuts. Pour into 2 8-inch well greased and floured layer pans. Bake for 30 minutes in 350° oven. This cake stays fresh for a week if covered; it also freezes well.

Be sure to toast the pecans . . . what a difference.

COCOA COFFEE FROSTING:

6 Tb. butter
1 egg yolk
3 cups powdered sugar

1½ Tb. Droste cocoa
1 tsp. cinnamon
1½ Tb. hot coffee

Cream butter, add egg yolk and blend. Sift dry ingredients together and add with the coffee. If necessary add a bit more coffee. Beat in mixer at slowest speed for about 45 minutes. (Yes, 45 minutes.)

This icing is lovely. You'll be surprised how much it tastes like cooked icing.

CORDELL DOUGHERTY

FRESH APPLE CAKE

Serves: 8-10   Oven: 325°

4 cups apple, diced (peeled,
  optional)
2 cups sugar
1 cup salad oil
2 eggs, well beaten
1 tsp. vanilla

2 cups flour
1 tsp. soda
2 tsp. cinnamon
1 tsp. salt
1 cup chopped nuts
  (optional)

Combine sugar, oil, eggs, and vanilla; add diced apples. Sift together flour, soda, cinnamon, and salt; add to apple mixture and mix thoroughly. This will be a thick batter. Add nuts; mix again. Pour into a greased and floured 8 x 8-inch square pan or a loaf pan. Bake at 325° for 90 minutes. Test cake with a toothpick. Run knife around edge to loosen; remove from pan to cool.

MRS. JOHN R. GROBMYER, III

COCA-COLA CAKE

Serves: 12   Oven: 350°

2 cups flour
2 cups sugar
1 cup butter
2 to 3 Tb. cocoa
1½ cups miniature marshmallows

1 cup Coca-Cola
½ cup buttermilk
2 eggs, beaten
1 tsp. soda
1 tsp. vanilla

Combine flour and sugar. Heat butter, cocoa, marshmallows, and Coca-Cola until marshmallows melt. Pour over flour mixture; mix thoroughly. Beat together buttermilk, eggs, soda and vanilla; add to flour mixture and mix well. This will be a thin batter. Bake in a greased and floured 9 x 13-inch pan at 350° for 30 to 35 minutes. Ice while hot.

COCA-COLA ICING:

½ cup butter
2 Tb. cocoa
6 Tb. Coca-Cola

1 lb. powdered sugar
1 cup pecans, chopped and toasted

Combine butter, cocoa and Coca-Cola; heat to boiling. Pour over powdered sugar, after beating well, add nuts. Spread over hot cake.

MRS. A. HOWARD STEBBINS, III

DIANE'S CHOCOLATE SHEET CAKE

Serves: 18-20   Oven: 400°

3 cups sugar
3 cups flour
4¾ Tb. cocoa
1½ cups water
¾ cup shortening

¾ cup margarine
3 eggs
¾ cup buttermilk
1½ tsp. soda
1½ tsp. vanilla

In a large bowl mix sugar, flour and cocoa. Bring to a boil water, shortening and margarine. Mix well the dry mixture and boiling mixture. Add soda and vanilla to buttermilk. Add buttermilk and eggs to batter, mixing thoroughly. Bake in a greased and floured 11 x 16-inch pan for 25 minutes at 400°. Test cake with a toothpick. Ice the cake while it is warm.

COCOA-NUT ICING:

½ cup margarine
3 Tb. cocoa
⅓ cup milk

1 tsp. vanilla
1 lb. powdered sugar
½ to 1 cup pecans, toasted

Bring ingredients to a boil. Cool slightly. Ice while cake is warm.
Rich and delicious.

MRS. WILLIAM CASTLES
TULSA, OKLAHOMA

WHITE CHOCOLATE CAKE

Serves: 12   Oven: 350°

4 oz. white chocolate, broken
  into small pieces
½ cup boiling water
1 cup butter, softened
2 cups sugar
4 egg yolks, unbeaten

1 tsp. vanilla
2½ cups cake flour, sifted
½ tsp. salt
1 tsp. baking soda
1 cup buttermilk
4 egg whites, stiffly beaten

Melt chocolate in water; set aside to cool. Cream butter and sugar until fluffy. Add egg yolks one at a time to creamed mixture, beating well after each addition. Add vanilla and chocolate; then blend. Sift together flour, salt and baking soda; add alternately with buttermilk to chocolate batter, beating well after each addition. Beat the egg whites until stiff; fold into batter. Line three 8-inch cake pans with waxed paper; pour in batter. Bake at 350° for 25 to 30 minutes. Cool cake for 10 minutes; then ice with White Chocolate Frosting.

WHITE CHOCOLATE FROSTING:

4 oz. white chocolate, melted
  and cooled
Dash of salt
2 Tb. butter, softened

¾ cup powdered sugar
2 Tb. hot water
1 egg yolk
½ tsp. vanilla

Combine all ingredients; beat well with an electric mixer. Frost only the top of each layer and stack layers.

DATE NUT CAKE

Serves: 18-20   Oven: 300°

1 lb. dates, chopped
1 lb. nuts, chopped
1 cup flour
2 tsp. baking powder,
  rounded
½ tsp. salt
4 eggs, separated
1 cup sugar

Dash of salt
1 tsp. vanilla
1 lb. candied cherries or small
  jar maraschino cherries,
  drained and chopped
  (optional)
Whipped cream

Sift together flour, baking powder and salt. Sprinkle over dates and nuts. Beat egg yolks; add sugar and mix well. Beat egg whites until stiff; adding a dash of salt and vanilla, fold into egg yolk mixture. Add floured dates and nuts. Mix well. Bake in a greased and floured tube pan at 300° for 1 hour. Test with a toothpick or a broomstraw. Serve with whipped cream.

This is a great stand-in for fruit cake.

MRS. GARRETT BROWN

FIESTA BANANA CAKE

Serves: 12   Oven: 350°

½ cup butter
2 cups cake flour
1 tsp. baking powder
1 tsp. soda
¾ tsp. salt
1⅓ cups sugar

½ cup buttermilk
1 tsp. vanilla
1 cup ripe bananas, mashed
2 eggs, unbeaten
½ cup nuts, chopped

Sift together flour, baking powder, soda, salt, and sugar; add to softened butter. To this mixture add ¼ cup buttermilk and bananas; mix until all flour is dampened. Add eggs, nuts and remaining milk; beat 1 minute. Bake at 350° for 25 minutes in two greased and floured 9-inch cake pans.

BANANA ICING:

1 banana, mashed
2 Tb. butter
2 Tb. cream
1 tsp. vanilla

¾ to 1 lb. powdered sugar
½ can angel flake coconut
(optional)

Beat banana; melt together butter, cream, vanilla and add to banana. Mix in powdered sugar until you get spreading consistency. Add coconut, if desired. Spread between layers and on top and sides of cake. Sliced bananas between layers is a nice extra touch.

RUSSELL HOLCOMB

CARROT CAKE

Serves: 18-20   Oven: 350°

1½ cups salad oil
2 cups sugar
5 eggs
2 cups flour
2 tsp. baking powder
1 tsp. soda
2 tsp. cinnamon

1 tsp. salt
2 tsp. vanilla
2 cups grated carrots or
   2 jars Jr. baby food carrots
1 cup pineapple, crushed and
   drained

In a large bowl mix oil and sugar; add eggs one at a time, beating well after each addition. Sift together flour, baking powder, soda, cinnamon and salt. Add this in small amounts to egg mixture until all ingredients are well blended. Add vanilla. Blend in carrots and pineapple. Bake in 3 greased and floured 9-inch pans at 350° for 30 to 40 minutes. Cool cakes.

CREAM CHEESE ICING:

8-oz. pkg. Philadelphia
   Cream cheese, softened
½ cup butter, melted

2 tsp. vanilla
1 lb. powdered sugar

Blend all ingredients well. Spread between layers and on top of cake.

MRS. HARLEY CROWDER

CRANBERRY CAKE

Serves: 12   Oven: 325°

2½ cups flour, sifted	1 cup whole cranberries
1 cup sugar	1 cup nuts, chopped
1 tsp. salt	Grated rind of 2 oranges
1 tsp. soda	2 eggs, beaten
1 tsp. baking powder	1 cup buttermilk
1 cup dates, diced	¾ cup salad oil

Sift flour; then measure it. Sift again with sugar, salt, soda and baking powder. Stir into flour mixture the dates, cranberries, nuts and orange rind. Combine beaten eggs with buttermilk and oil; add to flour and fruit mixture. Mix thoroughly. Bake in a greased and floured 9 x 5-inch loaf pan for 1 hour at 325°.

ORANGE GLAZE:

¾ cup orange juice   ¾ cup sugar

Place baked cake, still in pan, on a wire rack. Heat orange juice and sugar until sugar is dissolved. DO NOT BOIL. Pour this mixture over hot cake. Let stand for 30 minutes before removing cake.

A great holiday cake.

MRS. J. RUSSELL COOK
HUNTINGTON, WEST VIRGINIA

BROWNIE DATE LOAF

Serves: 16-18   Oven: 350°

1¼ cups flour, sifted	½ cup water
¾ tsp. soda	6-oz. pkg. semi-sweet
½ tsp. salt	chocolate morsels
8-oz. pkg. dates, pitted and	2 eggs, slightly beaten
chopped	½ cup orange juice
¾ cup brown sugar, packed	½ cup milk
½ cup margarine	1 cup nuts, chopped

Sift together flour, soda and salt; set aside. Combine dates, sugar, margarine and water in a saucepan. Heat, stirring constantly, until dates soften. Remove from heat; stir in chocolate morsels and eggs. Add sifted dry ingredients to chocolate mixture alternately with milk and orange juice. Blend thoroughly. Stir in nuts. Bake in a greased and floured 9 x 13-inch pan at 350° for 25 to 30 minutes.

MRS. JACK W. SMITH

ORANGE RIND LOAF CAKE

Serves: 10-12   Oven: 350°

1 cup raisins
1 cup nuts
Rind of 2 oranges
½ cup shortening
1 cup sugar

2 eggs
1 tsp. soda
1 cup buttermilk
1 tsp. salt
2 cups flour

Grind together raisins, nuts and orange rind. Cream shortening and sugar. Add eggs, mix well. Add soda to buttermilk and add alternately with dry ingredients. Add ground raisins, nuts and rind. Mix thoroughly. Bake in greased and floured large loaf pan for 40 to 50 minutes, or until toothpick comes out clean. While warm and still in pan, glaze with:

1 cup sugar   1 cup orange juice

Heat these together and slowly pour over cake until all is absorbed.

MRS. JOHN M. OSTNER

PINEAPPLE CAKE

Serves: 20   Oven: 375°

2 cups sugar
2 cups flour
2 tsp. soda
2 eggs, beaten

8¼-oz. can crushed pine-
  apple
1 tsp. vanilla

Mix dry ingredients. Add eggs, undrained pineapple and vanilla; mix thoroughly. Pour into a 13 x 9-inch greased and floured cake pan. Bake at 375° for 30 minutes.

ICING:

½ cup butter
1 cup sugar
1 cup evaporated milk

1 cup pecans or almonds,
  chopped

Boil the butter, sugar and milk for 7 minutes, stirring occasionally. After icing has cooked, stir until slightly cooled. Add nuts. Pour over cake while it is still warm. Cut into squares for easy serving.

Best the second day! It's not a beautiful cake, but oh so delicious.

MRS. JAMES B. KALMBACH
DALLAS, TEXAS

LEMON PINEAPPLE LAYER CAKE

Serves: 12   Oven: 350°

1½ cups sugar
½ cup butter
2½ cups cake flour
3 tsp. baking powder
½ tsp. salt

1 cup milk
1 tsp. vanilla
5 egg whites
¼ tsp. salt
¼ tsp. cream of tartar

Cream sugar and butter until fluffy. Sift together flour, baking powder and ½ teaspoon salt. Add sifted ingredients alternately with milk to creamed mixture; add vanilla. Beat egg whites and ¼ teaspoon salt partially; then add cream of tartar; continue beating until whites hold their shape. Fold into batter. Grease and flour 2 9-inch layer pans; pour into batter and bake at 350° for 20 to 25 minutes. Cool cakes. Frost with Lemon Pineapple Filling.

LEMON PINEAPPLE FILLING:

5 egg yolks
2 lemons, juice and rind
Small can of crushed pineapple, undrained

3 Tb. flour
1½ cups sugar
1 lump butter

Mix all ingredients. Cook until it thickens to a custard consistency. Let cool; then use to cover tops of layers and sides of cake.

MRS. STANLEY K. BRADSHAW, JR.

SPECIAL CHEESECAKE

Serves: 20   Oven: 350°

CRUST:

14 Zwieback crackers
½ cup butter, melted

½ cup sugar

Mix three ingredients together. Line bottom of a large cheese cake pan (9½ x 3-inch).

FILLING:

3 lbs. cream cheese, softened
6 eggs
½ cup plus 2 Tb. flour
2½ cups sugar

1½ cups heavy cream
1 tsp. vanilla
Juice of 1 lemon

Mix all ingredients well and pour into crust lined cake pan. Place a pan with an inch of water in it under cake while baking. Bake at 350° for 1 hour or until cake begins to brown on top. Then turn off oven and let cake remain in oven for 30 minutes with oven door closed. Chill before unmolding. This makes a large rich cake which serves at least 20. It also freezes beautifully.

This is an old family recipe passed on to me by my aunt, Mrs. Jack Carnes.

MRS. JAMES R. WALT

PRUNE CAKE

Serves: 12-15   Oven: 325°

1 cup prunes, chopped	1 tsp. soda
2 cups sugar	1 tsp. cinnamon
1 cup salad oil	1 tsp. cloves
3 eggs	½ tsp. salt
2 cups flour	1 cup buttermilk

Cut up prunes; soak overnight in enough water to cover. Combine sugar and oil; let stand 5 minutes. Add eggs, mix well. Combine flour, soda, spices and salt. Add to sugar mixture, alternating with buttermilk. Add drained prunes. Pour into a 9 by 13-inch greased and floured pan. Bake in 325° oven for 45 to 55 minutes or until toothpick inserted in center comes out clean.

MRS. CARL A. ROSENBAUM
SCOTT, ARKANSAS

CARAMEL ICING:

2 cups brown sugar	1 tsp. vanilla
⅛ tsp. salt	1 Tb. light cream
4 Tb. butter	1 cup pecans, chopped
⅔ cup milk	

Combine brown sugar, salt, butter and milk in a heavy saucepan. Cook to soft ball stage or 235° on a candy thermometer. Cool and beat until thick. Add vanilla and 1 tablespoon or more cream to make spreadable. Add nuts.

This is also delicious on spice cakes of any kind.

MRS. ROBERT L. DORTCH, JR.

OATMEAL CAKE

Serves: 12   Oven: 350°

1 cup quick cook oats	2 eggs
1½ cups water, boiling	1⅓ cups flour
1 cup brown sugar	1 tsp. soda
1 cup sugar	1 tsp. cinnamon
½ cup shortening	

Pour boiling water over oats; set aside. Cream sugars and shortening. Add eggs to creamed mixture, beating well. Mix flour, soda and spice; add to creamed mixture; then add oats. Mix thoroughly. Bake at 350° for 40 minutes in a greased and floured 8 x 13-inch pan. Add topping to hot cake.

TOPPING:

½ cup butter	1 cup nuts, chopped
1 cup brown sugar	1 cup coconut
1 Tb. cream, heavy	

Cook all ingredients together for 1 minute. Pour over warm cake.

MRS. ED CHERRY, JR.
JONESBORO, ARKANSAS

GERMAN CHEESECAKE

Serves: 8-10   Oven: 250°

½ cup butter, melted   ⅓ cup flour
6-oz. pkg. Zwieback   3 Tb. lemon juice
½ cup brown sugar   ½ tsp. vanilla
1 Tb. cinnamon   1 cup heavy cream
4 eggs, beaten   2 lbs. cottage cheese
1 cup sugar   1½ tsp. grated lemon rind
¼ tsp. salt

Finely crush Zwieback; add melted butter, brown sugar and cinnamon. Mix well and set aside. To well-beaten eggs, beat in sugar, flour, salt, lemon juice and vanilla; add cream and beat at cake mixing speed. Drain off at least half the liquid in cottage cheese and either press cheese through ricer or blend in a blender until very smooth. Add cottage cheese; beat for 5 minutes at cake speed; add lemon rind. Line the bottom of an 8-inch spring form pan with half the Zwieback mixture. Gently pour batter on top; then top with remainder of Zwieback mixture. Bake for 1 hour at 250°; turn off oven, open door and leave cheesecake in oven for 1 hour. Chill at least 6 hours before removing mold. Suggest a cookie sheet under cake pan while baking to avoid dripping in oven. This cheesecake can be frozen for 2 months if you have the will power to leave it.

MRS. SIDNEY A. NEWCOMB

IRISH POTATO CAKE (GERMAN CHOCOLATE)

Serves: 12   Oven: 375°

1 cup shortening   1 tsp. cinnamon
2 cups sugar   ¼ tsp. allspice
4 eggs   ¼ tsp. nutmeg
1 cup warm mashed potatoes   3 Tb. cocoa
1 tsp. soda   1 tsp. vanilla
1 cup buttermilk   ½ cup pecans, chopped
2½ cups flour

Cream shortening and sugar. Add eggs one at a time and beat well after each addition. Add warm potatoes. Add soda to buttermilk. Add spices to flour. Alternate adding sifted dry ingredients and buttermilk to creamed mixture. Beat after each addition. Stir in vanilla and pecans. Bake in two greased and floured 9-inch pans at 375° for 35 to 40 minutes.

GERMAN CHOCOLATE ICING:

1 cup sugar   3 egg yolks, beaten
½ cup heavy cream   1 cup pecans, chopped
¼ cup butter   1 cup angel flake coconut

Cook sugar, cream, butter and yolks together until thick. Add pecans and coconut; blend well. Spread between layers and over cooled cake.

MRS. GILBERT BUCHANAN

ITALIAN CREAM CAKE

Serves: 18-20   Oven: 350°

2 cups sugar
½ cup butter, softened
½ cup shortening
5 eggs, separated
1 tsp. soda

1 cup buttermilk
2 cups flour, sifted
1 cup angel flake coconut
1 tsp. vanilla

Cream sugar, butter and shortening. Add egg yolks, beating after each addition. Dissolve soda in buttermilk and add alternately with flour to egg mixture. Add coconut; fold in stiffly beaten egg whites; add vanilla. Pour into three 8-inch greased and floured cake pans. Bake at 350° for 25 to 30 minutes. Cool cakes.

ICING:

1½ lbs. powdered sugar, sifted
8-oz. pkg. Philadelphia cream cheese, softened

½ cup butter, soft
1½ tsp. vanilla
1 cup pecans, chopped
Milk to moisten

Mix butter and cheese; add sugar, vanilla and nuts. Moisten with milk to spreading consistency. Ice only tops of layers.

MRS. J. F. SAWYER
BENTON, ARKANSAS

PECAN CAKE

Serves: 12   Oven: 325°

2 cups sugar
2 cups butter
6 eggs
¾ oz. pure lemon extract
4 cups flour, sifted

1 tsp. baking powder
8-oz. pkg. dates
4 cups pecan halves
1 lb. whole candied cherries

Cream sugar and butter together. Beat eggs until lemon colored, and add to the butter mixture. Mix well. Add lemon extract, flour, and baking powder. Mix. Dredge dates, pecans, and cherries with flour and add to mixture. Grease and flour an angel food tube pan and pour in cake mixture. Bake for 2 hours in 325° preheated oven. Test with cake straw. Cool the cake until it can be removed from pan, but is still warm. Glaze with the following mixture.

GLAZE:

2 cups sugar
1 cup orange juice

1 tsp. grated orange rind
1 tsp. grated lemon rind

Cook the glaze in a heavy saucepan until it will spin a thread. Drizzle over slightly warm cake.

Delicious substitute for fruit cake.

MRS. W. RANDALL BYARS

RUM CAKE

Serves: 12-15   Oven: 350°

1 cup seedless raisins	1 tsp. cinnamon
2 cups water	½ tsp. allspice
2 tsp. soda	1 tsp. nutmeg
¾ cup shortening	1 tsp. cloves
1½ cups brown sugar	1⅓ cups nuts, broken
2 eggs, separated	4 Tb. rum
2 cups cake flour	2 tsp. vanilla

Boil raisins, uncovered, in the water until liquid is reduced to 1 cup (about 20 minutes). Cool and add soda to raisin water. Cream shortening, add sugar a little at a time, then beaten egg yolks. Next add raisins and raisin water alternately with dry ingredients which have been sifted together. Add nuts, vanilla and rum. Lastly add stiffly beaten egg whites. Bake in 2 greased and floured 9-inch layer pans at 350° for 30 minutes. Cool cakes and frost.

RUM FROSTING:

1 lb. powdered sugar	2 Tb. rum
1 egg	1 tsp. vanilla
½ cup soft butter	

Break whole egg into sugar. Add rest of ingredients. Beat until light. Spread between and over layers.

MRS. RAYMOND COOK

HOLIDAY JAM CAKE

Serves: 18-20   Oven: 300°

1 cup butter	½ tsp. nutmeg
2 cups sugar	½ tsp. ground cloves
3 eggs, separated	1 cup seedless blackberry jam
½ cup buttermilk	1 cup broken pecans
1 tsp. soda	1 cup seedless raisins
3 cups sifted flour	1 cup dates, quartered
1 tsp. cinnamon	lengthwise
½ tsp. allspice	

Cream butter and sugar. Beat egg yolks until thick and pale in color, add to creamed butter and sugar. Dissolve soda in buttermilk; beat into butter, egg and sugar mixture. Gradually add flour, spices and jam, alternating jam with dry ingredients. Fold in stiffly beaten egg whites by hand. Roll fruit and nuts in a little flour and add to batter. Line bottom of large tube pan with heavy brown paper. Grease and flour pan and liner well. Bake in preheated 300° oven for 3 to 3½ hours. Test with toothpick or broomstraw. Invert on rack to cool. When thoroughly cool, cake may be stored in a tin box with apples or wrapped in a soft cloth sprinkled with bourbon, brandy or sherry.

It is better when aged and will keep in a cool spot for 6 weeks.

MRS. ROBERT B. ROACH

DARK FRUIT CAKE

Yield: 20 lbs.   Oven: 225° — 275°

1 lb. butter, softened
1 lb. sugar
1 dozen eggs
1 lb. flour
3 tsp. cinnamon
2 tsp. allspice
2 tsp. cloves
1 tsp. nutmeg
1 tsp. salt
1½ cups dark corn syrup

½ cup sherry or whiskey
4 lbs. mixed chopped fruit, candied
2 lbs. dates, pitted and chopped
4 lbs. raisins
3 11-oz. pkgs. currants
2 lbs. pecans, shelled
1 lb. almonds, shelled and slivered

In a large mixing bowl, cream butter and sugar, then eggs one at a time, beating well after each addition. Sift flour and spices and salt together; add alternately with corn syrup and sherry to the batter. In a very large pan mix the fruit, nuts, raisins and currants until mixture is uniform. Add the batter; then mix thoroughly. Round fruit cake tin or square bread or loaf pans are greased and lined with waxed paper which has also been greased. Paper should completely cover all parts of pan. Fill pans to within one inch of top and press down evenly and firmly into corners. Cover with greased waxed paper and with greased aluminum foil caps over tops of pans. Place pans in a 225° oven for 2 hours with pans of steaming water in bottom of oven. Then remove pans of water, aluminum foil tops, and waxed paper tops. Bake at 275° about 45 minutes until cakes are slightly dry looking and lightly browned. Watch carefully so as not to burn cakes. Remove cakes from pans, remove waxed paper, allow to cool, then wrap in plastic wrap and foil. Makes twenty pounds. Cakes will keep in a cool place for 3 months, after then refrigerate.

This was my grandmother's receipe!

MRS. GUS FULK, III

MOTHER-IN-LAW'S CAKE

Serves: 18-20   Oven: 325°

1 box white cake mix
3¾-oz. box lemon instant pudding

¾ cup salad oil
10 oz. 7-UP
4 eggs

Mix first 4 ingredients. Add eggs one at a time, beating well after each addition. Pour batter into a greased and floured Bundt or tube pan; bake at 325° for 50 minutes or until done. Remove cake from pan while warm. Drizzle glaze over warm cake, if desired.

LEMON GLAZE:

5 Tb. lemon juice

1½ cups powdered sugar

MRS. WILLIAM RALPH COOK
WYNNE, ARKANSAS

PLUM PUDDING (GREAT GRANDMOTHER BLACKMAN'S)

Serves: 10-12

1 lb. ground suet	2 tsp. nutmeg
2¼ cups flour	2¾ tsp. allspice
8 oz. bread crumbs	Grated rind and juice of
1½ cups sugar	2 lemons
1½ 11-oz. boxes currants	4 oz. brandy
1 lb. raisins	6 eggs
½ lb. mixed peel	Milk for mixing, about 3 Tb.
4 oz. almonds, chopped	

Have suet ground fine, then chop with a knife until as fine as possible. Add the flour a little at a time as you chop. Fine grind raisins and peel. Mix suet, flour, raisins, peel and currants; add all other ingredients and mix thoroughly with your hands as you would a meat loaf. When completely mixed, divide into 4 one quart greased pudding or pyrex molds. Molds must have a lip. Cover tops of bowls with greased paper (paper bag cut to fit top of bowl). Take a square piece of sheeting, cover top of bowl and tightly tie string around under the lip. Take corners of cloth and tie in a knot above bowl; this is your handle for lifting and lowering into kettles. Boil 6 to 7 hours on a trivet in covered kettles. (Water should boil gently. Add more boiling water as needed.) When pudding is done (cake tester inserted comes out clean) remove mold to wire rack; uncover and let cool completely in mold. To store, invert and lift off mold. Wrap in plastic wrap, then in foil. Will keep in refrigerator several weeks. To serve: return to mold, cover and resteam as directed above for an hour until pudding is thoroughly heated. Remove from mold, place on a heatproof serving dish. Heat 3 tablespoons of rum or brandy and pour over pudding. Set aflame as you carry to the table. Serve with Hot Sherry Sauce.

HOT SHERRY SAUCE:

½ cup butter	¼ cup sherry
1 cup sugar	

Cream butter and sugar. Stir these ingredients over heat; permit to boil. Remove at once. Add sherry.

In England, the Traditional Plum Pudding contains goodies for everyone: button for the bachelor, ring for the next married, thimble for the old maid, closed safety pin for the next child and nickles, dimes and quarters for the kids. These may be boiled and mixed into the batter. The Plum Pudding is served on Christmas Eve with flaming brandy and a sprig of holly.

MRS. WILLIAM T. GILMORE, JR.

THE PRESIDENT'S CAKE

Serves: 18-20　　　　　　　　　　　　　　Oven: 350°

1 box buttercake mix
½ pt. sour cream
¾ cup salad oil
½ cup sugar

4 eggs
3 Tb. brown sugar
2 tsp. cinnamon
½ to 1 cup chopped pecans

Mix together first 4 ingredients; add eggs one at a time, beating well after each addition. Grease and flour Bundt or tube pan. Put almost half of the batter in the pan. Mix brown sugar, cinnamon and nuts. Sprinkle over batter in pan. Carefully add remainder of batter. Bake at 350° for 60 to 80 minutes. Cool for 20 to 30 minutes then remove from pan. Glaze the cake.

GLAZE:

1 cup powdered sugar
1 tsp. vanilla

Enough milk to make thin glaze

This is delicious. Place on a cake stand and watch it dwindle away.

MRS. WENDELL TACKETT
MEMPHIS, TENNESSEE

CINNAMON COFFEE CAKE

Serves: 18-20　　　　　　　　　　　　　　Oven: 350°

1 box yellow cake mix
3¾-oz. box vanilla instant
　pudding
⅔ cup salad oil
¾ cup water

4 eggs
1 tsp. vanilla
1 tsp. butter flavoring
½ to 1 cup brown sugar
¼ cup chopped nuts

FILLING:

¼ cup sugar

2 tsp. cinnamon

Mix first 7 ingredients for 8 minutes. Grease and flour Bundt pan. Cover bottom of pan with brown sugar, sprinkle chopped nuts over brown sugar. Alternate cake batter and a sprinkling of filling mixture in three layers. Bake at 350° for 40 to 50 minutes.

GLAZE:

1 cup powdered sugar
½ tsp. vanilla

½ tsp. butter flavoring
Enough milk to thin glaze

Glaze with ½ of mixture while hot and still in pan. Cool cake for several minutes, then remove from pan. Top cake with remaining glaze.

MRS. W. C. SCHROEPFER, JR.

APRICOT NECTAR CAKE

Serves: 18-20   Oven: 325°

1 box yellow cake mix   ¾ cup salad oil
3-oz. box lemon gelatin   4 eggs
¾ cup apricot nectar   2 Tb. lemon juice
1 tsp. vanilla

Mix ingredients together, adding eggs one at a time, beating well after each addition. Beat for 5 more minutes. Pour into greased and floured Bundt or tube pan, bake at 325° for 55 minutes. This cake is delicious plain, but may be glazed or soaked. To soak, poke holes, with an ice pick, in the hot cake while still in pan. Pour over cake a mixture of:

1 cup powdered sugar   Dash of salt
½ cup lemon juice

Remove from pan immediately. For a top glaze, remove warm cake from pan and drizzle on top a mixture of:

1 cup powdered sugar   Dash of salt
2 Tb. lemon juice

MRS. JOHN W. REX

STRAWBERRY CAKE

Serves: 12   Oven: 350°

1 box white cake mix   10-oz. box frozen straw-
3-oz. box strawberry gelatin   berries, thawed
1 cup salad oil   1 cup coconut
½ cup milk   1 cup chopped pecans
4 eggs

Mix dry ingredients. Add oil and mix; add milk and mix. Add eggs one at a time, beating well after each addition. Add strawberries, coconut and nuts. Grease and flour three layer pans. Bake at 350° for 20 to 25 minutes. Cool in pans for 10 minutes, remove cake, cool thoroughly.

STRAWBERRY ICING:

½ cup butter, very soft   1 lb. powdered sugar
10-oz. box frozen straw-   ½ cup chopped pecans
    berries, thawed, well   ½ cup coconut
    drained

Cream butter and sugar gradually in small amounts. Add strawberries, pecans and coconut. Mix well. Spread between layers and let drizzle down sides of cake.

MRS. JACK GARDNER

APPLESAUCE JAM CAKE

Serves: 18-20   Oven: 350°

1 box applesauce cake mix
3¾-oz. pkg. butterscotch
  instant pudding
1 cup water
¾ cup salad oil

4 eggs
½ cup seedless black raspberry or strawberry
  preserves
1 cup nuts, chopped

GLAZE:
1½ cups powdered sugar   Juice of 1 lemon

Blend cake and pudding mixes with water and oil. Add eggs one at
a time, beating well after each addition. Fold in preserves and nuts.
Bake in a greased and floured tube or Bundt pan at 350° for 50 to
60 minutes. Test cake with toothpick. Cool cake for 5 minutes;
remove from pan; glaze cake while still warm with juice of lemon
and powdered sugar.

RUM CAKE

Serves: 18-20   Oven: 325°

1 box yellow cake mix
3¾-oz. box instant vanilla
  pudding
½ cup salad oil

½ cup water
½ cup rum, light, dry
4 eggs

Mix first 5 ingredients together and beat well. Add eggs one at a
time, beating well after each addition. Pour batter into a greased
and floured Bundt or tube pan. Bake for 1 hour at 325°. Prepare
glaze 15 minutes before cake is done. Remove cake from oven. Poke
holes in cake with an ice pick; pour glaze over cake while still in
pan. Completely cool cake before removing from pan. Cake ages
well, may be made days in advance and freezes well, too.

RUM GLAZE:
1 cup sugar
½ cup butter

¼ cup rum, light, dry
¼ cup water

Combine ingredients in pan and boil gently 1 minute.

MRS. JAMES C. ROBINSON, JR.

SHERRY CAKE

Serves: 18-20   Oven: 350°

1 box yellow cake mix
3¾-oz. box vanilla instant
  pudding
4 eggs

¾ cup salad oil
¾ cup sherry
1 tsp. nutmeg
Powdered sugar

Combine all ingredients; mix for 5 minutes at medium speed. Pour
into a greased and floured Bundt or tube pan. Bake at 350° for 45
minutes. Cool 5 minutes; remove from pan. Sprinkle with sifted
powdered sugar.

MRS. CHARLES MCDADE

ANGEL TOFFEE CAKE ROLL

Serves: 16   Oven: 375°

1 angel food cake mix   6 or 7 oz. Heath Toffee bars,
10-oz. carton non-dairy   crushed
   whipped topping   ½ to 1 cup powdered sugar
   (or whipped cream)

Line two 17 x 11-inch pans with waxed paper. Mix cake according to package directions. Spread batter evenly in two pans. Place oven rack 4 to 5 inches from bottom of oven. Bake one sheet at a time at 375° for 11 to 13 minutes or until light golden brown on top. When done, turn out onto a kitchen towel that has been dusted with powdered sugar. Peel off the waxed paper and roll up cake in the towel. Leave rolled until completely cool. Repeat with second sheet. When cool, unroll and spread whipped topping or whipped cream over complete surface, ½ inch thick. Sprinkle crushed toffee bars over surface and lightly reroll. Cover and refrigerate. Each roll may be sliced into 8 slices for serving.

MRS. A. BRUCE CARTER

CAKE ICINGS

HEAVENLY WHITE FROSTING

4½ cups sugar   6 egg whites, stiffly beaten
1 cup water   ⅓ cup powdered sugar
6 Tb. light corn syrup

In a saucepan mix sugar, water and corn syrup; cook to soft ball stage (238° on a candy thermometer). To egg whites, which have been beaten stiff but not dry, slowly add hot sugar mixture, thoroughly beating until icing is like cream. Then add powdered sugar.

This icing goes deliciously on any cake!

Variations:
Add instant coffee, rum, crème de menthe or any flavor you like.

For angel food cakes, flavor with juice and rind of any fruit you choose. Garnish with slices of fruit or berries.

Chiffon, layer or angel food cakes, after icing, may be drizzled with melted chocolate or sprinkled with chopped nuts or fresh or toasted coconut.

Before icing your cake, split layers and fill with pudding or pie filling, such as lemon filling with yellow cake.

Do your own thing!

CHOCOLATE FUDGE FROSTING

2 oz. chocolate	2 Tb. butter
1½ cups sugar	1 Tb. corn syrup
7 Tb. milk	½ tsp. salt
2 Tb. shortening	1 tsp. vanilla

Bring ingredients, except vanilla, to a rolling boil, stirring constantly. Continue stirring and boil for 1 minute. Cool. Add vanilla. Beat to spreading consistency.

Delicious on white or chocolate cake.

MRS. STANLEY K. BRADSHAW, JR.

CARAMEL ICING

3 cups sugar	1 tsp. vanilla
1 cup milk	1 Tb. butter
1 Tb. light corn syrup	1 Tb. cornstarch (optional)
Pinch of salt	

Put 2½ cups sugar, milk and corn syrup into top of double boiler; let come to boil. Stir and watch carefully to prevent burning. Put ½ cup sugar into iron skillet and heat until brown or caramelized. When both mixtures are equally hot, pour caramelized sugar into milk mixture. Cook until a soft ball forms when dropped in cold water. Add salt, vanilla and butter. Stir; then cool a little, then beat until thickened. (If icing is not thick enough, add 1 tablespoon cornstarch moistened with milk, then continue to beat.)

MILDRED BELL

SUGAR PLUM FROSTING

¾ cup brown sugar	2 egg whites, stiffly beaten
¾ cup white sugar	¼ tsp. salt
4 Tb. hot water	½ tsp. almond extract
2 Tb. strong coffee	¼ tsp. baking powder
¼ tsp. cream of tartar	

In a saucepan, boil sugars, water, coffee and cream of tartar until the mixture spins a thread (248° on a candy thermometer). Remove from heat, pour very slowly into stiffly beaten egg whites; beat until thick. Add salt, almond extract and baking powder; beat to spreading consistency. Ice the cake generously.

ORANGE BUTTER ICING

½ cup butter, softened	1 tsp. vanilla
1 orange, ground peel and all	Orange juice
1-lb. box powdered sugar	

Beat all ingredients, except orange juice, at high speed until smooth, adding orange juice to spreading consistency.

MRS. COOPER JACOWAY

BUTTER FROSTING

½ cup butter
2½ cups powdered sugar
¼ tsp. salt

3 to 4 Tb. milk
1 tsp. vanilla

Cream butter, sugar and salt, in small amounts, beating continuously. Add milk to spreading consistency and vanilla.

Variations:
Add fruit juice instead of milk plus 2 teaspoons rind of the fruit.
Add any flavoring you choose instead of vanilla.
Add 2 tablespoons instant coffee.
Add 2 squares melted bitter chocolate.
Add 3 tablespoons mashed banana plus 1 tablespoon lemon juice.
Do your own thing!

WHIPPED CREAM FROSTING

1 cup cream, heavy
2 tsp. sugar

½ tsp. of any chosen
flavoring

Beat together in a bowl until thick. Spread lavishly on any kind of cake and refrigerate. Garnish with chopped nuts or fresh fruit.

SMALL CAKES

CARAMEL MERINGUE BARS

Yield: 40-60 small bars   Oven: 350°

¾ cup soft butter
½ cup brown sugar, packed
½ cup sugar
3 eggs, separated
1 tsp. vanilla
2 cups sifted flour
1 tsp. baking powder

¼ tsp. salt
¼ tsp. soda
6-oz. pkg. semi-sweet
  chocolate bits
1 cup coconut, flaked
¾ cup chopped nuts
1 cup brown sugar

Blend butter, ½ cup brown sugar, granulated sugar, egg yolks and vanilla. Beat 2 minutes with electric mixer, scraping bowl constantly. Sift flour, baking powder, salt, and soda. Stir into creamed mixture until thoroughly mixed. Spread or pat dough into greased 9½ x 13-inch pan. Sprinkle with chocolate bits, coconut, and nuts. Beat egg whites until frothy. Add 1 cup brown sugar. Beat until stiff but not dry. Spread on top of chocolate mixture and bake for 35 to 40 minutes at 350°. Cool. Cut into bars.

MRS. MARION BECHTEL
VENICE, FLORIDA

BROWNIES (ICED)

Yield: 25 squares   Oven: 350°

½ cup margarine	1 cup flour, sifted
3 squares bitter chocolate	½ tsp. salt
2 cups sugar	1 tsp. vanilla
4 eggs	

Melt margarine and chocolate over low heat in heavy saucepan. Let cool. Drop into cooled mixture sugar and stir until well mixed. Add eggs one at a time and mix well. Add flour, salt and vanilla. Grease and flour a 9 x 13-inch pan. Bake 25 to 30 minutes at 350°. Do not overcook.

FROSTING:

¼ cup margarine	1½ tsp. vanilla
1 square bitter chocolate	1½ tsp. lemon juice
1 cup powdered sugar	1 cup pecans, chopped
1 egg	

Melt margarine and chocolate over low heat. When melted add powdered sugar. Remove from heat and stir. Add egg and mix well. Add vanilla and lemon juice. Add nuts. Spread on brownies while warm.

MRS. ROBERT M. BRAMBL
MINNEAPOLIS, MINNESOTA

CHOCOLATE DEVILS

Yield: 15-18 squares   Oven: 350°

4 oz. bitter chocolate	¼ tsp. salt
1 cup butter	½ cup pecans, chopped
4 eggs	1 cup semi-sweet chocolate
2 cups sugar	bits
2 tsp. vanilla	16 to 20 marshmallows
1 cup flour, sifted	

Melt chocolate and butter. Beat eggs until lemon colored. Gradually beat in sugar until fluffy. Stir in chocolate and butter mixture and vanilla. Blend in flour, salt, nuts, and chocolate bits. Bake in a greased 9 x 13-inch pan for 30 minutes at 350°. Remove from oven and dot with marshmallows. Return to oven long enough to melt marshmallows. Spread them and let cool.

FUDGE FROSTING:

2 cups powdered sugar	⅛ tsp. salt
½ cup cocoa	1 tsp. vanilla
¼ cup butter, soft	5 to 7 Tb. milk

Blend sugar, cocoa, butter, salt and vanilla. Add milk to make spreadable.

MRS. LEONARD THOMPSON

CHEESE BARS

Serves: 12   **Oven: 350°**

CRUST:

⅓ cup margarine, melted   Dash of salt
⅓ cup brown sugar, packed   ½ cup nuts, broken
1 cup flour

Cream melted margarine and brown sugar together. Add flour, salt, and nuts. Mix until crumbly. Pat into a square pan and save one cup mixture for topping. Bake 15 minutes at 350°.

FILLING:

¼ cup sugar   1 Tb. lemon juice
8-oz. pkg. cream cheese   ½ tsp. vanilla
1 egg   Dash of salt
2 Tb. milk

Mix above ingredients together and beat well. Spread over crust and add one cup topping. Bake at 350° for 25 minutes. After cooled keep in refrigerator.

This recipe may be doubled and placed in a pan 8 x 12 x 2.

A nice change from the usual chocolate bar.

MRS. JOE BATES

CREAM CHEESE BROWNIES

Yield: 18 squares   **Oven: 350°**

4-oz. pkg. German sweet   ½ cup plus 1 Tb. flour
  chocolate   1½ tsp. vanilla
5 Tb. butter   ½ tsp. baking powder
3-oz. pkg. cream cheese   ¼ tsp. salt
1 cup sugar   ½ cup nuts, chopped
3 eggs   ¼ tsp. almond extract

Melt chocolate with 3 tablespoons butter over low heat, stirring constantly. Cool. Cream remaining butter with cream cheese until soft. Gradually add ¼ cup sugar. Blend in 1 egg, 1 tablespoon flour, and ½ teaspoon vanilla. Set aside.

Beat remaining eggs until thick. Gradually add remaining sugar. Add baking powder, salt, and remaining flour. Blend in cooled chocolate mixture, nuts, almond extract, and remaining vanilla. Measure 1 cup chocolate batter and set aside.

Spread remaining chocolate batter in a greased 9-inch square pan. Top with cheese mixture. Drop measured chocolate batter from tablespoon onto cheese mixture; swirl to marbleized. Bake at 350° for 35 to 40 minutes. Cool. Cut and store in refrigerator.

MRS. SMITH GROBMYER

CANADIAN SQUARES

Yield: 20-25 bars

CRUST:

½ cup butter
¼ cup sugar
1 egg
⅓ cup cocoa
1 tsp. vanilla

2 cups graham cracker
  crumbs
4-oz. can coconut (flaked)
½ cup chopped pecans

Melt butter. Blend in other ingredients. Press into 9 x 14-inch pan.

FILLING:

¼ cup soft butter
2 Tb. vanilla instant pudding
  mix

3 Tb. milk
2 cups sifted powdered sugar

Cream butter. Blend in other ingredients. Spread over first mixture. Chill.

TOPPING:

3 oz. semi-sweet chocolate   1 Tb. butter

Melt chocolate and butter over low heat. Spread quickly over chilled mixture. Chill. Let sit at room temperature for 5 minutes before cutting into bars.

MRS. JOE BUCHMAN

CHESS CAKES

Serves: 24   Oven: 350°-325°

¾ cup butter
1½ cups flour, sifted

3 Tb. sugar

Cream butter, stir in flour and sugar. Smooth with fingers into an 11 x 7-inch pan. Bake at 350° for 15 to 20 minutes or until lightly brown.

FILLING:

3 eggs, separated
2¼ cups dark brown sugar,
  packed
½ tsp. vanilla

1 cup pecans or walnuts,
  coarsely chopped
½ cup powdered sugar

Beat yolks; add sugar gradually until thick and soggy looking. Add vanilla and nuts. Whip egg whites stiff, fold in thoroughly. Pour filling over baked base; bake another 40 minutes at 325°. Sprinkle with sifted powdered sugar. Cool, cut in 1½-inch squares.

Tastes rich and delicious!

MRS. MILFORD DAVIS, JR.

CARAMEL FUDGE SQUARES

Yield: 9 squares   Oven: 375°

½ cup margarine   1 cup flour
1 cup brown sugar (packed)   1 tsp. baking powder
1 egg   1 cup chopped nuts

Cream margarine and brown sugar. Add egg and beat well. Sift flour and baking powder together and add to mixture. Fold in nuts. Spread in small, greased square pan. Bake at 375° for 25 to 30 minutes. Allow to cool and cut into squares.

MRS. BERT PARKE

LEBKUCHEN

Yield: 25 bars   Oven: 325°

3 egg yolks   1 cup dark "Brer Rabbit"
1 whole egg   syrup
¾ cup sugar   Nuts (optional)
1½ cups flour   4 tsp. bourbon
1 rounded tsp. baking powder   1 oz. bitter chocolate, melted
1½ tsp. cinnamon   in 2 Tb. margarine
½ tsp. allspice   Powdered sugar (optional)
½ tsp. ground cloves

Cream egg yolks and whole egg with sugar until smooth. Add dry ingredients and syrup and mix thoroughly. Add nuts, if desired. Add bourbon, melted chocolate and margarine; mix well.

Pour into greased baking pan 10 x 13 x 1½-inch. Bake at 325° for 25 minutes or until toothpick can be withdrawn without sticking. Garnish with powdered sugar while hot, if desired.

Men love this dessert.

MRS. HERBERT BESSER

COOKIES AND CANDIES

COOKIES

RICH BUTTER COOKIES

Yield: 5 dozen   **Oven: 375°**

1 cup butter	2½ cups flour
1½ cups sugar	1 tsp. baking soda
1 egg	1 tsp. cream of tartar
1 tsp. vanilla	¼ tsp. salt

Cream butter; add sugar gradually, creaming until fluffy. Add unbeaten egg, vanilla. Beat well. Sift together dry ingredients. Blend with creamed mixture. Drop by teaspoons onto ungreased cookie sheet. Bake at 375° for 8 minutes.

Easy, chewy and good!

MRS. JAMES N. COOK

MOLASSES SUGAR COOKIES

Yield: 3 dozen   **Oven: 375°**

¾ cup shortening	2 cups flour
1 cup sugar	½ tsp. cloves
¼ cup molasses	½ tsp. ginger
1 egg, beaten	1 tsp. cinnamon
2 tsp. baking soda	½ tsp. salt

Melt shortening in a 2 or 3 quart saucepan over low heat; cool. Add sugar, molasses, and egg; beat well. Sift together soda, flour, cloves, ginger, cinnamon, and salt and add to molasses mixture. Mix well. Chill. Form dough into one inch balls, roll in granulated sugar and place on a greased cookie sheet 2 inches apart. Bake at 375° for 8 to 10 minutes.

CINNAMON STRIPS

Yield: 48 strips   **Oven: 350°**

1 cup butter, less 1 Tb.	1 cup sugar
2 egg yolks	2 egg whites
2 cups sifted flour	1 cup finely chopped nuts
1 Tb. cinnamon	

Grease a large cookie sheet. Mix together butter, egg yolks, flour, cinnamon, and sugar; pat mixture out on cookie sheet. Pour unbeaten egg whites over dough. (I take my fingers and spread the egg whites and it is easier to smooth the top.) Pour off excess egg white. Sprinkle nuts over top and pat them in a little or they will fall off when baked. Bake at 350° about 25 minutes, depending on thickness. Cut into desired lengths and remove from cookie sheet to cool. Store in tins.

MRS. SLOAN CUMMINS
PINE BLUFF, ARKANSAS

KOULORGIA
(Coffee Cookies)

1 lb. clarified butter	6 cups flour
1½ cups sugar	4 tsp. baking powder
4 eggs	Beaten egg
3 tsp. vanilla	Sesame seeds

After clarifying butter, pour in a bowl and refrigerate until set. Remove from refrigerator and cream butter and sugar. Add eggs one at a time, beating well after each. Add vanilla. Sift flour and add baking powder. Combine with butter mixture and mix well (probably with your hands). Refrigerate until dough sets. Remove dough and roll small balls into pencil-size strips, fold over and twist into any form desired. Brush with beaten egg and sprinkle with sesame seeds. Bake at 350° for 20 minutes.

MRS. GEORGE POLYCHRON

BROWN SUGAR CHEWS

Yield: 36 cookies   Oven: 325°

1 egg white	Pinch of salt
1 cup brown sugar	¾ cup nuts, chopped
1 Tb. flour	

Beat egg white until stiff froth; add brown sugar and continue beating. Stir in flour and salt. Fold in pecans. Drop by small teaspoons on buttered cookie sheet and bake at 325° for 10 minutes.

Partly cool before removing from cookie sheet.

Delicious served with homemade ice cream.

SAND TARTS

Yield: 5 dozen   Oven: 350°

1 cup real butter	1 tsp. ice water
6 Tb. powdered sugar	½ cup chopped nuts
2 cups flour	

Cut butter into flour and sugar mixture. Add ice water and nuts. Work up well. Drop by teaspoon onto baking sheet. Bake at 350° for 10 to 12 minutes. Roll in powdered sugar while hot. They will be slightly brown when done.

Freezes or keeps in tin.

MRS. DOUGLAS BRANDON

PECAN DREAMS
Yield: 2 dozen　　　　　　　　　　　Oven: 350°
- ½ cup butter
- 2 Tb. sugar
- 1 cup flour
- 1 cup nuts, ground
- 1 tsp. vanilla
- Powdered sugar

Cream butter and sugar; add remaining ingredients and mix together. Roll in balls. Bake on greased cookie sheet for 15 to 20 minutes at 350°. Roll in powdered sugar while hot and again when cool.

MRS. JAMES VERNON FLACK

ALMOND ROCA COOKIES
Yield: 4 dozen squares　　　　　　　Oven: 350°
- 1 cup butter
- ½ cup brown sugar
- ½ cup sugar
- 1 egg yolk, beaten
- 1 tsp. vanilla
- 2 cups cake flour
- 10 oz. milk chocolate bar, melted
- 1 cup almonds, finely chopped

Cream butter, brown sugar, and white sugar together until light and fluffy; add beaten egg yolk and vanilla. Add flour and mix thoroughly. Spread mixture thinly on a greased cookie sheet. Bake 15 to 20 minutes at 350°. Spread the melted chocolate bar on warm cookies and top with almonds. Cut cookies while warm. Refrigerate. These cookies are best the day they are made.
Variation: You may substitute pecans for the almonds.

PRALINE GRAHAMS
Yield: 2 dozen　　　　　　　　　　　Oven: 350°
- 1 cup margarine
- 1 cup light brown sugar
- Dash salt
- 1 cup pecans
- 24 graham crackers

Mix margarine, brown sugar, and salt and boil for 2 minutes ONLY. Remove from heat and stir in pecans. Place graham crackers close together on greased cookie sheet. Pour cooked mixture over crackers. Bake at 350° for 10 minutes. Watch carefully!

MRS. ED T. ALLEN
CROSSETT, ARKANSAS

CHOCOLATE CHIP GOODIES
Yield: 12 bars　　　　　　　　　　　Oven: 350°
- 6-oz. pkg. semi-sweet chocolate chips
- 1 can condensed milk
- 1½ cups graham cracker crumbs
- 1 tsp. almond extract

Mix and bake in a greased 8-inch square pan for 25 minutes at 350°. Cool slightly and cut into squares before completely cool.
Variation: A cup of coconut and/or a cup of nuts may be added.

MRS. BART ROACH

COOKIES

POTATO CHIP COOKIES

Yield: About 3 dozen   **Oven: 325°**

2 cups flour
1 cup shortening
1 cup brown sugar
1 cup white sugar
1 tsp. soda

2 eggs
2 cups crushed potato chips
6-oz. pkg. chocolate or butterscotch chips

Cream first six ingredients and mix well. Add crushed potato chips and package of chocolate or butterscotch chips. Mix well. Roll into balls the size of walnuts. Place on cookie sheet and bake at 325° for 10 to 12 minutes.

MRS. CHARLES S. RULE

MERINGUE SURPRISES

Yield: Approximately 3½ dozen   **Oven: 300°**

2 egg whites
1 tsp. vanilla
⅛ tsp. salt

½ cup sugar
6-oz. pkg. semi-sweet chocolate morsels

Combine egg whites, vanilla and salt. Beat until stiff but not dry. Beat in sugar gradually until stiff and satiny. Fold in chocolate morsels. Drop close together on greased cookie sheet. Bake in 300° oven for 30 minutes.

Variation: Use 6-oz. package mint chocolate morsels and/or use ¼ cup chopped nuts.

CHOCOLATE-PECAN KISSES

Yield: 40 cookies   **Oven: 375°**

1 cup butter
1 pkg. (5¾ oz.) milk chocolate kisses
1 cup powdered sugar

1 tsp. vanilla extract
2 cups sifted flour
1 cup finely chopped pecans

In large bowl of electric mixer, let butter stand at room temperature until softened. Remove paper from chocolate kisses. Preheat oven to 375°. At medium speed, beat butter, ½ cup powdered sugar and the vanilla until light and fluffy. At low speed, beat in flour and nuts until well combined. Divide dough into 40 equal parts. Shape each part around a chocolate kiss, to make a ball, being sure to cover candy completely. Place on ungreased cookie sheet. Bake 12 minutes, or until cookies are set but not brown. Let stand 1 minute, removing from cookie sheet. Cool slightly, then roll in powdered sugar. Reroll in sugar before serving.

MRS. JOHN R. FLETCHER

GRAMMA COOKIES

Yield: Approximately 3 dozen   Oven: 350°

6-oz. pkg. chocolate chips	1 cup flour
½ cup sugar	½ tsp. soda
½ cup butter	½ tsp. salt
1 egg slightly beaten	1 cup chopped nuts
¼ cup cold water	

Melt ½ package of chocolate chips in a double boiler. Cream butter and sugar. Add one egg and cold water. Mix flour, soda and salt and add to other mixture. Add melted chips and blend well. Add other ½ package of chips and nuts last. Drop by spoonfuls. Bake at 350° about 10 minutes or until done.

MRS. JOE C. BARRETT
JONESBORO, ARKANSAS

SKILLET COOKIES

Yield: 4 dozen

½ cup margarine	2 tsp. vanilla (or lemon
8 oz. dates, pitted	extract)
¾ cup sugar	2 cups rice krispies
2 Tb. milk	1 cup pecans
2 egg yolks	1 cup coconut, flaked

Melt margarine slowly; add dates, sugar, milk and egg yolks; cook 10 minutes, stirring constantly, over low heat. Remove from heat; add vanilla, rice krispies and pecans. Mix well and shape into balls. Roll in flaked coconut.

MRS. PHILIP MCMATH

BROWN LIZZIES

Yield: 3 dozen   Oven: 250°

½ lb. candied cherries	⅓ cup dry wine or whiskey
3 cups pecans	1½ tsp. baking soda
½ lb. seedless raisins	2 Tb. milk
2 slices candied pineapple	1½ cups flour
¼ lb. citron	½ tsp. allspice
¼ cup margarine	½ tsp. nutmeg
½ lb. brown sugar	½ tsp. ground cloves
2 eggs, beaten	

Chop first five ingredients into medium sized pieces. Cream margarine and brown sugar. Add beaten eggs; mix well. Stir in wine. Dissolve soda in milk; stir into creamed mixture. Sift flour with spices. Sprinkle half over fruit; stir remainder into batter. Mix fruit and nuts until well coated; add to batter.

Drop by teaspoons onto well greased cookie sheet. Bake at 250° for 25 to 30 minutes.

MRS. C. RAY WILLIAMS

WALNUT HERMITS

Yield: 6 dozen   **Oven: 375°**

1 cup shortening
2 cups brown sugar
2 eggs
3½ cups sifted flour
1 tsp. baking powder
1 tsp. soda
½ tsp. salt

2 tsp. cinnamon
1 tsp. nutmeg
½ cup buttermilk
1 cup chopped walnuts
2 cups raisins
1 cup chopped dates

Cream together shortening, brown sugar and eggs. Add the dry ingredients and milk to creamed mixture. Add walnuts, raisins and dates. Drop on greased cookie sheet. Bake at 375° for 10 to 12 minutes.

MRS. JOHN M. OSTNER

CANDIES

ALMOND BUTTER CRUNCH

1½ cups butter
2 cups sugar

3½-oz. pkg. blanched,
chopped almonds

Put butter and sugar in a heavy saucepan with a candy thermometer. Cook over high heat, stirring constantly to prevent burning, until the mixture reaches 245°. Add almonds and continue cooking and stirring until it reaches 300°. Turn out on heavily buttered cookie sheets and spread as thin as possible with the bowl of a buttered spoon. Let cool completely. Wipe off excess butter with a dish towel. Turn the candy out by holding it upside down close to a counter top and slightly flexing the cookie sheet. Wipe excess butter off the other side. Break into bite-size pieces and enjoy.

BILL LEWIS

AUNT BYRD'S BRITTLE

Yield: 2 lbs.

1 cup sugar
½ cup light corn syrup
¼ cup water

1½ cups raw peanuts with
red skins
1 tsp. soda

Combine sugar, corn syrup, water, and peanuts in a heavy skillet and boil until thick and light brown (15 to 20 minutes) ; stir frequently while cooking. Add soda and mix well. Quickly pour into a buttered pan and spread thin. When cool, break into bite-size pieces. Store in a tin box tightly covered.

MRS. GIL BUCHANAN

SPICED NUTS

1 cup sugar
1 tsp. salt
4 Tb. water

½ tsp. cinnamon
2 cups toasted pecan halves

Mix sugar, salt, water and cinnamon together; cook until it spins a thread when dropped from a spoon. Remove from heat and add warm toasted nuts. Toss with fork until all nuts are coated; quickly separate nuts on a cookie sheet. Cool and store in tins. May be frozen but serve at room temperature.

My favorite!

MRS. SLOAN CUMMINS
PINE BLUFF, ARKANSAS

CREAMY PRALINES

3 cups sugar
1 cup buttermilk
¼ cup light corn syrup
Pinch of salt

1 tsp. soda
1 tsp. vanilla
1 qt. pecans

Combine sugar, buttermilk, corn syrup and salt in a very large pan (it will foam considerably when soda is added) and bring to a boil. Add soda, stir and cook until soft ball is formed when dropped in cold water (about 238° on a candy thermometer). Add vanilla. Beat until color changes and candy thickens. Stir in pecans. Drop by teaspoons on greased cookie sheet. Cool till set.

GLADSTONE SPOTTS

APRICOT SNOWBALLS

Yield: 2 dozen

24 dried apricots
10 oz. flaked coconut
1 cup sugar

2 tsp. orange juice
Powdered sugar

Put apricots through medium blade of food grinder. Mix ground apricots with coconut, granulated sugar and orange juice. Blend well. Shape mixture into ¾-inch balls. Roll in powdered sugar. Store in tightly covered container.

MRS. CHARLES MCDADE

ORANGE PECANS

2 cups sugar
½ cup water
Cream of tartar, pinch

Grated rind of one orange
1 Tb. orange juice
2 cups pecan halves

Cook sugar, water and cream of tartar for five minutes after it begins to boil. Cook for a few seconds then stir in orange rind and orange juice. Beat with spoon until creamy. Stir in pecan halves and mix well. Pour mixture on buttered platter to harden.

MRS. ROBERT M. EUBANKS, JR.

ORANGE BALLS

Yield: 4 dozen

3 cups crushed vanilla wafers
1 cup powdered sugar
6-oz. can frozen orange juice, thawed

2 Tb. butter
1 cup chopped nuts
1 cup coconut

I prefer to chop nuts and vanilla wafers in the blender, but this is not necessary. You may do it by hand, if you like a coarser texture. Blend all ingredients together well. Moisten hands and roll mixture into ball the size of large marbles. Chill before serving. They may be rolled in powdered sugar if you like.

MRS. W. Y. HESTER

HEATH BAR CANDY

Yield: About 35 squares

2 cups sugar
1 lb. butter
1 cup pecans, chopped

10 to 12 Hershey Bars
½ cup pecans, chopped

Mix sugar, butter and nuts in a medium iron skillet and stir constantly over medium-low heat. Substance will become light brown, smell caramalized, and spoon tracks will show as you stir. Cook until it reaches the hard crack stage when dropped in cold water (300° on candy thermometer).

Pour mixture on a small cookie sheet with sides. Spread evenly and place Hershey Bars on top. Spread the bars as they melt to cover surface. Sprinkle with ½ cup chopped pecans. Allow to cool slightly before cutting in one inch squares. Let cool completely on cookie sheet. Separate and serve.

MRS. JOHN Y. BONDS

CANDY BALLS

Yield: 2 pounds

2 lbs. powdered sugar
1 can condensed milk
1 tsp. vanilla
1 to 2 pts. pecans, chopped

½ cup margarine
2 cans coconut
12 oz. semi-sweet chocolate
3 oz. paraffin

Mix sugar, milk, vanilla, pecans, margarine and coconut until well blended. Chill mixture. Roll into small balls and chill hard. Melt chocolate and paraffin in double boiler. Roll chilled balls in chocolate mixture and place on waxed paper to dry and cool.

MRS. JACK C. GARDNER

PERFECT DIVINITY

Yield: 40 pieces

2½ cups sugar	2 egg whites
½ cup light corn syrup	1 tsp. vanilla
½ cup water	½ cup nuts, chopped
¼ tsp. salt	Pecan halves

Mix sugar, corn syrup, water, and salt in a 2 quart saucepan. Stir only until sugar dissolves. Cook until a small amount of mixture forms a hard ball when dropped in cold water (260° on candy thermometer). Remove from heat.

Beat egg whites to stiff peaks. Gradually add syrup to egg whites, beating at high speed with electric mixer. Add vanilla. Beat until candy holds its shape. If desired, add nuts. Drop by teaspoons on waxed paper. Top with pecan half.

MRS. WILLIAM A. MAY

CARAMEL CANDY

2 cups sugar	13-oz. can evaporated milk
1 cup butter	1 tsp. vanilla
1¼ cups light corn syrup	1 cup chopped nuts, optional

Place sugar, butter, corn syrup, and one-half of the evaporated milk in a large saucepan. Boil slowly, stirring constantly. When mixture comes to a good rolling boil, add the remainder of the milk. Continue stirring and watch carefully to keep mixture from sticking to pan and burning. Test by dropping some in cold water. When a firm ball forms (about 240° on candy thermometer) remove from fire. Add vanilla and nuts, if desired. Pour into a greased dish 8 x 12 x 2-inch and allow to cool. Cut in squares. Wrap in individual pieces of waxed paper or place waxed paper between layers of candy and store in a tin box.

MRS. R. E. JACK BUSH, SR.

FUDGE

4 cups sugar	2 cups semi-sweet chocolate
13-oz. can evaporated milk	chips
1 cup butter	1 tsp. vanilla
2 cups marshmallow creme	1 cup nuts, chopped

Butter sides of a heavy 3 quart saucepan. Add sugar, milk, and butter. Cook over medium heat to a soft ball stage (236° on candy thermometer) stirring constantly. Remove from heat; add chocolate chips, marshmallow creme, vanilla and nuts. Beat until chocolate melts. Pour into a buttered 13 x 9 x 2-inch pan. Score while warm. Cut when cool and firm.

MRS. CHARLES MCDADE

CARAMEL FUDGE CANDY

3 cups sugar
1 cup cream, light
¼ cup butter

⅛ tsp. soda
1 tsp. vanilla
1 cup pecans, chopped

Place 2 cups sugar and cream in a large pan. Place 1 cup sugar in a heavy iron skillet. Start both pans on medium high heat, stirring the melting sugar constantly with a wooden spoon and the sugar and cream frequently. Lower the heat under melting sugar so it will melt but not brown too much. When the sugar is melted, add it to the other boiling mixture; lower the heat and stir to mix. Raise heat to medium high and cook until it forms a ball in cold water. Remove from heat, add butter and soda. Sit until butter melts then add vanilla. Beat with spoon or mixer until glossy and fairly thick. Add nuts and pour into greased platter.

Sounds difficult—is not! Makes great icing when not cooked so long. If too hard, add a little cream.

MRS. TYNDALL DICKINSON

INDEX

A

ACCOMPANIMENTS, 258-262
 Brandied Apricot Jelly, 260
 Bread and Butter Pickles, 261
 Cranberry Jelly, 259
 Cranberry Port Jelly, 260
 Curried Fruit, 258
 Hot Fruit, 259
 Kosher Dill Pickles, 261
 Pepper Jelly, 260
 Pickled Eggplant, 262
 Pickled Mushrooms and
  Artichokes, 262
 Port Wine Jelly, 260
 Quick Pickled Peaches, 261
 Strawberry Preserves, 259
 Sterilizing Jars, 259
Acorn Squash with Cranberries, 215
Almond Butter Crunch, 328
Almond Log, 275
Almond Pound Cake, 295
Almond Roca Cookies, 325
Angel Delight Dessert, 277
Angel Toffee Cake Roll, 314

APPETIZERS, 3-24
 Barbecued Party Franks, 16
 Bell Pepper Cheese Dip, 12
 Blue Cheese Ball, 10
 Braunschweiger Ball, 13
 Cantaloupe Dill Dip, 4
 Cheese Crispies, 8
 Cheese Fondue, 11
 Cheese Puffs, 9
 Cheesy Chicken Wings, 15
 Cherry Tomato Canapé, 5
 Chicken Liver Paté, 14
 Chicken Liver Spread, 14
 Chinese Egg Rolls, 17
 Chipped Beef Roll-Ups, 19
 Cocktail Ham Balls, 19
 Crab Rolls, 22
 Cream Cheese Caviar Mold, 13
 Curry Dip for Vegetables, 4
 Devilish Ham Puffs, 19
 Dill Weed Dip, 3
 Easy Shrimp Dip, 21
 Egg and Olive Cheese Spread, 9
 Ella's Cheese Straws, 8
 Glazed Pecans, 24
 Guacamole, 3
 Hibachi Steak, 18
 Hot Crab Spread, 23
 Hot Curried Crab Dip, 23
 Hot Jalapenos Cheese Dip, 12
 Hot Shrimp and Cheese Dip, 21
 Liverwurst Mold, 14
 Mexican Bean Dip, 13
 Mexican Cheese Dip, 12
 Mushrooms, Bacon Filling, 6
 Mushrooms, Cheese & Herb
  Filling, 6
 Mushrooms, Crabmeat Filling, 6
 Mushrooms, Parmesan Filling, 7

 Mushrooms, Sherry Cream
  Filling, 7
 Nachos, 7
 Nutty Soybeans, 24
 Oriental Franks, 16
 Parmesan Sticks, 8
 Pickled Mushrooms, 5
 Pickled Shrimp, 20
 Raw Vegetables to Dip, 3
 Rosy Radishes, 5
 Sauerkraut Balls, 20
 Sausage and Chestnut Balls, 16
 Sausage, Cheese Crumbles, 16
 Sausage Pinwheels, 15
 Seafood Cocktail Sauce, 256
 Sherry and Blue Cheese Dip, 10
 Shrimp Potpourri, 21
 Shrimp Spread, 22
 Snappy Cheese Log, 9
 Spicy Vegetable Dip, 4
 Spinach Crabmeat Dip, 22
 Steak Tartare, 18
 Stuffed Mushrooms, 6
 Swedish Meat Balls, 18
 Tangy Cheese Spread, 10
 Tiny Corn Fritters, 7
 Tipsy Watermelon, 4
 Wild Duck Cocktail Spread, 15
 Wine Cellar Cheese, 11
Apple and Sweet Potato Casserole, 208
Apple Cake, Fresh, 298
Apple Crisp, 265
Apple Pancakes, 71
Apple Pie, Dutch, 292
Applesauce Jam Cake, 313
Apples, Baked Supreme, 265
Apricot Bread, 65
Apricot-Cottage Cheese Salad, 235
Apricot Ice, 269
Apricot Jelly, Brandied, 260
Apricot Nectar Cake, 312
Apricot Snowballs, 329
Arkansas Spinach Rockefeller, 213
Armenian Marinade, 171
Artichoke and Spinach Casserole, 184
Artichoke Hearts, Carrots, and
  Mushrooms, 193
Artichoke, Potage Creme de, 46
Artichokes Alsation, 184
Artichokes and Mushrooms,
  Pickled, 262
Artichokes, Fresh, 185
Artichoke, Shrimp and Salad, 240
Artichokes Stuffed with Lamb, 170
Asparagus and Broccoli, Dressing
  for, 254
Asparagus Casserole, 185
Asparagus, Chinese, 186
Asparagus, Marinated Salad, 223
Asparagus, Molded Salad, 223
Asparagus Soup, 46
Asparagus, Sweet and Sour, 223
Asparagus with Lobster Sauce, 101
Aspic (see Salads)
Aspic, Lamb & Cucumber, 240

Aspic, Tomato, 233
Aunt Byrd's Brittle, 328
Aunt Mary's Pecan Pie, 290
Avocado and Grapefruit Mold, 224
Avocado Dip, Guacamole, 3
Avocado Mousse, 224

B

Bachelor's Barbecue Lamb, 169
Baegels, 61
Baked Acorn Squash, 215
Baked Apples Supreme, 265
Baked Barley with Mushrooms, 186
Baked Crab Meat Sandwich, 98
Baked Custard with Raspberries, 280
Baked Eggs in Cheese Sauce, 79
Baked Onions, 202
Baked Onions Parmesan, 202
Baked Sole, 105
Baked Squash with Bacon, 215
Baked Steak with Mushrooms, 154
Baked Stuffed Onions, 176
Baked Tomato Verdis, 217
Baking Powder Biscuits, 63
Banana Cake, Fiesta, 301
Banana Cream Pie, 291
Banana Daiquiri, 30
Banana Icing, 301
Banana Nut Bread, 66
Bananas Burgundy, 265
Bananas Foster, 266
Barbara's Potted Duck, 134
Barbecued Brisket, 152
Barbecued Party Franks, 16
Barbecue Lamb, Bachelor's, 169
Barbecue Sauce, Carrie's, 252
Barbecue Sauce for Chicken, 129
Barbecue Sauce for Duck, 134
Barbecue Sauce for Ham, 176
Barley, Baked with Mushrooms, 186
Basic Bread Dressing, 128
Basic Quiche, 79
Basic Recipe for Wild Ducks, 133
Bavarian Breakfast Rolls, 70
Bean Dip, Mexican, 13
Bean, Hot Salad, 225
Beans, Green (see Green Beans)
Bean Soup, 37
Bean, Swedish Salad, 224
Bean, Sweet and Sour, 225
Bearnaise Sauce, 252
Beef (see Meats)
Beef and Ham Birds in White
  Wine, 155
Beef Burgundy Flambé, 159
Beefsteak Au Roquefort, 153
Beef Tenderloin, 149
Beer Batter for Fried Shrimp, 89
Beer Beef Stroganoff, 160
Beet Ring Mold, 225
Bell Pepper Cheese Dip, 12
Bell's Roquefort Dressing, 245
Beouf Bourguignon, 159

BEVERAGES, 27-34
Banana Daiquiri, 30
Bloody Mary, 29
Bridge Day Mint Tea, 27
Citrus Punch, 28
Coffee Brandy, 34
Cranberry Slush, 30
Do Ahead Daiquiri, 29
Gin Fizz, 31
Glögg, 31
Grasshopper, 32
Hot Buttered Cranberry Punch, 28
Hot Buttered Rum, 33
Iced Russian Tea, 27
Instant Spiced Tea, 27
Magnolia Manor Julep, 32
Mimosa, 30
Mocha Punch, 33
Mrs. Witt's Egg Nog, 32
Mulled Cider, 28
Quantity Bloody Mary Mix, 29
Rum Runner's Punch, 33
Syrup, Simple, 30
  (in Banana Daiquiri recipe)
Whiskey Sour Punch, 31
Yellow Birds, 30
Billie's Cabbage Roll, 165
Bing Cherry Salad with Coca Cola, 235
Biscuits, Baking Powder, 63
Biscuits, Cheese, 63
Biscuits, Lou's Buttermilk, 63
Biscuits, Sourdough, 73
Blackeyed Peas Creole, 204
Bloody Mary, 29
Bloody Mary Mix, Quantity, 29
Blueberry Pancakes, 71
Blue Cheese Ball, 10
Blue Cheese Dip, Sherry, 10
Boiled Custard, 280
Bordelaise Sauce, 252
Bourguignon, Beouf, 159
Braided Poppy Seed Bread, 56
Brandied Apricot Jelly, 260
Brandy Alexander Pie, 286
Brandy Pudding Sauce, 256
Bran Muffins, 64
Bran, Six-week Muffins, 64
Braunschweiger Ball, 13
Bread and Butter Pickles, 261

BREADS, 51-73
  Breads, Quick
    Apple Pancakes, 71
    Apricot Bread, 65
    Baking Powder Biscuits, 63
    Banana Nut Bread, 66
    Bavarian Breakfast Rolls, 70
    Blueberry Pancakes, 71
    Bran Muffins, 64
    Cheese Biscuits, 63
    Cheese Puffs, 9
    Cheese Roll, 71
    Cheese Spooned Bread, 69
    Cornbread, 68
    Corn Cakes, 68

Corn Sticks, 69
Cranberry Bread, 66
Crepes, 70
Date Muffins, 64
German Pancakes, 70
Ginger Cheese Muffins, 65
Hushpuppies, 69
Lemon Bread, 66
Lou's Buttermilk Biscuits, 63
Mexican Cornbread, 68
Orange Bread, 67
Pancakes, 71
Peabody Hotel Muffins, 65
Prune Loaf, 67
Pumpkin Bread, 67
Six-Weeks Bran Muffins, 64
Sour Cream Coffee Cake, 71
Spoon Bread, 69
Waffles, 71
Yorkshire Pudding, 63
Breads, Sourdough
Biscuits, 73
Bread, 72
English Muffins, 73
Pancakes, Blueberry, 73
Starter, 72
Breads, Yeast
Baegels, 61
Braided Poppy Seed, 56
Brown, 53
Cheese, 55
Cinnamon Ring, 54
Dill, 54
Elizabeth Young's Homemade, 52
French, 53
Hot Cross Buns, 62
Monkey, 54
Oatmeal, 56
Onion Buns, 62
Party Rolls, 60
Patio Herb, 55
Raisin, 57
Refrigerator Dinner Rolls, 60
Rye, 57
Sally Lunn, 59
Sticky Buns, 61
Stuffed Sour Cream, 58
Wheat Germ, 59
Whole Wheat, 58
Breast of Chicken Honduras, 119
Bride's Salad, 236
Bridge Day Mint Tea, 27
Brisket, Barbecued, 152
Brisket Roast with Beer, 152
Broccoli and Asparagus, Dressing
for, 254
Broccoli Casserole, 189
Broccoli Casserole, 189
Broccoli, Crepes Theodora, 191
Broccoli Mushroom Casserole, 190
Broccoli Soup, 37
Broccoli Vinaigrette, 226
Broccoli Waddile, 190
Broccoli, Zesty Mold, 226
Broiled Chicken Temple Bells, 116

Brown Bread, 53
Brownie Date Loaf, 302
Brownies, 317
Brown Lizzies, 327
Brown Sauce, Basic, 251
Brown Sugar Chews, 324
Brown Sugar Loaf, 296
Brunch Eggs, 80
Brussels Sprouts Salad, 226
Brussels Sprouts, Sour Cream—
Bacon Sauce for, 190
Buns, Hot Cross, 62
Buns, Onion, 62
Buns, Sticky, 61
Butter Frosting, 316
Buttermilk Pound Cake, 295
Butterscotch Nut Pie, 286
Butterscotch Sauce, 256

C

Cabbage Potpourri, 192
Cabbage Roll, Billie's, 165
Cabbage Stroganoff, 192
Cabbage, Sweet and Sour, 192
Caesar Salad, 227

CAKE ICINGS
Banana, 301
Butter, 316
Caramel, 305
Caramel, 315
Chocolate, 296
Chocolate, 317
Chocolate Fudge, 315
Chocolate Mallow, 297
Cocoa Coffee, 298
Coca-Cola, 299
Cocoa-Nut, 299
Cream Cheese, 301
Fudge, 317
German Chocolate, 306
Heavenly White, 314
Lemon Pineapple, 304
Orange Butter, 315
Rum, 308
Strawberry, 312
Sugar Plum, 315
White Chocolate, 300
Whipped Cream, 316

CAKES, 295-314
Cakes
Almond Pound, 295
Angel Toffee Cake Roll, 314
Applesauce Jam, 313
Apricot Nectar, 312
Brown Sugar Loaf, 296
Brownie Date Loaf, 302
Buttermilk Pound, 295
Carrot, 301
Chocolate Pound, 296
Cinnamon Coffee, 311
Coca-Cola, 299
Cordell's, 298

Cranberry, 302
Dark Fruit, 309
Date Nut, 300
Diane's Chocolate Sheet, 299
Fiesta Banana, 301
Fresh Apple, 298
German Cheesecake, 306
Holiday Jam, 308
Irish Potato, 306
Italian Cream, 307
Lemon Pineapple Layer, 304
Mission Sunday Fudge, 297
Momma's Gingerbread, 297
Mother-in-Law's, 309
Oatmeal, 305
Orange Rind Loaf, 303
Pecan, 307
Peggy's Pound, 295
Pineapple, 303
Plum Pudding, 310
Prune, 305
Rum, 308
Rum, 313
Sherry, 313
Special Cheesecake, 304
Strawberry, 312
The President's, 311
Tunnel of Fudge, 296
White Chocolate, 300
Small Cakes
   Brownies (Iced,) 317
   Canadian Squares, 319
   Caramel Fudge Squares, 320
   Caramel Meringue Bars, 316
   Cheese Bars, 318
   Chess Cakes, 319
   Chocolate Devils, 317
   Cream Cheese Brownies, 318
   Lebkuchen, 320
Camping Chicken, 113
Canadian Squares, 319
Canapé, Cherry Tomato, 5
Canapes (see Appetizers)
Candied Yams, 207

CANDIES, 328-332
   Almond Butter Crunch, 328
   Apricot Snowballs, 329
   Aunt Byrd's Brittle, 328
   Candy Balls, 330
   Caramel, 331
   Caramel Fudge, 332
   Creamy Pralines, 329
   Fudge, 331
   Heath Bar, 330
   Orange Balls, 330
   Orange Pecans, 329
   Perfect Divinity, 331
   Spiced Nuts, 329
Candy Balls, 330
Canlis Special Dressing, 242
Canlis Special Salad, 227
Cantaloupe Dill Dip, 4
Caramel Candy, 331
Caramel Fudge Candy, 332

Caramel Fudge Squares, 320
Caramel Ice Cream Dessert, 272
Caramel Icing, 305
Caramel Icing, 315
Caramel Meringue Bars, 316
Caraway Green Beans, 187
Carbonade of Beef Flamande, 158
Carrie's Barbecue Sauce, 252
Carrot Cake, 301
Carrot Casserole Supreme, 193
Carrot Ring, 194
Carrots, Artichoke Hearts, and
   Mushrooms, 193
Carrots di Prossedi, 194
Carrots-In-Honey Au Gratin, 193
Carrots, Marinated, 194
Carrots, Saucy, 195
Cauliflower Au Gratin, 195
Cauliflower, Italian, 195
Cauliflower Salad, 227
Cauliflower Slaw, 228
Cauliflower, Tangy, 196
Caviar Mold, Cream Cheese, 13
Caviar, Red Molds, 239
Celery Amandine, 196
Celery Au Gratin, 197
Celery, Crunchy, 197
Celery, Mushroom, and Water
   Chestnut Casserole, 197
Celery with Almonds, 196
Champagne Sauerkraut for Duck, 138
Charcoal Broiled Fish, 106
Charcoal Broiled Quail, 140
Charlotte Russe, 281
Cheese and Eggs (see Eggs and
   Cheese)
Cheese and Shrimp Dip, Hot, 21
Cheese Ball, Blue, 10
Cheese Bars, 318
Cheese Biscuits, 63
Cheese Bread, 55
Cheesecake, German, 306
Cheesecake, Special, 304
Cheese, Cream, Caviar Mold, 13
Cheese Crispies, 8
Cheese Crumbles, Sausage, 16
Cheese Dip, Bell Pepper, 12
Cheese Dip, Blue & Sherry, 10
Cheese Dip, Hot Jalapenos, 12
Cheese Dip, Mexican, 12
Cheese Fondue, 11
Cheese Log, Snappy, 9
Cheese Puffs, 9
Cheese Roll, 71
Cheese Souffle, 78
Cheese Spooned Bread, 69
Cheese Spread, Egg and Olive, 9
Cheese Spread, Tangy, 10
Cheese Straws, Ella's, 8
Cheese, Wine Cellar, 11
Cheesy Chicken Wings, 15
Cherries Jubilee, 267
Cherries Supreme, 266
Cherry Sauce for Pork Roast, 173
Cherry Tomato Canapé, 5

Chess Cakes, 319
Chess Meringue Pie, 287
Chestnut Dressing, 128
Chicken (see Poultry), 109-126
Chicken Adolphus, 120
Chicken and Wild Rice Casserole, 122
Chicken Breasts with Shrimp
  Sauce, 117
Chicken Cacciatore, 123
Chicken Chablis, 113
Chicken Dana, 120
Chicken Indienne, 112
Chicken Kiev, 114
Chicken Korean, 118
Chicken Liver Paté, 14
Chicken Livers in Onion Crepes, 126
Chicken Liver Spread, 14
Chicken Livers with Madeira
  Sauce, 125
Chicken Paprika, 119
Chicken Parisienne, 118
Chicken Richelieu, 116
Chicken Spaghetti, 123-124
Chicken Surprise, 121
Chicken Tetrazzini, 124
Chicken Wings, Cheesy, 15
Chicken with Chipped Beef, 117
Chicken with Pecans, 118
Chili, 163
Chilies Rellenos, 198
Chinese Asparagus, 186
Chinese Egg Rolls, 17
Chinese Fried Rice, 208
Chipped Beef Roll-ups, 19
Chocolate Cake, White, 300
Chocolate Chip Goodies, 325
Chocolate Cookie Crust, 287
Chocolate Cream Pie, 291
Chocolate Devils, 317
Chocolate Fudge Frosting, 315
Chocolate Ice Box Dessert, 273
Chocolate Ice Cream, 271
Chocolate Ice Cream Dessert, 274
Chocolate Icing, 296
Chocolate Icing, 317
Chocolate Igloo Dessert, 275
Chocolate Mallow Icing, 297
Chocolate-Menthe Dream, 281
Chocolate-Pecan Kisses, 326
Chocolate Pecan Pie, 289
Chocolate Pie, French, 288
Chocolate Pot de Creme, 273
Chocolate Pound Cake, 296
Chocolate Roll, 276
Chocolate Sauce, 276
Chocolate Sauce, 294
Chocolate Sundae Pie, 289
Chocolat, Fondue Au, 276
Chopstick Tuna, 105
Chowder, Clam, 44
Chowder, Shrimp, 44
Cider, Mulled, 28
Cinnamon Coffee Cake, 311
Cinnamon Ring, 54
Cinnamon Strips, 323

Citrus Chiffon Pie, 294
Citrus Punch, 28
Clam Chowder, 44
Claret Sauce, 271
Coca-Cola Cake, 299
Coca-Cola Icing, 299
Cocktail Ham Balls, 19
Cocoa-Coffee Frosting, 298
Cocoa-Nut Icing, 299
Coconut Cream Pie, 291
Coconut Pie, Toasted, 288
Coffee Brandy, 34
Coffee Cake, Cinnamon, 311
Coffee Cake, Sour Cream, 71
Coffee-Cocoa Frosting, 298
Coffee Tortoni, 277
Cold Cucumber Soup, 38
Cold Curry-Crab Soup, 38
Cold Spinach Soup, 44
Cold Tomato Soup, 47
Company Brussels Sprouts, 191
Consomme, Quick, 47

COOKIES, 323-328
  Almond Roca, 325
  Brown Lizzies, 327
  Brown Sugar Chews, 324
  Chocolate Chip Goodies, 325
  Chocolate-Pecan Kisses, 326
  Cinnamon Strips, 323
  Gramma Cookies, 327
  Koulorgia, 324
  Meringue Surprises, 326
  Molasses Sugar, 323
  Pecan Dreams, 325
  Potato Chip Cookies, 326
  Praline Grahams, 325
  Rich Butter, 323
  Sand Tarts, 324
  Skillet, 327
  Walnut Hermits, 328
Coq au Vin, 121
Coquilles St. Jacques, 101
Cordell's Cake, 298
Cornbread, 68
Cornbread, Mexican, 68
Corn Cakes, 68
Corn Fritters, Tiny, 7
Corn Pudding, 198
Corn Souffle, 198
Corn Soup, Fresh Cream of, 37
Corn Sticks, 69
Cottage Cheese-Apricot Salad, 235
Cottage Cheese Dressing, 242
Cottage Cheese Salad, 228
Cottage Cheese, Tomato Loaf, 234
Country Cured Ham, 175
Country Noodle Casserole, 202
Crab (see Fish and Shellfish)
Crab, Cold Curry Soup, 38
Crab Dip, Hot Curried, 23
Crab Meat and Rice Casserole, 96
Crab Meat Dip, Spinach, 22
Crab Meat Eggs Au Gratin, 78
Crab Meat Imperial, 95

Crab Meat Mornay, 95
Crab Meat Salad Casserole, 97
Crab Meat Sycamore, 95
Crab or Shrimp Gaylord, 96
Crab Pie, 99
Crab Rolls, 22
Crab-Shrimp Pie with Bechemel
  Sauce, 98
Crab Spread, Hot, 23
Crab Supper Pie, 99
Cracker Pecan Pie, 285
Cranberry Bread, 66
Cranberry Cake, 302
Cranberry Cashew Salad, 236
Cranberry Jelly, 259
Cranberry Onions, 201
Cranberry Port Jelly, 260
Cranberry Punch, Hot Buttered, 28
Cranberry Salad, 236
Cranberry Slush, 30
Cream Base for Cream Pies, 291
Cream Cheese Brownies, 318
Cream Cheese Caviar Mold, 13
Cream Cheese Crust, 290
Cream Cheese Icing, 301
Cream of Mushroom Soup, 41
Cream Puffs, 278
Cream Puff Shells, 278
Cream Sauce (see White Sauce), 251
Creme de Menthe Pie, 287
Creamed Onion Soup, 41
Creamed Spinach, 213
Creamy Dressing, 243
Creamy Pralines, 329
Creole Duck, 133
Creole Oysters, 102
Crepes, 70
Crepes of Crab Meat Maryland, 100
Crepes Theodora, Broccoli, 191
Crepes with Sour Cream and
  Strawberries, 270
Crown Pork Roast, 172
Crumbled Pears, 269
Crunchy Celery, 197
Cucumber, Cold Soup, 38
Cucumber, Easy Soup, 47
Cucumber, Lamb and Aspic, 240
Cucumbers, Dilled in Sour Cream, 228
Cucumbers Stuffed with Ham, 239
Cup Baked Eggs, 78
Currant Jelly Sauce, 137
Curried Crab Dip, Hot, 23
Curried Fruit, 258
Curried Rice, 208
Curried Shrimp Sauce, 255
Curry, Cold Crab Soup, 38
Curry Dip for Vegetables, 4
Curry Dressing, 243
Curry, Shrimp, 91
Custard, Baked with Raspberries, 280
Custard, Boiled, 280

D

Daiquiri, Banana, 30

Daiquiri, Do Ahead, 29
Dark Fruit Cake, 309
Date Muffins, 64
Date Nut Cake, 300

DESSERTS (see Cakes, Pies, Cookies, Candies), 265-320
Almond Log, 275
Angel Delight, 277
Apple Crisp, 265
Apricot Ice, 269
Baked Apples Supreme, 265
Baked Custard with
  Raspberries, 280
Bananas Burgundy, 265
Bananas Foster, 266
Boiled Custard, 280
Caramel Ice Cream Dessert, 272
Charlotte Russe, 281
Cherries Jubilee, 267
Cherries Supreme, 266
Chocolate Ice Box, 273
Chocolate Ice Cream Dessert, 274
Chocolate Igloo, 275
Chocolate Pot de Creme, 273
Chocolate Roll, 276
Coffee Tortoni, 277
Cream Puffs, 278
Crepes with Sour Cream and
  Strawberries, 270
Crumbled Pears, 269
Fondue au Chocolat, 276
Forgotten Torte, 279
French Mints, 273
Fresh Fruit Shortcake, 268
Granny Parkin's Ice Cream, 271
Ice Cream Bombe, 272
Japanese Orange, 267
Lemon Ice Cream, 270
Les Oranges Aux Liqueurs, 268
Meringue Shells, 278
Midge's Party Torte, 274
Orange Macaroon Pudding, 267
Peach Mold, 269
Sherry Cooler, 280
Spiced Fruit Compote, 266
Strawberry Squares with Claret
  Sauce, 271

DESSERTS, QUICK, 281-284
Chocolate-Menthe Dream, 281
Fresh Fruit Ice, 284
Frozen Berry Cream, 283
Frozen Whipped Cream, 283
Fudge Sundae Pie, 282
Lemon-Berry Cream, 281
Lemon Ice Box Pie, 282
Lemon Ice Cream Pie, 283
Peach Angel, 282
Refreshing Desserts, 284
Strawberries-Drambuie, 281
Strawberry Pie, 282
Deviled Corn and Crab Meat, 97
Deviled Crab, 94
Deviled Eggs and Asparagus, 80

Devilish Ham Puffs, 19
Diane's Chocolate Sheet Cake, 299
Diane's Rice Pilaf, 209
Dill Beans, 187
Dill Bread, 54
Dill Dip, Cantaloupe, 4
Dilled Cucumbers in Sour Cream, 228
Dilled Macaroni Salad, 230
Dill Pickles, Kosher, 261
Dill Weed Dip, 3
Dips (see Appetizers)
Divinity, Perfect, 331
Do Ahead Daiquiri, 29
Dolmades, 169
Dove (see Wild Game)
Dove a la Como, 139
Dove in Wine, 140
Do Your Own Thing Soup, 48
Dressing, Basic Bread, 128
Dressing, Chestnut, 128
Dressing for Broccoli and
    Asparagus, 254
Dressing for Turkey, 130
Dressing, Rice, 127
Dressing, Sausage, 133
Drinks (see Beverages)
Duck (see Wild Game)
Duck Bigarade, 129
Duck Casserole, 137
Dumplings, Potato, 155
Dutch Apple Pie, 292

E

Easy Blender Mayonnaise, 244
Easy Cucumber Soup, 47
Easy Shrimp Dip, 21
Egg and Olive Cheese Spread, 9
Egg Croquettes, 81
Egg Nog, Mrs. Witt's, 32
Eggplant Casserole, 199
Eggplant Casserole (Ratatouille), 200
Eggplant, Oriental Stuffed, 199
Eggplant, Pickled, 262
Eggplant Souffle, 200
Egg Rolls, Chinese, 17

EGGS AND CHEESE, 77-85

    Baked Eggs in Cheese Sauce, 79
    Basic Quiche, 79
    Brunch Eggs, 80
    Cheese Souffle, 78
    Crab Meat Eggs Au Gratin, 78
    Cup Baked Eggs, 78
    Deviled Eggs and Asparagus, 80
    Egg Croquettes, 81
    Eggs and Cheese Continental, 81
    Eggs Hussarde, 82
    Eggs Obstaculos, 80
    Florentine Eggs En Cocotte, 82
    Fluffy Omelet, 83
    Green Eggs and Ham, 81
    Party Eggs, 83
    Ramekin Forestier, 84

    Scrambled Eggs Chasseur, 83
    Stuffed French Loaf, 84
    Welsh Rarebit, 85
Eggs and Cheese Continental, 81
Eggs Hussarde, 82
Eggs Obstaculos, 80
Elizabeth Young's Homemade
    Bread, 52
Ella's Cheese Straws, 8
English Muffins, Sourdough, 73

F

Fiesta Banana Cake, 301
Filet, Savory Stuffed of Beef, 154
Finger Lickin' Shrimp, 89
Firepit Steak Sauce, 253

FISH AND SHELLFISH, 87-107

    Baked Crab Meat Sandwich, 98
    Baked Sole, 105
    Beer Batter for Fried Shrimp, 89
    Charcoal Broiled Fish, 106
    Chopstick Tuna, 105
    Clam Chowder, 44
    Cold Curry-Crab Soup, 38
    Coquilles St. Jacques, 101
    Crab Meat and Rice Casserole, 96
    Crab Meat Eggs Au Gratin, 78
    Crab Meat Imperial, 95
    Crab Meat Mornay, 95
    Crab Meat Salad Casserole, 97
    Crab Meat Sycamore, 95
    Crab or Shrimp Gaylord, 96
    Crab Pie, 99
    Crab Rolls, 22
    Crab-Shrimp Pie with Bechemel
        Sauce, 98
    Crab Supper Pie, 99
    Creole Oysters, 102
    Crepes of Crab Meat
        Maryland, 100
    Curried Shrimp Sauce, 255
    Deviled Corn and Crab Meat, 97
    Deviled Crab, 94
    Finger Lickin' Shrimp, 89
    Fish Fillets Provencial, 106
    Garlic Scampi, 89
    Gumbo, 39
    Immediate Shrimp, 90
    Lemon Wild Rice with Shrimp, 91
    Lobster Sauce for Asparagus, 101
    Louisiana Seafood Soup, 43
    Lulla's Oysters, 103
    Nancy's Deep Sea Chowder, 43
    Oysters Dunbar, 103
    Oysters on the Half Shell, 102
    Pickled Shrimp, 20
    Salmon Croquettes, 104
    Salmon Loaf, 105
    Salmon Souffle, 104
    Scalloped Oysters, 102
    Scallops Newburg, 99
    Seashell Crab Casserole, 96

Shrimp and Artichoke Heart
   Casserole, 92
Shrimp Bake in Avocado, 93
Shrimp Chowder, 44
Shrimp Creole, 93
Shrimp Curry, 91
Shrimp de Jonghe, 90
Shrimp Harpin, 91
Shrimp Jambalaya, 94
Shrimp Potpourri, 21
Shrimp Remoulade, 90
Shrimp Rockefeller, 92
Shrimp Sauce for Flounder, 106
Southern Fried Catfish, 107
Stuffed Lobster Tails
   Thermidor, 100
Stuffed Oysters, 103
White Clam Sauce for
   Spaghetti, 104
Winkum, 97
Fish Fillets Provencial, 106
Florentine Eggs En Cocotte, 82
Fluffy Omelet, 83
Fondue Au Chocolate, 276
Fondue, Cheese, 11
Forgotten Torte, 279
Fowl (see Poultry)
Franks, Barbecued Party, 16
Franks, Oriental, 16
French Bread, 53
French Chocolate Pie, 288
French Dressing, 243
French Mints, 273
French Peas, 204
Fresh Apple Cake, 298
Fresh Artichokes, 185
Fresh Cream of Corn Soup, 37
Fresh Fruit Ice, 284
Fresh Fruit Shortcake, 268
Fresh Mushrooms, 200
Fresh Peach Custard Pie, 292
Fresh Strawberry Pie, 292
Fried Onion Rings, 203
Fried Quail, 140
Frostings (see Cake Icings)
Frozen Berry Cream, 283
Frozen Fruit Salad, 237
Frozen Roquefort Dressing, 246
Frozen Whipped Cream, 283
Fruit Cake, Dark, 309
Fruit, Curried, 258
Fruit, Frozen Salad, 237
Fruit, Hot, 259
Fruit Salad, 237
Fruit Shortcake, Fresh, 268
Fruit, Spiced Compote, 266
Fudge, 331
Fudge Chocolate Frosting, 315
Fudge Frosting, 317
Fudge Sauce, 257
Fudge Sundae, 257
Fudge Sundae Pie, 282

G

Game (see Wild Game)
Garden Vegetable Skillet, 220
Garlic Cheese Grits, 201
Garlic Scampi, 89
Gazpacho, 38
German Cheesecake, 306
German Chocolate Icing, 306
German Pancakes, 70
German Potato Salad, 231
German Rouladen, 155
German Salad Dressing, 244
German Slaw, 232
Gin Fizz, 31
Gingerbread, Momma's, 297
Ginger Cheese Muffins, 65
Gingersnap Crust, 283
Gipsey's Stuffed Chicken, 115
Glazed Pecans, 24
Glazed Pork Chops, 175
Glenleigh Tavern Dressing, 244
Glögg, 31
Goose (see Wild Game)
Goulash, Hungarian, 158
Gourmet Delight Pheasant, 142
Graham Cracker Crust, 285
Gramma Cookies, 327
Granny Parkin's Ice Cream, 271
Grapefruit, Avocado and Mold, 224
Grapes with Sweetbread Salad, 240
Grasshopper, 32
Green and Gold Salad, 237
Green Beans Amandine, 187
Green Beans Au Gratin, 188
Green Beans, Caraway
Green Beans, Dill, 187
Green Beans Supreme, 188
Green Beans with Swiss Cheese, 188
Green Eggs and Ham, 81
Green Goddess Dressing, 244
Green Pea Salad, 231
Green Salad, 229
Grilled Oriental Chicken, 120
Grilled Tomatoes with Rosemary, 217
Grits, Garlic Cheese, 201
Ground Beef (see Meats)
Guacamole, 3
Gumbo, 39

H

Ham (see Meats)
Ham and Beef Birds in White
   Wine, 155
Ham Balls, Cocktail, 19
Ham, Barbecue Sauce for, 176
Hamburger Stroganoff, 164
Ham, Country Cured, 175
Ham, Cucumbers Stuffed with, 239
Ham Fried Rice, 177
Ham, Pecan Stuffed, 176
Ham Puffs, Devilish, 19
Ham Salad, Hot, 177

Ham Sandwich, Hot, 178
Ham Sandwich, Open Face, 177
Hard Sauce, 257
Heath Bar Candy, 330
Heavenly White Frosting, 314
Herb Meat Loaf, 164
Herb, Patio Bread, 55
Herb Rice, 209
Hibachi Steak, 18
Hilda's Cream Dressing, 243
Holiday Jam Cake, 308
Holiday Pumpkin Pie, 293
Hollandaise Sauce, 255
Hors d'Oeuvres (see Appetizers)
Horseradish Sauce, 253
Hot Bean Salad, 225
Hot Buttered Cranberry Punch, 28
Hot Buttered Rum, 33
Hot Chicken Salad, 122
Hot Cross Buns, 62
Hot Curried Crab Dip, 23
Hot Crab Spread, 23
Hot Fruit, 259
Hot Ham Salad, 177
Hot Ham Sandwich, 178
Hot Jalapenos Cheese Dip, 12
Hot Potato Salad, 232
Hot Sherry Sauce, 310
Hot Shrimp and Cheese Dip, 21
Hungarian Goulash, 158
Hunter's Quail, 141
Hushpuppies, 69

I

Ice Cream Bombe, 272
Ice Cream, Caramel Dessert, 272
Ice Cream, Chocolate, 271
Ice Cream, Chocolate Dessert, 274
Ice Cream, Lemon, 270
Ice Cream, Lemon Pie, 283
Ice Cream, Peach, 271
Ice Cream, Strawberry, 271
Iced Russian Tea, 27
Immediate Shrimp, 90
Instant Spiced Tea, 27
Irish Potato Cake, 306
Irish Potato Soup, 43
Italian Beef Patties, 165
Italian Cauliflower, 195
Italian Cream Cake, 307
Italian Salad, 229
Italian Zucchini, 218

J

Jalapenos Cheese Dip, Hot, 12
Jam Cake, Applesauce, 313
Jam Cake, Holiday, 308
Japanese Orange Dessert, 267
Jellied Madrilene, 47
Jellies (see Accompaniments)
Jelly, Brandied Apricot, 260
Jelly, Cranberry, 259

Jelly, Cranberry Port, 260
Jelly, Pepper, 260
Jelly, Port Wine, 260

K

Kentucky Derby Pie, 287
Kingdom-Come Duck, 138
King Ranch Casserole, 122
Kosher Dill Pickles, 261
Koulorgia, 324
Kraut Salad, 229

L

Lamb (see Meats)
Lamb and Cucumber Aspic, 240
Lamb Stew, 170
Lasagne, 166
Lebanese Stew, 160
Lebkuchen, 320
Leek-Potato Casserole, 206
Leek Soup, 40
Leg of Lamb, 168
Lemon Berry Cream, 281
Lemon Bread, 66
Lemon Cream Pie, 291
Lemon Ice Box Pie, 282
Lemon Ice Box Pie, Sky-High, 293
Lemon Ice Cream, 270
Lemon Ice Cream Pie, 283
Lemon Pineapple Icing, 304
Lemon Pineapple Layer Cake, 304
Lemon Pudding Salad, 238
Lemon Sauce, 257
Lemon Sauce, 297
Lemon Wild Rice with Shrimp, 91
Lentils, Polish Sausage and, 179
Les Oranges aux Liqueurs, 268
Lettuce, Wilted, 235
Lima Beans, 189
Liverwurst Mold, 14
Lobster Sauce for Asparagus, 101
London Broil, 153
Louisiana Seafood Soup, 43
Lou's Buttermilk Biscuits, 63
Lulla's Oysters, 103

M

Macaroni, Dilled Salad, 230
Macaroon, Orange Pudding, 267
Magnolia Manor Julep, 32
Main Chance Low Calorie
    Dressing, 245
Margarella, 123
Marie Schulte's Duck Casserole, 137
Marie Schulte's Rice Casserole, 209
Marie's Kentucky Fried Chicken, 111
Marinades (see Meats)
Marinated Asparagus Salad, 223
Marinated Blackeyed Peas, 204
Marinated Carrots, 194

Marinated Duck Breasts, 136
Mayonnaise, Easy Blender, 244
Mary Ann's Orange Sauce for
    Duck, 128
Meatball Casserole, Spicy, 167
Meat Balls, 163
Meat Balls, Swedish, 18
Meat Loaf, Herb, 164

MEATS, 147-180
  Beef
    Baked Steak with Mushrooms, 154
    Barbecued Brisket, 152
    Beef and Ham Birds in White
        Wine, 155
    Beef Burgundy Flambé, 159
    Beefsteak Au Roquefort, 153
    Beer Beef Stroganoff, 160
    Beouf Bourguignon, 159
    Brisket Roast with Beer, 152
    Carbonade of Beef Flamande, 158
    German Rouladen, 155
    Hungarian Goulash, 158
    Lebanese Stew, 160
    London Broil, 153
    Old Fashioned Beef Ragout, 157
    Our Town Stew, 161
    Paprika Beef Roll, 156
    Pot Roast Dubonnet, 150
    Roast Beef Teriyaki, 150
    Roast Beef with Coffee, 149
    Sauerbraten, 151
    Savory Stuffed Filet of Beef, 154
    Spaghetti Sauce di Cocco, 157
    Standing Rib Roast, 149
    Steak Diane, 153
    Steak, Hibachi, 18
    Tenderloin, 149
    Wine Marinade for Shish
        Kabob, 156
  Ground Beef
    Billie's Cabbage Roll, 165
    Chili, 163
    Dolmades, 169
    Hamburger Stroganoff, 164
    Herb Meat Loaf, 164
    Italian Beef Patties, 165
    Lasagne, 166
    Meat Balls, 163
    Moussaka, 168
    Spaghetti Sauce, 166
    Spicy Meatball Casserole, 167
    Steak Tartare, 18
    Stuffed Mushroom Casserole, 167
    Stuffed Peppers, 162
    Swedish Meat Balls, 18
    Tallerini, 164
    Tim's Cheese 'n Butter
        Burgers, 162
  Lamb
    Armenian Marinade, 171
    Artichokes Stuffed with
        Lamb, 170
    Bachelor's Barbecue Lamb, 169
    Dolmades, 169

Lamb Stew, 170
Leg of Lamb, 168
Moussaka, 168
  Marinades
    Armenian Marinade, 171
    Bachelor's Barbecue Lamb, 169
    Hibachi Steak, 18
    London Broil, 153
    Teriyaki, 150
    Wine Marinade for Shish
        Kabob, 156
  Pork
    Barbecue Sauce for Ham, 176
    Beef and Ham Birds in White
        Wine, 155
    Cherry Sauce for Pork Roast, 173
    Cocktail Ham Balls, 19
    Country Cured Ham, 175
    Crown Pork Roast, 172
    Glazed Pork Chops, 175
    Ham Fried Rice, 177
    Hot Ham Salad, 177
    Hot Ham Sandwich, 178
    Open Face Ham Sandwich, 177
    Pecan Stuffed Ham, 176
    Polish Sausage and Lentils, 179
    Pork Chops in Wine, 174
    Pork Chops with Artichokes, 174
    Ruth's Pork Chops with
        Sauerkraut, 174
    Sausage and Rice Supreme, 179
    Scrapple Von Kolnitz, 178
    Stuffed Pork Chops, 173
    Sweet and Sour Pork, 173
    Sweet and Sour Ribs, 175
  Veal
    Pressed Veal, 242
    Veal Parmigiana, 171
    Veal Scalloppine, 172
Sweetbread Salad with
    Grapes, 240
Sweetbreads New Yorker, 180
Meringue Crust, 288
Meringue Shells, 278
Meringue Surprises, 326
Mexican Bean Dip, 13
Mexican Cheese Dip, 12
Mexican Cornbread, 68
Midge's Party Torte, 274
Mile High Pie, 294
Mimi's Casserole of Zucchini,
    Eggplant, and Tomatoes, 219
Mimosa, 30
Miniature Pecan Pie, 290
Mint Julep, Magnolia Manor, 32
Mission Sunday Fudge Cake, 297
Mocha Punch, 33
Mocha Topping, 285
Molasses Sugar Cookies, 323
Molded Asparagus Salad, 223
Momma's Gingerbread, 297
Monkey Bread, 54
Mornay Sauce, 253
Mother-in-Law's Cake, 309
Moussaka, 168

Mrs. Witt's Egg Nog, 32
Muffins, Bran, 64
Muffins, Date, 64
Muffins, Ginger-Cheese, 65
Muffins, Peabody Hotel, 65
Muffins, Six-Weeks Bran, 64
Muffins, Sourdough English, 73
Mulled Cider, 28
Mulligatawny Soup, 39
Mushroom and Shrimp Sauce, 256
Mushroom, Broccoli Casserole, 190
Mushroom Casserole, 201
Mushroom Casserole, Stuffed, 167
Mushroom, Celery, and Water
  Chestnut Casserole, 197
Mushroom, Cream of Soup, 41
Mushrooms and Artichokes,
  Pickled, 262
Mushrooms and Chicken Livers, 124
Mushroom Sauce, 253
Mushrooms, Carrots, and Artichoke
  Hearts, 193
Mushrooms, Fillings for, 6-7
Mushrooms, Fresh, 200
Mushrooms, Pickled, 5
Mushrooms, Stuffed, 6
Mustard Sauce, 254

N

Nachos, 7
Nancy's Deep Sea Chowder, 43
Nancy's Russian Dressing, 247
Nectar Dressing, 245
Noodle Casserole, Country, 202
Nuts, Spiced, 329
Nutty Soybeans, 24

O

Oatmeal Bread, 56
Oatmeal Cake, 305
Oil and Vinegar Dressing, 245
Okra and Tomatoes, 203
Okra Fritters, 203
Old Fashioned Beef Ragout, 157
Onion Buns, 62
Onion, Creamed Soup, 41
Onion Rings, Fried, 203
Onions, Baked, 202
Onions, Baked, Parmesan, 202
Onions, Baked Stuffed, 176
Onions, Cranberry, 201
Onion Soup Gratinéed with Cheese, 40
Open-faced Breast of Chicken Sand-
  wich with Remoulade Sauce, 125
Open Face Ham Sandwich, 177
Orange Balls, 330
Orange Bread, 67
Orange Butter Icing, 315
Orange, Japanese Dessert, 267
Orange Macaroon Pudding, 267
Orange Pecans, 329
Orange Rind Loaf Cake, 303

Orange Salad, 238
Orange Sauce for Wild Duck, 139
Oranges aux Liqueurs, 268
Orange-Spinach Toss, 238
Oriental Franks, 16
Oriental Stuffed Eggplant, 199
Our Town Stew, 161
Oysters (see Fish and Shellfish)
Oyster Bisque, 42
Oysters Dunbar, 103
Oysters on the Half Shell, 102

P

Pancakes, 71
Pancakes, Apple, 71
Pancakes, Blueberry, 71
Pancakes, Blueberry Sourdough, 73
Pancakes, German, 70
Pancakes, Potato, with
  Applesauce, 206
Paprika Beef Roll, 156
Parmesan Sticks, 8
Parmigiana, Veal, 171
Party Cheese Potatoes, 205
Party Eggs, 83
Party Rolls, 60
Paté, Chicken Liver, 14
Patio Herb Bread, 55
Peabody Hotel Muffins, 65
Peach Angel, 282
Peach Custard Pie, Fresh, 292
Peach Ice Cream, 271
Peach Melba, 279
Peach Mold, 269
Peach-Pickle Salad, 238
Peaches, Quick Pickled, 261
Pea, Green Salad, 231
Peanut Brittle, Aunt Byrd's, 328
Pears, Crumbled, 269
Peas a la Durkees, 230
Peas, Blackeyed, Creole, 204
Peas, French, 204
Peas, Marinated Blackeyed, 204
Pea, Split Soup, 42
Pecan Cake, 307
Pecan Dreams, 325
Pecan Pie, Aunt Mary's, 290
Pecan Pie, Miniature, 290
Pecans, Glazed, 24
Pecans, Orange, 329
Pecan Stuffed Ham, 176
Peggy's Pound Cake, 295
Pepper Jelly, 260
Peppers, Stuffed, 162
Perfect Divinity, 331
Perfect Pastry, 285
Pheasant with Gravy, 142
Pickled Eggplant, 262
Pickled Mushrooms, 5
Pickled Mushrooms and
  Artichokes, 262
Pickled Peaches, Quick, 261
Pickled Shrimp, 20
Pickles, Bread and Butter, 261

Pickles, Kosher Dill, 261
Pie Crust Hints, 284

PIE CRUSTS
  Chocolate Cookie, 287
  Cream Cheese, 290
  Gingersnap, 283
  Graham Cracker, 285
  Meringue, 288
  Perfect Pastry, 285
  Pie Crust Hints, 284
  Stir-n-Roll, 285
  Vanilla Wafer, 289

PIES, 284-294
  Aunt Mary's Pecan, 290
  Banana Cream, 291
  Brandy Alexander, 286
  Butterscotch-Nut, 286
  Chess Meringue, 287
  Chocolate Cream, 291
  Chocolate Pecan, 289
  Chocolate Sundae, 289
  Citrus Chiffon, 294
  Coconut Cream, 291
  Cracker Pecan, 285
  Cream Base for Cream Pies, 291
  Creme de Menthe, 287
  Dutch Apple, 292
  French Chocolate, 288
  Fresh Peach Custard, 292
  Fresh Strawberry, 292
  Fudge Sundae, 282
  Holiday Pumpkin, 293
  Kentucky Derby, 287
  Lemon Cream, 291
  Lemon Ice Box, 282
  Lemon Ice Cream, 283
  Mile High, 294
  Miniature Pecan, 290
  Sky-High Lemon Ice Box, 293
  Strawberry, 282
  Toasted Coconut, 288
  Tutti-Frutti, 291
Pineapple Cake, 303
Pineapple-Lemon Layer Cake, 304
Plantation Squash, 216
Plum Pudding, 310
Poivrade Sauce for Venison, 144
Polish Sausage and Lentils, 179
Pollo en Jugo de Naranja, 111
Poppy Seed, Braided Bread, 56
Poppy Seed Dressing, 246
Pork (see Meats)
Pork Chops in Wine, 174
Pork Chops with Artichokes, 174
Port Wine Jelly, 260
Potage Crème d' Artichoke, 46
Potato Cake, Irish, 306
Potato Casserole, 205
Potato Chip Cookies, 326
Potato Dumplings, 155
Potatoes Anna, 205
Potatoes, Party Cheese, 205
Potatoes, Scalloped, 207
Potatoes, Twice Baked, with Corn, 207

Potato, German Salad, 231
Potato, Hot Salad, 232
Potato, Irish Soup, 43
Potato-Leek Casserole, 206
Potato Pancakes with Applesauce, 206
Potato Salad, 231
Potato, Sweet, and Apple
  Casserole, 208
Pot-au-Feu, 42
Pot Roast Dubonnet, 150

POULTRY, 109-130
  Barbecue Sauce for Chicken, 129
  Basic Bread Dressing, 128
  Breast of Chicken Honduras, 119
  Broiled Chicken Temple Bells, 116
  Camping Chicken, 113
  Cheesy Chicken Wings, 15
  Chestnut Dressing, 128
  Chicken Adolphus, 120
  Chicken and Wild Rice
    Casserole, 122
  Chicken Breasts with Shrimp
    Sauce, 117
  Chicken Cacciatore, 123
  Chicken Chablis, 113
  Chicken Dana, 120
  Chicken Indienne, 112
  Chicken Kiev, 114
  Chicken Korean, 118
  Chicken Livers in Onion
    Crepes, 126
  Chicken Livers with Madeira
    Sauce, 125
  Chicken Paprika, 119
  Chicken Parisienne, 118
  Chicken Richelieu, 116
  Chicken Spaghetti, 123-124
  Chicken Surprise, 121
  Chicken Tetrazzini, 124
  Chicken with Chipped Beef, 117
  Chicken with Pecans, 118
  Coq au Vin, 121
  Duck Bigarade, 129
  Gipsey's Stuffed Chicken, 115
  Grilled Oriental Chicken, 120
  Hot Chicken Salad, 122
  King Ranch Casserole, 122
  Margarella, 123
  Marie's Kentucky Fried
    Chicken, 111
  Mary Ann's Orange Sauce for
    Ducks, 128
  Mushrooms and Chicken
    Livers, 124
  Open-faced Breast of Chicken
    Sandwich with Remoulade
    Sauce, 125
  Pollo en Jugo de Naranja, 111
  Rice Dressing, 127
  Roasted Rock Cornish Hens, 125
  Rock Cornish Hens/Orange
    Raisin Sauce, 126
  Rum Sauce for Chicken, 254
  Sauteed Chicken Supreme, 113

Sesame Chicken, 115
Sesame Chicken Fondue, 112
Stuffed Chicken Breasts, 114
Stuffed Rock Cornish Hens, 127
Turkey with Honey & Ginger
    Glaze, 127
Pound Cake, Almond, 295
Pound Cake, Buttermilk, 295
Pound Cake, Chocolate, 296
Pound Cake, Peggy's, 295
Praline Grahams, 325
Preserves, Strawberry, 259
Pressed Veal, 242
Prune Cake, 305
Prune Loaf, 67
Pumpkin Bread, 67
Pumpkin Pie, Holiday, 293
Punch, Citrus, 28
Punch, Hot Buttered Cranberry, 28
Punch, Mocha, 33
Punch, Rum Runners, 33
Punch, Whiskey Sour, 31

Q

Quail (see Wild Game)
Quantity Bloody Mary Mix, 29
Quiche, Basic, 79
Quiche, Spinach, 214
Quick Consommé, 47
Quick Pickled Peaches, 261

R

Rabbit Stew, 142
Radishes, Rosy, 5
Ragout, Old Fashioned Beef, 157
Raisin Bread, 57
Raisin Sauce, 254
Ramekin, Forestier, 84
Rarebit, Spinach, 214
Raspberry Sauce, 258
Ratatouille (Eggplant Casserole), 200
Raw Vegetables to Dip, 3
Red Caviar Molds, 239
Red Hot Squash Casserole, 216
Refreshing Desserts, 284
Refrigerator Dinner Rolls, 60
Relishes (see Accompaniments)
Ribs, Sweet and Sour, 175
Rice Casserole, Marie Schulte's, 209
Rice Casserole, Wild, 211
Rice, Chinese Fried, 208
Rice, Curried, 208
Rice Dressing, 127
Rice, Ham Fried, 177
Rice, Herb, 209
Rice O'Brien, 210
Rice Pilaf, Diane's, 209
Rice Potpourri, 210
Rice Potpourri, Wild, 212
Rice Ring with Water Chestnuts and
    Mushrooms, 210
Rice Salad, 232

Rice Spinach Casserole, 214
Rice Supreme, Sausage and, 179
Rice Surprise, 211
Rice, Wine, 211
Rich Butter Cookies, 323
Roast Beef Teriyaki, 150
Roast Beef with Coffee, 149
Roast, Crown Pork, 172
Roasted Quail, 140
Roasted Rock Cornish Hens, 125
Roast Venison with Poivrade
    Sauce, 144
Rock Cornish Hens/Orange Raisin
    Sauce, 126
Rock Cornish Hens, Roasted, 125
Rock Cornish Hens, Stuffed, 127
Rolls, Party, 60
Rolls, Refrigerator Dinner, 60
Roquefort, Bell's Dressing, 245
Roquefort Cheese Dressing, 246
Roquefort, Frozen Dressing, 246
Rosy Radishes, 5
Rum Butter Sauce, 258
Rum Cake, 308
Rum Cake, 313
Rum Frosting, 308
Rum, Hot Buttered, 33
Rum Runner's Punch, 33
Rum Sauce for Chicken, 254
Russian Dressing, Nancy's, 247
Russian Tea, Iced, 27
Ruth's Pork Chops with
    Sauerkraut, 174
Rye Bread, 57

S

SALAD DRESSINGS, 242-247

    Bell's Roquefort, 245
    Canlis Special, 242
    Cottage Cheese, 242
    Creamy, 243   \
    Curry, 243
    Easy Blender Mayonnaise, 244
    French, 243
    Frozen Roquefort, 246
    German Salad, 244
    Glenleigh Tavern, 244
    Green Goddess, 244
    Hilda's Cream, 243
    Main Chance Low Calorie, 245
    Nancy's Russian, 247
    Nectar, 245
    Oil and Vinegar, 245
    Poppy Seed, 246
    Roquefort Cheese, 246
    Seafood Cocktail, 256
    Sour Cream, 247
    Thousand Island, 247

SALADS, 223-242
    Fruit
        Avocado and Grapefruit Mold, 224
        Avocado Mousse, 224

Bing Cherry with Coca Cola, 235
Bride's, 236
Cottage Cheese-Apricot, 235
Cranberry, 236
Cranberry-Cashew, 236
Curried Fruit, 258
Frozen Fruit, 237
Fruit, 237
Green & Gold, 237
Hot Fruit, 259
Lemon Pudding, 238
Orange, 238
Orange-Spinach Toss, 238
Peach-Pickle Salad, 238
Strawberry Salad, 239
Meat
Cucumbers Stuffed with Ham, 239
Hot Chicken, 122
Hot Crab Meat, 97
Hot Ham, 177
Lamb & Cucumber Aspic, 240
Pressed Veal, 242
Red Caviar Molds, 239
Sweetbread Salad with
    Grapes, 240
Shrimp & Artichoke, 240
Shrimp Mold, 241
Tuna Salad Loaf, 241
Vegetable
Beet Ring Mold, 225
Broccoli Vinaigrette, 226
Brussels Sprouts, 226
Caesar, 227
Canlis Special, 227
Cauliflower, 227
Cauliflower Slaw, 228
Cottage Cheese, 228
Dilled Cucumbers in Sour
    Cream, 228
Dilled Macaroni, 230
German Potato, 231
German Slaw, 232
Green Pea, 231
Green, 229
Guacamole, 3
Hot Bean, 225
Hot Potato, 232
Italian, 229
Kraut, 229
Marinated Asparagus, 223
Molded Asparagus, 223
Peas a la Durkees, 230
Potato, 231
Rice, 232
Swedish Bean, 224
Sweet and Sour Asparagus, 223
Sweet and Sour Bean, 225
Tabbooli, 233
Tomato Aspic, 233
Tomato-Cottage Cheese Loaf, 234
Tomatoes Babiche, 234
Tomatoes Stuffed with Garden
    Vegetables, 233
Tomatoes Vinaigrette, 234
Wilson's Pantry, 230

Wilted Lettuce, 235
Zesty Broccoli Mold, 226
Sally Lunn Bread, 59
Salmon Croquettes, 104
Salmon Loaf, 105
Salmon Soufflé, 104
Sand Tarts, 324
Sandwich, Baked Crab Meat, 98
Sandwich, Open-faced Breast of
    Chicken with Remoulade Sauce, 125
SAUCES, 251-258
Basic White Sauce, 251
Dessert
Brandy Pudding, 256
Butterscotch, 256
Chocolate, 276
Chocolate, 294
Claret, 271
Fudge, 257
Fudge Sundae, 257
Hard, 257
Hot Sherry, 310
Lemon, 257
Lemon, 297
Peach Melba, 279
Raspberry, 258
Rum Butter, 258
Vanilla, 258
Fish
Bechemel Sauce for Crab-Shrimp
    Pie, 98
Curried Shrimp, 255
Remoulade, 89
Remoulade Sauce, for Open-faced
    Breast of Chicken
    Sandwich, 125
Seafood Cocktail, 256
Shrimp and Mushroom, 256
Shrimp Sauce for Flounder, 106
Tartar, 255
Meat
Avgolemono, 169
Barbecued Brisket, 152
Barbecue Sauce for Chicken, 129
Barbecue Sauce for Duck, 134
Barbecue Sauce for Ham, 176
Bearnaise, 252
Bordelaise, 252
Brown Sauce, Basic, 251
Carrie's Barbecue, 252
Cherry Sauce for Pork Roast, 173
Currant Jelly Sauce for Duck, 137
Firepit Steak, 253
Horseradish, 253
Mary Ann's Orange Sauce for
    Ducks, 128
Mornay, 253
Mushroom, 253
Mustard, 254
Orange Raisin Sauce for Cornish
    Hens, 126
Orange Sauce for Wild Duck, 139
Poivrade Sauce for Venison, 144
Raisin, 254
Rum Sauce for Chicken, 254

Sauterne, 170
Sherry, 180
Spaghetti, 166
Tomato Sauce, Basic, 251
Vegetable
Dressing for Broccoli and Asparagus, 254
Easy Blender Mayonnaise, 244
Hollandaise, 255
Lobster Sauce for Asparagus, 101
Sour Cream-Bacon Sauce for Brussels Sprouts, 190
Vinaigrette, 255
White Clam Sauce for Spaghetti, 104
Saucy Carrots, 195
Sauerbraten, 151
Sauerkraut Balls, 20
Sausage and Chestnut Balls, 16
Sausage and Lentils, Polish, 179
Sausage and Rice Supreme, 179
Sausage Cheese Crumbles, 16
Sausage Dressing, 133
Sausage Pinwheels, 15
Sauteed Chicken Supreme, 113
Savory Goose, 141
Savory Stuffed Filet of Beef, 154
Scalloped Oysters, 102
Scalloped Potatoes, 207
Scalloppine, Veal, 172
Scallops Newburg, 99
Scrambled Eggs Chasseur, 83
Scrapple Von Kolnitz, 178
Seafood (see Fish and Shellfish)
Seafood Cocktail Sauce, 256
Seashell Crab Casserole, 96
Senegalese Soup, 48
Sesame Chicken, 115
Sesame Chicken Fondue, 112
Sheet Cake, Diane's Chocolate, 299
Sherry and Blue Cheese Dip, 10
Sherry Cake, 313
Sherry Cooler, 280
Sherry Sauce, Hot, 310
Shish Kabob, Wine Marinade for, 156
Shortcake, Fresh Fruit, 268
Shrimp (see Fish and Shellfish)
Shrimp and Artichoke Heart Casserole, 92
Shrimp and Artichoke Salad, 240
Shrimp and Cheese Dip, Hot, 21
Shrimp and Mushroom Sauce, 256
Shrimp Bake in Avocado, 93
Shrimp Chowder, 44
Shrimp, Crab Pie with Bechemel Sauce, 98
Shrimp Creole, 93
Shrimp Curry, 91
Shrimp de Jonghe, 90
Shrimp Dip, Easy, 21
Shrimp Harpin, 91
Shrimp Jambalaya, 94
Shrimp Mold, 241
Shrimp or Crab Gaylord, 96
Shrimp, Pickled, 20

Shrimp Potpourri, 21
Shrimp Remoulade, 90
Shrimp Rockefeller, 92
Shrimp Sauce for Flounder, 106
Shrimp Spread, 22
Simple Syrup, 30
(see Banana Daiquiri)
Six-Weeks Bran Muffins, 64
Skillet Cookies, 327
Sky-High Lemon Ice Box Pie, 293
Slaw, Cauliflower, 228
Slaw, German, 232
Smothered Dove Breasts, 139
Smothered Quail, 141
Snappy Cheese Log, 9
Souffle, Corn, 198
Souffle, Eggplant, 200
Souffle, Salmon, 104

SOUPS, 37-48

Asparagus, 46
Bean, 37
Broccoli, 37
Clam Chowder, 44
Cold Cucumber, 38
Cold Curry-Crab, 38
Cold Spinach, 44
Cold Tomato, 47
Cream of Mushroom, 41
Creamed Onion, 41
Do Your Own Thing, 48
Easy Cucumber, 47
Fresh Cream of Corn, 37
Gazpacho, 38
Gumbo, 39
Irish Potato, 43
Jellied Madrilene, 47
Leek, 40
Louisiana Seafood, 43
Mulligatawny, 39
Nancy's Deep Sea Chowder, 43
Onion, Gratineéd with Cheese, 40
Oyster Bisque, 42
Pot-au-Feu, 42
Potage Créme d'Artichoke, 46
Quick Consommé, 47
Senegalese, 48
Shrimp Chowder, 44
Spinach, 46
Split Pea, 42
Spring, 44
Tomato, 45
Vegetable, 45
Vichyssoise, 46
Watercress, 46
Sour Cream-Bacon Sauce for Brussels Sprouts, 190
Sour Cream Coffee Cake, 71
Sour Cream Dressing, 247
Sourdough Biscuits, 73
Sourdough Blueberry Pancakes, 73
Sourdough Bread, 72
Sourdough English Muffins, 73
Sourdough Starter, 72
Southern Fried Catfish, 107

Soybeans, Nutty, 24
Spaghetti, Chicken, 123-124
Spaghetti Sauce, 166
Spaghetti Sauce di Cocco, 157
Special Cheesecake, 304
Spiced Fruit Compote, 266
Spiced Nuts, 329
Spicy Meatball Casserole, 167
Spicy Vegetable Dip, 4
Spinach and Artichoke Casserole, 184
Spinach and Cheese Casserole, 213
Spinach, Cold Soup, 44
Spinach Crabmeat Dip, 22
Spinach, Creamed, 213
Spinach Madelaine, 212
Spinach, Orange Toss, 238
Spinach Quiche, 214
Spinach Rarebit, 214
Spinach Rice Casserole, 214
Spinach Rockefeller, Arkansas, 213
Spinach Soup (variation), 46
Split Pea Soup, 42
Spoon Bread, 69
Spooned Bread, Cheese, 69
Sportsman's Delight, 134
Spring Garden Medley, 186
Spring Soup, 44
Squash, Acorn, with Cranberries, 215
Squash, Baked Acorn, 215
Squash, Baked with Bacon, 215
Squash Casserole, 216
Squash Casserole, Red Hot, 216
Squash Casserole, Yellow, 215
Squash, Plantation, 216
Standing Rib Roast Beef, 149
Steak, Baked with Mushrooms, 154
Steak Diane, 153
Steak Sauce, Firepit, 253
Steak Tartare, 18
Stew, Lamb, 170
Stew, Lebanese, 160
Stew, Our Town, 161
Sticky Buns, 61
Stir-n-Roll Crust, 285
Strawberries, Crepes with Sour
    Cream, 270
Strawberries-Drambuie, 281
Strawberry Cake, 312
Strawberry Ice Cream, 271
Strawberry Icing, 312
Strawberry Pie, 282
Strawberry Pie, Fresh, 292
Strawberry Preserves, 259
Strawberry Salad, 239
Strawberry Squares with Claret
    Sauce, 271
Stroganoff, Beer Beef, 160
Stroganoff, Hamburger, 164
Stuffed Chicken Breasts, 114
Stuffed French Loaf, 84
Stuffed Lobster Tails Thermidor, 100
Stuffed Mushroom Casserole, 167
Stuffed Mushrooms, 6
Stuffed Oysters, 103
Stuffed Peppers, 162

Stuffed Pork Chops, 173
Stuffed Rock Cornish Hens, 127
Stuffed Sour Cream Bread, 58
Stuffed Tomatoes Hollandaise, 217
Sugar Plum Frosting, 315
Swedish Bean Salad, 224
Swedish Meat Balls, 18
Sweet and Sour Asparagus, 223
Sweet and Sour Bean Salad, 225
Sweet and Sour Cabbage, 192
Sweet and Sour Pork, 173
Sweet and Sour Ribs, 175
Sweetbread Salad with Grapes, 240
Sweetbreads New Yorker, 180
Sweet Potato and Apple Casserole, 208

                      T

Tabbooli, 233
Tallerini, 164
Tangy Cauliflower, 196
Tangy Cheese Spread, 10
Tartare, Steak, 18
Tartar Sauce, 255
Tea, Bridge Day Mint, 27
Tea, Instant Spiced, 27
Tea, Russian Iced, 27
Tenderloin, Beef, 149
Teriyaki, Roast Beef, 150
The President's Cake, 311
Thousand Island Dressing, 247
Tim's Cheese 'n Butter Burgers, 162
Tiny Corn Fritters, 7
Tipsy Watermelon, 4
Toasted Coconut Pie, 288
Toffee, Angel Cake Roll, 314
Toffee Topping, 279
Tomato Aspic, 233
Tomato Canapé, Cherry, 5
Tomato, Cold Soup, 47
Tomato-Cottage Cheese Loaf, 234
Tomatoes and Okra, 203
Tomatoes Babiche, 234
Tomatoes, Grilled with Rosemary, 217
Tomatoes, Stuffed, Hollandaise, 217
Tomatoes Stuffed with Fresh
    Corn, 218
Tomatoes Stuffed with Garden
    Vegetables, 233
Tomatoes Vinaigrette, 234
Tomato Sauce, Basic, 251
Tomato Soup, 45
Tomato Verdis, Baked, 217
Top of the Stove Duck, 135
Torte, Forgotten, 279
Torte, Midge's Party, 274
Tortoni, Coffee, 277
Tuna Salad Loaf, 241
Tunnel of Fudge Cake, 296
Turkey with Honey and Ginger
    Glaze, 127
Tutti-Frutti Pie, 291
Twice Baked Potatoes with Corn, 207

V

Vanilla Sauce, 258
Vanilla Wafer Crust, 289
Veal (see Meats)
Veal Parmigiana, 171
Veal, Pressed, 242
Veal Scalloppine, 172
VEGETABLES, 183-220
  Acorn Squash with
    Cranberries, 215
  Arkansas Spinach
    Rockefeller, 213
  Artichokes Alsation, 184
  Artichoke and Spinach
    Casserole, 184
  Asparagus Casserole, 185
  Baked Acorn Squash, 215
  Baked Barley with Mushrooms
    and Almonds, 186
  Baked Onions, 202
  Baked Onions Parmesan, 202
  Baked Squash with Bacon, 215
  Baked Tomatoes Verdis, 217
  Blackeyed Peas Creole, 204
  Broccoli Casserole, 189
  Broccoli Mushroom Casserole, 190
  Broccoli Waddile, 190
  Cabbage Potpourri, 192
  Cabbage Stroganoff, 192
  Candied Yams, 207
  Caraway Green Beans, 187
  Carrot Casserole Supreme, 193
  Carrot Ring, 194
  Carrots, Artichoke Hearts,
    and Mushrooms, 193
  Carrots-in-honey Au Gratin, 193
  Carrots di Prossedi, 194
  Cauliflower Au Gratin, 195
  Celery Amandine, 196
  Celery Au Gratin, 197
  Celery, Mushroom and Water
    Chestnut Casserole, 197
  Celery with Almonds, 195
  Chilies Rellenos, 198
  Chinese Asparagus, 186
  Chinese Fried Rice, 208
  Company Brussels Sprouts, 191
  Corn Casserole, 198
  Corn Pudding, 198
  Country Noodle Casserole, 202
  Cranberry Onions, 201
  Creamed Spinach, 213
  Crepes Theodora, 191
  Crunchy Celery, 197
  Curried Rice, 208
  Diane's Rice Pilaf, 209
  Dill Beans, 187
  Eggplant Casserole, 199
  Eggplant Souffle, 200
  French Peas, 204
  Fresh Artichokes, 185
  Fresh Mushrooms, 200
  Fried Onion Rings, 203
  Garden Vegetable Skillet, 220

  Garlic Cheese Grits, 201
  Green Beans Amandine, 187
  Green Beans Au Gratin, 188
  Green Beans Supreme, 188
  Green Beans with Swiss
    Cheese, 188
  Grilled Tomatoes with
    Rosemary, 217
  Herb Rice, 209
  Italian Cauliflower, 195
  Italian Zucchini, 218
  Lima Beans, 189
  Marie Schulte's Rice
    Casserole, 209
  Marinated Blackeyed Peas, 204
  Marinated Carrots, 194
  Mimi's Casserole of Zucchini,
    Eggplant, and Tomatoes, 219
  Mushroom Casserole, 201
  Okra and Tomatoes, 203
  Okra Fritters, 203
  Oriental Stuffed Eggplant, 199
  Party Cheese Potatoes, 205
  Plantation Squash, 216
  Potato Casserole, 205
  Potato-Leek Casserole, 206
  Potato Pancakes with
    Applesauce, 206
  Potatoes Anna, 205
  Ratatouille
    (Eggplant Casserole), 200
  Red Hot Squash Casserole, 216
  Rice O'Brien, 210
  Rice Potpourri, 210
  Rice Ring with Water Chestnuts
    and Mushrooms, 210
  Rice Surprise, 211
  Saucy Carrots, 195
  Scalloped Potatoes, 207
  Sour Cream-Bacon Sauce
    for Brussels Sprouts, 190
  Spinach and Cheese Casserole, 213
  Spinach Madelaine, 212
  Spinach Quiche, 214
  Spinach Rarebit, 214
  Spinach Rice Casserole, 214
  Spring Garden Medley, 186
  Squash Casserole, 216
  Stuffed Tomatoes
    Hollandaise, 217
  Sweet and Sour Cabbage, 192
  Sweet Potato and
    Apple Casserole, 208
  Tangy Cauliflower, 196
  Tomatoes Stuffed with
    Fresh Corn, 218
  Twice Baked Potatoes
    with Corn, 207
  Wild Rice Casserole, 211
  Wild Rice Potpourri, 212
  Wine Rice, 211
  Yellow Squash Casserole, 215
  Zucchini Au Oeufs, 219
  Zucchini Squash with
    Sour Cream, 218

Vegetable Dip, Curry, 4
Vegetable Dip, Dill Weed, 3
Vegetable Dip, Spicy, 4
Vegetable Soup, 45
Vegetables to Dip, Raw, 3
Venison (see Wild Game)
Venison and Ale, 145
Venison Stew, 144
Venison Swiss Steak, 143
Vichyssoise, 46
Vinaigrette Sauce, 255

W

Waffles, 71
Walnut Hermits, 328
Watercress Soup, 46
Watermelon, Tipsy, 4
Welsh Rarebit, 85
Whipped Cream Frosting, 316
Wheat Germ Bread, 59
Whiskey Sour Punch, 31
White Chocolate Cake, 300
White Chocolate Frosting, 300
White Clam Sauce for Spaghetti, 104
White Frosting, Heavenly, 314
White Sauce, Basic, 251
Whole Wheat Bread, 58
Wild Duck Button Willow, 135
Wild Duck Cocktail Spread, 15
Wild Duck Deluxe, 136
Wild Duck in Apple Juice and
    Brandy, 135
Wild Duck in Barbecue Sauce, 134
Wild Duck in Sherry, 136
Wild Duck Stucky, 138

WILD GAME, 131-146

Barbara's Potted Duck, 134
Basic Recipe for Wild Ducks, 133
Champagne Sauerkraut for
    Duck, 138
Charcoal Broiled Quail, 140
Creole Duck, 133
Currant Jelly Sauce, 137
Dove a la Como, 139
Dove in Wine, 140
Duck Casserole, 137
Fried Quail, 140
Gourmet Delight Pheasant, 142
Hunter's Quail, 141
Kingdom Come Duck, 138
Marie Schulte's Duck
    Casserole, 137
Marinated Duck Breasts, 136
Orange Sauce for Wild Duck, 139
Pheasant with Gravy, 142
Rabbit Stew, 142
Roasted Quail, 140
Roast Venison with Poivrade
    Sauce, 144
Sausage Dressing, 133
Savory Goose, 141
Smothered Dove Breasts, 139

Smothered Quail, 141
Sportsman's Delight, 134
Top of the Stove Duck, 135
Venison and Ale, 145
Venison Stew, 144
Venison Swiss Steak, 143
Wild Duck Button Willow, 135
Wild Duck Cocktail Spread, 15
Wild Duck Deluxe, 136
Wild Duck in Apple Juice and
    Brandy, 135
Wild Duck in Barbecue Sauce, 134
Wild Duck in Sherry, 136
Wild Duck Stuckey, 138
Wild Goose, 141
Wild Turkey Steaks, 143
Wild Goose, 141
Wild Rice Casserole, 211
Wild Rice Potpourri, 212
Wild Turkey Steaks, 143
Wilson's Pantry Salad, 230
Wilted Lettuce, 235
Wine Cellar Cheese, 11
Wine Marinade for Shish Kabob, 156
Wine Rice, 211
Winkum, 97

Y

Yams, Candied, 207
Yellow Birds, 30
Yellow Squash Casserole, 215
Yorkshire Pudding, 63

Z

Zesty Broccoli Mold, 226
Zucchini Au Oeufs, 219
Zucchini, Italian, 218
Zucchini Squash with Sour Cream, 218

The Junior League of Little Rock, Inc.
Post Office Box 7421
Little Rock, Arkansas 72207

Send me............ copies of **Little Rock Cooks** at $5.00 per copy, postpaid. Enclosed

is my check or money order for $............................ .

Name..

Street..

City...State...........................Zip...................

Check if gift wrapping is desired .   .   .   .   ☐
Make check payable to:
JUNIOR LEAGUE OF LITTLE ROCK — COOKBOOK

The Junior League of Little Rock, Inc.
Post Office Box 7421
Little Rock, Arkansas 72207

Send me............ copies of **Little Rock Cooks** at $5.00 per copy, postpaid. Enclosed

is my check or money order for $............................ .

Name..

Street..

City...State...........................Zip...................

Check if gift wrapping is desired .   .   .   .   ☐
Make check payable to:
JUNIOR LEAGUE OF LITTLE ROCK — COOKBOOK

The Junior League of Little Rock, Inc.
Post Office Box 7421
Little Rock, Arkansas 72207

Send me............ copies of **Little Rock Cooks** at $5.00 per copy, postpaid. Enclosed

is my check or money order for $............................ .

Name..

Street..

City...State...........................Zip...................

Check if gift wrapping is desired .   .   .   .   ☐
Make check payable to:
JUNIOR LEAGUE OF LITTLE ROCK — COOKBOOK